8-2-61   56-5857   Powell

GOODBYE TO UNCLE TOM

J. C. Furnas

1 9 5 6

WILLIAM SLOANE ASSOCIATES

NEW YORK

GOODBYE TO UNCLE TOM

Grateful acknowledgment is made to The Macmillan Company, New York, for permission to quote from "Simon Legree, A Negro Sermon," from *Collected Poems,* by Vachel Lindsay; and to Harper & Brothers, New York, for permission to quote from "Heritage," by Countee Cullen.

Library of Congress Catalog Card Number: 56–5857

Second Printing, May 1956

FOR ANNE ANDERSEN
WHO LIKED IT EARLY

"Indeed I tremble for my country when I reflect that God is just; that His justice cannot sleep forever."

—THOMAS JEFFERSON *of Virginia discussing slavery in 1784.*

"Slavery brings the judgment of heaven upon a country. As nations cannot be rewarded or punished in the next world, they must be in this.

—GEORGE MASON *of Virginia discussing slavery in 1787.*

Contents

Acknowledgments

Before final revision this entire text was read by an American Negro well situated for wide acquaintance with current problems in race relations and with Negroes' needs and programs in handling them. Exceptions taken were few and small. Most of them have been observed in revision. In general approval was high.

The last sections (Negroes are . . . and Clarity Begins at Home) similarly were read by an eminent anthropologist. His exceptions were also few and small. Some are now reflected in the text. Both these experts were assured that they would not be identified. The reader has my word for it that they are excellently well qualified.

Thanking individuals in print for help on such books as this is risky. Somebody always gets left out. Will all who gave me advice or information—and there are hundreds of them —take this, please, as personal and hearty thanks?

Institutions that have been helpful include the Princeton

University Library; the New York Public Library; the Harvard College Library; the British Museum; the Northwestern University Library; the Library of the Harvard Club of New York City; the Hunterdon County Library; the Flemington Free Library; the Royal Empire Society; the Charleston Library Society; the Public Library of Cincinnati and Hamilton County; Colonial Williamsburg; the Louisiana Historical Society; the Museum of the City of New York; the Virginia State Library; the Virginia Historical Society; the New York Historical Society; the Historical and Philosophical Society of Ohio; the Cincinnati Art Museum; the Marshall-Wythe Law School of William and Mary College; the United States Department of State; Her Majesty's Colonial Office; the Farrell Lines.

Every page reflects my wife's skills as researcher, editor and whetstone to an extent that amounts practically to collaboration.

J. C. Furnas

Prologue

Curiosity once caused me to pay a quarter for a grimy secondhand copy of *Uncle Tom's Cabin,* a book that I had missed reading, had never even held in my hand before. In spite of fine type and poor paper it proved unexpectedly interesting.

Fifteen years later the devil put it into my head to write a book to acquaint Europeans, particularly Britons, with some of the things they should know, and seldom do, when seeking to evaluate Americans and American ways and things. The scheme was eventually given up partly because Americans presumably had little need for such a book and, in view of the testy tone of my tentative outlines and drafts, Britons would hardly care to buy it. The other reason was less crass: When my planning got round to the Negro problem in the United States, confidence deserted me. The more I strove to block out the pertinent issues and chart the areas of required information, the plainer it grew that on this subject I was shockingly ill prepared to instruct anybody, not even myself.

This was disconcerting, since I had occasionally been closer to several stripes of Negro than is usual among white Americans and had had unusual opportunities to observe interracial frictions outside the United States. My grasp of the basic sociology of the modern American Negro was, no doubt, as sound as that of the next respectful reader of Myrdal's *An American Dilemma,* all four pounds of it. Try as I might, however, until the sense of mental frustration was physically oppressive, I could not bring into focus the strange plight of the American Negro. Once you really considered it, it was, in the most literal sense, inconceivable. Yet I was well aware of and accustomed to the fact that, in many other contexts too, the world can be even more cruel than it is stupid.

About rye whiskey, the two-party system, soft-sprung automobiles and combination in restraint of trade I was prepared to be as trenchant—and as glib—as you please. But pondering Harlem and Mound Bayou, Mississippi, reduced me to saying nervously to my hypothetical European readers: "In parallel circumstances you people would have done no better. When it all started, in fact, you were we and we were you. Besides, look at South Africa."

However peevish, that was tenable as far as it went; but it could not be said to go far. Then it occurred to me that at least one probable cause of the American intellectual block on the subject was within arm's reach, third shelf from the top—*Uncle Tom's Cabin.* I remembered being puzzled by my first reading of this most widely circulated and perhaps most influential novel ever published. Its flavor had been so curiously illiberal for a book of such renown with reputedly liberal consequences.

Rereading renewed this impression and showed me that its basic content, the assumptions that it made and proliferated and confirmed by fictitious examples, were still fundamental—far below rational thought—in white Americans' feelings about Negroes. Was this book actually as ill advised as it now sounded? Was there ever, I wondered, adequate reality beneath these notions of Harriet Beecher Stowe's about "the African race" and how Negroes fared "at the South?" And if the data and attitudes worked into this book had always been as unreliable as, on the face of the little I knew, they seemed to be, might not much of our mental dyspepsia on the subject come of the way we have all along let a work of fiction—and a cheap one, too—guide our thinking and, even more important, our feeling?

Such questions set me seeking the actualities involved as of today and as of the heyday of *Uncle Tom* a hundred years ago. How well did Mrs. Stowe know her subject matter? What was it really like to be an antebellum slave? How did *Uncle Tom* come to be the permanent blueprint of white Americans' attitudes toward Negroes? And if there is, or ever was, an "African race," what can intelligibly be said about it?

Pursuit of those issues took me to strange places—Ripley, Ohio; Sierra Leone; Butler's Island, Georgia; Barbados, and many others, some charming, some not—and eventually into a firm conviction that the more I explored this book and its queer creatrix, the less I should wonder that the nation Mrs. Stowe tutored is still so confused about Negroes. She meant well, more or less. Fortunately she was a plucky little woman and probably holds up better than most under her perpetual task of paving the place with the proverbial materials.

What follows is what I learned on the way to de-confusion. Bits or parts of it may annoy some American Negoes, among them better men than I. Certain details, such as the high likelihood of "black blood" in many white Southerners, will unquestionably annoy Southern readers. But, except as they will sometimes be people whom I know and like, I am not much concerned. Not having spent generations under a fraudulent curse of Canaan, Southerners have less excuse for ingrown emotions. I even feel little need to apologize to Negroes for findings that rub the wrong way, except as they re-

flect occasions when, in spite of earnest precautions, I have
shown inadequate knowledge, judgment or charity. In my
field—that of reporting to the general reader—one calls things
the way they are seen by a witness experienced in allowing
for the pretensions of experts as well as for the misapprehen-
sions of the man in the street and the illusions of the actors
in social tangles.

Mrs. Stowe herself was quite as confused as anybody. She
sometimes asserted that God was the actual author of *Uncle
Tom's Cabin,* though precisely what she meant by that was
never clear. Soon after the book was published, she told a
friend that He had sent her visions, apparently a sort of
magic-lantern scenario of tableaux, to develop and connect
up. Forty years later, when she was senile and verging on
megalomania in a fashion that her normal behavior had often foreshadowed, she wrote on the flyleaf of a new edition:
"The Spirit of the Lord is upon me, because He hath
anointed me to preach the gospel to the poor . . . sent me
to heal the broken-hearted, to preach deliverance to the captive . . . to set at liberty those who are bruised."

By then it was thirty years since she had done much for
any good cause. So what she had had in mind all along may
have been like what happened to the disciples at Pentecost—
a sort of possession by a divine afflatus that would make her
and her work more than life-sized. This fits the history of
her book. It went all over the world on the winds of emotion, like the volcanic dust from Krakatoa, and spoke her
mind abroad in just about all the tongues for which fonts of
type existed.

It could have been, though it probably was not, modesty
that caused her thus to enlist God as collaborator; she

might have sought diffidently to renounce personal credit, since the consequences of what she wrote were on a scale arguing an order of things that even underwriters admit to be an "act of God." *Uncle Tom* was a verbal earthquake, an ink-and-paper tidal wave. Nowadays a writer attributing his work to God would be either blasphemous or suspect of grave mental illness. But in Mrs. Stowe's time such a statement was not necessarily pathological in the daughter of an eminent and self-righteous Yankee theologian. The Rev. Dr. Lyman Beecher and most of his many children felt something more positive, more exhilarating than mere surrender in "Lord, not my will but Thine be done." On their lips this showed a magnanimous willingness to let other authority see what It could do. Even Mrs. Stowe's official biographer-descendants wrote, "It was a necessity of her mind to persuade herself that some higher end was sought in everything that she did from raising potatoes to writing a book."

Whatever she meant in 1852, her book had a calamitously large hand in making sure that a dividing Union would wreak on itself the overdue justice that Jefferson had shrunk from contemplating sixty-eight years before. By the epoch of *Uncle Tom*, Mrs. Stowe's Lord seems to have worked back to his Old Testament phase, bent on an eye for an eye and the wiping out of armies. For every Negro slave hustled ashore filthy and naked in North America, a white man was to die in fratricidal violence; for every misbegotten excuse for treating men like things, a white man would lie festering in a fly-fetid hospital; for every free Negro treated as subhuman by Northerners reproaching the South for the crime of slavery, a Yankee would succumb to some foul camp disease; for every mulatto sold to strangers by his own cousins, a white child would be orphaned. The score had long accumulated, and compounding interest had long since dwarfed the principal.

In 1851 Mrs. Stowe had the delusion that her book would promote healing of the already deepening rift between the two segments of the nation. In her chronic confusion she wrote: "To you, generous, noble-minded men and women of the South, whose virtue, magnanimity and purity of character are the greater for the severe trial it [*sic*] has encountered—to you is her appeal."* Since she accomplished the diametric opposite of this objective, she may not have been as much in God's confidence as she had assumed.

Lincoln's Second Inaugural hesitantly suggested that God might see fit to credit the agony of the Civil War as expiation and strike a clean balance. But, thanks in a considerable degree to Mrs. Stowe's book, even that hope was futile. The very background and character of His chosen instrument, the very popular touch that made her fiction so effective, caused her to set down—and so broadcast and perpetuate—notions that would create fresh debts of viciousness as fast as the old ones were paid. *Uncle Tom* would never have burned on and on had it not been compounded of the misconceptions, Southern and Northern, the wrongheadednesses, distortions and wishful thinkings about Negroes in general and American Negroes in particular that still plague us today. They might not plague us quite so sore if Mrs. Stowe had not so persuasively formulated and thus frozen them.

A sense of this well-meant falseness, this treacherous help, may underlie the fact that American Negroes have made her titular hero a hissing and a byword. Many of them would rather be called "nigger" than "Uncle Tom." An astute Negro preacher already felt some of this a hundred years ago, saying "that resistance to tyranny was obedience to God . . . hence . . . the only drawback to the matchless Uncle Tom of Mrs. Stowe was his virtue of submission to tyranny—an

---

* Her son and grandson wrote: "Mrs. Stowe wished to be more than fair to the South . . . to show that the fault was not in the Southern people but in the system. . . . Great was her surprise when from the whole South arose a storm of abuse." (Stowes, *Harriet Beecher Stowe,* 141)

exhibition of grace which [the speaker] did not covet."* By
now, a Negro source tells me, "Uncle Tom" as epithet has
expanded from "its earliest connotation . . . a boot-licking,
servile type of Negro in . . . his relationship with whites,
also a yes-man to anything proposed by whites which did not
seem to favor Negroes. Now it may mean a weakling or a
coward, a traitor, a wily manipulator, one who engineers a
race sell-out or one who for any reason failed to 'speak up'
for his race at an important point. There is also the connotation of general disgust. . . ."

Thus to use "Uncle Tom" is unfair to the figure that Mrs.
Stowe created. Given the basic Christian virtues, her Uncle
Tom would be a credit to any race in any context. It was
not Christ who said that resistance to tyrants was obedience
to God—on which more later. But the current meanings of
the epithet may well have grown, sub- or supra-logically, from
Negroes' general uneasiness about the overtones of Mrs.
Stowe's irresponsibly sententious book and the crude plays
concocted from it.

The pity of it is that, if human beings were only born
consistently blind, by now there well might be no serious
Negro problem among us children of the Sermon on the

---

* Letter of William C. Nell to the *Liberator* (Woodson, *Mind of the
Negro;* 338). This attitude was then rare among free Negro leaders.
The Colored National Convention of 1853, led by Frederick Douglass,
called the book "plainly marked by the finger of God." (Quarles,
Frederick Douglass; 123) William Wells Brown, a conspicuous fugitive
slave, evinced no misgivings about it. (Woodson, *op. cit.;* 360) Nearer
our own day, Paul Laurence Dunbar's sonnet on Mrs. Stowe was most
grateful. James Weldon Johnson was generously shrewd about the
content of the book, Uncle Tom included. (*Autobiography of an Ex-
Coloured Man;* 41-42) Langston Hughes's preface to a 1952 edition
shows no trace of mistrust. These are exceptions, however. The epithet
is apparently also used among Negroes (largely of West Indian background) in England. (Richmond, *Colour Problem;* 278) I was surprised
to find so few white respondents to my questionnaire (described on
p. 36) aware of its being so used. Fewer than a third answering had
ever heard of such a thing.

Mount and the Declaration of Independence. As things are, however, we still see Negroes and their plight all too consistently through Mrs. Stowe's always flawed and long obsolete spectacles. In the most august study of these matters, Gunnar Myrdal concluded that "the status accorded the Negro in America represents . . . a century-long lag in public morals. In principle the Negro problem was settled long ago; in practice the solution is not yet effectuated."

In my view Mrs. Stowe's book had more to do than any other single factor with this moral disgrace. Or, if this seems to accord an individual too much weight, take it the other way, and all this needs writing just the same. Say that her sins of ignorance and presumption merely typified the unrealized sins of her time, which she foisted on us, which we have yet to slough off. For either reason this book must be discursive, looping here, shooting off at apparently impertinent angles there, achieving only the consistency of saying things that badly need saying. But it will always have Mrs. Stowe somehow in mind. Her role is similar to that of the front wall of a squash court: wherever the ball goes, it always starts from there, and, once that point is played out, the next starts from there again.

We had our warning. The rules state plainly that the children's teeth will be set on edge. God works in mysterious ways. Directly, as thousands still read *Uncle Tom*—as they do —indirectly as millions who never read it feel its residual influence on what others do and say, at many subtle and permeating removes, Mrs. Stowe's book is still His instrument for punitive ends. It would all be fair as fair if this "century-long lag" to which *Uncle Tom* contributed so much were not so tragic for the Negroes.

LICK AND
A PROMISE

1 *Mrs. Scribble-in-Haste*

"One suspects that those who regard 'Uncle Tom' as a grotesque saint capable only of drugging his race into genteel apathy have not read Uncle Tom's Cabin.*"*
—JORGENSON, Uncle Tom's Cabin as Book and Legend

When carving *The King and I* out of *Anna and the King of Siam,* Rodgers and Hammerstein made much of the Siamese court lady who learned English, read *Uncle Tom* and grew obsessed with it, translated it into Siamese and renamed herself "Harriet Beecher Stowe Son Klin." The result was a pseudo-Siamese ballet, "The Small House of Uncle Thomas," to amuse millions of paying customers. In it a Siamese-style Eliza fled pursued by dog-masked dancers urged on by King Simon of Legree and eventually found refuge in the cabin of an Uncle Thomas with a kinky blue wig and a minstrel-show black mask.* In the end a Siamese-style Eva, who had previously taken little part in the pantomime conversation, ascended to a Siamese-style heaven.

---

* Mr. Hammerstein tells me that he knows of no Negro protest of this light-hearted but definite use of the clown stereotype of the Negro. As this is written, shooting is soon to begin on the Twentieth Century-Fox version of *The King and I.*

All this was staged with charm. But a prosy spectator brooded over it afterward. He wondered if, after almost a century of progressive mayhem and dilution, this was the end of the road. After *The King and I*, could anything more conceivably happen to *Uncle Tom's Cabin?* It had already been a stage vehicle for John L. Sullivan—for an all-child troupe—an opera—a musical show for the Duncan Sisters —a Players' Club revival—and later been readapted all over again for the stage by George Abbott. This rhetorical question was answered in 1953 by a report that a Communist-angled production in Budapest "deflated Uncle Tom to a meek, Bible-reading, secondary figure, and added a narrator [who] explains that Simon Legree is really a Wall Street villain, true today as he was in the age of slaves. 'Do you, children, wish to side with Simon Legree or with the camp of peace led by the Soviet Union?' . . ." There was much to brood about, in fact, in "The Small House of Uncle Thomas." Those dogs now—they were no part of the story that so affected Lady Son Klin. In the book that Mrs. Stowe wrote and polyglot millions read, the slave dealer could find no dogs suitable for pursuing Eliza. The bloodhounds tradition, wholly of-the-stage-stagey, was not even necessary to the unprecedented success of the first stage versions.* Nor was it Simon Legree who pursued. His role was not to rave and curse as he saw Eliza flitting over the ice out of reach but to buy Uncle Tom in New Orleans, hundreds of miles from frozen rivers and flog him to death on a Deep South plantation.

To reproach the authors of *The King and I* with these anomalies would be stuffy. Fantasy is fantasy and sometimes fun. But these elements spontaneously included in their ballet did wryly illustrate the likelihood that not one spec-

---

* Mrs. Cordelia Howard Macdonald, who created the role of little Eva, mentioned this to actors in the Players' revival of 1933; they said that the public would not accept the play without the dogs. (Interview in *Christian Science Monitor,* October 11, 1933.)

tator in a thousand with the *Uncle Tom's Cabin* circuit of his memory thus jogged was aware of anything wrong. The world's essential impression of the old warhorse was well summed up for me by a lady recently trying to remember the play as she had seen it in childhood: "An old Negro with white hair, and a big man in a black coat with a whip. It was sad." Certainly everybody knows the gist of *Uncle Tom's Cabin:* bloodhounds . . . Eliza crossed the ice . . . or was it Little Eva? No, Little Eva went to Heaven to soft music . . . Uncle Tom died . . . Simon Legree . . . Wasn't that about all?

Unhappily for Negroes and the world in general, there was far, far more to Mrs. Stowe's tale than these tags still sticking to the popular mind. Since her thronging errors of fact or approach are seldom traced to this extraordinary book as their long-outmoded source and authority, we need another look at it. Even synopsis of this monument of hasty propaganda has regrettable overtones. Here is the story that you may only think you know: *Plot*

Arthur Shelby, gentleman-farmer, with a large establishment in the Bluegrass, has a slave foreman named Tom—pious, able, loyal, husband of the Big House cook and father of several comic-relief children, not at all the quavering Ol'-Uncle-Ned type of the Tom-show but robustly in the prime of life. Later in the book, for instance, he is shown picking cotton at double speed to help ailing fellow slaves on Legree's Red River plantation.

Other focal characters are George Harris and Eliza, his wife, both slaves but so near white that they can "pass" while escaping. Intelligent, cultivated Eliza is personal maid to Mrs. Shelby. George is a skilled mechanic, able to make practical inventions, but kept at drudgery tasks by his owner, a neighboring farmer, who considers him "uppity" and wantonly mistreats him. The pair have a clever and pretty little boy child Harry.

Goaded beyond discretion by his coarse master, George has

determined to run away to Canada, where British law excludes slavery and protects fugitives: ". . . if any man tries to stop me, let him take care, for I am desperate. I'll fight for my liberty to the last breath I breathe." He disguises himself as a gentleman traveler with an obviously Negro fellow runaway posing as body servant and gets safe out of slave territory with help from a kindly Kentuckian to whom he had once been hired out.

Simultaneously a slave trader named Haley uses some awkward obligations of Shelby's to force him to hand over ownership of Tom and little Harry, a transaction that outrages Mrs. Shelby. "This is God's curse on slavery!" she breaks out, "a bitter, bitter, most accursed thing!—a curse to the master and a curse to the slave! I was a fool to think I could make anything out of such a deadly evil. . . ."

Shelby, too, is sick at heart, but it is sell or go bankrupt. Eliza overhears his dealings with Haley, warns Tom that he has been sold, and runs away with little Harry, hoping somehow to rejoin George in Canada. Haley's vigorous pursuit is sabotaged by Shelby's slapstick slave boys. Even so, he reaches the Ohio River, boundary of freedom, so hard on Eliza's heels that she must scramble, with her child in her arms—the famous scene!—from floe to floe over the ice-clogged river.

Sympathetic Ohioans, including a senator who votes for fugitive-slave laws but cannot practice the severity that he preaches, pass her on to the Underground Railroad, manned chiefly by Quakers. George joins her at an Underground station in Indiana. In further flight they and their escort must once stand and fight professional slave catchers. (One of them, Lawyer Marks, became a featured comic role in the Tom-show-to-be.) The fugitives win clear and, passing as white and disguising Harry as a girl and Eliza as a man, reach Canada by lake steamer. George works as a mechanic, studies at night and does very well. But he eventually determines to shift himself and family to Liberia, the West African colony for free and freed American Negroes. His reason is his new sense of solidarity with "the oppressed, en-slaved African race. . . . I would wish myself two shades darker rather than one lighter. . . . The desire and yearn-ing of my soul is for an African *nationality*. . . . The Afri-can race has peculiarities, yet to be unfolded in the light of civilization and Christianity, which if not the same with those of the Anglo-Saxon, may prove to be, morally, of even higher type."

That is Plot One—a standard chase scenario with the dawn of a new day breaking in the last frames. Plot Two is con-nected with it only by common origin in Shelby's business difficulties and at the end, when minor actors in Plot Two prove to be relatives of both George and Eliza.

Eliza and Tom's wife Aunt Chloe, who is woefully like Aunt Jemima, have urged him to run away before Haley can sell him "down the river." Tom refuses on the ground that, unless he is thus sacrificed, the whole establishment will be broken up and all the slaves, not just two, will suffer. Besides "Mas'r always found me on the spot—he always will." Tom is all the readier with this decision because he is a sin-cere Christian, sure of the Lord's promise to assuage all anguish in the hereafter.* This consistent and dignified pi-ety makes Plot Two an able and sometimes touching tract apart from its ostensible purpose of exposing the miseries attendant on slavery.

Haley ships Tom and other slaves bought for the dread New Orleans market on a southbound Ohio steamboat. Dur-ing the trip a slave girl whom he buys away from her hus-band and then deprives of her baby drowns herself overside. The passengers include the wealthy and finically intelligent Augustin St. Clare, of New Orleans, his ethereal little daugh-ter Evangeline, soon to be "Little Eva," and his spinster

---

* Mrs. Eastman, whose *Aunt Phillis's Cabin* was best of the anti-*Uncle Tom* novels, uttered unladylike snorts about Tom's piety, suggesting that Shelby should have kept him until he died "and then sold him bone after bone to the Roman Catholics." (p. 266)

cousin Ophelia, a severe Yankee who is coming South to manage St. Clare's household for his hypochondriac wife.

Tom the saintly slave and Eva the saintly child make friends. Eva falls overboard and Tom rescues her. At her instance St. Clare buys him as coachman and Eva's special pet and protector. In the St. Clare town house in New Orleans, which Mrs. Stowe makes ludicrously luxurious, and at the country place on Lake Pontchartrain, the relation grows idyllically close. Tom and Eva read the Bible and sing hymns together. Even the cynical St. Clare develops a deep sense of Tom's virtues, though he cannot quite manage the conversion that Tom so respectfully urges on him. He can only renounce late carousing.

It is presently plain that Eva is dying of tuberculosis, a disease that in Mrs. Stowe's time was sentimentally associated with delicate spiritual gifts. Just before Eva dies in a high odor of sanctity, she commends Tom to St. Clare's promise of freedom for him and assures all that she will meet them up above. None of this is quite as crudely blasphemous as the Tom-shows were to be. But Mrs. Stowe did make Eva a sort of paper-doll Christ of the wrong sex: ". . . when I saw those poor creatures on the boat . . . ," Eva tells Tom, "and a great many other times, I've felt that I could be glad to die, if my dying could end all this misery. I *would* die for them, Tom, if I could." And she was certainly assigned, on Mrs. Stowe's recommendation, to a literal and facile Heaven: ". . . in the heart of Eva, a calm, sweet, prophetic certainty that Heaven was near: calm as the light of sunset, sweet as the bright stillness of autumn, there her little heart reposed, only troubled by sorrow for those who loved her so dearly."*

Meanwhile Miss Ophelia, prodding her patron-cousin

* In fairness to Mrs. Stowe it should be pointed out that generally her descriptions of Eva, particularly the passages quoted above, are among the worst she ever wrote.

about the iniquities of slavery, learns that he can denounce the "peculiar institution" more bitterly than any Yankee:

> This cursed business . . . because my brother Quashy is ignorant and weak, and I am intelligent and strong . . . I may steal all he has, keep it, and give him only . . . so much as suits my fancy. . . . Because I don't like work, Quashy shall work. Because the sun burns me, Quashy shall stay in the sun . . . shall lie down in every puddle, that I may walk over dry-shod. . . . Talk of the *abuses* of slavery! . . . The *thing itself* is the essense of all abuse! And the only reason why the land doesn't sink under it . . . is because it is *used* in a way infinitely better than it is. . . . When I have reflected that every brutal, disgusting, mean, low-lived fellow I met was allowed by law to become absolute despot of as many men, women and children as he could cheat, steal or gamble enough money to buy—when I have seen such men in actual ownership of helpless children, of young girls and women—I have been ready to curse my country, to curse the whole human race!

The grammar is shaky, but this tirade is a tonic corrective to the spun-sugar handling of Eva.

St. Clare nevertheless ridicules Miss Ophelia's wish that slaveowners might improve Negroes morally and intellectually. He maintains that such improvement is impossible under the degradations inevitable in slavery. On a sardonic whim he buys and gives Miss Ophelia a brutalized, quasi-animal Negro she-waif named Topsy for moral and intellectual experiment. Here Miss Ophelia is hampered not only by Topsy's simian habits but even more by the Northerner's physical shrinking from Negroes: ". . . she'd as soon have a toad touch her," says Topsy with bitter truth. Southern-born Eva does not feel so, can show Miss Ophelia how to gain Topsy through a love that ignores color of skin. St. Clare points the moral with monosyllabic true eloquence: ". . . if we want to give sight to the blind," he tells his perplexed cousin, "we must be willing to do as Christ did—call them to us and put our hands on them."

Prejudices erased, Miss Ophelia finally takes Topsy home with her for a proper rearing in Vermont. The others' destinies are all dreadful. St. Clare dies of a wound received when he intervenes in a barroom brawl. He has neglected to have Tom legally freed; now it is too late. Tom freely forgives him. As widow, the callous Marie St. Clare breaks up the household and sells all house slaves, Tom included. He is bought by Simon Legree, Yankee-born quondam pirate, who owns a cotton plantation in the new country up the Red River and shows a fist "hard as iron from knocking down niggers." He plans to make Tom a "driver"—a slave foreman over field gangs—and assistant in his stated policy of working slaves to death in a few years and then buying replacements as cheaper in the long run than any coddling.

Tom is deprived of all but his Bible, a bit of Eva's hair and a keepsake dollar that George Shelby, growing son of his former owners, gave him on leaving Kentucky. The atmosphere of Legree's plantation is melodramatically degenerate in a sort of premonitory travesty of William Faulkner. The Big House built by Legree's predecessors is already falling down. Legree is often savagely drunk, alternately abusing and hobnobbing with Sambo and Quimbo, his incumbent drivers. His quadroon mistress, Cassie, whom he fears because she reputedly dabbles in black magic, has just been set to field work as penalty for defying him. Her successor is to be Emmeline, a pretty and unwilling mulatto girl bought at the same sale as Tom.

To start Tom as driver, Legree orders him to flog a slave too ill to work. Tom refuses: "I'm willing to work, night and day . . . while there's life and breath in me; but this yer thing I can't feel it right to do;—and mas'r, I *never* shall do it—*never!* . . . I'll die first." This earns him a heavy flogging. Capitalizing on her privileges, Cassie takes what care of him is possible. She is planning for Emmeline and herself an escape led into by a most implausible hocus-pocus of ghosts in the attic that presently persuades Legree that the two have already run away. He assumes that Tom knows about it and threatens to have his blood drop by drop unless he tells all. Tom, who knows nothing about it anyway, begs him not to damn himself by needless cruelty:

"Mas'r," he says, "if you was sick, or in trouble, or dying, and I could save you, I'd *give* ye my heart's blood. . . . O Mas'r, don't bring this great sin on your soul! It will hurt you more'n it will me! Do the worst you can, my troubles'll soon be over; but, if you don't repent, yours won't *never* end!" Disregarding such triumphant charity, Legree knocks him down and has the drivers flog him beyond hope of survival. All the while Tom prays for their souls and actually effectuates the conversion of even these expertly brutalized monsters.

While Tom is still lingering, enter George Shelby, newly come of age and bent on buying Tom back as his father had promised when selling him. So Tom dies aware that his folks had not forgotten him. The young fellow knocks Legree down for sneering at his threats of prosecution for Tom's death. The plantation slaves help to bury Tom. Kneeling in the grave, George swears that "from this hour, I will do *what one man can* to drive this curse of slavery from our land."

Cassie and Emmeline play even more heavily on Legree's superstitions and bad conscience to make their actual escape. En route they meet George Shelby whom Cassie identifies as Tom's friend and confides in as a likely ally. He escorts them on board a northbound steamboat. During the trip Cassie proves to be Eliza's long-lost mother. A freed West Indian octoroon in the next cabin proves to be George Harris's long-lost sister. No strawberry marks are involved.

All in all, much story. Synopsis makes it sound livelier than it is. The narrative is clogged with debate and exposition, but the Finns, Peruvians and Japanese who eventually read it had no reason to complain that it lacked action.

The official account of how Mrs. Stowe launched on writing it brought in one of the reasons for her implication of God. Early in 1850 she visited her brother Edward, a committed Abolitionist, in Boston. To her he introduced Josiah Henson, an able runaway who later claimed to have been the original of Uncle Tom. This was dubious in any definite sense, but Henson's piety and manner of escape may have supplied general suggestion. Later that year, in response to a letter from brother Edward's wife, urging her to write "something that will make this whole nation feel what an accursed thing slavery is," she is said to have fiercely pledged herself: "I will write that thing if I live!" Then, at a communion service in Brunswick, Maine: "Suddenly, like the unrolling of a picture scroll, the scene of the death of Uncle Tom seemed to pass before her. . . ." The same day she roughed it out and read it to her children, whom it moved to hysteria. Then she put it away until she found her husband dripping tears over it and "Largely at his suggestion . . . determined to write a serial story, the climax of which was to be the death of Uncle Tom." Much of this could be near truth. Calvin Stowe wept readily; the scene in question has power. But one must be cautious in listening to Beechers. They tended strongly to confuse what might picturesquely or advantageously have occurred with what actually did.

In one sense the thing was bound somehow to be written. Therein lies what intelligible reason there may be for Mrs. Stowe's reference to God as her collaborator. The tradition of handling sociological materials in fiction as easy-steps-for-the-public's-feet was already well established. And already two lady writers of international reputation—Harriet Martineau of England and Fredrika Bremer of Sweden—had noted, while visiting America, that fugitive slaves offered admirable opportunity for fictioneering. Miss Bremer, who represented much common sense, as well as the Victorian tradition of the refined lady novelist, had even elected "American women who have hearts and genius—the American mother" to exploit the opportunity and had accurately predicted that "the history of a fugitive pair," properly narrated, would "reduce all the prudential maxims of statesmanship to dust and ashes, and produce a revolution in the old widely-praised Constitution itself."

If Calvin Stowe's high-strung wife had known in advance of Miss Bremer's specifications—they were published after *Uncle Tom*—she need not have hesitated. She was an "American mother" right enough, with five little Stowes to prove it. Any child of her father—Lyman Beecher, the great Calvinist theologian and controversialist—had "heart and genius" by definition. And according to her own lights Harriet Beecher Stowe was an experienced writer, that is, she earned pin-money and servant hire by writing for the religious and antislavery press certain moral short stories, lay sermons, verses and chatty bits. One of these had dealt with a runaway slave, a decent master and a Quaker connected with the Underground Railroad. She had lived eight years in Cincinnati, a principal center of the UGRR, within sight of slave territory just across the river in Kentucky. She had even once spent a week end in Kentucky. Astonishing as it sounds, this was the basis of it all. She was describing slavery and the slave country from only a single visit of perhaps three days a few miles into Kentucky, which, she herself admitted, was not at all representative of the Deep South, where her story was concentrated.

In the middle of writing *Uncle Tom* she had to beseech Frederick Douglass, an eminent fugitive slave, to find someone to tell her how a cotton plantation looked and operated. True, she was steeped in Abolitionist propaganda, some of which, especially Theodore Weld's compilation *Slavery as It Is,** contained reliable information. Her brother Charles, hoping to evade the family destiny that every Beecher must be a preacher, had worked in New Orleans and returned with grim details, probably authentic enough, such as Legree's talk of "knocking down niggers." But by any modern standards she utterly lacked direct knowledge for Plot Two and, for Plot One, had adequate background on only the Underground Railroad episodes.

Nevertheless, when offering to write an antislavery story for the Abolitionist *National Era,* to which she was already a contributor, she glibly misrepresented her merchandise, telling the editor, an old acquaintance from Cincinnati, that her basis would be "observation, incidents which have occurred in the sphere of my personal knowledge, or in the knowledge of my friends," and assured him that she had had "ample opportunity for studying the negro character." She meant that in Cincinnati she had known some free Negroes and a few runaways, a highly preselected group originating in atypical slave states. She carried on the deception by tucking into *Uncle Tom* bits to persuade the unwary that she knew the South well: Thus the second chapter opens: "The traveller in the South must often have remarked that peculiar air of refinement . . . a particular gift of the quadroon and mulatto women. . . ." And halfway through, she very knowingly remarks: "There is all the difference in the world in the servants of Southern establishments, according

---

* Angelina Grimké Weld told her daughter that Mrs. Stowe said that she kept Weld's book "in her workbasket by day and slept with it under her pillow . . . till its facts crystallized into Uncle Tom." This would be clear from internal evidence without such direct testimony. *Slavery as It Is* has not had its due as a force forming antislavery opinion. In its first year alone, 1839, it sold close to 100,000 copies. (Barnes, *Anti-Slavery Impulse;* 231.)

to the character and capacities of the mistresses who have brought them up." * Such innuendo deceived even bilious Barrett Wendell into assuring his students that Harriet had most of her background for *Uncle Tom* from "personal ex- perience . . . the local sentiment aroused . . . may gener- ally be accepted as true." No doubt, as so often occurs when wishful statements are often repeated, she came to believe it herself. Late in life she elaborated for James Lane Allen, the Kentucky novelist who had asked why she had been so polite to Kentucky slaveowners, how she "visited somewhat extensively in Kentucky and . . . saw many counterparts of the Shelbys. . . ."

But then it probably never occurred to the staff of the *Na- tional Era,* when commissioning *Uncle Tom,* to ask how re- cently she had inspected conditions up the Red River or whether houses in New Orleans were really so like stage sets for *Lalla Rookh.* In that day people were less exacting in such matters. Byron set plots in the South Pacific, Scott in Palestine, without ever having even coasted past those regions: Prescott had never visited Peru; whereas our re- porter-minded times rightly put great stress on on-the-spot data even in fiction. The lower standards of Mrs. Stowe's time help to explain how her readers could ignore both Southern and Northern protests of her standing as witness to what the South and slavery were like. Outside the United States this issue can hardly be said even to have existed. The French knew that slavery existed in America; this Mme. Beecher-Stowe was American; it was assumed that she knew all about it. Attacks on her reliability, however shrewd, could not discourage the throngs of Britons and other Euro- peans who greedily bought and read her book.

Even a novelist-with-a-purpose can occasionally fudge de-

---

* One flat lie in *Uncle Tom:* her assertion that "for many years" be- fore passage of the Fugitive Slave Act of 1850 she had "avoided all reading upon or allusion to . . . slavery." That would have been utterly impossible for anybody in the circles in which she moved.

tail with small harm done, and to object is pedantic. It is un-important that the craggy rocks in the middle of a plain where the slave catchers brought Mrs. Stowe's fugitives to bay would be hard to find in Indiana, though readily avail-able in a scenic warehouse. But descriptions of whole social groups and situations that depend for their interest on their claim to be well grounded, whether admittedly fictional or not, can be vicious when those claims are false. Creative li-cense is no excuse in the novel-with-a-purpose. If it were, Mrs. Stowe, herself a character whom John Bunyan might have named Mrs. Scribble-in-Haste, would not have felt so strong a need to overstate—to be polite about it—her qualifi-cations to describe and prescribe.

Soon she had some excuse in the Southern attack on *Uncle Tom,* supplemented by that of Northern friends of the South. Seldom valid, it was usually brutal or condescending, arrogant, sneering, sometimes obscene. Mrs. Stowe did not take it peacefully. The Beechers were confident that God was in their camp and that they did well to smite traducers hip and thigh. Under this heavy fire she prepared and pub-lished an elaborate factual justification called *A Key to Un-cle Tom's Cabin.* Its mass of double-columned type assembled the advertisements for runaways "dead or alive," the in-stances of children sold away from mothers and of slaves tor-tured to death that showed how everything in *Uncle Tom*— and worse—could have happened as described, a point that few have ever sought to deny. Even so oleaginous an apol-ogist for slavery as the Rev. Dr. Nehemiah Adams averred that Georgia slaveholders could "parallel most of the abuses" adduced in *Uncle Tom* and "in speaking of some bad master . . . would say, 'He is a real Legree.' "

Mrs. Stowe's self-protective impulse was natural, her mar-shaling of evidence was capable. But she twistily presented these data as the research materials used in *Uncle Tom.* Her title page said: "Presenting the original facts and documents upon which the story is founded . . . ," and the text exploits her one foray across the Ohio as few trips so short have ever been worked: ". . . the writer . . . while on a journey through Kentucky," "while travelling in Kentucky a few years since," "while the writer was travelling in Kentucky many years ago. . . ." Those passages occur within a few pages. To the Duchess of Sutherland, an august British friend and sympathizer of hers, Mrs. Stowe wrote that the *Key* was "made up of the facts, the documents, the things which my own eyes have looked upon and my hands have handled, that attest this awful indictment upon my country." Actually, of course, the pressure of supplying weekly installments would have ruled out adequate research if she had considered such work necessary. Practically every item in the *Key* was sought out *ad hoc* after *Uncle Tom* was finished.

At the time she resented having thus to convince people that she could speak with authority of what she actually knew so little about. She wrote to Eliza Follen, a noted Yankee good-causer: ". . . till I began the examinations of facts to write [*A Key*], much as I had thought I knew before, I had not begun to measure the depth of the abyss. . . . I was obliged to spend three months in what were to me the most agonizing researches. . . . All that consoled me was that I was bearing the same kind of suffering that Christ bore. . . ." Research can be dull, as writers know, sometimes arduous, but seldom comparable to what one hears of crucifixion. Sacrilege aside, it was all in the exact spirit of the King of Hearts' ruling—verdict first, evidence later.

Five years after beginning *Uncle Tom* she set to work on another antislavery novel, *Dred: A Tale of the Great Dismal Swamp*. It exploited much of the material included in the *Key*, particularly legal decisions illustrating the inconsistency of justice with the values of slavery. But you can't make a story out of judicial opinions, so blithely Mrs. Stowe plunged into the swamp of her choice, towing behind her hundreds of thousands of readers without first warning them that she had never been there before either.

No doubt it was Longfellow's verses about runaway slaves in the Great Dismal, which she inserted in the *Key,* that attracted her to this setting. It was known otherwise that fugitives had set up semipermanent settlements in this great morass between tidewater Virginia and amphibious North Carolina. Dred, her fanatical chief refugee, reflects what Mrs. Stowe had read of Nat Turner, leader of the bloody slave insurrection round Suffolk, Virginia, on the northern margin of the Great Dismal, twenty-five years earlier. He was also shown as son of Denmark Vesey, the free Negro insurrectionist of Charleston. All this pointed toward her setting her story in northeastern North Carolina, a long-settled region bordering the Great Dismal to the southward. But she had never visited either Virginia or North Carolina and, in view of the way the South had taken *Uncle Tom,* might have been well advised not to go there to see what they were like.

The remedy was promptly at hand in a new book: Olmsted's *Journey in the Seaboard Slave States,* first of his fine studies of the slavery South. His careful accounts of his travels in the Carolinas encouraged her to daub away at her poor whites, mulatto overseers, camp meetings and plantation life, incapable of suspecting that she was as ill advised as a portraitist consenting to work solely from description. Her slapdash temperament may even have kept her from noticing how scrupulously Olmsted made it clear that his material on the Great Dismal itself, some of which she borrowed with hardly any rewriting,* was all secondhand, merely

---

* Mrs. Stowe's debt to Olmsted would be plain generally even without such parallel passages. She "began . . . *Dred* . . . the end of February, 1856." (Wilson, *Crusader in Crinoline;* 410.) She had already read the *Seaboard Slave States,* or at least the *Independent* carried her endorsement of the book on January 21, 1856. (Schlesinger, introduction to

recording what those who had worked or hunted runaways in the area told him. So, when she finally got her action shifted into the swamp to justify the striking title of the book, her background was actually thirdhand. It shows it. Her Great Dismal is as artificial as a stage tree, about as sinister as a blueberry patch.

Dred sold well, 150,000 copies the first year in the United States and even better in England, where Queen Victoria admired it and Miss Martineau pronounced it superior to *Uncle Tom*, a most questionable judgment. But, though dramatized with some success both sides of the water, it never became embedded in American folklore as did its predecessor. Its sole present interest lies in further demonstration of Mrs. Stowe's irresponsibility and of the closeness with which her attitudes reflected—or created, or followed, as you please—the mind of her time; for *Dred* wholly blackens and deepens the negative aspects of *Uncle Tom*. Unlike Legree, its villain comes to no bad end, but flourishes as symbol of an outrageous South, unregenerate and still to be punished, a device that distressed Queen Victoria. Religion as spiritual refuge for the slave is shown as helping pitifully few: "where one soul is raised to higher piety, thousands are crushed in hopeless imbecility." And where did she learn that? From Olmsted's doubts of the efficacy of conversion among slaves and his dismayed descriptions of "dull, idiotic, and brute-like" field hands "with their usual besotted expression. Clumsy, awkward, gross, elephantine . . . pouting, grinning, and leering at us," whom he found from Virginia southward.

One after another *Dred* closes doors that in *Uncle Tom*

Cotton Kingdom; xxvi.) Perhaps she had read Olmsted's original letters, from which the book was compiled, in the New York *Times* as they appeared. She probably knew Olmsted personally; at least she had given him a letter of introduction to Cassius M. Clay in November, 1853. (*Lincoln Herald,* June, 1946.) The only alternative to the theory of her having borrowed heavily from Olmsted (legitimately enough) is that she endorsed his book without reading it.

sometimes admitted faith or at least charity if not hope. The old Roman of a Southern judge must publicly expound law that outrages his own decent instincts. The poor-white wench gloats over possession of her first slave. The Southern clergy pass by on the other side. Mrs. Stowe has no more illusions about reconciling the North and South through allying right-eous Northerners with Southerners of foresight and good will. All that her good Southerners can do for their slaves is to colonize them in Canada. She is, in fact, on the verge of calling down lightnings on Sodom on the usual grounds. Or, to shift the locale, though she has never visited Babylon, she is intuitively sure that, weighed in her own infallible bal-ances, that proud city would prove worse than wanting. Her definitive biographer called *Dred* a "broadside of hate." And so it was.

For better or worse, *Uncle Tom* had made her the locus of Northern conscience on slavery and intersectional problems; so in 1856 her rancorous pessimism was ominous. The Beech-ers' legend has it that, when she was presented to Abraham Lincoln, he almost affectionately called her "The little lady who wrote the book that made this great war." If this actu-ally occurred, the suggestion has weight, since Lincoln's sense of public relations was superb. But perhaps "hastened" would have fitted better. It accords better with modern ap-proaches to see Mrs. Stowe as a series of lenses reflecting and concentrating light and heat on materials already smolder-ing. Editors generally agree that the secret of problem-novel best sellers is that they appear just when the public is ready for the content concerned—that, in effect, *Main Street* would have been only a *succès d'estime* in 1910. Certainly the moral theories and social misconceptions that Mrs. Stowe crammed into *Uncle Tom* soon became tools to shape the attitudes of herself and her swarming readers toward the actual re-sults of the Fugitive Slave Act and squatter sovereignty. As the witty lady said of another wrongheaded catalyst, Mrs. Stowe invented nothing but set everything on fire.

This theory of timing is good enough to interpret her loss of temper between *Uncle Tom* and *Dred* as betokening a corresponding shift in the emotions of her mass public. The North's uneasiness about slavery, latent but looming for generations and due somehow to manifest itself some time, had been precipitated by *Uncle Tom*. In the four years between it and *Dred*, mounting Southern aggressiveness had chafed sore places, drawn and then slashingly underscored lines of cleavage. The political parallel was the national advent, in the same year as *Dred*, of the Republican party, inevitably as sectional as slavery.* A meaningful dialogue in *Dred* concludes: "Well," the hero tells his Southern crony, "there's one element of force left out of your calculation . . . God. . . . I believe he is alive yet."

Indeed he was. Within a few years he would muffle his knife-thin mouth in a Mosaic beard and pass himself off as John Brown, the other great hastener.

But hastening is not causing. Hence it cannot be said that, even though her sins of irresponsibility were great, Mrs. Stowe's book did more good than harm. The Civil War was probably inevitable. At least the slaves were going to be freed somehow some time, and that, with or without formalized shooting, would precipitate a cataclysmic crisis. What Mrs. Stowe—and John Brown—did was not to create the forces that would free the slave but to make sure that North

---

* Rhodes (*History of the United States*, I; 278) called *Uncle Tom* "one of the most important causes" of Republican victory in 1860, explaining: "The mother's opinion was a potent educator in politics between 1856 and 1860 . . . boys in their teens in one year were voters in the other." Woodrow Wilson (*Division and Reunion;* 181) said that *Uncle Tom* "a subtle instrument of power . . . played no small part in creating the anti-slavery party."

and South went into their crisis in the least promising state of mind.

Condition contrary to fact is bad historical manners. It did rain before Waterloo; Booth did aim true; warning was disregarded the morning of Pearl Harbor. The shortcomings of Mrs. Stowe and *Uncle Tom* can nevertheless be usefully illuminated by speculating on what might have happened if Frances Anne Kemble Butler had not had domestic woes.

I introduce her here for deliberately invidious comparison with Mrs. Stowe. Fanny Kemble's personal style and convinced pride came from England's greatest dynasty of actors, even the women members being received in good houses. Her brains, beauty and wayward integrity were all her own, but she was Mrs. Siddons's niece, John Kemble's niece, Charles Kemble's daughter, and it is embarrassing even to think of how Mrs. Stowe's sanctimonious horror of the stage would have appeared to this brilliant and beautiful lady who was also a stage player of immense ability. Say that she was what all bright and ambitious girls have wished to be since 1800, only she managed not to be mawkish about it.

In her late teens she toured the United States, delighting packed houses in classic and semiclassic roles and then, as soon as she had sent home enough money to get her remarkable family out of current difficulties, married Pierce Butler, a young Philadelphian of wealth and aristocratic Southern connections. The intellectual Sedgwicks of Stockbridge, Massachusetts, had made great friends with her and fired her to sympathy with slaves. When Butler went South to supervise his family's rice and cotton plantations in the Sea Islands of Georgia, the Sedgwicks urged Fanny to go along and play ministering angel to the hands. Butler did not oppose this plan. The marriage was still newish and Fanny was smashingly lovely and in any case not at all the sort of woman readily opposed.

All the following year she wrote to Elizabeth Sedgwick, by prearrangement, long journal letters describing actual con-

ditions on Butler's and St. Simon's islands, an epitome of the
sanitation, morality, religion and economy of somewhat superior low-country slavery. This record was the more poign-
ant because the evident futility of the ministering angel business wrung her with frustration. Fanny here was also the
qualified witness that Mrs. Stowe was not—no few-days visitor touring the South to round out a book of travels and getting Treatment A from planters to whom one had letters,
but the planter's wife living the facts season in and season
out. The noisome slave hospital, the cynically lecherous overseer, the shiftless slave mothers, the sales that broke up marriages, the degenerating effect on her own child of thus living among slaves were for her not matters of propaganda
hearsay or even inquisitive acquaintance but immediate experiences, immediately described, smells and sunsets inter-
mingled. The Butler's Island establishment has now disappeared, all but the ruined chimneys of the rice mill. Let-
tuce has replaced rice on its wide fields, but it is not dead.
Combine her book with the brimming river and the expan-
sive swamp, and it all lives again.

That comes of her work's having an aesthetic integrity denied *Uncle Tom*. Being of deeper cultivation, intelligence
and emotional potential than Mrs. Stowe, she wrote with
sweep and pungency that the other's pattering method and
occasionally well-swung phrase never approached. Even in
debate, where Mrs. Stowe was strong, the comparison must
be unfavorable. Fanny's preface on her civilized reprehen-
sion of slavery, which, she candidly warned, was written before she went South, couples a man's slashing logic with a
woman's nimbleness in turning issues inside out to show
their unsuspected prickles. And the magnetic actress had the
further, and no doubt unfair, advantage of an extraordinary
personality, sensitive, vigorous, willful, witty and twitchy as
the fine horses that she loved to ride hell for leather. Barring
a few contemporary misconceptions about heredity, as when
she ascribed a mulatto slave's troubles to "the mutinous

white blood," she is astonishingly modern and can be read today with few precautions. She describes slaves as

> . . . diabolically cruel to animals . . . they seem to me as a rule, hardly to know the difference between truth and falsehood. These detestable qualities, which I constantly hear attributed to them as innate and inherent in their race, appear to me the direct result of their condition. The individual exceptions among them are, I think, quite as many as would be found, under similar circumstances, among the same number of white people.

Even when seeking after deep emotion, she did not idealize her materials:

> In one miserable hut I heard that the baby was just dead; it was one of thirteen, many of whom had been, like itself, mercifully removed from the life of degradation and misery to which their birth appointed them; and whether it was the frequent repetition of similar losses, or an instinctive consciousness that death was indeed better than life for such children as theirs, I know not, but the father and mother, and old Rose, the nurse, who was their little baby's grandmother, all seemed apathetic, and apparently indifferent to the event. The mother merely repeated over and over again, "I've lost a many; they all goes so"; and the father, without word or comment, went out to his enforced labor.

For once a blurb was accurate when Harper's announced this as "the most powerful anti-slavery book ever written." Its scope was narrow—the flat, oozy Sea Islands, all muck and sky, where isolated gangs of slaves worked large plantations under conditions unlike those on small Piedmont cotton farms or in sleazy Arkansas river settlements. But anyone reading it thenceforth knew what was bad about slavery with an intimacy that Mrs. Stowe never approached. And it sold magnificently well on both sides of the Atlantic. Only it had stayed too long in Elizabeth Sedgwick's desk.

The Sedgwicks had urged Fanny to publish these letters soon after she broke with Butler, several years before Mrs. Stowe envisioned *Uncle Tom*. But Fanny was a burned child. Her previous book on her impressions of the United States had been too widely taken amiss. She also shrank from publishing data that she could have learned of only in her private capacity of planter's wife. And, even if these considerations had not obtained, she hesitated further to annoy Butler, whose potential right to take away her children always haunted her. So *A Journal of a Residence on a Georgian Plantation* did not reach booksellers until May, 1863, when the fat had long been popping in the fire and the Negroes' cause was already speciously summed up in the mythical figures jauntily celebrated by Dr. Holmes: "Uncle Tom and Old John Brown." Her reason for finally publishing was hope that her book would strengthen Britons who opposed British support to the Confederacy. The gesture was probably futile, since the Palmerston government had renounced positively countenancing the South several months earlier.

The pity of it is that publication in 1848, say, an election year with the slavery issue hot from the implications of the Mexican War, might have seen sales even larger than were achieved in 1863. The notoriety of her previous book would have been much fresher in people's recollections, and there would have been less feeling of "Oh, another book about slavery" as a brake on sales. And it is really not at all unlikely that, had Fanny's *Journal* made such a roaring success before 1851, Mrs. Stowe might never have felt that *Uncle Tom* wanted writing. I do not contend that the *Journal* would ever have gone as far as Mrs. Stowe's work. It would not have appealed so strongly to potential admirers of Eva. It lacked the claptrap of Legree's stagey rantings about his mother. Nevertheless, it was anything but a dry survey. A recent biographer of Fanny justly says that "Preacher London, Psyche and Venus, Jack and Headman Frank are as alive as any characters in Mrs. Stowe's melodrama." Person-

ally I find them much more so. And even though Lady
Son Klin might not have fallen in love with the *Journal,* it
might well have been so widely read and so widely de-
nounced and might have proved so effective a lightning rod
for Mrs. Stowe's and her friends' emotions that she would
have had small occasion to seek to outdo it in fiction. As it is,
the relative renown of the two books is absurdly out of balance, about in inverse proportion to their respective merits:
Of sixty-one of my questionnaire respondents who had read
Uncle Tom's Cabin, only two had read the *Journal.**

The South would certainly have got out bell, book and
candle for her in 1848. To this day many pretty open-minded
Southerners cannot forgive her; it particularly irks them that
she recorded, with no betraying emphasis, that the Sea Island
planters, who were certainly well-to-do "quality," lived lives
that, to a gently reared Englishwoman, seemed sordid, messy
and inane.† But actually her book might have been some-

---

* This questionnaire about *Uncle Tom* and allied subjects was sent to
several hundred personal acquaintances, allowing them to be anonymous if they preferred. The results were scientifically negligible, of
course. But they often did give interesting informal cross sections of the
opinions of a happenstance group of Americans, well educated as
a rule, of the sort who make up articulate public opinion—writers,
newspapermen, editors, publishers, spiced with doctors, lawyers, artists,
scientists, businessmen and the wives and daughters of same. It will be
referred to in the text as occasion arises.

† Daniels (*A Southerner Discovers the South;* 314) felt that Fanny must
have been both "talented and evil-tempered in her righteousness so to
sting the planters . . . with her descriptions for the abolitionists of
their depravity and oppression." The sting is easily explicable if you
think of a professional Southerner reading Fanny's account of a visit
to the beautiful daughter of an ex-governor of Georgia: ". . . the residence of this princess . . . was like all the planters' residences that
I have seen, and such as a well-to-do English farmer would certainly
not inhabit. Occasional marks of former elegance or splendor survive
sometimes in the size of the rooms, sometimes in a little carved wood-
work about the mantel-pieces . . . but all things have a Castle Rackrent-
air of neglect, and dreary, careless untidiness, with which the dirty,

thing of a friend in disguise for the South. It fostered few
of the misconceptions that helped to make a tragic failure of
Reconstruction; whereas a great modern historian concludes:
"No small part of the incredible optimism with which the
North later approached the task of converting slaves into voters, self-dependent citizens, and legislators, thinking it could
be done overnight, is chargeable to the impression diffused
by Mrs. Stowe." Pierce Butler's much-hated wife could never
have written to the Duchess of Argyle or anybody else as
Mrs. Stowe did in 1862:

> . . . whether God be with us or not, I know He is with the
> slave, and with his redemption will come the solution of our
> question. . . . I wish [Southerners] no ill, feel no bitterness.
> . . . We don't expect any more of *them,* but if slavery is
> destroyed, one generation of education and liberty will efface
> these stains.

That Sunday-school superficiality was what ailed much of
Mrs. Stowe's message. It is notable further that Fanny Kemble
encouraged none of the other tendentious errors that *Uncle
Tom* saddled on the nation. Her book has no condescending
profundities about "the African race"; no tunnel-vision concentration on the difficult but minor problem of "white as
you are"; no wistful dwelling on the possibility of removing
the Negro problem by removing the Negroes; no misleading
emphasis on the slave as a freedom-craving Spartacus or a
desponding potential suicide; no temptation to the stage to
cheapen the Negro by tawdry hippodroming of the super-
ficialities of a third-rate novel. And on the positive side

---

barefoot negro servants are in excellent keeping." (*Georgian Plantation;*
116.) Phillips, the brilliant historian of slavery, stayed Southerner
enough to scold Fanny and her evidence while using it: ". . . she registered her horror of slavery in advance, and the resulting record is
gloomy enough . . . the new mistress herself repudiating the title, was
more irritable and meddlesome than helpful." (*American Negro Slavery;*
251.)

Fanny told much that her readers could not otherwise learn (certainly not from Mrs. Stowe*) about the severe cultural handicaps of slaves that probably would require generations to eradicate.

Thus, if the nation had had the opportunity to focus on her book instead of on *Uncle Tom,* it might have floundered into the Civil War with a better chance of doing clearer thinking now and again about the South and slavery. In a crisis even a small advantage can be crucial. This consideration leads to bitter thoughts about Mrs. Stowe's well-meant irresponsibilities. To our great emotional and economic cost, we have had to live with the consequences of them for over a century now, and the end is not yet.

---

* Fanny prepared an elaborate letter to the London *Times* defending *Uncle Tom* against charges of exaggeration, then decided not to submit it because she mistrusted the patent pro-Southerner bias of the paper. Eventually it appeared as Appendix to her *Journal* in 1863.

2 *The little lady who . . .*

*"All Mrs. Stowe's books . . . illustrate . . . the absolute
necessity of making over the world on the New England
model."* —BRADFORD, Portraits of American Women

*"Even in New England, where there is . . . more wisdom
and virtue than in any other part of the United States. . . ."*
—*George Cabot to Timothy Pickering, quoted in*
HENRY ADAMS, Formative Years

In spite of a biography or two every generation and a mildly
successful play about her in 1943,* the literate mind is al-

---

* That is, *Harriet,* by Florence Ryerson and Colin Clements, a chipper
bit of fiction that starred Helen Hayes and showed Mrs. Stowe hating
"the noise, the arguments and confusion [of the Beechers]. . . . Pa
and Catherine always crusading for some cause. . . ." Actually Mrs.
Stowe showed few if any signs of such sentiments. The play seems bent
on making her a watered-down Barrie heroine, aimed at the secondary
woman's magazine market, an intense madcap, primly rebellious, with
charmingly uninhibited children. She is even shown as broadminded
about the theater, saying that, to put her message over, she would consent to see *Uncle Tom* dramatized if her consent were necessary. See
p. 260 for the facts that this coolly jettisons. There are offstage noises
from slave-hunting mobs outside the Stowes' house in Cincinnati
and of another mob demonstrating against Mrs. Stowe personally and
hurling a copy of *Uncle Tom* through her parlor window in, of all
hotbeds of proslavery feeling, Andover, Massachusetts! The one thing
to be said for this sort of thing is that Hollywood does biographical
films even worse. And this script at least makes Henry Ward Beecher
out as just as unpleasant a specimen as he probably was.

most as vague about Harriet Beecher Stowe as it is about her astounding book. Oh, yes, worthy little woman . . . wrote *Uncle Tom's Cabin* . . . started the Civil War . . . titles of other books not readily recalled . . . pious . . . did the words of "The Battle-Hymn of the Republic"—no, that was somebody else—Julia . . .

Actually she was a character created by Louisa M. Alcott: the ugly duckling gradually evincing talent in a Yankee context, committed to a world where women doughtily make do because men are shiftless, though pretentious and important, gamely scribbling hack work to eke out the family purse. Call her Jo March with a small-boned skeleton, curly hair, many children, and a touch of megalomania.

Like most people's, her life was intimate and corporeal, and either trivial or terrifying, depending on which details are stressed. She loved dogs and wrote of them charmingly. John Ruskin, Nathaniel Hawthorne, George Eliot and Oliver Wendell Holmes variously liked or admired her, or said that they did. She was good-natured, if demurely self-conscious, about rearing a large family on little money. In her prosperity she used her gains with engaging foolishness and was intensely loyal to her tribe in spite of their afflicting her with a whited sepulcher of a brother, a psychopathic half-sister, an alcoholic son and a daughter addicted to morphine.

Specifically she was a younger daughter, by his first wife, of the Rev. Dr. Lyman Beecher, a figure as important among theologians in his day as Reinhold Niebuhr is in ours. With numerous brothers and sisters Harriet Beecher was reared under this ponderous shadow in Litchfield, Connecticut, a town still handsome and then a highland center of New England culture. By an abortive sort of semicoincidence, John Brown, of Harpers Ferry fame, was born eleven years earlier in Torrington, only six miles away. Beechers thought well of themselves. In 1853 a biographical sketch prefacing a minor work of Mrs. Stowe's, which must have passed under her eye in proof, asserted, "The family to which Mrs. Stowe belongs, is more widely and favorably known than almost any other in the United States." Elder sister Catherine was a pioneering educationist and bluestocking. All her seven brothers became ministers; the most eminent was Henry Ward Beecher, who spread the family renown first as a mighty pulpiteer and then as the most conspicuous adulterer in American history.

At about the time of Harriet's maturity Lyman Beecher took most of his family, including her, to assist and applaud as he founded a new theological seminary in Cincinnati, thus giving her *almost* firsthand knowledge of slavery. There in her mid-twenties she married a recently widowed and fustily learned young theologian, Calvin Stowe, whose first wife had been an intimate of wife number two. Harriet Beecher bore him many children and, apparently, little grudge for his shortcomings as breadwinner. She survived him, living to a great old age encumbered by a pathetic senility.

Many such personal data have meanings only remote or obscure; whereas Mrs. Stowe's rearing, education, crotchets and aesthetic and intellectual attainments are most pertinent to her effect on an unlucky world. Our main concern is with what a garrulous contemporary called "the foremost woman in America," the literary property who set herself down in thirty-odd volumes of fiction, polemics, travel, pious verse, lay sermons and simpering twaddle. She was a twin, but not always an identical twin, of the woman who cohabited with Professor Stowe, that potent but flabby bedfellow, and so yearningly idealized healthy, cultivated spinsterhood.

"No Jewish maiden ever grew up with a more earnest faith that she belonged to a consecrated race, a people specially called and chosen of God for some great work on earth."
—STOWES, Harriet Beecher Stowe

The salient fact about her is almost too easily identified: She was a Yankee, not in the Southerner's sense of born north of Mason and Dixon's line or the European's sense of "Yank" as "American outsider," but in the salt-codfish, white-steeple, close-bargaining and plain-living sense applied by gentiles to old-stock New Englanders and by no means always with flattering connotations.

Modern Yankees are less articulate about the scandalous way the rest of the nation neglects New England's standard of behavior. This may mean that they have grown less assured of their cultural prerogatives. Five generations ago they showed no such hesitancy. They may also have been better justified because Yankee textbooks, parsons, missionaries, shipbuilders, skippers, industrialists, reformers, prophets and writers then consistently led the nation in both intellectual and economic enterprise. An impartial observer would have had ample reason to suspect that, in some terms or other, these were unusual people. But the Yankees could never let their universal genius earn its own laurels. They knew themselves to be a touch too special for ordinary accounting and firmly believed that their primacy in so many fields was founded on divine mandate as well as on practical ability. The early New Englanders' contention that they were God's chosen remnant intended to establish His designs in the wilderness, with assistance from miracles at His discretion, was no mere pious snuffling. Outsiders might take it for heartening metaphor, but the Yankee knew that it meant literally what it said. Lyman Beecher set out for Cincinnati in precisely the spirit of a World Health Organization doctor taking hookworm control to a backward people.

This point of view was often most distinguishable in parsons, who were New England's elder statesmen as well as priests, their prestige manifest in both influence and silver-headed canes. Telling others what to do in matters secular as well as spiritual was the natural and particular function of the Yankee minister. His prototypes were John Calvin and John Knox, always so diligent in their self-appointed business of standing before kings, and, further back, the Old Testament judges. The Calvinist, who takes pride in denouncing himself with special harshness, feels entitled to apply the same whip of scorpions to others. And parsons' children might share this urge even when, being female, they could not hope to stand in pulpits. Hence parsons' children were often especially Yankee-minded. They had special reason to value the traditions and institutions that made their fathers aristocrats ex officio and trained themselves in an austere and rewarding narcissism.

Thus Mrs. Stowe's peroration to *Uncle Tom,* calling on the "men and women of America" to take action about slavery, mentions only two Northern states outside New England— New York and Ohio, both already heavily infiltrated with Yankees. Otherwise, she apostrophizes the "Farmers of Massachusetts, of New Hampshire, of Vermont, of Connecticut, who read this book by the blaze of your winter-evening fires —strong-hearted, generous sailors and ship-owners of Maine —is this a thing for you to protect and countenance?" The implication is stronger for being inadvertent; hope of decency centers in New England. In allowing that scoundrels may also be found in New York and London, she goes on: "Nay, take the purest district in New England. . . ." Consider her loving descriptions of Miss Ophelia's Vermont home, always calm, clean and orderly without visible effort, so the non-Yankee wonders as at an enchanted palace per-

petually "redd-up" by spirits. And consider Miss Ophelia
herself, with her standing verdict of "Shiftless!" on each successive instance of the sloppiness that, Mrs. Stowe knew
only by hearsay, however accurately, slavery had saddled on
the South.

She was on sound ground in calling slavery necessarily
cruel, degrading and wasteful, but she could not refrain
from going on, in effect, "Look at us Yankees! How much
better to do things our way!" Sometimes she was chauvinis-
tic, as when extolling the heroes of Reconstruction as those
"noble men . . . [who] have just consummated . . . the
sublimest national and moral reform the world ever saw . . .
tracing their descent in lineal blood to the Puritan parentage
or, like Garrison, spiritually born of the eternal influences
which they left in the air of the society they moulded."

Some of these tactless comparisons between Yankees and
those who dwelt in outer darkness were not unjustified, but
they were a poor basis for treating the national cancer of
slavery, present in only one section but threatening the
welfare of the whole organism. No doubt the nation's conscience needed rousing on the point. But the chosen instrument for rousing it should not have been a Litchfield dog-
matist's child trained to refer all phenomena to benchmarks
set up for all time north and east of Greenwich, Connecticut.

Description tends to overstress this cocksure parochialism.
The category Yankee also included Olmsted, the soundest reporter on the slave states; R. H. Dana, the most level-headed
Abolitionist; and Theodore Weld, the most decent doctrinaire ever to espouse Abolition. Nor was Mrs. Stowe an extreme example. She was never a "kiver-to-kiver" Abolitionist in the grim and altogether Yankee manner of Garrison
and Phillips and of such Yankee emigrants to Ohio as Gid-
dings and John Brown. She consented to Abolitionist lionizing after the triumph of *Uncle Tom* and was as shrill as
anyone during the Civil War. But she never disowned sister
Catherine's *Essay on Slavery and Abolitionism* of 1837, which

called Abolitionists un-Christian and even cowardly. To the orthodox "nigger-lover," as the rabble named the Abolitionist, slavery was a salient angle in the forts of folly, to reduce which would expedite carrying the whole work. True, Mrs. Stowe did set St. Clare talking like a German student of 1848 about irresistible stirrings among the masses, of which slaves' unrest was only part.* But she lacked the temperament for the complete syndrome of Garrison's Friends of Universal Reform summed up by Seldes as "woman's suffrage, temperance, non-resistant pacifism, prison reform, justice to the redman . . . attacks upon state lotteries . . . radical ideas on education, spiritualism, keeping the Sabbath holy, and the sinlessness of humanity."

The typical Abolitionist female was prim little Lucy Stone wearing the Bloomer costume, refusing to take her husband's name, lecturing on Abolition tonight, tomorrow on the "Demon Rum," next night on woman's rights; whereas Mrs. Stowe was something of an amateur Tory, as befitted the daughter of a man who took it as black personal tragedy when Connecticut disestablished the Puritan church. Her quasi-autobiographic novel, *Poganuc People,* scolded the "pauper population of Europe," the people about whom Emma Lazarus later wrote the verses on the base of the Statue of Liberty, for swarming in to undermine Yankee thrift and self-respect. On immoral yellowback French novels—apparently including those of Balzac and Flaubert—her *Pink and White Tyranny* sounds like Anthony Comstock. Sister Catherine, though favoring women teachers in public schools, opposed woman's suffrage, and so did Harriet. She followed brother Henry when he took up the cause of temperance, then meaning prohibition and regarded as liberal, but not zealously enough always to resist the wine when it was bubbly. Though she had a drift toward being a crank, she worked it off by

---

* It was probably this flavor of amateur Jacobinism, not that of Protestantism, that got *Uncle Tom* banned in Papal Rome. (Rhodes, *History of the United States,* I; 278.)

way of phrenology, spiritualism, homeopathy, hydropathy, a formidable list but liberal-trending only in the phrenologist's teaching, important in social history, that people aren't responsible for what they do.

Even in *Dred,* for all its bad temper, Mrs. Stowe did try, as Garrison and company never did, to see slavery through national spectacles. Her Southern assailants identified her with the North in general instead of with New England in particular.* But all the while the chronic Yankee underneath felt comment for others' good to be a pleasure, however disguised as "the duty of rebuke which every inhabitant of the free States owes to every slave-holder." Like Martha Hawkins in *The Hoosier Schoolmaster,* Mrs. Stowe was likely to describe how things were or were not done "at the East" every time she opened her mouth. Only in her novels of New England could this regional self-glorification be gracefully affectionate.

The overweeningness of the Yankee parson was another hazard in her intellectual path. All writers touching on fact are doomed to write to some extent as if pretending to omniscience. The degree to which they resist this tendency— none is altogether guiltless—gauges their intellectual integrity, that tool of their trade corresponding to a carpenter's level. By any such criterion Mrs. Stowe was hopeless, abjectly so. She apparently never even recognized that the temptation to this sin existed. Unwary readers of her work might readily assume that she was at the same time a psychologist, a physician, a geneticist, a theologian and a geographer. On Asiatic cholera in *Dred,* for instance, she assumes the airs of an 1850 authority on tropical epidemiology. The disease, she avers, "has many forms of approach and development. One, and the most deadly, is that which takes place when a person has long and gradually imbibed the fatal

---

* Perhaps this merely meant that the South, as parochial as New England and even worse informed, was not aware that any such distinction could be made.

poison of an infected atmosphere, and the resisting powers of nature have been insidiously and quietly subdued . . ." and so on. Then she goes out of her way to sneer at a doctor who takes "animalculae" seriously as a possible cause of cholera. No doubt she owed her reader a lay summary of what then passed for knowledge of the disease and was in no position to know that "animalculae" was a lucky shot plump on target. But she need not have taken this gravely and consideredly judicious tone. In *Uncle Tom* she had been just as pontifical about tuberculosis.

Not all of this came of being Lyman Beecher's daughter. She had been further brought to presumption by being set, as an ill-grounded, bony child of fourteen, to teaching Latin at Catherine Beecher's school for girls in Hartford. At sixteen she was teaching elementary theology, and at twenty-odd, having never been outside the northeastern quadrant of the then much smaller United States, she wrote a textbook on geography. Still, minister and schoolmarm are often closely akin, and both kinds of preceptor were then conspicuous among the exports from, and spokesmen for, New England.

The effect was notably unfortunate when Mrs. Stowe came to share brother Henry's admiration for phrenology—the psychological fad of a century ago that shows salutary parallels to the renown of psychoanalysis in our own time. These two best-known Beechers were not alone in liking the theory that the exterior shape of the skull signifies the properties and capacities of the brain within. Many another reputedly intelligent American or Briton of the day was most respectful about how cranial bumps showed amativeness, philoprogenitiveness, approbativeness and other polysyllabic qualities into which, no doubt in self-deceiving good faith, Gall and Spurzheim dissected the human spirit. Mrs. Stowe was only in the fashion of the day among the well informed when filling *Dred* with phrenological jargon.

She also dragged mesmerism into her glib generalizations

about "the African race," and so did many other lady novelists. But unfortunately Mrs. Stowe's effect on posterity would
be heavier than that of Fanny Fern and Grace Greenwood.
She was a self-appointed catalyst hoping to reduce a major
social disgrace, and her action would leave deeper marks than
theirs. So it was a serious matter when her intellectual gullibility about phrenology and other intellectual fads, which she
disguised as learned ponderings, tricked her and her readers
into deepening their belief in the half-baked racism of that
time. With appalling generosity Mrs. Stowe stuffed *Uncle
Tom* with sweeping statements about a kind of "African
race" that can never have existed in comparison with an
"Anglo-Saxon race" that never did either. Some of this is
really extraordinary. When made at home in the St. Clare
mansion, Tom is

> . . . in a beautiful place, a consideration to which his
> sensitive race are never indifferent. . . . If ever Africa shall
> show an elegant and cultured race . . . life will awaken
> there with a gorgeousness and splendor of which our cold
> western tribes faintly have conceived. In that far-off mystic
> land of gold, and gems, and spices, and waving palms, and
> wondrous flowers, and miraculous fertility will awaken new
> forms of art, new styles of splendor; and the negro race, no
> longer despised and trodden down, will perhaps show forth
> some of the latest and most magnificent revelations of human
> life. Certainly they will, in their gentleness, in their lowly
> docility of heart, their aptitude to repose on a superior mind
> and rest on a higher power, their childlike simplicity of af-
> fection, and facility of forgiveness.*

---

* She was not the only lady fictioneer guilty of such stuff. Here is
Sara J. Hale, popular novelist and editor of *Godey's Lady's Book,* in
Liberia: or, Mr. Peyton's Experiments, pp. 182-185: "Africa is the home
of the leviathan, the behemoth, the unicorn, the giraffe, the antelope,
the elephant, the lion, the buffalo . . . the home, too, of the mysterious
negro races yet lying dormant in the germ, destined, perhaps, to rule
this earth when our proud Anglo-Saxon blood is as corrupt as that of

Such rhapsody about poverty-stricken, skinny-soiled West Africa had much to do with good people's organizing to send freed slaves to die of infections and malnutrition in Sierra Leone and Liberia. Insidiously commingled here is also a flavor of Southerners telling how and why the "darky" is so dear to his white folks and can always so touchingly count on their taking care of him. It takes genius, perhaps a specifically female genius, thus to mix these two attitudes without a hint of transition. In one form or another racism was always tempting Mrs. Stowe's inrushing feet. When St. Clare's harsh brother scoffs at the lesson of Haiti on the grounds that the whites whom the slave insurrection wiped out were "not Anglo Saxons," which is in itself indicative of how strangely people thought of such matters in that day, St. Clare replies:

> Well, there is a pretty fair infusion of Anglo Saxon blood among our slaves now. . . . Plenty . . . have only enough of the African to give a sort of tropical warmth and fervor to our calculating firmness and foresight. If ever [slave revolt] comes, Anglo Saxon blood will lead the day. Sons of white fathers, with all our haughty feelings burning in their veins, will not always be bought and sold and traded. They will rise, and raise with them their mother's race.

Presumably well-informed people of good will indulged in such talk throughout Mrs. Stowe's long life. It is still all too readily acceptable among their descendants. She did not invent the crude old notion that emotional bents and intellectual potentials are as much matter of racial as of family inheritance. She was only one of many salient figures taking such doctrine for granted long before de Gobineau, the accepted whipping boy for racism, published his *Essai sur l'in-*

---

the descendants of Homer. . . . does the dark race, in all the varieties, possess a capacity of understanding and living out the deep laws of the world's ruler, Christianity, as the offspring of the followers of Odin never did, and never can, understand and act it?"

égalité des races humaines in 1855.* She not only anticipated
the warped Frenchman but probably did far more damage
than he ever managed. His readers were few if eventually influential; hers were fantastically many, and not from strata
usually accessible to intellectuals' nonsense at either first or
second hand.

No doubt what coaxed these millions into reading was the
emotional debauches clustered round Tom and Eva. But, like
others who knew only the ostracized Northern Negro, these
same readers must already have developed vague notions of
an innate Negro inferiority. Numbers of them, specially in
the Middle West, had parents or grandparents from the
South, bringing along a taken-for-granted race prejudice and
its attendant contemptuous folklore. Now this mordant
melodrama of Mrs. Stowe's provided these millions with an
apparently authoritative racist doctrine to plump out their
previously inchoate notions. The fact is that she invited her
unprecedentedly huge public to subscribe to the very terms
in which the harshest Southerners justified slavery, the very
terms that, if he ever were emancipated, would most tragically
handicap the American Negro.

I cannot show how many accepted this invitation. I do not
contend that Mrs. Stowe's non-Southern readers retained her
racist teachings as a matter of conscious learning. But her
books are the only racist propaganda known to have been
read favorably by very many at that time, and their effect
must always have been to instill or to strengthen racist ideas.
The victims unquestionably thought themselves generously
and mercifully moved against slavery. So they were. But this

---

* At least once she verged on knowing better. In London she met
Samuel Ringgold Ward, full-blooded and very black American Negro
preacher, and commented: "All who converse with him are satisfied that
there is no difference between the African and other men." (*Sunny
Memories of Foreign Lands*, II; 105.) She was wrong about that, too, of
course. But for once she was generalizing in the other direction, and
between her two positions the probable facts got bracketed.

was the generosity and mercy of antivivisectionists rather than of champions of fully *human* rights for fully human beings. People of Mrs. Stowe's mind about "the African race" were, so to speak, subscribing to the SPCA rather than to the Declaration of Independence.

The devil could have forged no shrewder weapon for the Negro's worst enemy; Mrs. Stowe's book was obviously decent and Christian, obviously warm with hopes of helping poor people with dark skins. Nevertheless, it became a principal occasion for Negroes to say, "God deliver us from our friends." As her work soaked into the common mind, fostering cheap sagacity about alleged racial traits down to our own day and affecting millions who have never read *Uncle Tom* or seen a Tom-show, it has sadly clogged the efforts of modern good will, acting on sounder information, to persuade people that this kind of racist idea does not hold water.

What does hold water, so far as is now known, will be gone into later. For the moment, take this as the most deleterious result of the lady's habit of not knowing what she was talking about.* In tinkering with society, good will is not enough.

How could the poor woman have known better in 1850? I do not know. But, in circumstances that made Negroes look much more like animals than any Mrs. Stowe ever met, Fanny Kemble now and again clearly saw and crisply stated the abject speciousness of the racist's case.

---

* Within a year of finishing *Uncle Tom,* she was under fire because she had not made sure of the data before defending her new friend the Duchess of Sutherland against charges of countenancing harshness to Highland tenants. This would make a book in itself, but at least one can say there is nothing in the charge of Moray McLaren in *The Scots* that the Duchess bribed Mrs. Stowe to write a book exonerating the Sutherland dynasty. Years later she was unconscionably abused for publicly accusing Lord Byron of incest (a charge now widely accepted as true) and mustering available proofs only when challenged. Here she thought she was defending Lady Byron, another of the greatly valued noblewoman friends that *Uncle Tom* brought her.

Even her religion helped to trip Mrs. Stowe. By rearing and temperament she was bound to consider Christian rewards in the next world fair recompense for suffering in this. And what she had seen of Negroes combined with much that she heard to suggest that the "African race" had a special, glorious talent for Christianity. Tom survives each ordeal with his loving charity intact. His and Eva's comradeship in devoutness, which is usually taken to be mere Victorian lacework, actually symbolizes the intimacy of fellowship in Christ that, on the other side of the grave, assuages such mundane trials as innate racial differences. Mrs. Stowe here says that beyond Jordan the inexplicable superiorities and inferiorities of sinful life will disappear. But she was *not* denying that, after the fashion of this world, Tom is Eva's racial inferior. She could have agreed with the Southern Presbyterians in 1843 that "The sons of Ethiopia, whatever may be said of their natural stupidity . . . have ever shown a ready disposition to stretch forth their hands to God" or with the decent Southern attitude on this issue as formulated by the late Howard W. Odum that "the Negro is just a Negro and must be kept in his place, but he is as dear in the sight of God as a white person."

She sometimes hinted that, in making Negroes especially apt for salvation, God justified His having given them the docility (her word) and nearer-the-animal qualities that enabled whites to exploit them. (I apologize for using these hymn-book terms, but they were real a hundred years ago and even now fall readily into place if one allows them just to flow over the consciousness.) Being as little children, Negroes were by definition potentially of such as the Kingdom of Heaven. It might even be that God was contemplating using Negroes to show Anglo-Saxons (that stiff-necked and disreputable generation!) how the handicapped might best their betters in what counts up yonder. This reverent travesty on the Beatitudes ironically recalls the fact that Christianity began as a cult of the underprivileged who understandably yearned for pie in the sky. It was Embree's skilled anthropological opinion that Christianity is a religion especially well suited to slaves.

Mrs. Stowe was at least sure that, whatever their innate dimness, Negroes had souls, a point disputed in the South, usually by innuendo. Here she was the eternal missionary, arrogating to the objects of her benevolence spiritual privileges at the same time that she condescended to them. In her view the damage to Negro souls consequent on slavery's denying them the opportunity to hear and accept the Gospel was the worst of the whole system. She thought of the plight of the slave as a sort of spiritual malnutrition. Cassie tells Tom in his agony, " . . . it can't be that the Lord will lay sin to our account. He won't charge it to us when we're forced to it; he'll charge it to them that drove us to it." "Yes," says Tom, "but that won't prevent us from growing wicked. If I get to be as hardhearted as that ar' Sambo, and as wicked, it won't make much odds to me how I come so. It's the *bein' so*—that ar's what I'm dreadin'."

That noble and subtle speech should have made Lyman Beecher proud of his daughter. She never created a sound Negro character. It is simply untrue, though an eminent historian said it, that "Mrs. Stowe was felicitous in her description of the negro character." But she did black up an ideal, simple Christian and depict him undergoing what Negroes too frequently experienced under slavery. The modern American Negro who resents *Uncle Tom's Cabin* has small reason to resent Tom specifically. He was dutiful to master and forgiving unto seventy times seven, not because of truckling instincts but because he was a true Christian. Present-day Negro distaste for him means only current lack of sympathy with Christian values. Few modern Protestants would write a problem novel offering increased chance of Christian salvation as a principal reason for relieving an oppressed class. Yet that is just what Mrs. Stowe did, and a hundred years ago it made sense.

That her Christianity is the best thing about *Uncle Tom* probably reflects the fact that this field was really familiar to her. In her daily life she was no better Christian than the next person. She could lie and deceive. She absent-mindedly misapplied money given her for the slaves* and was uncharitable about Pharisaical divines. But the woman who wrote that reply of Tom's had the root of Christianity—the slashing doctrine that excuses are impertinent; that, when the roll is called up yonder, it is just you and God for it. It was unfortunate that her real religiousness merely helped further to confirm so many in their—and her—opinion that, whatever the status of Negroes in the next world, they were inferior here below. Her insistence that they had special talent for religion sounds too much like people who say, with hasty courtesy, that mongrel dogs are often more intelligent than those with pedigrees.

She did not allow other-worldliness to distract her from the need for doing things about slavery. The last chapter of *Uncle Tom* proposed laws to prohibit the breaking up of slave families and the sale of slave women to brothels and lascivious masters; outlawry of interstate slave trade; repeal of the Fugitive Slave Law of 1850; and revision of state statutes and constitutions to permit education of slaves and admission of sworn slave testimony against whites. None of this

---

* Of almost $20,000 thus acquired in England, some $500 went to Frederick Douglass for a vocational school for Negroes. (*Life and Times of . . .;* 247-253.) Her only accounting for the rest was to tell a biographer that it went "to educate several former slaves." (Wilson, *Crusader in Crinoline;* 371.)

was original with her, but the combination was shrewdly thought out. Among them these measures might have gone far toward smothering slavery within a couple of generations; for the Border States relied heavily on selling human surplus to the cotton states, and masters prevented from separating families would soon have found themselves feeding and clothing intolerable accumulations of their slaves' progeny.

On the last page of *Uncle Tom* an oracular paragraph combined fervent religion with a strangely modern note of social prophylaxis: "This is an age of the world when nations are trembling and convulsed . . . and is America safe? Every nation that carries in its bosom great and unredressed injustices has in it the elements of this last convulsion. . . . O, Church of Christ, read the signs of the times!" *

This makes just as much sense today as it did in 1852. But Mrs. Stowe was not calling for immediate emancipation, the *ruat caelum* specialty of the Garrisonites. At times she even showed an uneasy suspicion that the bulk of slaves were not in condition to look after themselves creditably in all respects, but it was a very small suspicion, and unfortunately she neglected to enlarge on it for her many readers.

"*. . . of the merits of* Uncle Tom's Cabin *as a work of art I have no desire to speak.*" —KEMBLE, Journal of a Residence on a Georgian Plantation

Mrs. Stowe always wrote hastily, seldom revised, usually left punctuation to the printer. With sounder technical habits she might have written fairly well. Histories of American litera-

---

* She was thinking, of course, of the turbulent recent year of 1848 in Europe, with its international pandemic of revolutions and the harsh readjustments that followed.

ture always treat her with a respect difficult to account for on strictly literary grounds, however. Perhaps there is a feeling that to leave her out, since she did not really write too badly and was so deep a social influence, would be absurd. And quite right—so it would.

Her long suit was a sort of slipshod momentum. But she could also believe that she was still telling a story when actually floundering in verbose circles. Time and again she set up a situation or *motif* and then neglected, or forgot, to work it out, often when to do so would have furthered her effect. At intervals, however, her way of just slapping down one line after another, like the late Emmeline Grangerford, became perceptibly airborne, particularly in dialogue—if it was not Negro dialogue. Though in Cincinnati she had had some acquaintance with Negroes fresh from the South, her Negro characters, with the possible exception of Milly in *Dred,* all sound like the Stella Dallas of soap opera. Literally as well as figuratively Yankee was the only idiom in which she was at home.*

Her skill in dialectic, often prominent, she also owed to Lyman Beecher, a renowned debater who trained his children, both sexes, in forensic cut-and-thrust like an old tomcat teaching his kittens feint and dodge and pounce. When St. Clare and his brother or Clayton and the parsons in *Dred* discuss slavery, the clashing arguments break as clean as harness racers and show their paces without a hint of stumble. The terms are elementary, like those of good high-school debating. Mrs. Stowe had small grasp of the hard-to-define factors—what we would now call the "cultural" aspects of slavery —underlying the exasperations, special pleadings, fears and hypocrisies with which the South defended the "peculiar

---

* Wilson (*Crusader in Crinoline;* 164) came to the conclusion that even Topsy's signature line " 'Spect I growed" was Yankee-derived as a favorite humorous locution of Calvin Stowe's picked up by his wife as a trait for a Louisiana Negro child.

institution." But it is a pleasure, of a lawyerish sort, to read these dialogues. Even the pompous vocabulary does not muffle the sword play. And when Mrs. Stowe was admittedly preaching a sermon, as in the concluding chapters of the *Key* on the incompatibilities of slavery with Christianity, she showed brilliantly that it was no accident that Beecher rhymed with preacher.

It is customary to think a priori about persons who make influential things. A device, book, play or cult becomes pandemic, and comment on its creator is thenceforth committed to a mystical sort of awe. The scope of the thing created is taken to argue greatness in the creator. This is a poor position, even when applied to such men as Leonardo da Vinci, Darwin, Tolstoi. In almost all instances it leads to glorification of the petty—and of the pathological. Let no one reasoning from the scale of *Uncle Tom* be tempted to think: "All this picking Mrs. Stowe apart is clever. But in last analysis she must have been quite a woman and often risen to greatness—else why was her book so cataclysmic, her mark so difficult to efface?"

In my view it was cataclysmic and catalytic too precisely because this was a smallish person, small personally as well as physically, glib, lazy-minded, a common denominator of millions of the brains and consciences of her time. Not a *least* common denominator, since only a substantial talent could formulate her content aptly and palatably. She may well have been literally an "unusual woman." After all, few of her lady contemporaries had such remarkable careers. Fewer still can have had her minor degree of intelligence, and many would have been far worse spoiled by the lionizing that she received. But it is no use trying to make her a Fanny Kemble or a Jane Addams. Idealizing Mrs. Stowe is like trying to admire a composite photograph of all the Yes-respondents in a public-opinion poll. The gist of the attitude explored is most important. But the oracle, study her as generously and favorably as you may, is not distinguished.

Such analysis is worth while only as it picks out elements that dull or sharpen the effect of *Uncle Tom*. The French saw that clearly, taking their cue from Gautier as to the aesthetic standing of the book: ". . . art in the customary sense has nothing to do with it. Such works are outside criticism; the one thing to consider is their effect." The *Journal des Débats* recommended it as "full of tears and fire," with certain pages presenting "all the elements of a revolution." This was astute. So was the other Parisian critic who said that this book numbered the days of slavery in the American South.* Would that French judgment of American books and affairs were always so keen! Three thousand miles from Harpers Ferry these acute aliens saw the meaning of *Uncle Tom*, as millions of Americans themselves as yet did not. Sound or not, honest or not, Mrs. Stowe was making her countrymen aware of what they had not known they were feeling. She was bringing out their emotional patterns as the chemical that develops a photograph brings out images latent in the silver salts.

---

* All these citations from Lucas, *La littérature anti-esclavagiste* . . . One dissenting French reviewer called the book "a long and boring Methodist declamation" and scolded his compatriots for rushing to buy it while disregarding currently available translations of *Vanity Fair*. It is interesting to note that, when his secretary bought him a twenty-five-cent copy from a railroad candy-butcher, Thackeray refused to read *Uncle Tom;* he said that he thought that "stories founded on such painful themes were scarcely within the legitimate purview of story-telling," a point probably sounder than the secretary's stuffy style makes it sound. (Crowe, *With Thackeray in America;* 34-35.) Dickens praised *Uncle Tom* sniffily: "If I might suggest a fault in what has so much charmed me, it would be that . . . you seek to prove too much. . . . I doubt there being any warrant for making out the African race to be a great one." (Gilbertson, *Harriet Beecher Stowe;* 160.)

French readers paid small heed to these predictions. They were busy swooning over the death of Eva and admiring her synthetically debonair father in a fashion that throws a curious light on the French reputation for sophistication. Literary big guns of immense calibre joined the great public in a fantastic enthusiasm. It is not too startling to find George Sand pantingly and prolixly endorsing *Uncle Tom,* several times dubbing its creatrix saint and angel. Heine's overwrought approval can be digested. But it is another matter to find Flaubert the mordant, the austere, the finicky, the surgical, admitting that he found "des jolies choses" in *La case de l'Oncle Tom.* That was certainly the peak of what the boulevards were calling *l'oncletomerie.*

These French were only doing what the whole world was doing or soon would be. Never mind *Gone with the Wind* or *The Pilgrim's Progress;* this was the textbook example of a super-super best seller owing its success to being applied to a situation like a blowtorch to a kerosene can. British booksellers needing no delay for translation jostled one another to get out immense pirated editions; the one that paid Mrs. Stowe some royalties was among the least successful. The Parisian hacks who knew enough English to rush into print with six or seven rival translations* soon had counterparts in Germany, Italy, Spain, Russia, Scandinavia. In time the book appeared in Welsh, Wallachian, Wendish, Arabic and Armenian. German publishers got out at least seventy-five editions plus eleven abridgments for children. This "Onkeltomerei" still survives in an Onkel Tom Strasse in the Zellen-

---

* This usually meant heavy cutting. The version still sold in the Bibliothèque Verte (Hachette) omits much pious matter about Eva and much of St. Clare's radical talk. The unsigned preface holds surprises for American readers. It gives as principal cause of the Civil War the North's jealous wish to wreck Southern prosperity by getting the slaves freed and asserts that Texas entered the Union as part of the Compromise of 1850.

dorff district of Berlin† and in several imitations from Germans who had never seen the United States. *Am Red River; oder, Sklavenleben in Nord-Amerika,* for instance, retained the names of Mrs. Stowe's characters but altered their natures: an Eva helps her father to torture Negroes; a Harriet is a wicked woman slaveowner. In this welter of exploitation things confused easily: Cruikshank's illustrations to a British edition show Uncle Tom reading his Bible on Legree's plantation with a background of conical African huts and coco palms.

One reason for the hullabaloo was unpalatably simple: To the supracultural appeal of sentiment and melodrama was added a familiar special flavor—the standing eagerness of the Old World to read or hear the worst, whether authentic or not, about the New. Calvin Stowe finally winded this odor in British adulation of his wife and mentioned it acidly at a public meeting in her honor. It helps to explain the otherwise fantastic fact that *Uncle Tom* sold three times as well in Britain as in its own country. To this day Britain and the Continent continue to read it in that misguided approach to American literature that keeps Jack London and Upton Sinclair so prominent on the other side of the Atlantic. A Scottish writer recently called *Uncle Tom* "that widely distributed nursery book." Hungarian Communists not long ago got out a children's edition selling well enough to call for a second printing. Apparently it persists on the shelves of most European households of some cultivation. Two years ago I was astounded to learn from shipmates of numerous nationalities on an Antwerp-to-Africa freighter that it was still required reading for Dutch, German and Swiss schoolchildren within the last generation. Though it can also be found, usually optional, on American high-school reading lists, only three Americans answering my questionnaire had read it as

† I owe Onkel Tom Strasse to my good neighbor, Craig Thompson. The rest about the German reaction is mostly from MacLean, *Uncle Tom's Cabin in Germany,* an admirable and intelligent piece of research.

a school assignment, whereas in the ship in question practically all the officers and passengers knew it as a school text, required reading.

Early infection thus acquired from a piece of fiction that was unreliable even in its own time must greatly further European exaggeration of the plight of the American Negro. It would be just as sound for American school children to read *Oliver Twist* as current briefing on the plight of the underprivileged Briton. But we Americans cannot deny that, much as things have changed and little as Europe ever knew about it, the reality is still disgraceful. Scoffing at wanton ignorance does not make the American Negro's present situation easier to live with. Though lynching is practically dead, though the Supreme Court is bold, Jim Crow lives on, feeling his age a bit but hearty still. Our concern here is not transatlantic gullibility and stupidity but how Harriet Beecher Stowe's book happened to become Jim Crow's good friend.

Nobody has ever known how many Americans read *Uncle Tom,* even up to the outbreak of the Civil War. The serialization was lent from hand to hand until the good rag paper of the *National Era* disintegrated. The same happened to the book. "I got two copies," recalled A. M. Kennedy of Union City, Indiana, a non-Garrisonian Abolitionist, ". . . and circulated them . . . until they was worn out. Many converts was the result." Southern efforts to keep the book out were futile because the South could no more enforce censorship than she could her laws against Negro literacy. Alabama burned shipments of it, Maryland jailed a free Negro preacher for having a copy. But Olmsted saw it sold openly on a Mississippi steamboat. A bookseller in Columbia, South Carolina, complained that he could not keep up with demand for it. It was read aloud in Georgia to large and inquisitive white audiences, and Mrs. Chesnut, salty chronicler of the "quality" during the Civil War, read it several times. So, to judge from the talk that she recorded, did most of wartime Richmond. A former slave of Jefferson Davis's brother remembered that a copy was smuggled into the slave quarters on the plantation and literate slaves read it aloud to the others; that word of this reached the Big House, where Missis had heard of *Uncle Tom* but had no way of obtaining a copy, and so Master borrowed it from the slaves for her to read. You don't have to believe that tale to see that it means very good things about Joe Davis's Hurricane Plantation.

It is five generations since the presses ran the first installment in the *National Era,* but only now is the furore really slacking off. Of my questionnaire respondents above the age of thirty-five (few were Southerners), three out of four had read *Uncle Tom.* The incidence of readers was highest over sixty, of course, but even so a majority of those over forty-five had read it.* Two out of three readers had got it off the family bookshelves. Nor need this have been the result of browsing among the relics of a bygone day in grandpa's library. For several American publishers find it still pays to keep the old warhorse available. From fragmentary information obtained from most of them, I should guess conservatively that its annual sales today in the United States are at least 8000 copies—after 104 years.

I hope that the buyers include few parents imitating the European error of giving their children, as a traditional *must* like *Alice in Wonderland,* this well-meaning, dilutely vulgar, subtly tainted piece of cultural subversion. Asked to assess *Uncle Tom* as of today, Miss Mary Eakins, of the

---

* The questionnaire also asked what other notable American literary monuments of the same era had been read. The results were strange. For the whole group only *House of the Seven Gables* and *Evangeline* (both school-list favorites) outranked *Uncle Tom* in "readership." He ran a dead heat with *Moby Dick* and *Fall of the House of Usher* and far outstripped such magnificent reading of high prestige as *Walden* and *Two Years Before the Mast.*

Center for Children's Books, University of Chicago Library, replied:

> [It] probably has a place in high school libraries as an original document . . . in American history . . . has no place in an elementary school collection, nor should it be recommended for general reading in high schools. . . . Mrs. Stowe has employed most of the stereotypes to which there is the greatest objection . . . immature readers will not recognize the book as a social document but will accept it at its face value . . . it can do much harm in perpetuating stereotypes and fostering misunderstandings.

Mrs. Stowe deserves this place on the index expurgatorius of modern education because to an unholy extent the text, topics and doctrine of her sermon still shape our attitudes toward Negroes. The unwary reader of *Uncle Tom* now, as then, probably comes away from it with something like this:

Slaveowners are (or were) cultivated gentlemen, well off to wealthy and uneasy or indignant about slavery, or they are (or were) snarling brutes of paranoid tendency and criminal background. Class One inhabit large, slave-cultivated plantations or urban palaces of more than Oriental splendor with amusingly shiftless slave servants. Their wives are either high-minded ladies of great sensibility or spoiled sadists. Slaves themselves, when markedly of "African race," are either gentle and pellucidly Christian or diabolically brutalized. When markedly tinged with "white blood," they are far more intelligent, enterprising and sensitive and show it by running away in great numbers. Slave women usually run away either because their children have been sold away from them or because master has assailed their virtue. Northerners are much to blame for an un-Christian repugnance toward Negroes, for black skins contain souls of which Heaven is solicitous. But one must not expect full intelligence and refinement from many members of this innately handicapped "African race," a term that can dispense with definition since everybody knows more or less what it means. The fact is, "Africans" are genetically endowed with natures nearer "the animal" than ours. The best thing for them and for the part-white spawn of miscegenation would be a good Yankee-style vocational education with religious trimmings, followed by colonization in Africa, that rich and beautiful and fortunately very distant land of their mistreated ancestors. . . .

The hypothetical reader could hardly have his confidence worse abused. Nor is he an altogether negligible figure. In the year 1953 my questionnaire respondents clearly showed vestiges of some of the above. Their guesses as to how many slaves the South lost through running away were fantastically high. Almost half of them thought that admixture of "white blood" should mean higher intelligence among those classed as Negroes—a position certainly erroneous as thus stated, though the right of it must take careful investigation in a later chapter and still defy definite opinion. About one in six believed that Negroes tend to be happier in dependent or subordinate status. About the same proportion, not necessarily the same respondents, thought kindly of some kind of colonization for American Negroes, supposing it otherwise practical.

"Did any of all this make any sense in its own day?" was a question we started out with. At least looking into it can no longer hurt Mrs. Stowe's feelings. These sixty years she has lain inactive beside Calvin Stowe in an Andover churchyard. What makes investigation advisable now is that, were she resurrected tomorrow, she would feel far too much at home among our current notions about Negroes.

SLAVERY WAS . . .

"Sir, slavery is a thing which cannot be hid; it is not a dry rot, which you can cover with the carpet until the house tumbles about your ears; you might as well try to hide a volcano in full eruption; it is a cancer in your face."
—JOHN RANDOLPH *of Roanoke*

Born north of the Ohio forty years after Appomattox, I was late for acquaintance with former slaves. One I did know well, if children ever know adults well. Thought back upon, she seems to have been the most integrating influence in my childhood.

Her work was everything but laundry and dressmaking in our household. I recall little about her with police-court precision. She was not African-dark, but her face was broad Negro with bright little eyes, her build was stubby and sturdy; I have seen bush Liberians who might have been her sons. She must have been born soon after 1845, for she was old enough before Emancipation to have been set to iron the wash and mature enough to have tempted young master. Threats with a hot flatiron quelled him. By the time she came to us, she had been widowed of a husband of whom she always spoke with affectionate honor and, by working days, had been able to rear a large and self-respecting family in Louisville.

She had chronic arthritis, and her little bedroom off our kitchen was aromatic with liniment. Even her Bible smelled of it. But her creaky joints did not keep her from occasionally playing a shuffly little dance game that she called "Peep-O Rabbit" or from working doughtily, efficiently and with a huge good will that frayed only when she was to do something in a way other than her own. Ours was a household of monotonous fare. She had a free hand only in the children's breakfasts and delighted in ringing unexpected changes on prunes, oatmeal and eggs. Looming through the swinging door, with a flourish she would announce that this morning the Palace Hotel was serving pancakes and stand to watch us eat with the air of a horse-loving groom listening to a colt's feeding.

When gay she might gabble a wonderful rigmarole about how "They was Ringwood, Springwood, Dasher and Dan, the old bitch and nine pups, but the best ole dog I ever had, one night he et his belly full of mush and milk, turned his heels up to heb'n and died like a lamb," which we valued highly. It could have been an infiltration of minstrel-show material? No such suspicion was possible about her flavorsome but shapeless tales, of which I recall strangely little. There was one about a man who killed a booger, which should have been a head louse, of course, but its skin was unaccountably large enough to be hung to dry on a fence, and there were awesome complications when the booger returned and resumed its skin for some witchy purpose. At the time my mental picture of the booger was of something like a flayed ape.

On her afternoon off she usually visited the Idle Hour, a local movie theater that admitted Negroes. She called it the "Idle Hoover" because the name was lettered Roman style: IDLE HOVR. We knew what she saw only when the bill had included a Chaplin. Then we heard all about it. "Kickinest man I ever see!" she would crow and gasp between paroxysms of relish. She felt the same intimacy of gusto in Dickens whom, with an instinct that I still think shrewd, I set her to reading. *Nicholas Nickleby* was her favorite and Ralph Nickleby the character whom she discussed most. She would mutter and grumble about "That ole Nickle*by!*" until he acquired actuality greater than his creator ever gave him.

She drew us children by a sort of gravitation, the lighter attracted to the mass of higher density. We were always under her feet and she tolerated us with a good nature that astounds me when I recall her temper. Ah, she was a person. There was every bit as much thunder as butter in her. The whole family of us were, in a sense, afraid of her; only we children had the advantage of her sympathy. At a word, gesture or notion that she found unbecoming—and her standards were subtle and high—her mouth and eyes would lower, her skin actually darken, or so it seemed, her gestures grow extravagant and tense with power as she thumped the rolling pin or lashed her mop at the floor. The more she felt the less she said, but until the offense was corrected and the storm blown over, everybody in that house walked Spanish.

She never struck us, though a blow would often have been fair and from her we might well not have resented it. When she flourished that massive right arm and said, "Boy, I break the crystal yo' watch!" it was understood to mean merely "Calm down." But those earnest tempers of hers were formidable. She was formidable. One night when our parents were out and she was skylarking with us, I ran into a clothes closet and pulled the door shut after me. It jammed. She hauled on the outside knob and it came off in her hand. A neighbor was telephoned to for help. When he did not appear as soon as she thought reasonable, she fetched the crowbar-poker from the cellar and ripped that door out of the frame in about three seconds of powerful leverage. Coming upstairs a few minutes later, the rescuing neighbor met her with the poker still in her hand and the light of battle still in her little eyes. He said afterward that his first impulse had been to turn and run.

She died back home with her family in Louisville, God rest her soul. None of this conveys her pride, her strong sweetness, like wild dark honey, her scathing mother wit and the knotty richness of her speech. With ampler opportunity this woman could have commanded an army or founded a colony. There is no reason whatever to confuse her with the *Gone with the Wind* sort of "mammy." And she was only a fair-to-middling cook. It was the fun not the flavor that we valued in those breakfasts.

Our town then had the largest Negro-white ratio in the North. Southerners probably outnumbered Yankees among the forebears of local people, certainly among mine. The public schools that I attended had a few Negro pupils ignored even more completely than if they had been invisible. I knew of a Negro dentist in town but never saw a Negro with social or economic status above that of trusted servant until I was eighteen years old and away from home for good. Reared in this quasi-Dixie atmosphere, I had much to unlearn about Negroes. I cannot promise, I can only hope, that I have unlearned most of it. In the process I have met Negro chiefs of state, tribal emperors, scholars, soldiers, administrators and scientists. This was only a powerless and underpaid old woman able barely to read her Bible and get through the *Pickwick Papers* in the course of a year or so. But thanks to having known her I never needed telling, while unlearning, that a Negro can manifest superlative integrity, acumen and power of personality. *Uncle Tom's Cabin* contained nothing at all like her.

Such people are rare anywhere. There were probably few like her in ante bellum Kentucky. I do not know just where she was born, but it is tantalizingly possible that she was a bright-smiling little slave child in the very neighborhood that Mrs. Stowe so fatefully visited, the very neighborhood where some of my own people once owned slaves. Her likes were probably fewer still farther South, where Negroes received even less stimulus. In exploring what slavery was actually like we should not lean much on individual exceptions. But keep her in mind all the same as the more representative evidence streams past. When such as she could come out of slavery even as exceptions, the worst thing about the whole institution must have been the way it smothered and aborted human raw material of impressive quality.

1   *The crime of color*

"Some day history may record with amazement that a man's whole life was once determined by the color of his skin. —RICE, I Came Out of the Eighteenth Century

NOTE: *Data in the following main section (through the chapter entitled* Darling Nelly Gray) *derive principally, though by no means exclusively, from either Negro sources, or Southern sources, or sources highly sympathetic to the traditional South. To remind the reader of such derivation, a boldfaced capital N appears at the end of the citation from a Negro source. A boldfaced capital S appears at the end of the citation of a Southern or Southern-sympathizing source. It is believed that the device will be helpful in unobtrusively reminding the reader just who is talking.*

Olmsted, the great clinician-reporter on slavery, made a neat point: he said that the slave's situation was that of "a convict in a dockyard," * that is, at forced labor. This analogy fits

---

* J. S. Buckingham, the English traveler and reformer, made the same point most devastating in *Slave States of America*, I; 399-400. U. B. Phillips, who knew a great deal about slavery, though born too late to see it, was a Southern witness who came close: "The plantation force was a conscript army, living in barracks and on constant 'fatigue.' . . . The field hands were privates, with no choice but to obey, unless, like other seasoned soldiers, they could dodge the duties assigned." (*Life and Labor in the Old South;* 196.) The difference is that an army, even of conscripts, presumably serves some abstract national purpose under public auspices. Phillips later saw the slave-manned plantation as a sort of compulsory school for savages, with "the function of a modern social settlement, setting patterns of orderly, well-bred conduct which the negroes were encouraged to emulate," with "a vigor of discipline which democracy cannot possess." (*American Negro Slavery;* 342-343). For fairness to this great historian-researcher the whole context should be read; but at best it is rather offhand. The Olmsted statement is in the preface to *An Englishman in Kansas* as quoted in *Cotton Kingdom;* 574.

better than most. At the time he wrote—the era of the slave power's greatest leverage, soon after *Uncle Tom* was published—the system did amount to the sentencing of the individuals of one group by those of another to perpetual dependence and servitude, an order of deprivation that in most free societies is usually the second most severe penalty for crime. In this case the crime was that of being darker, poorly organized and mandatorily ignorant. A colonization-minded parson investigating a slave depot in Washington in 1835 conscientiously recorded that the premises were as clean and orderly as those of the District's penitentiary, which he had visited a few days before, but "the situation of the convicts at the penitentiary was far less deplorable than that of these slaves, confined for the crime of being descended from ancestors who were forcibly reduced to bondage." From despair of making it sound tenable in any other way, spokesmen for the South had long laid on Noah and God the responsibility for this lunatic harshness.

In American slavery most, not all, of the wardens were more or less humane. Tasks exacted were usually tolerable, often mitigated by lax standards of performance. The standard of living afforded the convicts sustained life and apparently left margin for considerable fecundity. And it was a great alleviation that, unlike prisoners in a work gang, even unlike many Roman slaves,* most American Negro slaves had ready access to women. The wardens' personal needs often enlisted special "trusties" off the rockpile to become craftsmen or house servants. There was even a sort of tied-parolee system. Best of all perhaps—only those who have been

---

* Recent commentators on American slavery may hint that Roman slavery was better, particularly because it freely admitted manumission and had no color as caste-class criterion. This can be taken for what it is worth only after reading the rebuttal of Jefferson, a classicist with first-hand knowledge of American slavery. (*Notes on Virginia;* 146 *et seq.* See also Phillips, *American Negro Slavery;* 341-342; Ballagh, *History of Slavery in Virginia;* 33; Becker, *Gallus; passim.*)

slaves could know—the slave was usually born under sentence, knew nothing of a former freedom and so may have felt his plight less keenly than a man, however stupid or antisocial, imprisoned after being born free. In parallel, people assume— and correctly, one always hopes—that feral animals born in captivity find their situations less irksome for that reason.

But the essentials of convicthood were unmistakable: In his own person or that of an ancestor, whether his enslaver was African or European, the slave had been arbitrarily sentenced. Within the slave system he could seldom maintain for long any illusions of tenuous subfreedom. His only practical recourse against abuse was the desperate step of mutiny, whether flight or rebellion. His sole constructive hope lay in a sort of pardon, manumission, which sprang from the master's unilateral willingness to forgive him as individual for his people's crimes as listed above. And by Olmsted's and Mrs. Stowe's day, laws checking manumission were many and fairly effective.

All this is too analytical. Thus described, slavery could never have been countenanced by any society with post-medieval Western ideas, least of all by white settlers in America. But accident, interest and arbitrary cultural notions based on common misconceptions cajoled our forebears into not only indicting a whole people but condemning it and even its unborn posterity to penal servitude for unlimited generations. In the face of behavior so flagrant, mere outcry is not enough. Better to begin by asking how such an outrage came to be.

Well, our ancestors were less squeamish than we are about forced labor. The unblushing slavery of the lowest order of whites common in medieval Europe was still close to people's minds when the New World was being settled. In some parts of England wife selling might still occur.* Slaves plus con-

---

* Little, *Negroes in Britain;* 72. On this, of course, Hardy based *The Mayor of Casterbridge.* Sale was at public auction after display of the wife with a rope round her neck in token of proffer.

victs were the principal motive power of Moslem and Christian military shipping in the Mediterranean. Apprenticeship bound the young to a kind of tutorial slavery hedged with legal cautions, true, but long-lasting and, under a severe master, often rigorous. Not so long ago many American communities "bound out" pauper children, orphans and such to work for room and board until of age. The press gang that legally shanghaied recruits for the Royal Navy was taken for granted in national emergencies. An anthropologist studying the British aspects of the matter explains, "Probably the popular attitude saw nothing extraordinary in a Negro being a slave, even in England, not because he was black, but because the rights of human beings, irrespective of colour, were apt at the time to be defined rather in terms of social and economic status than of humanity."

There was certainly small humanity in the indenture system that populated much of North America as "at the same time a labor-supply and an immigration agency." **s** By this arrangement the underprivileged Briton or German mort-

---

s *This is the first instance of the device described at the beginning of this section for indicating testimony from Southerners or those sympathetic to the South. Such boldfaced capital* **s**'s *close the material indicated. A similar boldfaced* **N** *will mean testimony from Negroes.*

---

gaged four or five years of his economic future to pay his passage to America with some hope of improving his circumstances. Once he signed, there was no drawing back. Such indentured servants were segregated under guard until shipped and, on arrival on the other side of the ocean, were auctioned off for the cost of transportation plus profit. Speculators buying these redemptioners in lots for sale upcountry were called "soul drivers" with no complimentary intent, and men from Mars ignorant of the language could hardly have distinguished between these and actual sales of slaves. Wherever their fates lay, whether in the tiny port towns or the new clearings of the back country, these whites were pretty much convict-style slaves for their stated terms, fed and clothed as the purchaser liked, obligated to any work assigned, disciplined with the lash and pursued by the law when they ran away, as they often did.

The system was obviously well adapted to disposal of low-grade or dangerous or inconvenient persons. The government approved, though sometimes it attempted perfunctory regulation, as shipmen drummed up paupers and unwanted children for "the plantations" on a basis of cynical speculation. Imprisoned debtors might be released on condition that they migrate under indenture. Such people were problems at home; the New World needed labor. It was a brutal age. Emigration of the recalcitrant Scots-Irish of Ulster was officially encouraged. Rebels captured under the Duke of Monmouth or the successive Pretenders were herded off to America for what they might fetch at the pier head.* Persons of some skill or education who had fallen on hard times might thus go westward—one hears of dancing and fencing masters, silversmiths and builders' artisans under indenture; Edmund Pendleton's indentured emigrant ancestor was a schoolmaster of gentle lineage. But on the whole those consignments of the dislocated must have ranged lower in personal quality than the home average.

People were then even likelier than they are now to confound the rebellious or the helpless with the criminal. It troubled few when the courts began to mingle pickpockets, forgers, prostitutes into this stream of quasi slaves. It cost the government only three to five pounds a head passage money

---

* This, and much of what follows, applies as much to the British West Indies as to the mainland colonies. Barbados, for example, got the lion's share of Sedgmoor prisoners; their descendants are still distinguishable locally as "redlegs," the local white trash. Montserrat got so many Irish that the local Negroes used to be said to speak with a marked brogue.

to dump into mainland North America, between 1717 and 1775, nearly 50,000 persons fallen foul of the law but not quite seriously enough for hanging. Sentences ran three to seven years of such transportation or, more severely, "transportation for life." Such numbers bulked dismayingly large in the sparsely populated colonies. Benjamin Franklin protested that sending these scum to America to mend their ways was like sending American rattlesnakes to Britain to unlearn their venomous habits, but it did small good. Transportation swept the rogue, the trollop and the mental case under the rug, so to speak, and masters paying good sugar or tobacco for them in Annapolis, Savannah or Basse-Terre made sure that they expended many useful foot-pounds of energy before their freedom came due or they died in harness of malaria, yellow fever or "the flux."

The French used the same means to people Louisiana, as witness *Manon Lescaut*. *Moll Flanders* shows how the system was taken for granted, and Stevenson exploited it in the kidnapping of David Balfour as a "twenty-pounder," for when transatlantic demand was lively and supply low, outright "spiriting," as they called it, was resorted to. Male or female, vicious or just unlucky, stupid or fractious, mostly young or at their prime—other kinds of risk were hardly worth shipping—off they sailed below decks in conditions that made them die like flies. It can be assumed that as a rule only the sturdier survived—a rough and ready sorting out that, drastic as it was for them, may well have been salutary for the new country. The underfed men in gray or butternut who fought their hearts out at Shiloh and Franklin and made such dashing marches for Old Jack had many forebears among these ruthlessly screened misfits. Their current descendants, more prolific than Northerners, are still our major populational resource.

Perhaps close to half of the total white immigration to the colonies came somehow by means of indenture. New England, with choosier methods of recruiting, got fewest of this

sort.* Pennsylvania got more, some convicts but mainly the
ruggedly disgruntled Scotch-Irish and German refugees from
the religious turmoils and hideous wars of the Rhineland;
hence, of course, the "Pennsylvania Dutch." The South got
numbers of Scottish Highlanders, Scots-Irish, Swiss and Germans, immediately and by secondary infiltration as Pennsylvania's Irish and Dutch drifted southwestward between the
ridges into the Shenandoah, West Virginia, eastern Tennessee, the western areas of the Carolinas. But Dixie-to-be also
got most of the less promising human material. The main
flow of paupers, debtors, orphans, whores and minor felons
landed from Maryland southward because that region was
chronically hungry for mass labor for the large-scale production of indigo, naval stores and the tobacco that, says Wertenbaker, was to the South of 1750 what cotton was in 1850.†
Georgia was founded in a deliberate effort to inject some
coherence and decency into the movement while creating a
buffer between the British and the Spanish in Florida.**

---

* The largest such group reaching New England were Scots-Irish,
settling largely in New Hampshire; Horace Greeley, for example, came
of these people.

† Later tobacco was the standby of the small farmer in the noncotton
South of upland Carolina and Kentucky. Macmillan (*Warning from the
West Indies;* 66) thinks that the shift from tobacco to sugar was what
doomed Barbados to a dwindling white population, as sugar estates
enlarged under fewer and fewer owners. Yet tobacco was alos a big-
plantation crop in early Maryland and Virginia.

** The founders of Georgia ruled out alcohol and Negro slavery. The
motive for the second measure, says Brawley (*Short History of the
American Negro;* 12), was fear that Georgia would find it difficult to
"defend the other British colonies from the Spaniards . . . if it dis-
sipated its energies in guarding Negro slaves." In view of how peaceable
the Negro slaves were during the Civil War, the argument was ill
founded. But it is unlikely that Oglethorpe, principal founder of
Georgia, had firm antislavery principles; he had long acted as manager
of the Royal African Company, the backbone of the British slave trade,
and owned a Negro-stocked plantation in South Carolina. The movement to allow slavery in Georgia was strongly backed by George White-

Transportation went briskly on until the Revolution put a stop to Britain's using the American colonies as trash baskets. (So Britain promptly founded New South Wales as substitute and sent convicts there for another two generations.) The net effect is represented by an analysis of the population of the Baltimore area in 1752: 11,000 free whites (an indeterminate number of whom must have been indentured immigrants or convicts with their terms served out); 1000 white "servants" (that is, indentured); 500 to 600 felons under transportation; 116 mulatto slaves; 4027 Negro slaves; 196 free mulattoes. In 1852 Olmsted found a vestigial memory of it all in a Southern poor white inquisitive about immigrant labor up North, who assumed that these Germans and Irish were coming in on indenture to be bought and sold as, no doubt, his not too remote ancestors had been.*

It argues insensibility to treat an unlucky shopkeeper on a footing barely distinguishable from that of a convicted pimp. An age that jailed debtor, psychotic and footpad in the same fetid room would hardly scruple to utilize Negro forced labor when opportunity arose. The first Negroes sold as slaves in what would be the United States, in labor-hungry Jamestown in 1619, were booty from a Spanish prize taken by a British-manned Dutch privateer that was nine-tenths pirate.

---

field, the great Methodist evangelist, who applied the profits of his slave-staffed Carolina plantation to the support of an orphanage. (Flanders, *Plantation Slavery in Georgia;* 16.)

* Olmsted, *Cotton Kingdom;* 394. Goodrich says that, following an Indiana court decision of 1821, such indentures had pretty well died out in the United States by 1830. ("Indenture," *Encyclopedia of the Social Sciences.*) Andrews, *Colonial Folkways;* 187 *et seq.,* is a good summary of the movement of indentured servants and convicts. Smith's *Colonists in Bondage* is a fine specialized account. General historians usually tend to mention the scale of the movement and then expansively deny that the redemptioners and convicts were a specially poor lot, adducing the severity of poor laws and criminal laws of the day to indicate that they were far more sinned against than sinning. Australians make the same claim. It is comforting to try to agree with them.

As founding fathers Negro slaves were a year ahead of the
Pilgrims at Plymouth. This started a trickle that widened into
a river of slave manpower, which supplemented and then sup-
planted white labor entering under indenture or transportation.

The status of the "negar" was unclear at first. No written
and few customary stipulations dictated how long he should
serve before being loosed on his own or, indeed, whether he
should ever be freed. Andrews, historian of colonial America,
says that these early Negroes "were viewed in the light of
servants rather than of slaves . . . it is noteworthy how rarely
the word 'slave' was used in common parlance." Some imported Negroes secured freedom, as, for example, those whom
Director General Kieft of New Netherlands freed when their
service approached the twenty-one-year mark. Many were
never so favored, but there seems to have been a presumption
that Christian baptism, implying that the officiating clergyman was satisfied of his convert's adjustment to Western
values, carried freedom with it. This fitted with the notion,
first developed by the Pope to justify the Portuguese slave
trade, that the Negro's heathenism made him fair game for
export to countries where he could be infected with Christianity.

Socially things were equally confused. Though most shipments of slaves included a few women, the great majority of
imported Negroes was always male. Marriage, or anyway connection between Negro men and white women, usually convicts or under indenture, was not infrequent.* Sometimes a
Negro driver (slave foreman) used his office to force himself
on indentured white women, a precedent often reversed then
and later by white overseers in charge of Negro women. Soon

---

* Thus the maternal grandmother of Benjamin Banneker, Negro as-
tronomer of some reputation in the late eighteenth century, was a white
Englishwoman come to Maryland on indenture and married to an
African slave whom she had bought when her time was out and presently freed. (Williams, *History of the Negro Race in America,* I; 386.)

there were laws to discourage the growth of a new class of
free mulattoes, such as a Maryland statute of 1664 making
white women servants marrying Negroes serve their husbands'
masters for life, the issue of the union to be slaves for life.
When that set masters to encouraging such marriages, the
law was changed to free such women from indenture and
fine their masters for allowing them too much personal latitude.

Trial and error gradually crystallized these issues in unfortunate ways. The escape hatch of baptism and the possibility
of legal miscegenation were already ruled out or under heavy
fire in the late 1660's. In any case distinctions presuming
Negroes to be bond were likely to develop because a steady
supply of slaves for life was the handiest solution to the large-
scale planter's labor problem. This is always acute in a new
country. The small man willing to skin his own skunks and
carve out his own subsistence holding can manage with his
own and his family's labor without recourse to others. But
the pretentious man hoping to supervise others in a production unit large enough to afford him a gentlemanly living
grows annoyed when people fetched from the old country to
work for such as he soon drift away upcountry to open up
their own land. After an eloquent presentation of the relative
high cost and inefficiency of slave labor, Franklin asked rhe-
torically: "Why then will *Americans* purchase *Slaves?* Because
Slaves may be kept as long as a Man pleases or has Occasion
for their Labour; while hired Men are continually leaving
their Masters (often in the midst of his Business) and setting
up for themselves."

Indentured labor was hardly more stable. Wertenbaker
points out that the redemptioner "was bound for but four or
five years and then left to make his own bid for a farm and
prosperity." That was at best. A North Carolina missionary
explained that the planters preferred slaves because indented
servants "never stayed out the time for which they were indented." Such informal leave taking may have irked masters,

but it had gratifying aspects. It meant that on or before expiration of the stated term, unless the master juggled extra years into it, an art widely practiced, the Sedgmoor rebel, the Shoreditch whore, the kidnapped waif went free, and that, if they had the wit to shift for themselves in distant places where their pasts were untraceable, which was easy in a country with scanty communications, they could readily blend into the general white community. Until then they could be stigmatized as "runaways, thieves, disorderly persons, renegadoes." No doubt they were, as a group, not only underprivileged but also typically shiftless, ignorant, lazy, promiscuous, light-fingered, untruthful and dirty.

In view of where and how they were recruited, they could hardly have been anything else. But some did well anyway: Charles Thompson, secretary of the Continental Congress; George Taylor and Matthew Thornton, signers of the Declaration of Independence; and Adam Thoroughgood, a great Tidewater planter, had all been under indenture. In the 1850's a Scottish traveler met a Virginia blueblood who liked to tease an arrogant aunt by reminding her that "on the female side they were descended from a poor Irish girl, who had been transported, and purchased for a hogshead of tobacco on the banks of the James." At the other extreme, many, handicapped by the same shortcomings that had originally got them into trouble, drifted into founding the South's class of "white trash." The bulk of them, it can be assumed, became indistinguishable ingredients in the nation's human stockpot, forebears of practically every American who ever had an ancestor born west of Albany.

Not so the Negro. Nobody had signed anything but a bill of sale, if that, to protect him. His vulnerable status led to chattel slavery because that alone would make the gentleman-planter's labor force "mobile, regular, and secure." Nor did he have the protective coloring that showed through the redemptioner's grime. Whether conversion freed him in the early days or he stayed under the lash for life, his skin always betrayed the servile antecedents of him *and* his descendants, or most of them. That had not been the case with the thralls of the medieval lord a few centuries earlier. The human impulse to despise or fear the strikingly different might alone have initiated prejudice against him. Now to such color feeling, perhaps weaker in 1619 than it is now, was added his bad luck as principal heir to the caste contempt once applied to all forced labor.

"Nigger work" was not, as is often carelessly said, any kind of manual work. It was only what smacked of servility or gang labor under orders of a boss. **s** That was what the redemptioners had often been made to do alongside slaves fresh from Africa. No doubt most Negroes of this critical period were just as shiftless, ignorant, lazy, promiscuous, light-fingered, untruthful and dirty as the lower-grade white servants mentioned above. Slave ships and gang plantations made poor schools of manners and morals for illiterates abruptly shifted from one continent to another. But the point here is that this stereotype of the American Negro was intensified by being focused on a *born-conspicuous* group.

Well before the Revolution the Negro's status had altered tragically for the worse by growing more definite. Creeping custom, freezing into formal law, now made him a personal chattel, like horse or dog, presumed bond until proved free, disqualified from testifying against whites in criminal cases* and forbidden to possess weapons or to "lift his hand in opposition against any Christian white person." Few later Southerners had the intellectual courage of the Alabama Baptists who admitted Negro testimony on a par with that of whites in church trials "not on the ground that he is white or black, slave or free, but on the ground of the truthfulness of the witness, his acquaintance with the facts, and the integrity of his motives in giving it." **s**

---

* Jefferson approved of this disability for slaves because it spared them from the logical Roman assumption that the best way to take slave evidence was under torture. (*Notes on Virginia;* 149.)

Thus were consolidated a series of interlocking attitudes that the coming French and industrial revolutions would petrify. Since both those developments were, on the whole, liberalizing in net effect, this makes a curious story and the conventional versions of it do not always hold water.

The end of the American Revolution found the American Negro just about where he had been when it began—smothering under obloquy heaped on him by those seeking to escape from the shame of once having been forced labor themselves. The onus was lighter in the North because the Northern colonies had always had fewer slaves per capita and because, on the whole, their indentured white importees had been rebels and refugees rather than ne'er-do-wells and convicts. The number of Negroes in the South was temporarily reduced because so many had accepted British offers of freedom to slaves enlisting in the redcoats' labor corps. But where they remained they continued to impoverish the soil of Maryland and Virginia with tobacco culture, to carry out the shift to wheat, to tap the pines of the coastal forests and to grow rice and indigo in the Carolina lowlands. The Negro was considered particularly indispensable for indigo because the stuff stank so in processing that it was doubtful whether free labor would go near it; ˢ * and for rice because large-scale maintenance of the elaborate dikes, canals and ditches of rice plantations required large gangs of labor always on hand. ˢ

Small groups of slaves also followed restless or enterprising masters who pushed into the Shenandoah Valley or spilled

---

* Simkins, *History of the South;* 65. At this period, of course, American indigo was a dying enterprise. But the position of slaves in handling it helped greatly to make the Deep South planter slavery and gang minded, hence to make sure that slavery would be considered indispensable to cotton culture.

over the passes or down the Ohio into Kentucky and Tennessee. But, as the text books usually say, slavery was dwindling
north of Maryland, perhaps because it did not pay. "In New
England," says a Yankee historian, "to hold slaves was a mark
of dignity rather than of profit." * The Northern trend had
been toward one-family farming of diversified sustenance
crops, often utilizing a hired hand or limited-term servant but
with small use for a slave who ate 365 days a year by definition
and did no more than expert shirking could arrange.

At this time thoughtful Southerners, especially in Maryland
and Virginia, hoped that slavery would also dwindle in their
area. In spite of the high disproportion of men in slave-ship
cargoes, the Negro population of the elder South was steadily
growing, which had caused uneasy efforts to check the slave
trade well before the Revolution. And exhaustion of soil in
the early tobacco-growing regions meant less profit from slave
labor, usually inefficient and requiring very favorable conditions. Thus, finding slavery to be both encumbrance and
moral embarrassment, the great Virginians—Washington,
Jefferson, Patrick Henry, Madison, George Mason—led in de-
crying it, and the new-born Confederation was asked to bar
slavery from the new nation's national property, the unorganized area between the Appalachians and the Mississippi.

The proposal might well have succeeded had this been the
Federal government set up by the present Constitution of
1787, in which legislators vote as individuals. But this was
voting by state delegations. Nine were required for passage,
and only six voted aye, though by individuals the vote was
15 to 6 in favor, including two Southerners, Jefferson of Virginia and Williamson of North Carolina. Had this ballot gone
otherwise, Mrs. Stowe might never have had a Simon Legree
to write about. It was the Deep South cotton-states-to-be in
the area involved, particularly Alabama and Mississippi, that

---

* Hart, *Slavery and Abolition;* 53. The exception was Rhode Island,
with a sturdy development of large-farm slavery in the eighteenth
century.

committed the South to making slavery worse than it already was, or anyway crucial emotionally. As it was, slavery was ruled out of the unorganized area only *north* of the Ohio—the old Northwest Territory.*

This was in 1787. Certain French philosophers of the most benevolent sort were soon to deal the American Negro a heavy blow. There had always been risk of slave risings. Early in the eighteenth century New York had a dramatic, savagely put down (and possibly spurious) instance. The South had known sporadic outbreaks, though none as massive as the Jamaica Maroons' continuing defiance of the whites. Now, however, seizing on ideas and opportunities set up by the French Revolution, presently aided by Jacobin emissaries, the Negroes of San Domingo rose, slaughtered or drove out their white masters and, in spite of massive efforts to restore overseas rule, managed to retain an eventual independence.

The ominous reek of smoke and blood spread all over the slave-holding states. Doubtless spurred by unquiet conscience, American masters were determined that it should not happen here. Existing laws to protect whites were strengthened within state or local jurisdictions. Within the next forty years three ominous slave conspiracies—in Virginia, Gabriel's and Nat Turner's; in Charleston, Denmark Vesey's—had put relaxation of such laws out of the question.

Vesey was a literate, free Negro organizing both free Negroes and slaves. His literacy certainly helped him as or-

---

* Failure of the earlier measure has been described as more decisive than it actually may have been. Such a Federal bar would certainly have slowed down the spread of slavery. The Northwest Ordinance did keep slavery out of Illinois, even though at one time it looked as though pro-slavery agitation would carry the day. In any case, a Federal act would have immensely strengthened opponents of slavery at a critical juncture. But it is hard to assert that the land-hungry Cotton Kingdom could have been kept from taking slavery into the Indian lands of Mississippi and into the Alabama Black Belt by any Federal piece of paper. Georgia had her unscrupulous way with the Indians in defiance of Uncle Sam, because the Indians had land that King Cotton wanted.

ganizer, so legislation against schooling Negroes was soon widespread. His free condition might have been stimulus and bad example to the slaves with whom he tampered, so laws to make manumission difficult, to bar entry of free Negro outsiders and to harass those already resident with threats of seizure and sale for minor offenses appeared in many Southern jurisdictions. It could never be said of the Southland that it did not know how to lock the door after the horse was already obsolescent. Nat Turner's prestige as slave preacher let him use religious occasions to cloak his schemes, so meetings of Negroes were discouraged on the theory presented to Russell in 1861: "These preachings . . . 'do the niggers no good.' . . . 'they talk about things that are going on elsewhere and get their minds unsettled.' " Actually such measures were usually laxly enforced or altogether neglected, the South being incurably slipshod. Only a few years after Nat Turner, a Virginia judge called them "nearly dead letters upon our statute books, unless during times of excitement, or since the efforts of the abolitionists have reanimated them." But the moral intent was further to trammel the slave as the middle of the century—and *Uncle Tom*—approached.

Statesmen pondering these things conceived the famous "colonization movement" for settling free American Negroes in West Africa, not only to get rid of potential troublemakers but also to prepare a colony, called Liberia, for mass resettlement of slaves to be freed and immediately exiled. But the surplus of slaves and their dwindling utility were already on the way to cure. In 1793 Eli Whitney, a young Yankee seeking a post as tutor, learned in Georgia that the South needed a machine efficiently to clean the seeds from short-staple upland cotton. Hand cleaning, even with slave labor, made the crop hardly pay, and the existing "gin" for deseeding long-staple Sea Island cotton with wooden rollers (rather like those of a clothes wringer) only crushed short-staple seeds and stained the fiber an unsightly yellow. In all ingenious innocence Whitney perfected a device that cleaned upland cotton with revolving metal teeth and, with steam or mule power, could do the work of a hundred hands in a day.* Efficient laborsaving carding, spinning and weaving machinery for exploiting this improvement already existed. Henceforth the whole world could afford textiles of Southern upland cotton.

This sorcerer's apprentice thus committed his country to the Civil War. Rhodes and many a historian after him called it "more than probable that the invention of the cotton-gin prevented the peaceful abolition of slavery"; that is, it made slaves newly profitable by opening up to gang slavery a vast new industry. But this relation was not, as the textbooks usually imply, inevitable. At the time Southerners knew that free white labor could, if it wished, grow cotton efficiently on one-family farms. The cotton South could have developed like the corn Middle West with single families clearing and planting family-size farms for themselves to operate with only casual outside labor. But the gang system implicit in rice and indigo culture had made many Southerners gang minded. When pioneering cotton culture, they operated in the familiar terms of scores of slaves and thousands of acres; or, as Bancroft said, "the South deceived itself into believing that . . . cotton cultivation depended on the use of slaves." Alway wrong-headed, in fact, the South was insisting on mass-production organization of personnel long before mechanization put economic sense into such an approach. One detail, however, had

---

* Carter (*Lower Mississippi;* 202) calls Whitney "more lucky than brilliant," since he built on others' almost successful ideas. The South, he points out, was already so confident that the problem would be solved that 3,000,000 pounds of short-staple cotton were picked yearly. True as far as it goes, but it neglects the effect on world markets of the immense cheapening of cotton that came with the Whitney gin. Holt (*George Washington Carver;* 123) and others have a legend that Whitney got the germ of his idea from a clever Negro. The tale has no proof. There is no other reason why it should not be true. But it is probably wishful apocrypha, like the tale that Alexander Hamilton had "Negro blood." The mechanical cleverness of Negroes apropos of cotton gins is clear in an instance given in Sydnor, *Slavery in Mississippi;* 181.

unquestionable dollars-and-cents merit; the new staple gave the elder slave states a profitable and badly needed market for their surplus Negroes.

Westward went the cotton fields, westward across the Black Belt * of Alabama, into Mississippi (evicting the "civilized" tribes of Indians), across the big river into alluvial Arkansas and upper Louisiana and, within a generation, on into Texas.† And westward went the slaves, on the assumption that newly cleared fields for cotton would be useless without them. Virginians and Carolinians following the cotton boom brought along their gangs of Negroes to such effect that within twenty years the slave population of Mississippi quintupled. Slave prices in Memphis and New Orleans met temporary fluctuations to match general boom and panic, of course, but the general rising trend is clear. By 1845 prime male field hands brought $750 apiece from planter-buyers in the Southwest; by 1860 the same article was bringing $1500. Stay-at-homes in Virginia, Maryland and presently Kentucky found slavery at least paying for itself through the sale of human livestock to the cotton South.** In 1819 a Virginia slaveowner was already speaking of "the health of our Negroes, upon whose increase [*miserabile dictu*] our principal profit de-

---

* Originally applied to the state's central area of rich black soil. As heavy Negro population naturally followed, the color of the soil and of the slaves fused in the popular mind.

† Trans-Mississippi cotton planting, with its effect on the future of slavery, was another backlash from Haiti. It was French failure to regain Haiti that moved Napoleon to sell Louisiana to the United States.

** This has been questioned, for example, by Hart (*Slavery and Abolition;* 124) on the grounds that the census showed in Maryland and Virginia no "undue proportion of young Negroes . . . such as would have been evident if there had been a definite system of selling the adults." Given these data, this is a good common-sense point. But the general truth of the above statements in the text is unmistakable in the way that spokesmen for the South, to whose interests it would have been to minimize the domestic slave trade, vouched for its reality and importance in Southern economy. The above quotations and citations are merely a sampling out of many.

pends." **s** In the 1830's a Carolina planter advocated forcing slaves to keep themselves and quarters clean because that promoted fecundity and "their annual increase may be estimated as adding as much to my income as arises from all other sources." **s** A proslavery parson was soon writing that " 'he is gone to Virginia to buy Negroes' . . . is as often applied to a temporarily absent planter as 'he is gone to Boston to buy goods' to a New England country merchant." **s** During Virginia's conscientious effort of 1832 to slough off slavery, a scholarly proponent of the "peculiar institution" stated that the Old Dominion annually exported 6000 slaves, a crop crucial to her economy. By 1840 Kentucky was exporting the same number, and twenty years later the state had as many slave dealers as mule dealers in a day when Kentucky was to mules what Missouri would be later.

As large numbers of slaveowners came to depend on this domestic slave trade, it followed that thenceforth anybody calling slavery unwise, inhuman, wasteful, wrong, hypocritical or stupid, all of which it was, made a violent foe of a South committed to cotton as Brazil is to coffee and unable to envisage raising it in any other way than with plentiful slave labor. An anthropologist once pondered how much better advised that portentous young man would have been to invent the cotton *picker* in advance of the gin.* That might not have helped. The gin perpetuated slavery only because cultivation of the new crop was dominated by large-scale slaveowners' ideas of how to organize manpower. A recent historian of the South mentions with a learned grin how "tidewater aristocrats . . . learned by experience on exhausted lands that slavery was unprofitable and even morally wrong" only to be succeeded in power by "slave-holders of the back-country whose experience in the black lands of Alabama and Mississippi had convinced them that slavery was profitable and right." **s** Actually,

---

* Embree, *Brown Americans;* 146. The planter considered himself committed to slavery because it took so many people so long to keep the bolls of cotton harvested as they ripened all the way to frost.

as Dabneys of Virginia and Chesnuts of South Carolina moved troops of slaves inland to the expanding cotton belt and took up land, these two groups were often identical.

Within a few years of Eli Whitney's death, Britain had successively abandoned the African slave trade, West Indian slavery, the press gang and transportation of felons. The United States had renounced flogging in the armed forces and was giving up immigration financed by pledging future labor. The whole context of callous violence out of which slavery grew was collapsing. Yet, because attitudes born of the rice swamp profited a few and flattered many, every decade or so saw the South give the turnbuckles another twist in hopes that mounting internal tensions would hold anachronisms together.

Though entangled with the problems posed by *Uncle Tom,* all this, however, is not fundamental. The primary cause not of the Negro's plight but of its persistence, the detail that denied him a potential future like that of the flagrant whore and the undernourished debtor, was his color. And that biological vagary was the doing of Providence, not of Eli Whitney.

2 *Good to their niggers*

". . . not the worst slavery in the world, not a slavery that made all life unbearable, rather a slavery that had here and there something of kindliness, fidelity and happiness— but withal slavery, which, so far as human aspiration and desert were concerned, classed the black man and the ox together." —DU BOIS, The Souls of Black Folk

On the southern slope of the Sourlands stands a massive stone house built by Jerseyman forebears of mine in time for Lafayette to spend a night there in 1778, a visit duly commemorated by a tablet set into the north wall. The squat stone cottages nearby are said to have been slave quarters. No doubt they were, for central New Jersey once contained a fair number of slaves and the builders of these premises must have been well off in terms of the time. It was probably comfortable, if smelly, behind those thick stone walls with ample rations from a prosperous owner and firewood for the cutting and carrying.

Stone or brick slave quarters were occasionally known both North and South.* Log shacks were the rule, however, per-

---

* Thus, Hermitage Plantation, near Savannah, famous for its slave-made gray-brick, had brick quarters. (Matthews, *Aunt Phebe . . .* ; 107) Sydnor says that the brick quarters of the old Bailey place near Oxford, Mississippi, still stand. (*Slavery in Mississippi;* 42.) But even such a show place as Berkeley (Harrison's Landing) in Virginia had only log huts raised on cornerstones, according to the present owner.

haps replaced by frame-and-plank structures as the plantation prospered and the area developed sawmills; or planks were nailed over the logs. Neither kind of construction was durable. But old photographs and parallels drawn from current Negro housing in the South, viewed in the light of the accounts of old travelers and apologists for slavery, can still give a fair idea of the range and quality of slave housing.

Today's Southern plantation Negro is isolated on the plot that he farms. In 1850, however, he inhabited a row cabin in the quarters, near but not too near the Big House, where one existed. The area was usually unfenced, with the overseer's cottage—not so good as the Big House but far better than any slave's—at the head of two parallel rows of slave shacks in a perspective not unlike that of the Governor's Palace at Williamsburg. On smaller, less formally managed places the slaves lived closer by for convenience in supervision. ". . . log smokehouse back of the kitchen; three little log nigger cabins in a row t'other side of the smokehouse" were Huckleberry Finn's specifications for "one of those little one-horse cotton plantations and they all look alike." 5 Such edifices bore small resemblance to Uncle Tom's cabin, which Mrs. Stowe rashly described as buried in flowers and with *glass windows*. Many an ante bellum Southern white household went without glazing, and glass in Negro cabins was almost unheard of.*

So it was an airy life. Slaves often contracted tuberculosis (typically in the form of scrofula) but not from poor ventilation. The rough stone or clay-and-stick chimney was wide; the wooden shutters—supposing window holes cut—fitted poorly; the tightness of the walls, if of plank, depended on master's conscience, if of logs, on the inhabitants' persistence in renewing the clay chinking.† A physician-planter averred that his

---

* For exceptions, see Olmsted on a James River plantation (*Cotton Kingdom;* 42) and Allston (*South Carolina Rice Planter;* 346-350) as to a plantation near Georgetown, South Carolina.

† Sometimes the chinking was knocked out for coolness in summer, and then laziness prevented its being replaced as cold weather came on.

slaves had fallen ill when he housed them in solid brick cottages but flourished in log cabins with great fires in the fireplaces and outside air always moving in. ⁵ Circulation was even freer when the cabins were raised on cornerstones or wooden blocks with little pains taken to make the floors tight.

In the steaming Southern summers such housing kept off the sun and most of the rain and admitted what cooling air there was after sundown. But it aches one's bones to think of what it was like in the freezing or close-to-freezing Southern winter; even semitropical Natchez, after all, sometimes knew snowballing. Most of the heat of the fires must have gone up the gaping flue. The slave's winter outfit typically consisted of annual issue of a pair of shoes, enough sleazy woolen cloth for jacket and pants, or skirt and blouse, and a single woolen blanket to be worn Indian fashion or made into a sort of poncho as fancy dictated. ⁵ * Mattresses were mere aggregations of rags or shuck ticks—bags full of corn husks and an occasional end of cob to make it interesting—that can hardly have been smotheringly warm. The slave must actually have been chilly most of the time from the end of November to the middle of February, which may explain why he was always building little fires to squat by when waiting or loafing outdoors. In regions as wintry as the Shenandoah Valley, slave children went shoeless the year round until they reached the age of ten years or so. These conditions are nothing to which

* Ingraham, *Sunny South;* 86. Annual issue for 200 slaves on the Coffin plantation on St. Helena Island, South Carolina, was on the generous side: In spring 500 yards "men's blue cloth," 600 yards bleached shirting, 600 yards "stuff for women's underwear," 600 yards "gay calico for frocks," 100 "handkerchief pieces," 100 straw hats; in autumn 550 yards "woolen for men's clothes," 600 yards thinner ditto for women, 1200 yards unbleached cloth for shirts and underwear, 100 turban handkerchiefs, 100 warm caps, 200 pairs of shoes, 67 blankets, "and additional hose and flannels for the drivers, mechanics and house servants." For the rest no socks in the South Carolina winter! (Woofter, *Black Yeomanry;* 31.) Sometimes, however, knitting hose was one of the indoor tasks of women slaves. (Sydnor, *Slavery in Mississippi;* 27-28.)

human beings cannot adjust. The Patagonian Indians wore less and endured worse weather and lower temperatures for thousands of years. But these are the conditions that the apologist for slavery often adduced as being well housed and well clothed.

Planters drawing up ideal specifications for quarters recommended whitewash inside and out every year and a monthly clearing up of rubbish from below the floors. [s] A realistic Alabama master moved the cabins to fresh sites every two or three years to forestall epidemics arising from the noisome filth accumulated beneath. [s] Beaten-dirt floors in cabins flush with the ground cannot have been very sanitary either. Facilities for excretion were exactly the same for slaves as for horses and hogs and, not infrequently, for white folks too. Shingle roofs were a fire hazard, but fire meant small risk to the slave's person. He and his family had only to tumble out the door after a few moments of snatching up their meager belongings— Sunday clothes in a locked chest, some odd crockery, the ragged and fetid bedding. W. H. Russell, father of modern war correspondents, reported thus on living conditions on "Trescot plantation on Barnwell Island," a Sea Island establishment cognate to those that so distressed Fanny Kemble:

> The huts stand in a row, like a street, each detached with a poultry-house of rude planks behind it. . . . No attempt at any drainage or convenience exists near them, and the same remark applies to very good houses of white people in the south. Heaps of oyster shells, broken crockery, old shoes, rags and feathers were found near each hut. The huts were all alike windowless, and the apertures, intended to be glazed some fine day, were generally filled up with a deal board. . . . the whitewash which had once given the settlement an air of cleanliness was now to be traced only by patches which had escaped the action of the rain. . . . many of the doors were fastened by a padlock and chain outside. . . . [This last because slaves readily pilfered from one another.]

It all sounds much like what Booker T. Washington remembered as "typical" of his native region in upcountry Virginia—the dirt floors, the open window holes, **N** and so on.

N   *This is a sample instance of the use of boldfaced capital* **N**
*to close testimony from Negroes. As described before, similar use
of boldfaced capital* **s** *means testimony from Southerners or from
those sympathetic to the South. This is the last reminder on both.*

Withindoors privacy was scarce. Cubage varied from that
of a skimpy two-car garage to that of hutches twelve feet
square ventilated only by cracks between the logs. "Except for
the chimney," Olmsted wrote of one such, "I should have con-
jectured that it had been built for a powder-house or an icehouse—never for an animal to sleep in." Sixteen by eighteen
feet for a teeming Negro family swarming like pups in a
basket was considered roomy. About the lowest recorded ratio
of cabin to head of slaves was one to four on Jefferson Davis's
quixotically managed plantation. One authority considered
twenty-four cabins to 150 slaves—about one to six—
ample provision. **s** Some shacks had no partitions, others only
one, perhaps with a loft dormitory reached by a ladder for
children.*

To modern eyes better-than-average slave quarters would
have looked like a well-ventilated slum. Even in the 1830's a
slavery-hating Englishwoman saw them as "something be-

---

* The best-divided quarters that Olmsted saw were in South Carolina:
two-family cabins, each family with 400 square feet divided into three
rooms of 200, 100 and 100 respectively. (*Cotton Kingdom;* 184.) On the
Aiken plantation in the Edisto River country, Solon Robinson reported
two-family cabins, each family with two rooms and a loft. (Phillips,
American Negro Slavery; 252.) The Sparkman place near Georgetown,
South Carolina, had individual cabins eighteen by twenty-two, each
with a "hall" and two sleeping rooms. (Allston, *South Carolina Rice-
Plantation:* 346-350.)

tween a haunt of monkeys and a dwelling-place of human beings. . . . a walk through a lunatic asylum is far less painful." A few years later a countryman of hers wrote that whitewash on the quarters of a depressing plantation near Savannah did not make up for their "dirty, gloomy and wretched interiors. . . . The criminals in all the state-prisons of the country, that we had as yet seen, were better off in food, raiment, and accommodation, and much less severely worked." ". . . the housing of slaves," says an honest Southern scholar, "was more open to criticism than their food or even their clothing." [5]

He might have added, however, that in Mrs. Stowe's time the "lower orders" of Europe were hardly better off. Frederick Douglass, the conspicuous runaway slave from Maryland, said that the smallness and squalor of poor people's hovels in Ireland "represented much the same degradation as that of American slaves." Russell the realist described superior slave quarters on the Carrolls' principal plantation in Maryland as "palaces compared with the huts of Irish laborers." Many travelers whose feelings about slavery ranged from neutrality to hostility noted that cotton South slave housing compared well with facilities of the time for Scottish or Central European peasantry. And Olmsted, the sober Yankee, considered the galleried quarters on a certain Louisiana sugar plantation as equal to employer-furnished cottages for New England mill hands.

Consider further that the Southern poor white was seldom better housed than the slave. For that matter, most of your and my pioneer ancestors ate, slept, sweat and procreated in cubage of this order. The housing that Thomas Lincoln provided for his family while Abe was a growing boy was, in fact, inferior to what many masters afforded many slaves. And even in our own day it is still probably true that, as a great student of slavery concluded not long ago, many slave quarters were of "sounder construction and greater comfort than most of

the negroes in freedom have been able to command." ⁵ For
my part, I can never forget the fantastically rattletrap condition, inside and out, of representative Negro tenant houses
that I visited north of Vicksburg in 1940.

> "... *Spicy grove, cinnamon tree,*
> *What is Africa to me?"*
> —COUNTEE CULLEN, Heritage

Another kind of perspective comes from relating the American slave's situation and habits to those of his West African
ancestors. On engineering rather than moral grounds he
would have done well, for instance, to transplant the West
African hut structure. Privacy would have not been improved,
and the amusement-park look of the common West African
dwelling is neither good nor bad aesthetically, merely dull.
But those mud walls laid up on armatures of poles are cool
in tropic heat and should have been correspondingly warm in
North American winters.* The slave was in no position, how-

---

* Says Macmillan (*Warning from the West Indies;* 117): "The West
Indian has long abandoned the round African hut. . . . As in America
. . . framed cabins are the characteristic type of dwelling. . . . The
better examples are unexceptionable. For the poorer classes . . . it is a
disadvantage that the art of hut building has been lost." Wertenbaker
(*Old South;* 79) mentions that early Virginians found that wattle-and-
daub construction broke down quickly in the Southern climate. Yet
the slave's clay-and-stick chimney proved pretty durable in Southern
weather, and a close-to-African style of stockaded clay hut persisted on
the all-Negro, single-owner West Indian island of Barbuda up to two
generations ago. (Aspinwall, *Pocket Guide to the West Indies;* 219.)
Clay walls protected by light planking outside might have been excellent insulation from rain and frost. The best quarters were those of
"tabby," a shell-and-lime plaster, described in Flanders, *Plantation
Slavery in Georgia;* 152.

ever, to suit himself. He built and lived in whatever struck
the wardens as cheap and fit.

The only purely African domestic comforts that he kept, in
fact, were the immigrant vegetables, the collards, okra and
peanuts—which he might call "goobers" or "pinders," both
African words—that a cultural miracle had fetched across the
ocean for his garden patch.* Other such transatlantic heri-
tages, though numerous, were of small significance except in
superstition. Some Southern Negroes, usually women, still
carry things on their head, African-style. The use of African
pestle and mortar for pounding rice is said to persist in some
remote parts of the Carolina coast. Slave mothers working in
the field with their babies slung on the small of the maternal
back in the bight of a cloth told inquirers that the hazard of
snakes was their reason; they did not know that poor, over-
heated baby always rides that way in West Africa. Fanny
Kemble tried in vain to discourage the complementary custom, also still lively in West Africa, of keeping a steaming
woolen cap on baby, whatever the temperature. Slave women
often persisted in the "head tie," germ of the bandanna turban, which is still rife along the country roads of Alabama as
well as in advertisements showing Aunt Jemima. They often
stuck to the bare, dusty African dooryard, usually swept clean
in the Gold Coast but, under the demoralizations of slavery,
often unsightly with rubbish. Nor did the slave grasp the
point of shade trees. The West African hut village is usually
blindingly shadeless, and to this day many Negro shacks in
the South fry in the sun while the white man's Big House is

---

* I have found no historical explanation of how the seeds of okra, collards and so on got from Africa to the South. Slaves could hardly have
brought them, since no fresh-shipped slaves could have known that the
land he was going to lacked things so fundamental to life as he knew
it. Nor is it likely that early masters took the trouble to import
familiar vegetables to make their "people" happy. The only reasonable
possibility is that some African-born and subsequently freed Negro
seaman was homesick for these dishes and brought seed back with him.

buried in trees.* As for lack of privies, that too is good West Africa.†

North American winters soon weaned the slave from the admirable Guinea custom of bathing at least once a day, often with palm-oil-and-woodash soap. The cotton-chopping field hand was usually about as dirty as his clothes, which were too few to be spared for frequent laundry. Even humane masters might allow only a weekly "half-hour by sun" for slave women to do the family wash. Even if all hands wore the same clothes all week, little can be done in such a period. No doubt such discouragements underlay the complaint of a Carolina planter to a Yankee parson about his slaves as "doggedly averse to washing . . . can scarcely be more offended by anything than a compulsory system of bathing or washing their clothes. If not compelled to do it, they would never wash a garment from the time when it is put on new until it is worn out. Even house-servants must be watched like children, or most of them would neglect attention to cleanliness." **5**

Hence the American Negro's reputation for "negro funk" —a specially acrid odor taken to be innate. Since it is a traditional excuse for racist nonsense, this unpleasant subject is unavoidable in any effort to make sense about Negroes. It always has been so. In 1828 a fine lady in Charleston told Mrs. Hall, wife of a Royal Navy captain, that in summer she could

---

* A Negro boy once told Jonathan Daniels (*A Southerner Discovers the South;* 143) that the landlord discourages shade trees because their demand on moisture might "stunt the cotton" planted right up to Negro tenant shacks. Mr. Daniels is good enough to think well of my guess that this is afterthought accounting for a custom much older than intensive cotton culture.

† Sir Harry Johnston, touring the United States in 1904 after learning Africa inside out, thought it disgraceful that Southern slaveowners had not done more to break their chattels of the "indiscriminate defecation" that, he recalled, made "the outskirts of African towns noisome to a degree." (*Negro in the New World;* 18-20.) In this respect West Africa must have improved to some extent. At least as of 1953 it did not smell quite as richly as this implies it used to.

identify her house slaves sight unseen by their distinctive individual odors. ⁵ Dr. S. A. Cartwright, the eminent Louisiana
physician whose "scientific" pronouncements were of great
help to proslavery propaganda, believed that the healthier and
happier Negroes were, the stronger they smelled: "The skin
of a happy, healthy negro . . . emits the strongest odor when
the body is warmed by exercise and the soul is filled with the
most pleasurable emotions. In the dance called *patting juber*
the odor emitted from the men . . . is often so powerful as
to throw the negro women into paroxysms of unconscious-
ness." ⁵ A race-minded hysteric of the 1850's maintained that
this special odor was the last trait to disappear as miscegenation injected more and more "white blood"; it persisted from
one's great-grandmother in a sort of olfactory Nuremberg
Law.

Actually the American Negro's West African cousins, differing from him only in lacking much if any admixture of
"white blood," are ardent users of coarse, pink, carbolized
soaps made expressly for them by Unilever and competitors.
On a hot day a solid West African Negro crowd smells no
worse than any other crowd on such a day—not half so bad
as the pent-up passengers in a New York subway train in the
rush hour just after a thunderstorm. True, the Negro has
more sweat glands per square foot of skin than has the European, but that is no reason why the smell of his sweat should
grow stronger. In experiments with test tubes of sweat from
whites and Negroes, blindfold observers have been unable to
sort for rankness in any pattern corresponding to race; both
the least and the most offensive samples, as it happened, came
from whites. In this matter we can rely on Fanny Kemble's
impassioned common sense; she complained that her newly
assigned slave-maid was

> . . . so intolerably offensive in her person that it is impossible
> to endure her proximity. . . . About this same personal of-
> fensiveness, the Southerners . . . insist that it is inherent

with the race . . . one of their most cogent reasons for keeping them as slaves. But, as this very disagreeable peculiarity does not prevent Southern women from hanging their infants at the breasts of Negroes, nor almost every planter's wife and daughter from having one or more little pet blacks sleeping like puppy-dogs in their very bed-chambers, nor almost every planter from admitting one or several of his female slaves to the still closer intimacy of his bed, it seems to me that this objection . . . is not very valid. . . . I am strongly inclined to believe that ignorance of the laws of health and of decent cleanliness are the real and only causes of this disagreeable characteristic of the race. Thorough ablutions and change of linen, when tried, have been perfectly successful in removing all such objections; and if ever you have come into anything like neighborly proximity with a low Irishman or woman, I think you will allow that the same causes produce very nearly the same effects.

Brava, Fanny! *

The slave's problem with parasites was about what it had been for his forebears in Guinea. I know of only one master supplying the high-post bedsteads required for rigging mos-

---

* The attitude has numerous other friends in a position to speak: J. A. Froude, an ill-tempered colonialist, was revolted by the smell of the crowd at Jacmel, Haiti, but went on: "The wild African black is not filthy in his native state. He washes much and . . . at least tries to keep himself clear of vermin. The blacks in Jacmel . . . appeared to lose the sense which belonged to them in their wild condition." (*English in the West Indies;* 187-188.) Johnston (*Negro in the New World;* 11) was eloquent about the Negro's alleged "musky or goat-like smell," particularly from the armpit and groin; "Yet . . . this . . . is not as disgusting as that which proceeds from heated, unwashed Europeans and Asiatics. It is practically absent from many Africans who keep their bodies constantly washed. I mixed with many Negro crowds and assemblies in the United States and scarcely ever noticed a disagreeable smell." He was not being just antiracist about this, since he was very severe about newly landed immigrants and "the offensively dirty Chinese travelling in the public cars."

quito bars. **s** Transplanted West Africans had left the tsetse fly and sleeping sickness behind. But hookworm traveled along in their intestines and, in inadvertent revenge on their worst contemners, spread all over the South further to debilitate the shoeless and shiftless poor whites. It is also ironically possible that the water casks of slave ships and the blood streams of slaves and sailors brought to the New World the mosquitoes and virus that established Yellow Jack in South America and the West Indies—a most striking vengeance. The same could be true of malaria, which may have killed more people in our hemisphere than yellow fever ever did and has certainly caused far more—and more prolonged—misery.* Less subtle parasites can be taken for granted. Slaves often bought, or their masters supplied, fine-toothed combs, but slave children's heads were proverbially "lousy as a pet pig," **N** and the sight of friends picking over one another's heads was as familiar in Dixie as it still is in Polynesia.

The slave's table was about as good as his West African cousin's. (The table is figurative; he usually ate with his hands, buffet style, from a tin plate on his knees or right out of pot or skillet.) Rice areas afforded him the same staple as West Africa's. Cotton and tobacco country gave him equivalent starch in corn, issued shelled or on the ear, usually ground fresh daily for hoecake, grits or mush. With it came a weekly issue of smoked or salt pork, the renderings of which were more or less equivalent to the West African's palm-oil gravy. Molasses might be thrown in. Some plantations in Alabama and Georgia raised enough sugar cane to supply syrup to the hands; elsewhere sorghum came to serve this purpose. A

---

* Dr. W. H. Wright, of the U.S. National Microbiological Institute, finds the evidence for African origin of hookworm very strong. Yellow fever and malaria are not so certain, but the above text is probably justified. See Dr. Richard M. Taylor, in Strode, ed., *Yellow Fever* (1951), and Dr. Max Theiler, in Rivers, ed., *Viral and Rickettsial Infections of Man* (1952). Reciprocally the slave ships may have taken the jigger flea to Africa from South America. (*Science News-Letter*, March 13, 1954.)

Virginian witness recalled "a negro ration" as "a peck of meal, three pounds of bacon, and a pint of molasses weekly." s *
An Alabama planter defined proper diet for slaves as "3½ pounds of wholesome fat meat per week, bread [that is, corn bread] without stint or limit, molasses every Sunday, milk every day, butter occasionally, the privilege of raising chickens . . . one day's holiday and a feast every year when the crop is laid by." s That was generous. At the other extreme the Heyward rice plantation in South Carolina issued "the people" only cereals and vegetables and expected them to find their own meat or equivalent by hunting, trapping, fishing and raising hogs and poultry. s Beans, sweet potatoes, salt fish and starch vegetables, such as turnip and pumpkin, might replace the basic hog and hominy.

The able planter sought, at least in theory, to raise as much slave provender as possible on his own acres to avoid cash outlay.† Loud Bob Toombs, of Georgia, planter as well as politician, claimed that his place supplied all its own needs except salt and doctoring s—an obvious exaggeration, since it certainly also needed gunpowder and iron, but it shows the goal that was thought conceivable. In addition to cash-crop cotton, a sound operation like Bennett H. Barrow's in the

---

* Barringer, *American Negar*; 7. This checks with Olmsted, *Cotton Kingdom*; 483-484. For children's rations, see Frazier, *Negro Family in the United States*; 45.

† The Wetumpka, Alabama, *Argus* was scornful about the kind of cottonplanter who scorned this autarchic principle: "He wouldn't sell a chicken, nor a dozen eggs, nor a bushel of peaches, nor a colt for any consideration. He is above that! He raises cotton—he does. He rides in a six hundred dollar carriage, for which he is in debt. His daughters strum a piano that will never be paid for. He buys corn which he could raise for ten cents a bushel and pays sixty cents for it. . . . He could raise his own tobacco, yet he pays $3 a pound for Richmond scented. He could raise his own hogs, yet he patronizes Cincinnati. . . . He wants cotton goods and clothes for his plantation which he could make up at home. He orders them and feels 'large.' The year closes and he is up to his eyebrows in debt." (Quoted in Davis, *Cotton Kingdom in Alabama*; 182-183.)

Delta raised oats, hay, corn, peas, hogs, poultry, sheep, beef and tobacco for the hands. **5** Nutritionally the slave could have been much worse off. If the three M's—meat (largely salt and smoked pork), meal (corn meal) and molasses—could not sustain life, the South would long have been depopulated of both blacks and whites. The combination is now known to have had somewhat higher value in both minerals and vitamins than the white flour, beef and sugar that the slave would certainly have preferred.*

This combination was also superior, in both flavor and nutritives, to what hands before the mast got on the merchant vessels of the day. Some said that it compared well with European peasant diet, which I doubt. But the slave's supplementary edibles may well have raised his nutritional level above that of the Italian or Hungarian peasant of his time. He often could plant green stuff and sweet corn in an allotted garden patch, raise a few hens on pick-up scratch or the residue of an ample corn ration, catch an occasional catfish, trap coon, possum and rabbit. He was an ingenious and inveterate pilferer of house and plantation supplies. There is sound historical reason for the status of the chicken-stealing Negro in American folklore. "We stole so many chickens," a former slave told Fisk University researchers, "that if a chicken would see a darky he'd run right straight for the house." **N** Not infrequently a clever slave managed to steal, cook and consume undetected one of his master's or a neighbor's shoats. Former slaves' memories teemed with tales of how big Jim fooled the white folks in the matter of that missing sow. The great men,

---

* On the highly humane Poinsett plantation in South Carolina, Miss Bremer concluded that "under a good master," slaves were "much better provided for than the poor working people in many parts of Europe." Poinsett's slaves raised their own pork in pens next to their cabins, which implies both high corn rations and accentuation of local stenches, and seem to have been especially diligent in keeping the quarters clean. The same witness, and a good one, saw plenty elsewhere to persuade her that "under a wicked master," slaves could fall "into dire and hopeless misery." (*Homes of the New World*, I; 296.)

such as Jefferson and Mark Twain, who attributed Negro light-fingeredness to the degradation of slavery, not to racial delinquency, would be puzzled to account for the prevalence of the same trait among West African free Negroes today.* Yet this is no specific reproach to the Negro as a racial entity. It is something that usually happens when cultural streams of markedly different density come to mingle.

> *"I could see the slaves at work on either side of the road; their condition betokening, at a glance, the character of their owner, some being well fed, and hilarious in their dispositions; and others in rags, with their physical frames but poorly supported, and their spirits seemingly much depressed."*   —MACKAY, The Western World

The census is a faulty but eloquent test of slaves' welfare. A desperately unhappy nonliterate population usually fails to reproduce itself even when well fed and housed. That is prob-

---

* Jefferson, *Notes on Virginia;* 147: "That disposition to theft, with which they have been branded, must be ascribed to their situation and not to any depravity of the moral sense. The man in whose favor no laws of property exist, probably feels himself less bound to respect those made in favour of others. . . ." And Mark Twain (*Pudd'nhead Wilson;* 27-28): "They had an unfair share in the battle of life, and they held it no sin to take military advantage of the enemy—in a small way . . . not in a large one. They would smouch provisions from the pantry whenever they got a chance; or a brass thimble, or a cake of wax, or an emery-bag, or a paper of needles, or a silver spoon, or a dollar bill, or small articles of clothing. . . . A farm smoke-house had to be kept heavily padlocked, for even the colored deacon himself could not resist a ham. . . . But with a hundred hanging before him, the deacon would not take two—that is, on the same night." It is notable, however, that this same authority makes the King and the Duke consider it perfectly plausible that "the niggers" should have made away with old Peter Wilks's bag of gold totaling several thousand dollars.

ably why, until recently, the Polynesians were dying out and why the West Indian aborigines disappeared. To take this approach for what it is worth, it appears that sugar planters had usually treated slaves worst; large cotton planters better, but seldom well; and small owners, whether in the Deep South or the Border States, not too badly. Local testimony set at 2½ per cent the excess of deaths over births on Louisiana sugar plantations. 5 * Yet this grim ratio was not inseparable from cane culture: Russell found a crack sugar plantation in Louisiana that counted on 5 percent annual increase in slave population. So did well-run cotton plantations in alluvial Mississippi in the same latitude and climate. The Coupers sugar plantation in Georgia was notoriously healthy for slaves. The crucial difference must have been bad treatment. Conversely, slaves generally must not have been treated altogether too badly because one way or another the North American Negro population, both slave and free, showed a steady absolute increase from the time the first slaves were landed. Predictions of some decades past that Negroes were tending toward extinction naïvely—perhaps wishfully—reflected the fact that the *rate* of this increase was often lower than that of the whites.

A master owned his slave body and soul (if any) but did not necessarily use all his time and energy. On free Sundays slaves might earn cash by working for neighbors who needed help or (in coastal areas) by fishing and selling the catch to the master and other whites. N Corn accumulated from generous rations could be sold back to master or fed to the slave's hens, the eggs of which often made up the mistress's household supply, duly bought and paid for. Kind owners even permitted slaves to raise and market peanuts, melons, squash. One good-natured Georgia owner used to drive to town with one of his slaves and help him hawk vegetables and hand-woven baskets

---

* Collins, *Domestic Slave Trade in the Southern States;* 30. Jamaica, principal British sugar island, had a comparable local excess of deaths over births among slaves of 2 per cent.

up and down the streets. **s** Spanish moss from the boughs of
trees in the Deep South was gathered for mattress stuffing in
slaves' spare time and baled and sold on their behalf by helpful masters. **s**

Funds thus come by kept the slave in tobacco and bits of
finery. House servants, a caste haughtily distinct from field
hands, probably monopolized the white folks' cast-offs. But
the field hands could more or less clandestinely patronize the
wretched little stores set up on the roadside by poor whites
or recently landed European Jews settled down from being
peddlers and trying to accumulate capital for respectable
storekeeping in town.* Neither kind of merchant often asked
questions of a Negro swapping a side of bacon or a carpenter's
plane for whiskey or a few yards of calico. Each knew how to
advance a slave some enticing item on credit and then, by
threatening denunciation for previous pilfering, force him
into further thieving to cover the debt. In many jurisdictions
to do business with a slave without his master's consent was
illegal. But such laws were no better enforced than any others
in the "black codes." More realistically, slaves round Natchez
were allowed to flock to town on Sunday to go to church,
trade and gossip until a four-o'clock bell warned them to be
out of town in ten minutes. **s** Thereabouts slaves were not
allowed to raise and market the standard white cotton that
could have been stolen from the master's crop. They could

---

* Some investigators trace the American Negro's sporadic anti-Semitism
to slaves' experience with petty Jewish traders. Lyell, Charles Mackay
and Olmstead agree on their frequent presence and shady methods. But
in at least one case a Jewish trader was a Negro's good friend, acting
as front for self-purchase of a slave who had saved up the price of freedom. (Still, *Underground Railroad Records;* 23.) The slave needed little
encouragement to despise and mistrust the poor-white trader. The poor
white and he had been at feud ever since their ancestors had been forced
to worm tobacco together, and one of his songs made it clear: "Rather
be a nigger than a poor white man!" (Botkin, ed., *Lay My Burden
Down;* 242.)

plant and dispose of only the yellow-fibered Nankeen cotton, with which, though its great durability gave it local popularity here and there, few serious planters with their eyes on the world market cared to bother.

Many masters tried to forbid cash to their slaves, marketing their produce for them and paying them in orders on the store, feeling that handling money gave niggers "uppity" notions. Unlike many nonliterates, plantation slaves needed no training in the cash nexus. West Africans had currency, interest and formidable skills in close bargaining long before white men ever came troubling them. The American Negro knew just what it meant, was indeed proud of it, that master could get $900 cash for him any time. But since he could not. sell or mortgage himself, as he could have back in Africa, his money dealings tended to be on a very small scale. When Jim gave Colonel Grangerford's slaves ten cents for salvaging the raft, they " 'us mighty well satisfied, en wished some mo' rafts 'ud come long en make 'm rich ag'in." **s**

All this suggests a heterosexual penitentiary—issue clothes, issue food, issue quarters, small luxuries elaborately scrounged and, of course, gang labor. Irons were for punishment only, but the man with the whip was always there and the dogs specially trained for pursuing runaways were always on call nearby. At dawn or a little earlier the pulsing clang of iron on iron or the bray of a horn or the low of a conch shell brought "the people" tumbling frowsily into the equivalent of the company street. Good management rated able-bodied men and women "full" hands; feebler adults of both sexes and the stronger maturing boys and girls were "half" or "quarter" hands according to the overseer's or driver's rule-of-thumb ratings. The crippled or superannuated wove, spun, shelled corn. Planting of cotton seed was preceded by careful plowing, and much of the early cultivation was done by the one-mule plow with various attachments, an assignment reserved, with a touch of prestige, for the more responsible men and the most robust women. But hoeing was the average assignment. For cotton picking the plow gang fused with the hoe gang, and small children, plantation craftsmen and hobbling Aunty This and Uncle That joined in an all-hands-and-the-cat effort to get the crop in as swiftly as the bolls ripened. Individual norms were informally set for each picker, and, if the scales showed at the end of the day that his or her weight of cotton picked was materially below expectation, it required a very good story indeed to head off a curt order to lie down and take a licking.

The nature of cotton as a crop—and the master's lack of enterprise—committed the hoe gang to techniques already obsolete in 1850. Olmsted was impressed, however, by an all-woman hoe gang that he saw in the Louisiana cotton country: ". . . forty of the largest and strongest women I ever saw together . . . in a simple uniform dress of a bluish check stuff, the skirts reaching little below the knee; their legs and feet were bare; they carried themselves loftily, each having a hoe over the shoulder, and walking with a free, powerful swing . . . two of them rode astride on the plough mules . . . evidently a picked lot." "Evidently," indeed—the usual effect was tattered, dingy, sluggish, lumpy. "At work in the field," wrote Miss Bremer, "they look like figures of earth." Unhampered by their loose rags, the men in fraying straw hats, the women with kerchiefed heads, they advanced irregularly across the wide fields in successive "choppings" to thin the rows and, where the plow had been ineffective, to keep crab grass and other weeds from competing with King Cotton. Somewhere I have seen a cynical slave song about a deceitful master's telling a slave unwilling to be sold South that "they ain't no grass in Geo'gia."

Some overseers let the hands breakfast before going afield. More commonly they brought cold snacks and stopped work mid-morning to gnaw at them. Midday a mule cart fetched dinner, usually of corn bread and pork, eaten in the shade of the woods edging the field or under the midfield "weather

shed" * if there was one, and followed by a sweaty hour or so
of drowsing rest. Miss Bremer sampled such a field dinner on
a model plantation in South Carolina and found it good,
though the beans were seasoned too highly for her decorously
hygienic taste.

Much of the Southern countryside in which these "figures
of earth" toiled is not unlike West Africa now and must have
been more so then, in summer anyway: the same brushy old
fields, relics of the same slash-and-burn land use; the same
sluggish, dark-watered streams; the same look of being practically uninhabited; often the same blazing red dirt exposed
in cuts and gullies and powdering roadside vegetation with
what looks like rust. One hopes that, accidental and insignifi-
cant though it was, this likeness sometimes made a new-landed
exile feel a little more at home.

The detail to which those fresh from West Africa probably
had most difficulty adjusting was the *buckra*'s (West African
for "white man," surviving in the South) insistence on regular, steady labor day after day. Hour after hour the sun bore
down and the sweat exuded and dripped and the dust swirled
round naked black ankles as the hoes scuffed into the grassy
crust. On a fairly humane South Carolina plantation Mrs.
Hall remarked "no laughter or talking in the field, no sign
whatever of merriment or happiness; they seemed to work
on mechanically." She did not say what element in their situation should have made them merry. A Southern historian who
once "made a crop" of cotton—to my knowledge the only
historian so qualified—could say in favor of cotton chopping
only that "none of the work was beyond the strength of a
stripling and the sunshine, though very hot [in Georgia], was
never prostrating." 5

All day the water boy (who was sometimes a girl) toiled
back and forth from spring or branch, a gourd floating in his

---

* A large open shelter to make unnecessary the time-consuming trudge
to shade or quarters.

brimming bucket and the water slopping gratefully on his begrimed black feet. There was a song about how he could seldom keep pace with thirst. All day the driver shouted and scowled and now and again laid his whip where it would do the tired or the lazy the most good. If he knew his business, he could keep them singing the work songs that the slave developed early and copiously. But song or not, whip or not, habituation or not, outsiders noticed that the wavering rhythm of the hoes quickened or slackened in proportion to the nearness of the man with the whip. Even on well-run places the hoe gang's obvious intent was to stay as near as possible to a mere going through of motions.

Such bunch-hands organization was usual in cotton culture. Rice country preferred "tasking," each slave assigned a certain area to hoe or weed at his or her own pace, and the term "task" is still an informal measure of land in the Sea Islands.* Something rather like mass labor trouble could occur if a heedless master or new overseer too tactlessly altered a tasking basis of long standing. An earnest and vigorous slave starting work at dawn might be finished by two P.M. and have the rest of daylight for gardening, fishing, making things for sale. That was the one good thing about tasking. Otherwise, it obviously made for favoritism in assignment, unfair ratings, arbitrary punishment and high unlikelihood that many slaves would ever do more than the already low minimum. But then both systems necessarily limited production to the capacity of the weaker or lazier.

A hundred hands to the thousand acres was the proverbial cotton formula. [5] It reflected actuality no better than another glib calculation—that a prime field hand cost $100 for every

---

* Thus, in 1953, Samuel Hopkins Adams asked an Edisto Islander how much land he planted and was told: "I got me about fo'teen tasks, sah," a task working out to about a quarter acre. (*Ford Times,* October, 1953.) The task and gang systems were much mingled in Alabama cotton planting. (Davis, *Cotton Kingdom in Alabama;* 57.)

cent in the market price of cotton. The real working unit was
the number of hands that one man could effectively oversee—
say fifty. Efficient use of slaves as well as of cash required
planting as much acreage in corn as in cotton. The Georgia
practice, for example, was ten acres of each per hand. [s] In the
rich year of 1860 Isaac Croom, great man of Marengo County,
Alabama, raised 20,000 bushels of corn as well as the immense
crop of 1250 bales, say 300 tons, of cotton. Corn meant not
only bread but feed for hogs, poultry and horses and perhaps
supplementary cash income from neighboring planters caught
short of provisions.

Pat formulae are further misleading because they seldom
show whether effective "hands" or head of slaves on the place
is meant—a crucial point. Allow for fractional "hands," and
a working total of 100 means at least 150 persons in the field
gangs, plus at least 100 more specialists, old folks, children
below working age and house servants—say 250 Negroes on
the premises. Many a master did not know just how many
mouths he might be feeding at a given time. Nor was the bulk
of a 1000-acre plantation necessarily in either corn or cotton.
Sweet potatoes required much space, so did pasture for dairy
cows and the steers or sheep that the master might choose to
keep. The swamp and the woods, partly reserve for future
soil mining, partly essential fuel supply, accounted for hundreds of acres on each plantation. Both meant some steady
and much seasonal work in ditching, wood cutting, deaden-
ing, burning.

By non-Southern standards, remember, little of this was
well done or ever had been since William Byrd, the Virginia
patrician, wrote of how slaves "are even with their masters
and make him but indifferent crops, so that he gets nothing
by his injustice but the scandal of it." [s] An imaginative Mississippian tried to teach his field hands the most efficient stroke
for cotton chopping, but apparently he could not get far with
this motion-study approach. [s] A candid Virginian told Olm-

sted that one white farm hand in New Jersey did as much work as four slaves in the Old Dominion. Two cords of firewood a day was a standard task in Louisiana; in New York State whites were required to cut three. A fugitive from the Baltimore waterfront was amazed to see the Yankees in New Bedford unloading ships "with a capital of about sixty dollars in the shape of a good-natured old ox, attached to the end of a stout rope . . . [which] did the work of ten or twelve thousand dollars, represented in the bones and muscles of slaves, and did it better." N In relatively brisk Kentucky, George Combe, Scottish missionary of phrenology, concluded that "a vigorous German or British emigrant . . . performs more work than two slaves and . . . better." My favorite witness is Samuel Chamberlain, a British immigrant who saw much of the ante bellum South: "It makes a northern man nervous to see how them darkies would slip around. These slaves in Ky. Tenn. Va. and Md., the border states, well you could hardly see them stir in the morning when they were called out. . . . I never did see a slave do a hard day's work."

Forced labor is usually inefficient. Slave labor may have been especially so because it was toil without discernible future, even farther than the beehive from human values. The worker bee apparently goes at its destined chores with the passion of imperative instinct. The slave's primary motive was dully negative—to avoid punishment. Secondarily, but far behind, might come zest in manifesting skill or strength or a low-grade liking for the white man in charge. But in few cases could the slave tell himself, as could the soldier, the pressed seaman or most convicts, as he sat down with a vegetative grunt against the shady wall of the cabin, that there, at worst and least, was another day off his time. The exceptions would consist of slaves working on long-term arrangements for buying their own freedom, and those were rarer as Mrs. Stowe's great work approached its birth.

While production per man-hour, that key fact in any Western economy, was rising in the North, what with new ma-

chinery in both industry and agriculture* and the opening up
of rich Middle Western lands, it was probably falling, certainly not rising, in the South in spite of virgin cotton land
in Arkansas, upcountry Louisiana and eastern Texas. The
very fact of slaveowning was a brake on increasing the production per man-hour ratio, since the necessity for feeding slaves
meant the necessity for finding them things to do, often the
more time consuming the better. Thus a Southern historian
suggests that slavery encouraged the policy of wear-out-land-
and-clear-more because "it was convenient to employ slaves
in winter in clearing new fields." 5 Between the absolute low
efficiency of slave labor and relative lag behind Northern free
labor as it increased in efficiency, creeping bankruptcy was implicit in the Southern economy a decade before Sherman and
Sheridan devastated two of its principal productive areas.†
Consider the eloquent case of Farish Carter, richest man in
ante bellum Georgia, whose careful figures showed that, in
very good years, his cotton plantations netted him only 1 per
cent on his investment. 5 Strong cotton prices, which in turn
meant high prices for slaves, masked these trends. They were

---

* The McCormick reaper was actually invented in the Shenandoah Valley and used in Virginia wheat operations; Kentucky hemp might be
processed by machinery. But such exceptions were few and sporadic.

† Macmillan has gauged the effect of slave economy on the British West
Indies: "Bad planting . . . under-manuring are still very common, and
from the state of the soil today where scientific methods are neglected,
it is obvious that many estates, if not whole islands, must have been
exhausted by these vicious practices, and the defective methods played
a much larger part in the . . . 'decline of the plantation system' than
is generally admitted in what passes for history." (*Warning from the
West Indies;* 70.) Southerners doubting the above diagnosis of the ante
bellum South give figures showing per capita taxables higher in South
Carolina, say, than in Massachusetts. This neglects the fact that the
value of slaves was included in totals of Southern taxables. Had Massachusetts listed at comparable valuations all her factory workers, most
of her farm hands, and their wives and children, the figure would have
been quite different.

nevertheless an important aspect of the "house divided against itself."

Once driver or overseer was satisfied with the day's work, the gang straggled back to quarters caked with sweat and pulverized earth and perhaps, if the day had not been too smotheringly hot and things had otherwise gone tolerably, still improvising on their "quittin'-time song" or guffawing and breaking into infantile horseplay of the school's-out kind. On decent plantations the field hands often showed a certain slackjawed cheerfulness. They might even be got to sing starting for the field without breakfast, as well as during work and on the way home. Next day they would chop more cotton that looked exactly like yesterday's. Their work was not so monotonous as assembly-line work, for assignments varied seasonally and many slaves knew mattock, axe, shovel, oar and crowbar as well as hoe. But the assembly-line worker has off-the-job stimuli that the slave never dreamed of.

On some large plantations special crews ground the meal and cooked supper for all field hands, presumably weary and likely to scant themselves. But as a rule each household, whatever its members' functions, ground its own ration, with pecking-level bickerings over whose turn it was at the hand mill, baked its own pone and fried its own pork. Darkness meant bed, or what passed for bed, unless a bright moon and a mild night set off an evening of singing and dancing round a fire. Jefferson seriously maintained that Negroes "seem to require less sleep. A black after hard labour through the day, will be induced by the slightest amusements to sit up till midnight or later, though knowing he must be out with the first dawn of morning." [5] Since Sunday was usually a holiday and Saturday afternoon, or part of it, might be free, for even the less

heedless Saturday night might mean a frolic, with fiddle and
banjo going sixteen to the dozen. Drums, emotionally essential to the West African, were forbidden or discouraged because insurrectionists could use them for signaling.* But the
slaves could slake their thirst for percussion by hand clapping
and the use of the "bones"—beef ribs cleaned, polished and
knocked clunkingly together, furnishing the name of one
of the three principals of the minstrel show: Interlocutor,
Tambo and Bones.

This sub-African approach used both white man's music
and white man's instruments, just as the Polynesian did
with seaman's jigs, Portuguese guitars and missionary hymns,
vaguely approximating the words and subtly modifying
rhythms and melodies. At a Mississippi Delta wedding they
danced inside out to:

> Set to yo' partners, shocktumaloo,
> Shocktumaloo, my darlin!

This was the music that the minstrels conventionalized into
"Ethiopian" numbers for the white man's amusement, giving
the genius of Stephen Foster its occasion. Though practically
all minstrels were blacked-up whites, the slaves readily sang
minstrel-show coon songs partly because they liked them and
partly because the master often asked for them. As the hands
on a Carolina plantation gave out with "Oh, Susannah!" and
"Carry Me Back to Ole Virginny," Miss Bremer assumed that
she was hearing genuine Negro songs. Russell guessed better,
recalling a "real negro melody . . . as unlike the works of
the Ethiopian Serenaders as anything in song could be," sung
by Sea Island boatmen:

---

* The suppression was incomplete, of course. See Woofter, *Black Yeomanry; 36*, and Ingraham, *Sunny South; 105-106*, for minor exceptions.
The West Indies and the New Orleans area made much of drumming,
an art currently blooming in the West Indian "steel bands." Paine, *Six
Years in a Georgia Prison; 140*, gives the text of a Georgia law forbidding drums to slaves.

Oh your soul! Oh my soul!
I'm going to the churchyard to lay this body down!

Master was never so sure that slavery was right and proper
as when "the people" were summoned to the Big House to
sing for his family and guests and perhaps scramble for small
coins tossed over the gallery rail. They sang with such poign-
ant spontaneity and unquestionable enjoyment. Their teeth
and eyeballs gleamed so amusingly in the soft light from the
windows. There was such subservient good will in their rolling laughter and such leisurely good nature in the *r*-less,
vowel-heavy, elided speech (born of British rural dialects, it
is said*) that they shared with poor whites and their masters.
Why doubt that they were happy, especially since they had
so few adult responsibilities? ". . . if pleasure is correctly defined as the absence of pain," wrote Senator J. H. Hammond,
of South Carolina, an energetic spokesman for slavery and a
creditable example of humane slaveowning, "our slaves are
the happiest 3,000,000 of human beings on whom the sun
shines." s The point of view has lasted. In the 1920's a puzzled storekeeper in Albany, Georgia, considering how little a
certain Negro customer had on his mind, said to him: "Why,
you niggers have an easier time than I do." "Yassuh," said the
customer, "and so does yo' hogs." N
Long after slavery some of the survivors hankered back
after the fleshpots of Egypt: "My folks always said the best
time of their lives was the old plantation." N "If all slaves had
belonged to white folks like ours, there wouldn't been any
freedom wanted." N They remembered how at cornshuckings,
which were great interplantation festivals in some areas, the

* Americans in West Africa soon see that the "hush ma mouf" element
in Southern speech cannot be a carry-over from Africa through the
slave. But the staccato quality in Gullah talk, as distinct from that of
other Southern Negroes, which has some cognates in the West Indies,
could be African. In considering Southern speech I rely on Johnson, in
Botkin, ed., *Treasury of Southern Folklore;* Woofter, *Black Yeomanry;*
49, Greet, in Couch, ed., *Culture in the South.*

slaves would pick Master up and carry him round on their shoulders, singing "Rock me, Julie, rock me, . . ." N all the more melodiously for the whiskey that Master had supplied to make an occasion of a tedious chore. ". . . a crowd from Big Harper and a crowd from Little Harper and after we got through the shucking they'd give us whiskey, and there'd be plenty of fighting and the Little Harper white folks would take up for their darkys and the Big Harper white folks would do the same. I used to think them was the best times." N

"They said they had a good time," said a slave from the same part of Tennessee apropos of such frolics. "Anyway that was the only good time they had. . . . Their good times was so long between times." N Booker T. Washington asked a former slave woman in Kansas "if she would like to go back to the old days and live as she had lived on the plantation. 'Sometimes,' she replied, 'I feel I'd like to go back and see my old massa and missus'—she hesitated a moment and then added, 'but they sold my baby down South.' " N Disagreement with the fleshpotters could be much sharper: "Don't you believe no nigger," said another former slave, "when he say he ruther be no slave. Things happen then too awful to talk about." N Actually the facts of slaves' well-being seem greatly to have depended on which plantation and on what one calls happiness in human beings. A former slave just getting by was asked long after Emancipation whether he sometimes yearned for the security of slavery, and he answered, "Boss, dere's a kind of looseness about dis y'ere freedom which I kinder enjoys." N

3 *The sun shines bright*

". . . a slave-holder must be more or less of a despot in spite of himself; for the laws neither do, nor can they, effectually interfere in the details of discipline."

—CAPTAIN BASIL HALL, Travels in North America

To match his lack of status the slave usually lacked the dignity of a surname and might have to answer to "Boy!" to the age of forty. In overt contempt for slaves, the masters used "buck" and "wench" till they became trade terms, like "filly" and "shoat." Still worse taste lay in the continuing tradition of giving slaves classical names: Psyche, Venus, Chloë, to travesty Negro women; Pompey, Cicero, Scipio—on account of the "Africanus" tag, of course—to travesty Negro men. The Romans had done the same, naming slaves after ancient heroes, kings and queens: Jason, Priam, Midas, Croesus, Semiramis, Arsinoë; so did the French in the West Indies, the inventory of the estate of the Empress Josephine's mother listing Charlemagne, Ovide, Olympe, Radegonde, and more. The South mingled with these items from Lemprière and Suetonius some survivals from Africa, such as Cudjo and Cuffee. But on the whole slaves were called Andy and Jim like anyone else.*

---

* A Jamaican showed his scorn of American Revolutionary leaders and their sympathizers by naming various of his slaves Washington, Paine, Franklin, Burke, Fox. (Phillips, *American Negro Slavery;* 60.) The mat-

The cleavage between Big House and quarters, as sharp as
that between afterguard and forecastle in the old ships, was
alienating. Master might conscientiously ride out to inspect
the gang clearing new ground or the progress that Big Jack
and Caesar were making with the new sluice. But well-meant
inspection was not the same as the overseer's hourly petty contact with malingering, fornication, illness, squabbles and the
perpetual drag of a chronic, spontaneous slowdown for
which the whip was the only convenient recourse. And many
large slaveowners were absentee most of the year or permanently in Northern or Southern cities or even Europe.
Even when resident, the mistress and master had any kind of
informative contact only with the house staff. Russell described Carolina field hands as "apathetic, neither seeking
nor shunning us . . . master knew nothing about them."
Joel Chandler Harris, of *Uncle Remus* fame, saw that the
slaves who fecklessly followed Sherman were largely those
"who, by reason of their fieldwork, had not been on familiar
terms" **5** with their owners. Certainly, wherever master was
absent, negligent or easy, the overseer became the focus of
power as slaves felt it.

Overseers were not, as Southern legend had it and Mrs.
Stowe believed, ironically likely to be renegade Yankees.

---

ter of slave surnames is not simple. In Tennessee slaves used the master's
surname. (Fisk University *Social Science Source Document No. 1; 46.*)
As of Missouri, Mark Twain explained: "If Mr. Harbison owned a slave
named Bull, Tom would have spoken of him as 'Harbison's Bull,' but a
son or a dog of that name was 'Bull Harbison.' " (*Tom Sawyer;* 104.) In
the Carolina rice country: "Scarcely ever did a Negro choose the name
of his or her owner, but often took that of some other slaveholding
family of which he knew." This was not merely a matter of assuming
surnames after Emancipation; rather, "among themselves the slaves had
surnames, and immediately after they were freed the names came to
light." (Heyward, *Seed from Madagascar;* 98.) As for master's admitting
use of slave surnames, most inventories of slaves that I have seen carry
none. But that of Isaac Franklin's West Feliciana Parish (Louisiana)
plantations shows more slaves with surnames than without.

Most came from among Southern small farmers. ˢ Many, like
Harris's Bill Locke, were trying to amass capital for a few
Negroes and a farm, perhaps with a pack of dogs trained for
custom hunting of runaways. Some were hired for their
reputations for producing so many bales of cotton per hand.
Compensation consisted of housing, basic foodstuffs, and annual salary or a share of the crop or a percentage of book
profits,* all of which systems were usually bad for the land
and often for the slaves. The planter's maxim "Never change
overseers if you can help it" was a counsel of perfection. Turn-
over in this crude profession was ominously high. A model
planter in Alabama had had twenty overseers in twenty-three
years, and in general few remained more than two or three
years on a job. ˢ Hence few developed a sense of long-term
responsibility, thinking in terms of ruthless soil mining and
nothing more.

No one—slave, planter or visitor—approved of them. The
first feared and the others despised, or professed to despise,
this figure on horseback "with a big bull-whip tied over one
shoulder and under the other, scarf-fashion . . . rarely ad-
dressing a slave without cursing him in the same breath." ˢ
In the 1800's, John Bernard, the convivial and gentlemanly
actor, was assured that "the majority of outrages on slaves
have been chargeable entirely to these fiends of overseers
who, to gratify their own hellish humors, persuaded their
masters that rigor with the blacks was a necessary economy
of time and trouble." A Southern scholar explained not long
ago:

---

* Thus Benjamin L. S. Wailes of Mississippi hired a likely young overseer for $500 a year, a $2 bonus for every bale of cotton over 150 (the
previous year had brought only 120 bales), the "usual allowances of
sugar, coffee, and meat," use of a cow and free quarters. The man made
202 bales, but he handled the slaves badly and his fourteen-year-old
wife was a shocking slut, so he was fired. (Sydnor, *Gentleman of the Old
Natchez Region;* 112-150.)

The master was generally responsible [for cruelty to slaves]
only in the way that an absentee Irish landlord is responsible
for the condition of his tenants. The overseer in the one case,
the steward in the other, are the proximate cause of the suffering, it being perfectly possible for both slave-owner and
landlord to be humane and honorable men. s

A conscientious planter might erase the problem by dis-
pensing with overseers and supervising his own slaves with
the help of Negro drivers promoted from among them. Thus
Bennett Barrow gave up overseers by 1837. s A South Carolina cotton planter told an agricultural editor: "I have no
overseer, nor indeed is there one in the neighborhood. We
personally attend to our planting, believing that as good
manure as any, if not the best, we can apply to our fields, is
the print of the master's footstep." s A Virginia slaveowner
described overseers to Olmsted as "the curse of the country,
sir; the worst men in the community."

Post bellum fictions caught at this gratefully and made the
overseer "the uncondoned villain of the plantation cast." See
Thomas Nelson Page's *Red Rock* for the typical specimen. It
all makes one wonder to what extent the planter used the
overseer as whipping boy. Denouncing this subaltern as a
necessary evil enabled the master readily to evade his allegedly
benevolent and patriarchal responsibility for "my people."

In actual fact by no means all overseers were brutes. A
South Carolina patrician called one of his grandfather's overseers "that kindly hearted little man" and considered him an
intimate friend. s When a runaway slave killed a Mississippi
overseer who caught him lurking in the quarters, the plantation slaves had to be restrained from burning the killer alive,
which sounds as if they had some fondness for the victim. s
And a sturdy specimen of the class told Mrs. Chesnut, after
she had synopsized *Uncle Tom's Cabin* for him: "I never
knew a Negro to be murdered or burnt. But, if the marsters

are bad or drunken, look out. Slavery is a thing too unjust, too unfair to last. Let us take the bull by the horns, set 'em free, let 'em help us fight, to pay for their freedom." **s**

Yet do not conclude from such examples that many overseers did not deserve the generic foul reputation of their trade. The kind of man who applies for and stays on the post of boss guard in a prison is usually no nature's nobleman. Overseers often made the worse impression on outsiders because, whereas the master might suavely explain the virtues of slavery as a security system, his hired employee bothered less to gloss things over. The overseer of a great James River plantation readily told a Scottish traveler "that he was constantly obliged to use the lash, both to the men and women; that some he whipped four or five times a week, some only twice or thrice a month; that all attempts to make them work regularly by advice or kindness were unavailing. . . . many who . . . appeared attached to the family, would not work without occasional hints from the cowhide." Good masters instructed overseers to observe all practical decency in whipping women, and no doubt such stipulations were often observed. But there is also Olmsted's ugly record of being with a Mississippi overseer and the planter's adolescent son when a girl field hand was caught shirking in a gully; she was made to strip up her frock, lie down naked and take a lashing that even the overseer appeared to consider severe, while the boy and the visitor looked on. And a Virginia planter complained that his overseer invariably stripped every rag off a woman before he flogged her. **s**

On larger plantations it might well be such men, callous about Negroes and overeager for production, who determined whether Uncle Cudjo's rheumatics were severe enough to get him off work and whether Mandy really felt, or was only faking, abdominal pain three weeks after childbirth.* There was

---

* A genial planter told Olmsted (*Journey in the Seaboard Slave States*, I; 211) how "he had sometimes . . . made men go to work when they were really ill; therefore, when one of his people told him he was not

usually a "hospital" in which missis might take an interest. Sometimes it was cleaner than what appalled Fanny Kemble on Butler's Island, but sometimes it was even worse, as in the tumbledown squalor of the arrangements for superannuated slaves that Miss Bremer found near the fine Poinsett plantation. Many planters had the economic good sense to spend sums up to several hundred dollars a year on physicians' services for ailing slaves. $ Doctors in Natchez counted on such practice for a large part of their professional earnings; an eminent physician named Blackburn kept a special infirmary for slaves there. Resident doctors on plantations were not unknown, $ and prospering physicians who bought land and set up as planters often treated their own slaves. But there was also much amateur doctoring,* as implied in the redoubtable array of drugs that Isaac Franklin, the millionaire cotton planter, kept: jalap, calomel, morphine, laudanum, paregoric, quinine, alum, castor oil, flaxseed, ipecac, elixir vitriol, opodeldoc, sugar of lead, snakeroot, spirits of niter, hartshorn, Epsom salts, opium, prussic acid, tincture of cantharides, sul-

---

able to work, he usually thought, 'Very likely he'll be all the better for a day's rest, whether he's really ill or not,' and would let him off without being very particular in his examination. Lately he had been getting a new overseer, and . . . told him that was his way. The overseer replied, 'It's my way, too, now; it didn't use to be, but I had a lesson. There was a nigger one day at Mr. ———'s who was sulky and complaining; he said he couldn't work. I looked at his tongue and it was right clean, and I thought it was nothing but damned sulkiness so I paddled him, and made him go to work; but two days after, he was underground . . . a good eight hundred dollar nigger, and it was a lesson to me about taming possums, that I ain't agoing to forget in a hurry.' " One thing that made Olmsted so sound a reporter was his ability to catch and set down real talk even in idioms with which he was not originally familiar.

* Thomas Dabney of Mississippi treated "black tongue," a form of pellagra, by dosing his slaves liberally with port wine and mutton chops. It was a brilliant guess: the nicotinic acid in fresh meat relieves the particular vitamin deficiency that causes pellagra. (Smedes, *Southern Planter;* 28-29.)

phur, vermifuge, lunar caustic, and others. Merely skimming that list make one's belly ache.

In view of methods then prevalent among even well-trained physicians, the ailing field hand was probably better off in most instances without their help. But home practice also presented hazards, and not only that of master or missis prescribing hit or miss out of that kit of purges, painkillers and poisons. Some old slave woman might choose to act as plantation physician, midwife* and—more or less secretly—witch doctor. One such on a great Alabama plantation had an original formula for extreme cases: "I blisters 'em all over with red pepper, which cures 'em sure." **s** Particularly, no doubt, if it had been an acute case of malingering. Or the master might consult the plantation prescription book in which his predecessors had compiled "cures" much as if they were cooking recipes. Thus William P. Gould, of Alabama, wrote down what to do for corns, lockjaw and cancer, which, he said, responded well to dock-leaf poultices. **s**

Inhumane skepticism was often the overseer's only resource against the hospital's becoming a roost of malingerers. Here, as in most other matters, he had probably insisted on "full control, so far as the management of slaves [sic] are concerned," to quote an 1852 contract between an Alabama master and his overseer. **s** Divided authority means poor discipline. Undivided authority was also personally convenient. Master might allow no more than six lashes, might even put such instructions in the contract. **s** But who was to tell tales if, in the heat of anger out in the field, thirty felt more satisfactory? Missis might scold about the slaves' morals, but master might not care to lose an able overseer by too close inquiry into the paternity of the mulatto babies born to the likelier

---

* American slaves persisted in many of the violent and often ill-advised techniques of West African obstetrics. Perhaps the city Negro's dread of the hospital today (with concomitant tales of a lethal "black bottle") reflects the fact that the plantation sick bay, where laudanum was given to hopeless cases, was called a "hospital."

Negro girls. In one case, however, an overseer did get fired for being found in bed with two slave girls at once. **s** As far as possible most owners sought to disregard everything but the primary objective of the overseer institution: to raise more bales of cotton than would be necessary to meet the credit already advanced by broker-merchant-factor-agents against the crop.

As staff captain the overseer also chose, trained and backed up Negro drivers as his noncoms, perhaps permitting them to use a severity that they were encouraged to keep away from his and master's ken. Mrs. Stowe's depiction of Sambo and Quimbo as gargoyle-demons was not always justified. Some slaves in authority were able and humane. A few, such as Jefferson Davis's James Pemberton, became actual overseers. Within his educational limits Solomon, acting overseer of the Skirving place in South Carolina, must have been admirable. William Lumpkin's slave overseer Jerry was as reliable as he was huge—six feet eight, 320 pounds. **s** A former slave recalled how his "paw" had been driver over both plow and hoe gangs under a mean master who whipped him whenever he failed to whip his fellow bondsmen enough: "Paw'd come in when de dark come and put de whip on de flo', and set down in de chair. 'Nobody like de driver,' he say, and cry till de tears drop in de fireplace." **N** Oftener, it is too probable, however, the driver took bullying pride in his post and, for psychological reasons easily surmised, was hardly the field hand's best friend. One slave bossing another, Fanny Kemble observed, was "the worst of all tyrants."

That whip in the driver's black hand was a production tool as well as a symbol of authority. The lash had always played a large part in West African relations between Negro and Negro and in expediting the supply of slaves for the New World. It was familiar in colonial penology and in maritime discipline between white and white. The slave-owning free Negro—a rare but existent phenomenon—used the whip as liberally as anybody. For city-dwelling masters, professional floggers at the local jail did custom discipline at so much per lash. Or they might use the cob, a wooden paddle bored with holes to raise blisters.

It was pretty much taken for granted that the lash went with slavery, needing only to be controlled. William Gould's instructions to his overseers in Alabama required punishment to be "inflicted coolly and dispassionately, with a whip to be kept for that purpose. . . . Beating with a stick, the fist, or kicking are positively forbidden. Care is to be taken to proportion . . . the punishment to the offence, but in no case to desist until submission and penitence are manifested." ⁵ So the slave learned to start bellowing, "Oh, massa! Pray, massa!" with the first cuts in hopes of giving a strong impression of "submission and penitence." How often abuse of the lash—a strange word, for, as St. Clare said of slavery, the thing itself was an abuse—killed or crippled can never be known. When the overseer's dander was up, say when a skulking runaway was captured in the swamp after irksome pursuit, a hundred lashes might not seem disproportionate and laying them into him in the quarters might discourage other potential runaways. And since he was obviously a "bad nigger," of little further use on the place and difficult to sell, his possible death could be written off.

The laws of several Southern states did not find it murder when a slave died "under correction," a too logical principle laid down in a Virginian colonial statute: ". . . since it cannot be prepensed malice (which alone makes murther ffelony) should induce a man to destroy his own estate." ⁵ Seven generations later an Alabama slaveholder was convicted of whipping a slave to death in spite of the protests of a squeamish neighbor: verdict, manslaughter; penalty, two months and $500. ⁵ Some communities might have thought this severe; for instance, Natchez, where

Mr. Simon Murcherson had beat his man Arther very severely on Friday night with a Picket that he pulled off the

fence and that Picket had a Nail in it which stuck in the Poor
fellows head. . . . Inquest was held. . . . They looked at the
head, found it very much bruised. . . . the Law Seys that a
Dr shall have fifty dollars for Opening the head &c and no
One would say do it So they closed the man up again and
Said he Died with Congestion of the Brain. N

No doubt overseers disabling too many slaves would be
taken to task, since Negroes cost money and excessive brutality reduced their usefulness. Apologists for the South's
"peculiar institution" often maintained, in the spirit of that
Virginia statute, that the mere value of slaves necessarily kept
the wardens from severely abusing the convicts. The theory
left no room for exceptional individuals, such as old Adam
McWillie, of South Carolina, founder of a great family, who
"put Negroes in hogsheads, with nails driven in all round,
and rolled the poor things down hill. . . . My nurse told
me." S If economic value of the victims were automatic protection, societies for the prevention of cruelty to animals
would never have needed founding, nor would so many
Southern states have passed laws limiting punishments for
slaves and providing punishment for unusually flagrant slave
killings. But such laws counted for little on isolated plantations. Simon Legree was safe enough in laughing at George
Shelby's threat of prosecution for whipping Uncle Tom to
death, so long as there had been no white witnesses at the
scene.* Even in atypical Kentucky, says a sound local author-

---

* Since this book is not an abolitionist tract I have left out of the text
the grislier instances of brutality to slaves: here are three in chrono-
logical order: In 1660 a recalcitrant Maryland slave, described by the
overseer as "an ugly, yelling, beast-like brute" and given to running
away, was put in chains for some offense, whereupon he refused to work
and feigned fits; they whipped him a while, then poured hot lard down
his back and tied him to a ladder, leaving him thus in a cold wind so
long that he died of exposure. (Brackett, *Negro in Maryland;* 142.)
Master was acquitted, the jury mentioning insufficient evidence. Lilburn
Lewis of Livingston, Kentucky, a nephew of Thomas Jefferson, furious

ity, "Probably the darkest feature of the so-called black code was the fact that the slave's right of self-defense in the courts of the state amounted to virtually nothing more than legal fiction." **s**

A parson apologist for slavery asked a proslavery man what was the weightiest objection to the system and got an honest answer: "This irresponsible power. You cannot prevent its abuse while human nature is what it is. . . . certain masters and mistresses of slaves are the worst of tyrants." **s** Leonidas Polk, humane gentleman, Episcopalian bishop and able Confederate general, might punish chicken-stealing slaves merely by pillorying them with live chickens hung fluttering round their necks. **s** A Southern doctor might seek to persuade strangers that the standard field whip had a "soft-dry buckskin cracker" that stung without cutting or bruising, so a hundred lashes with it meant no more skin damage than ten with a cowhide. **s** But in his second-rate hotel in Charleston a British visitor saw the strapping landlady "give a young man, a servant, such a blow behind the ear as made him reel. . . . it was her daily or hourly practice to beat her servants, male or female, with her fist or with a thong made of cowhide." After whipping a girl until weary, she turned her over to the barkeep to finish. In Savannah Mrs. Hall learned that the slave chambermaid for whom she had rung could not answer because the landlady had just whipped her until she was unfit to be seen; next day blood on her neckerchief and cuts on her face were still visible. A purportedly humorous sketch in A. B. Longstreet's *Georgia Scenes* takes it for granted that the

---

at his slave George for breaking a valuable pitcher, took an axe and cut him up into pieces alive and then tried to burn them in the fireplace. (Rankin, *Letters on Slavery;* 62.) One occasionally encounters tales of "cat-hauling" as special punishment for slaves. Charles Ball, the runaway, who is a better witness than most runaways were, claimed to have seen it done on a Georgia plantation: The slave was held down with his back bared and then a cat was dragged by the tail the length of his back again and again, the claws ripping all the way.

slave nurse of the pretty young matron's baby will dodge apprehensively every time the mistress gives her any instructions. 5

Keep in mind, of course, that slaves on superior plantations were probably whipped no oftener and perhaps not even more severely than the planter's or overseer's own children; that there really were plantations without whipping; and that the barbarity of such discipline was less evident in those days to either public opinion or to the West African Negro, hence to the slave. An Abolitionist was shocked by the calm with which the other Negroes took a custom flogging of a girl in a New Orleans jail courtyard

> . . . surrounded by galleries . . . filled with colored persons of all sexes; runaway slaves, slaves committed for some crime, or slaves up for sale. You would naturally suppose they crowded forward, and gazed horror stricken at the brutal spectacle below. But . . . they did not; many of them hardly noticed it . . . many were entirely indifferent . . . some were laughing outright in the distant part of the galleries.

But indifference to a fact is not denial of it. The old slaves' memories of floggings in excess of any disciplinary need are unimpeachable. So are the advertisements of runaways noting heavily scarred backs and branded faces, slit and cropped ears.*

An "excellent British housekeeper" told a proslavery Scottish botanist traveling in Georgia that her experience convinced her that slaves would not work for the same motives

---

* Such cropping and branding were sometimes represented as intended to prevent misrepresentation and sale of incorrigibly turbulent slaves as docile. (Sellers, *Slavery in Alabama;* 244.) I suspect rather that they were just part of a cluster of anachronistic punishments inherited all at once from European example in the early colonial period, the others being the stocks, pillory and whipping post. Hart (*Slavery & Abolition;* 114) notes that whipping was conspicuous well into the postcolonial period of the South as a recognized legal punishment for white as well as Negro transgressors.

that prevailed on whites to do their economic duty; that she was "averse to reporting any of the darkies as requiring correction [that is, whipping]; but without the power of doing so, they would be utterly unmanageable." No doubt there was truth in it. Human beings reared under the lash are likely to be just that way. Think what the average overseer's personality must have been like, then of the provocation that the slaves' infantile inertia and carelessness must often have given him. Here is realistic comment from Captain Basil Hall, a civilized officer of the Royal Navy of the generation following that of William Bligh:

> The slave has, unfortunately, so few generous motives to stimulate him to work, that fear is necessarily . . . the chief ingredient into the discipline. . . . as their tasks are limited to what can be readily performed, it is in the power of any slave who chooses, to escape punishment for any length of time. But . . . when slaves are under the management of injudicious, unmethodical, dissipated, ill-tempered, or naturally cruel masters, of course the evils that ensue are too horrible to think of. But it ought to be recollected, in due fairness to slave-holders . . . that many ships of war, many regiments . . . to say nothing of schools, are often—as I have witnessed in all quarters of the globe—the scenes of as revolting tyranny as any rice or cotton plantation can well be.

Ideal slave discipline was set down by Hugh Davis, master of Beaver Bend cotton plantation in Alabama: After the day's work women to go straight to their cabins to sweep, fetch water and receive the family's cooked food from the cook's "carriers." (There seems to have been a communal kitchen.) After eating women might sew or knit but were "in no event to leave their house or yard to go visiting . . . no hand, man or woman, is to stay at the cook's shelter except the cook and suckling women engaged with their babies." At nine P.M. all hands to bed at the sound of the horn; bed check in five minutes and twenty lashes for anybody found not where he belonged. ⁵ It really sounds as if Mr. Davis had had experience in managing penitentiaries. James Tait, his fellow Alabaman and something of a model planter, recommended the daily practice of giving the last man out of quarters a whipping and laid down the friendly maxim: "Never talk to a Negro save on business." ⁵

This sort of convict camp had few equivalents for the library, radio, sports and other amenities with which modern society tries to mask the warping facts of penal life. Most field hands stagnated within the boundaries of the home place, for the patrol system originally set up to discourage insurrections spread pretty much all over the South. The slave could not leave his master's land without a written paper giving his name and identifying marks and whither bound and why, sometimes even specifying his route;* at least the ideal pass carried all that. Lack of some such paper was presumptive evidence that he was running away or otherwise up to no good, and the patrol—the "paddy rollers," said the slaves—whipped him on the spot or took him home for master to punish. Craftsmen and house servants on errands frequently got passes. A field hand seldom saw one unless he had a "broadwife," that is, a woman belonging on a nearby plantation. Then he might be permitted regularly to walk five or ten miles to spend Saturday night, perhaps Sunday too. The most liberal such leave I have found was from Saturday noon to Monday noon, with a twenty-mile walk each way involved. ⁵

---

* The possibility of forged passes was another reason why the South frowned on education for Negroes. Harrison Cary, of Washington, D.C., and Frederick Douglass, of Baltimore, both determined to learn to write in order to forge passes for themselves and others. (Still, *Underground Railroad Records;* 407; Chesnutt, *Frederick Douglass;* 13.) A free Negro arrested for having written a pass for a runaway in Natchez in 1850 was held in $2000 bail, an amount high for that time and place, indicating how seriously the crime was taken. (*Diary of William Johnson;* 717-718.)

Theoretically all whites did rotating service in the patrol, which was often tied into the militia system. Actually the well-to-do usually shirked and paid nominal fines. **s** In many places this left the overseers as backbone of patrolling. **s** Elsewhere, the county hired a regular patrol from among poor whites or small farmers, **s** thus giving young men from those strata a special taste for abusing niggers which until recently remained lively in Southern lynch mobs. These ill-disciplined parties of young fellows organized under community sanction, often passing the bottle freely while on their rounds, may well have been the nucleus suggestion for the Ku Klux Klan of post bellum renown. Well before the Civil War the paddy rollers bulked large in slave folklore. Fractious children were threatened with them. Ole Massa was mad at Sluefoot Tom so he gin him a pass and tole him he could go to town, but Tom he couldn't read and the paddy rollers cotch him and they look at his pass, and it say, 'Give this nigger hell,' so they gin him hell right there on the big road. **N**

None of this means that the patrols were efficient. One candid Southern historian of slavery calls them no better than a medieval town watch. **s** This was due only in part to slovenliness. The South was too sparsely settled, too masked with woods and swamps, its roads and paths too tortuous and vague for anything but a regiment in each county to have kept slaves from moving about a good deal. In the Civil War, the slaves' intimate knowledge of obscure trails was invaluable to Federal invaders, and there was only one way in which they could have acquired it. But the penalties were harsh when luck was poor, and, barring special personal reasons, few slaves cared to take the risks involved. After all, any given plantation was probably not unlike the home place—the same whiffs of hot bacon grease, the same yelping mongrel dogs, the same firelight flickering through the same un-chinked log walls.

"*Negroes are more ardent after their female; but love seems with them to be more an eager desire, than a delicate mixture of sentiment and sensation.*"
—JEFFERSON, *Notes on Virginia*

Once his stint was finished and his belly full of grits and fatback, the slave vegetated lumpily at the cabin door. It follows—and the evidence agrees—that his principal recreation was sexual intercourse. If psychiatrists are right about mental activity as a damper on potency, the slave must have been a mighty man. Indeed, Southern whites still credit him with formidable venereal prowess.* Except in the seasonal bursts of cotton picking and sugar grinding, his work was usually not overtiring; he was amply, if coarsely and monotonously, fed; he had little else to do after hours; and his opportunities were voluptuously wide.

Conscientious masters sought to infect the quarters with conventional notions of monogamy. The extreme case was that of Bishop Polk augustly marrying couples from among his own slaves, with one of his children holding the light in a special silver candlestick, provided that he was reasonably confident that the happy pair had not anticipated the parson.⁵ How he squared this with the South's refusal of legal recognition to marriage between slaves I do not know, but his intent was certainly decent. On his plantation up the Savannah River, Senator J. H. Hammond installed a sort of mar-

---

* All this ties in with the belief that Negroes' penes are larger than whites'. Montagu explores this inconclusively but solemnly in *Man's Most Dangerous Myth;* 241-243. So does Dollard in *Caste and Class in a Southern Town;* 161. Coon, Garn and Birdsell (*Races;* 62) cite relatively large genitalia as definite characteristics of both the West African Forest Negro and the Melanesian.

riage and divorce code, for he firmly believed that marriage
"adds to the comfort, happiness and health of those who
enter upon it, besides insuring a greater increase." **s** * With
both realism and irony a Kentucky minister observed slave
marriages with the revised proviso: "Till death or distance
do you part."

A fair number of strait-laced and humane slaveowners
probably did somehow provide a white clergyman for slave
weddings and a generous wedding feast; sometimes missis or
the young ladies were pleased to dress the bride. House
servants were likeliest to be so favored. Less responsibly, a
local slave preacher might be procured to tie the knot by
impressively gabbling scraps of the marriage service. Master
himself, somewhat sacrilegiously, might act as priest as well
as chief and hold the book and say what he considered fitting.
"On our plantation dere was no marriaging," a Sea Island
slave recalled. "De man and de woman just stood up in front
of Dr. Pope and he said 'Do you want dis man?' and 'Do you
want dis woman? All right, I will give you a house.'" **N** More
loosely still, master and missis would suggest that the intend-
ing couple "jump the broomstick," that is, step over a broomstick held across the cabin door, a folk ceremony adequate to
slave decencies. Or they might do so without white instance,

---

* Its founder thus summed up the Hammond system: "Permission must
always be obtained from the master before marriage, but no marriage
will be allowed with Negroes not belonging to the master. When sufficient cause can be shown on either side, a marriage may be annulled;
but the offending party must be severely punished. Where both are in
wrong, both must be punished, and if they insist on separating must
have a hundred lashes apiece . . . neither can marry again for three
years. For first marriage a bounty of $5.00, to be invested in household
articles, shall be given. If either has been married before, the bounty
shall be $2.50. A third marriage shall not be allowed, but in extreme
cases, or where both have been married before, no bounty shall be
given." (Quoted in Phillips, *American Negro Slavery;* 269.) So far as I
know these arrangements were unique. They must have been a great
trial to the Senator's overseers.

as a ritual joke enjoyed by all. Some candid master might admit that he "does not interfere with his slaves . . . further than is necessary for the good of his own interest. They may have two or three wives apiece so long as they do not quarrel about them. He says they have no morals or principles whatsoever." It was likely such an owner who ordered from a Charleston slave dealer "Ten or twelve wenches" aged twelve to eighteen years "for wives for his men" on an Alabama plantation. And far below are dark hints, not to be ignored, of isolated plantations where, on a probably false theory of fertility, master or overseer actively encouraged promiscuity to make sure that all women of breeding age did their biological duty.

When a slave "husband" lost his spouse by sale, even a fairly mealy-mouthed owner thought little of assigning him a new mate from among eligible women slaves. That made offspring likelier and reduced the chances of quarrels. The slaves concerned were usually willing enough. Among men on sale at the famous slave market at the Forks of the Road east of Natchez, a young coachman from Virginia told a visitor: "I lef' my wife in Richmond but I got new wife here in lot. I wish you buy her, master, if you gwine buy me." s Trying to secure the husband of a new-bought woman slave, Benjamin Wailes, of Mississippi, found that "Jack had found a more recent connection, & had no desire to go back to his former wife." s When the Dabneys moved from Virginia to the cotton belt, their Mammy Harriet, considerately given her option, decided to migrate with the family and leave her husband behind. s A sound summary was that of a slave trader questioned on a Potomac steamboat. Asked whether slave husbands and wives seemed to care when separated, he said, "Sometimes they don't mind it a great while, but at other times, they take on right smart for a long time."

It all slipped and adjusted more easily because of what Frazier called "the unromantic attitude of the peasant Negro toward sex and mating." N This was probably a result of the slave's relative lack of opportunity to dilute African attitudes with Western-style monogamy. Many must have been like the Tennessee slave woman who bore six children, each to a different father—three of her men had been sold away, one had died, two had "failed to make any lasting attachment. 'We all raise up without any reg'lar Pappy,' her daughter recalled, 'but we got 'long jus' fine!' " **N** In distant Guinea their remote forebears were polygamous and not rigid about that. Even chiefs might take infidelity as mere occasion for extorting petty damages, a tradition sometimes leading to a sort of fixed-fee prostitution.*

Neither sex found much value in premarital virtue as such, an attitude that probably came over in the slave ships. Lady Lyell brought her husband a revealing bit about an Alabama slave girl reared close under missis' wing whose shame over having borne a mulatto child disappeared after a visit to her mother, "a native African," who "assured her she had done nothing wrong, and had no reason to feel ashamed." Nor was the white man's example, as the early slaves saw it among slave dealers, colonial planters and redemptioners, impressively fastidious. The pioneer white master was likely to take his fun where he found it, at choice among his forced labor, black or white. His sons, grandsons and so forth often kept up the good old ways.

"Like the patriarchs of old," bitterly wrote Mrs. Chesnut, who held her head as high as any lady in South Carolina, "our men live all in one house with their wives and their concubines, and the mulattoes one sees in every family party resemble the white children. Any lady is ready to tell you who

---

* Little, *The Mende;* 142, has an extreme case of a Sierra Leone chief causing his minor wives to seduce young men so that he (husband) could exact from the sinners compensation in work or kind—a new version of the badger game, in fact. All this merely illustrates the relative lack of emotional store set on exclusive sexual relations among West Africans. It does not mean that, given adequate contact with other conventions, Negroes cannot value monogamy as highly as any people.

is the father of all the mulatto children in everybody's household but her own. Those, she seems to think, drop from the clouds." **S** Missis might tut-tut, but her writ hardly ran beyond the small group of house servants and, as this hints, sometimes not even there. A witness from Wilmington, North Carolina, said that it was the slave housemaids whom the young white boys particularly assailed. **S** And the average erotic morality of the quarters on large plantations was probably about like that of modern Hollywood. This may help to account for the luxuriant obscenities of American Negro folksong, which experts describe as the richest and most violent known to ethnology.

Instances of girl field hands of any attractiveness coming virgin to their "husbands" must have been very rare. The deflowering agency might be the overseer or young master, but more probably Polly's Joe or Bart the stableboy, who made a point of investigating such girls as soon as they reached puberty. James Madison told Miss Martineau that in the Virginia of his day slave girls were expected to become mothers by the age of fifteen; how they arranged impregnation was apparently their own affair. **S** Sixty years after Emancipation the illegitimacy rate on St. Helena, a South Carolina Sea Island, was responsibly estimated at some 30 per cent. A scholarly analysis of Negro ways in Alabama in the 1930's read: "Conditions are favorable to a great amount of sex-experimentation. . . . Whether or not sexual intercourse is an accepted part of courtship . . . no one is surprised when it occurs. When pregnancy follows . . . the girl does not lose status, perceptibly, nor are her chances for marrying seriously threatened." **N** But it would be a mistake to draw conclusions about concupiscence as a racial trait. Consider that a recent report on Australian girls, presumably of unmixed white racial origin, shows that, in 1951, "28% of all the year's firstborn children were conceived out of wedlock."

Master's share in all this—the aspect causing much lip licking from Tom Moore's time to our own—cannot be cleanly sorted out after so great a lapse of time exploited by liars on both sides. Senator Hammond, author of that slave divorce code, certainly lied when he said that "he who takes a colored mistress—with rare and extraordinary exceptions— loses caste at once." [5] Set this off against the absurd statement of Charles Stearns, Abolitionist ghost writer for several runaway slaves: ". . . one of the strongest motives . . . inducing [slaveholders] to maintain their iron grasp upon the unfortunate slaves, is because it gives them unlimited control over the person of the female slaves." But then Mrs. Chesnut, as quoted above, unquestionably knew what she was talking about and agreed pretty well with the summary of a modern Southerner:

> The slave-woman was to be had for the taking. Boys on and about the plantation inevitably learned to use her, and having acquired the habit, often continued it into manhood and even after marriage. . . . efforts to build up a taboo against miscegenation made little progress. I do not mean to imply . . . that it was universal . . . many men in the South . . . rigidly abstained from such liaisons and scorned those who indulged. Nevertheless, that they were sufficiently common is unquestionable.

Jefferson was only one of many eminent and sometimes aristocratic slaveowners who left mulatto offspring for their admirers to deny or ignore.* Sometimes their wills emanci-

---

* I am well aware that all Jeffersonians do not agree on this. But Miss Pearl M. Graham, who is said to have looked more thoroughly than anyone else into this aspect of Jefferson, is good enough to assure me that, dubious as much of the attached gossip probably is, "There can be no reasonable doubt that Jefferson had at least one slave mistress." Beyond that, accept as much as you like of Moore, who left posterity at least two versions of his bitter verses on the matter:

> *"The weary statesman for repose hath fled*
> *From halls of council to his Negro's shed,*

pated such by-blows.* William Thompson, Mississippi planter, settled in free-soil Ohio two separate families of slave mother and part-white children whom he had severally begotten on separate plantations. At the other extreme were authenticated cases of white master-fathers selling their own offspring, like the jolly South Carolinians with whom young Stuart traveled in the 1830's, gradually mellowing with brandy and talking more and more freely:

> The doctor asked the planter what could have induced him to stay at such and such a plantation during the unhealthy season. . . . He said . . . that half a dozen of the girls could no longer be trusted without husbands, for one of them had already been seized by the blacksmith . . . and he thought

---

> *Where blest he woos some black Aspasia's grace*
> *And dreams of freedom in his slave's embrace. . . ."*

and

> *"The patriot fresh from Freedom's councils come,*
> *Now pleased retires to lash his slaves at home;*
> *Or woo, perhaps, some black Aspasia's charms,*
> *And dream of freedom in his bondsmaid's arms. . . ."*

Or of Mrs. Trollope in *Domestic Manners of the Americans;* 72: "Mr. Jefferson is said to have been the father of children by almost all his numerous gang of female slaves. . . . it was his special pleasure to be waited upon by them at table, and the hospitable orgies for which his Montecielo [*sic*] was so celebrated, were incomplete unless the goblet he quaffed was tendered by the trembling hand of his own slavish offspring. I even heard it stated by a democratical admirer of the great man, that when . . . his children by Quadroon slaves were white enough to escape suspicion of their origin, he did not pursue them if they attempted to escape, saying laughingly, 'Let the rogues get off if they can; I will not hinder them.'"

* Sellers, *Slavery in Alabama*, has half a dozen such cases. Booker T. Washington (*Story of the Negro*, II; 22-23) mentions John M. Langston, P. B. S. Pinchback and Josiah T. Settle as Negro politicians of Reconstruction whose white fathers had been solicitous about them. Pinchback and his brother were sent to high school in Cincinnati; Settle's father brought his slave mistress North and freed and married her.

it was not only for his interest, but that of the plantation generally, that he would be the first husband. This . . . gave rise to a good deal of merriment . . . the doctor, who gave us similar accounts of his own management of his own slaves, admitted to the validity of the reason. . . . this planter was frequently waited on at table by his own children, and had actually sent some of them to the public market to be sold as slaves.

A planter planning to quit the South told Olmsted: "There is not a likely-looking black girl in this State that is not the concubine of a white man* . . . not an old plantation in which the grandchildren of the owner are not whipped in the field by his overseer." A strongminded Southern lady inadvertently said more than she meant in writing: "We love our slaves not as a miser loves his gold but as a father loves his children." **s**

No doubt house servants, in closer contact with Western ways and with more reason to imitate them, often developed toward self-respecting monogamy. But among underinfluenced and understimulated field hands this cannot have occurred typically ". . . among slaves," says an eminent Negro scholar, "the idea of chastity was undeveloped." **N** Chancellor Harper of the Supreme Court of South Carolina was polite about it:

In northern communities the unmarried woman who becomes a mother is an outcast from society. She has given birth to a human being who is commonly educated to a

---

* Cash (*Mind of the South;* 95) suggests that beneath the white man's lust for slave women was the way the "natural" Negro girl gave herself up to passion, as inhibited white wives did not. This may have been true of American-born slave girls. It probably has less pertinence to women slaves brought from Africa, since most West African female initiation cults excise the clitoris with the avowed purpose of reducing, if possible eliminating, pleasure in sexual congress. This is an instructive example of the healthily natural approach of the unspoiled savage to the glories of sex.

course of vice, depravity and crime. It is not so with the female slave. She is not a less useful member of society than
before . . . has not impaired her means of support nor materially injured her character or lowered her station . . . her
offspring is not a burden but an acquisition to her owner.
The want of chastity among slaves hardly deserves a harsher
name than weakness. **s**

After a second reading of *Uncle Tom's Cabin* Mrs. Chesnut
wrote: "These Negro women have a chance here that women
have nowhere else. They can redeem themselves—the 'im-
propers' can. They can marry decently, and nothing is remembered against these colored ladies. It is not a nice topic,
but Mrs. Stowe revels in it. . . ." **s**

As between slaves, quasi-permanent "marriages" punctu-
ated with cross-household dalliance could lead to quarrels
and mayhem—and to discipline, since useful hands were not
wantonly to be put out of working condition. However
achieved, pregnancies nevertheless called for praise and sometimes special privileges, for master usually agreed with most
slaveholders that fecund slave women were "if properly taken
care of . . . the most profitable to their owners of any others.
. . . It is remarkable the number of slaves which may be
raised from one woman in the course of forty or fifty years
with the proper kind of attention." **s** A Virginia-reared slave
twenty years of age was advertised in a Charleston paper in
1838 as already having produced two children and "very
prolific in the generating qualities . . . a rare opportunity
for any person who wishes to raise a family of strong and
healthy servants for their own use." **s** Such likely breeders
commanded premiums at auction over those still barren, an
economic fact that even the courts took into account.* Slave

---

* Sellers (*Slavery in Alabama;* 163) quotes the Supreme Court of Alabama in 1834: ". . . a jury would place a higher value on a female
slave promising issue . . . ." The principle was not universally accepted.
Ballagh (*History of Slavery in Virginia;* 98) says that slaveholders re-

women might be promised their freedom when they should
have produced five or ten children. A great Negro student of
his people says that "social status among Negro slave women
was in an important measure based upon their breeding
power," ᴺ a criterion probably to some extent reflecting consciousness of economic value. "Look, missis!" the grinning
slave women told Fanny Kemble. "Little niggers for you and
massa! Plenty little niggers for you and little missis!"

The potential cash value of slave babies as either salable
produce or eventual field hands on the old place was one reason why missis often looked after black women's progeny
pretty intimately. Other reasons were kindness and sense of
duty. All three applied because juvenile mortality was most
uneconomically and pitifully high among American slaves.
An intelligent Mississippi planter told Olmsted that not a
quarter of slave babies born were successfully reared—a ratio
appallingly high for even that septic day.* A minor cause of
this may have been the tenuous relation between mother and
child. For all her aching sympathy for slave women, Fanny
Kemble was reminded of "the short-lived connection between
the animal and its young." Mothers doing field work might
return to quarters at suckling time, or an elder child might
fetch the pickaninny to the field. An ante bellum Carolinian
recalled seeing "the slave women come from the fields to the
house of the old woman who took care of the small children
during the day, take their babies in their arms, nurse them,
and put them down without the least show of affection." ˢ

Conscientious planters developed a sort of despair about

---

garded "damage to service in childbearing and the cost of rearing the
infant . . . as involving a net loss." Perhaps it was a loss in actual fact.
But the evidence is overwhelming that, soundly or not, most planters
looked on fecundity in slave women as highly desirable economically.
* This informed guess is easier to accept because in West Africa even
today few health officers, doing their best in the absence of vital statistics, will try to maintain that infant mortality is lower than 50 per
cent, and it may well be a good deal worse than that.

slave-women's maternal instinct, or lack of it. One told Lyell that it was better to raise the children in batches instead of entrusting them to their negligent mothers, hence large plantations often assigned superannuated women to tend the smaller fry in a "child-house," ⁵ where they could be fed regularly, kept from hurting one another and occasionally washed. Awareness of such arrangements makes it easier to understand the various degrees of maternal solicitude observed among women slaves following Sherman's army: Some herded their children along at fearful cost in fatigue and disease; others abandoned any children who betrayed exhaustion; still others killed them as hampering nuisances. ᴺ

Word of a sick child in the quarters might bring missis to prescribe and, if the case looked serious, to sit up all night making sure that misunderstanding or negligence did not thwart her instructions to the mother. Missis might even supervise a daily meal for small Negroes crowding up to a trough to plunge their mouths into corn pone and buttermilk like so many little black pigs. ᴺ Such duties could be irksome. After midwifing a slave delivery most of the night, a great lady of South Carolina gave Russell his first hearing, by no means his last, of the classic plaint of the planter's wife: ". . . it is the slaves who own me. Morning, noon, and night, I'm obliged to look after them, to doctor them and to attend to them in every way." This cliché was as prevalent in the ante bellum South as "It's not the heat . . ." is in a New York summer. Similarly it had just enough truth in it for durability. Even Mrs. Stowe knew of it, causing Marie St. Clare to say: ". . . it's we mistresses that are the slaves down here. . . . Talk about our keeping slaves, as if we did it for *our convenience* . . . I'm sure, if we consulted *that,* we might let them all go at once." More honestly, Patrick Henry excused his slaveowning only by "the general inconvenience of living without them . . . I cannot justify it." ⁵

Those "little niggers for you and massa" went jaybird naked when small and even when approaching adolescence wore nothing but a flapping shirt of homespun tow linen or "boughten" osnaburgs, a coarse cotton cloth. But then at any age standards of slave dress were low, as we have already seen. When Tom Sawyer told Huck Finn to steal the Phelps's yellow gal's frock for a disguise, Huck reminded him: "Why, Tom, that'll make trouble next morning; because, of course, she probably hain't got any but that one." [5] The children ran wild in tenuous troops like sociable dogs, sometimes mobbing visitors with shrieking lack of inhibition and using the Negro child's engaging smile to extract pennies from them. Or they could be ferally timid. When "sent for to sing for us" on a small Carolina plantation,

> . . . they came very shyly, and by degrees; first peeping round the corners and from behind trees, oftentimes running away in spite of the orders of their haggard mammies, until they were chased, captured and brought back by their elder brethren . . . ragged, dirty, shoeless urchins of both sexes; the younger ones abdominous as infant Hindoos and wild as if just caught.

The "black women plowing in the field, with their scanty, dingy dresses, their walloping gait and vacant countenance" had themselves had little mothering except suckling. Until a child was grown enough to be handed a hoe and started in life as a quarter hand, it needed few skills but those of feeding, fighting and speaking the few hundred slurred, fragmented words necessary to a slave's daily concerns.* Only potentially higher intelligence distinguished small slaves from the pups littered by the old yellow hound-dog bitch that hung around the same shack. And that intelligence, though stub-

---

* Colonial planters preferred American-born slaves to fresh imports because it was harder to handle those knowing only the "Black English" of Guinea and the slave trade. (Andrews, *Colonial Folkways;* 10.) The richness of the American Negro's English is, I suspect, much the work of slave preachers literate enough to get vocabulary from the Bible. Some may have come of house servants' contact with whites.

bornly manifest in ability to learn to talk, as dogs cannot, was doomed to grope through life with little more deliberately applied stimulus than the pups got under training for coon and possum. An adult field hand had no cogent reason to learn any more than the difference between cotton and weed and how to say "Yassuh" and "Nossuh" and "Oddonocap'n" to every white man, grinning or hanging the head according to the white man's tone of voice but avoiding looking him square in the eye, which was considered uppity. A chimpanzee in a psychologist's laboratory has far more scope for showing what is in him.

The woman field hand may sometimes have loved the child she suckled just as she felt hunger or thirst—for a while. Or, if she were abnormally sensitive or met stimuli more personal than field work usually afforded, the relationship might expand toward what we would consider something nearer normal. Now and again on the "vendue table"—the Carolina term for the auction block—slave mothers pled to have their children sold with them, fought when they were taken away, grieved for them to the point of death, even poisoned the last child of a series to prevent its being sold away. N Such things as the bereaved slave mother of *Uncle Tom* jumping into the river really did happen. And Margaret Garner, captured in Cincinnati while running away with her children, slit the throat of one of them when she learned that slave catchers had surrounded their refuge,* an action as illuminating as a flash of lightning striking the slave system. But that sort of thing was rare, partly because efforts were really made in good faith to prevent sale of children away from mothers, partly because bereaved mothers were often pretty numb about it.

---

* The law handed her and the surviving children over for return to Kentucky but, according to one story, she managed to drown a child en route and was herself drowned in a steamboat accident. It sounds miserably probable. See varying accounts in *Reminiscences of Levi Coffin;* 558-567, and Blackwell, *Lucy Stone;* 183-184.

There is a ring of low-grade truth about the statement of the slave dealer to young Stuart that "He never . . . separated husband and wife, but some people did separate them as well as children, and then they had a crying scene, that was all." Abraham Lincoln wrote home that slaves he saw on an Ohio steamboat being taken South for sale were "the most cheerful and apparently happy people on board. One whose offense for which he had been sold was an over-fondness for his wife, played the fiddle almost continuously, and the others danced, sang, cracked jokes and played various games with cards all day long." A slave woman waiting to be sold told an inquiring traveler that her heart was "a'most broke" because she would never see her husband again but a few minutes later was seen laughing "as heartily as anyone" at the performance of a trick dog belonging to one of the spectators. This is distressing, but not surprising. Treating people as animals often makes something rather like animals of them. Under the conditions of slavery white women would probably have been just as regardless.

In view of such numbness in other respects it must be said —however callous it sounds—that master's or overseer's dealings with slave women whom they fancied cannot always have outraged finer feelings. Even among field hands, of course, tragic exceptions must have occurred. But when fidelity of slave spouse to slave spouse was no great matter, when the white man's prestige as tyrant-owner-chief-warden was so high, when a mulatto complexion was a social asset among slaves, as it still is among free American Negroes, distaste for fornication with massa was probably no stronger than it was in many a European peasant girl laid aboard by the lord of the manor in the twelfth century. "No moralist," wrote Rhodes, "would undertake to preach honesty to men who did not own their own labor, nor chastity to women who did not own their own bodies." The Southern white's approach to these issues was well summed up, with the right pimply snigger, by a Mississippian commenting on a Reconstruction scalawag who took up

with a mulatto girl and "stayed with her like a wife . . . lying by the thing don't do so well . . . that's different from
'taking a little and running.' " s

The wonder is that isolated plantations did not see more
miscegenation than actually occurred. The census of 1860
classes as Negroes persons known to have a Negro ancestor—
the definition of "American Negro" that we have been using in
this book. Of these only one in seven was set down as showing
"white blood," a ratio that must have been even lower in the
big-plantation country. Allegedly there was a higher rate of
Negro-white crosses in the Border States where the master's
lusts, it was hinted, were sharpened by awareness that, in
some markets, mulattoes and quadroons fetched higher prices.
However that may be, the charge, though common, cannot be
substantiated. It is known that the South's mixed-blood population centered in and about towns, not back in the plantation country.* This must mean that, on the whole, more
white men had more intercourse with more Negro women in
urban areas than in rural. Realistic accounts of slavery, particularly those of Phillips, abound in individual instances of
miscegenation on the plantation, but the odds of yellow
babies were nevertheless higher in Richmond, Wilmington,
Savannah and, God knows, in New Orleans.

Except in this gratifying respect the large plantation, source
of the wealth that made Charleston and Mobile charming,
was the milieu most degrading to the convicts and most bru-

---

* Reuter, *Mulatto,* quoted in J. T. Adams, *America's Tragedy;* 78-79.
This may have a supplementary explanation: Whites—and Negroes—
believed that admixture of "white blood" meant higher capacity; hence,
mulatto or quadroon boys and girls were likelier to be chosen for house
servants or craftsmen and hence were likelier to be taken to town or
sold or hired out to town dwellers.

talizing to the wardens. Jefferson Davis, owner of many Negroes, spoke sadly of how poor relations between master and slave usually were when "this species of property [was collected] into such masses that the owner is not personally acquainted with the individuals who compose it." **5** On big places better lives were likely for only the house servants and slaves trained as seamstress, spinster, cobbler, tanner, blacksmith, stableboy and, sometimes, engineer of cotton gin, sugar mill or steam ferry.

Once thus appealed to, slave ability could go far. In 1860 a cotton mill in Huntsville, Alabama, was completely in charge of a slave foreman who maintained and repaired all machinery and supervised all incoming materials and outgoing goods. Alabama River steamboats often carried slave pilots, and the schooners that served Carolina rice plantations had slave skippers. Wonderingly or sardonically outsiders used to report hearing masters generalize about Negroes' inherent stupidity and clumsiness only to boast, within ten minutes, of how Old Zeke, the plantation blacksmith, could weld a cracked plowshare as well as any Yankee, or how that yellow boy of mine at the mill can run more sugar a day than anybody for fifty miles up and down the Big River, suh. Part of this may reflect mere awareness that skills increased the value of a slave. In 1857, for instance, two Alabama slaves renowned as well drillers sold for a total of $4095. But another part may have come of generous impulses overriding conventional fallacies. A certain Virginian's will commended to his heirs his slave blacksmith as "one of the most respectable men, white or black, in the Commonwealth."

On a lowland plantation in Georgia, Lyell saw slave carpenters building a complicated canal lock with no guide but a rough sketch of master's, and a slave engineer handling a steam-powered rice mill with utter competence: "When these mechanics came to consult Mr. Couper on business, their manner of speaking to him is quite as independent as that

of English artisans to their employers." * This particular
master did not mouth nonsense about innate Negro inferiority. But for many others it was downright embarrassing
when, as the Civil War began, on several occasions subhuman
Negro slave engineers and crews lacking any initiative of
their own stole and ran small steam craft out to join the Federal blockaders.

The almost autarchic large plantation, with slaves busy at
forge, lathe, tan pit, bench, sawmill, loom, spinning wheel
and so forth, meant that thousands of more or less competent
slave specialists received human satisfactions from exercising
skills. So did Big House cooks, coachmen, bartenders, musicians. Special prestige was accorded the nurse (the much
famed "mammy"), the personal maid, master's body servant,
the butler—anyone, in fact, singled out for daintier duties.
Lesser household help alternated between loafing and
drudgery, but at least they saw more variety than went with
days or weeks of swinging axe or hoe. To some extent all
household servants got the immense stimulus of contact with
white ways—relatively immense, however ignorant master
and missis might actually be in civilized white folks' terms.
The small slave boy picked out of the troop of pickaninnies
for special brightness and set to keeping flies off the dinner
table with a great fan of peacock feathers (also a plantation
product) might learn something new every time a stranger
came to dinner, if only that there were such things as strangers and distant places for them to come from. Had the slave
still possessed an integrated culture of his own this would
sound stupidly patronizing. But within a generation or two

---

* *Second Visit to the United States,* I; 360. Two qualifications: (1)
Couper's father was Scots-reared, hence alien values somewhat diluted
standard Southern attitudes in the son; (2) the reader must not envisage anything rabidly equalitarian about the hat-in-hand relations of the
British mechanic to his employer in 1845. But it was probably in sharp
contrast with the slave's usual hangdog cringe.

the West African importee lost most of his own ways of doing. He was particularly crippled culturally by lack of the rigid custom patterns of West Africa of which only disconnected bits remained, a kind of dislocation often highly damaging to emotional development.*

Better quarters did not necessarily go with the prestige of house service. Some resident masters thought it risky to let slaves sleep on the premises and sent them back to the quarters when the day was finished. Others, especially in town, better served their own convenience and saved housing by the use of pallets on the kitchen floor for the house staff, the kitchen being often a separate building. A Yankee leasing a hotel in Savannah found that the five women cooks curled up nightly on the warm kitchen hearth and that the bootblacks' dormitory was a small closet half-full of boots. Asked about this kind of arrangement, the landlord of the best hotel said that niggers liked to sleep on the floor, why pamper them with beds? In a new town in Georgia a traveler found all the house servants sleeping on the floor, with only a blanket apiece for bedding. Uncle Tom's neat little chamber in the St. Clare

---

* This is a knotty question, of course. Herskovits (*Myth of the Negro Past, passim*) ably destroyed the older notion that the imported Negro slave was *utterly* cut off from a meager and weak cultural heritage in West Africa. But Herskovits's findings are much less significant for the slaves of the United States and their present Negro descendants than for those of the West Indies and Latin America. The richness and extent of the survivals of Africa that he found rise in number and intensity in the progression New Orleans . . . Trinidad . . . Haiti . . . Surinam . . . Brazil and, conversely, are most fragmentary in the non-Creole American South. Except round New Orleans the stateside Negro retained little but animal tales of the Uncle Remus kind, some shards of bush magic, hoe agriculture, a taste for carrying things on the head, neglect to take chastity seriously, and that was about all—nothing like the sub-African cultures of Haiti or the Surinam Maroons. In a 1948 edition Frazier, the great Negro sociologist, did not revise his considered statement (*Negro Family in the United States;* 15): "Probably never before in history has a people been so nearly completely stripped of its social heritage as the Negroes who were brought to America."

mansion was just an assumption of Mrs. Stowe's. As bachelor stable help he would probably have bunked in the hay or an empty stall.

Missis's personal maid might sleep across her door to be handy. For, unlike the field hand who was pretty much on his own when his task was done, the sleep-in house servant could never call his soul his own. Any minute, day or night, ole missis could sing out for him to do anything, from finding a missing chamberpot to bringing the bootjack for master returning mellow from court day at the county seat. Sometimes she kept her own cowhide to encourage promptness. So, in spite of prestige and perquisites, house servants might regret having been promoted. "I nursed and cooked sometimes," a former slave recalled, "but I liked the field work better. . . . We could talk and do anything we wanted to, just so we picked the cotton." **N**

Quality white folks often permitted a sycophantically impertinent freedom to pet house servants who were shown to outsiders as "undeniable proof of the general kindness with which their dependents are treated. It is as good a proof of it," wrote Fanny Kemble, kindling as she went along, "as the maudlin tenderness of a fine lady to her lap-dog is of her humane treatment of animals in general. . . . only the degradation of the many . . . admits of this favoritism to the few . . . which is perfectly consistent with the profoundest contempt and injustice, degrades the object of it quite as much, though it oppresses him less, than the cruelty practiced upon his fellows." There is a dismal logic about that. It applies even to Mrs. Stowe's point about the Northerners' ugly shrinking from contact with Negroes. One can be impressed by the way Thomas Dabney's daughter recorded twice, never turning a hair, that his slave Isaac frequently boasted of having been suckled by master's mother to use up her superfluous milk when she was nursing. **S** But a rabid professional Southerner flawed that in a slavering novel of Reconstruction, *The Leopard's Spots.* Its Yankee heroine remarks: "I've seen those beautiful southern children kiss their old black 'Mammy.' It made me shudder till I discovered that they did it just as I kiss Fido." s Then one recalls that Hawaiian noblewomen used to use puppies as nurslings.

House service was usually frowsy and inefficient. Outsiders with non-Southern ideas often deplored the whole system. At the Trescotts' on Barnwell Island Russell found a strange equivalent for the trim, clean maids of Britain: ". . . a child brings in my water and boots—an intelligent, curly-head little creature, dressed in a sort of sack, without any particular waist, barefooted. I imagined it was a boy, till it told me it was a girl." She asked him to buy her, describing herself as good at washing and sewing. Thackeray saw slavery as "the dearest institution that can be devised . . . fifteen negroes doing the work which John, the cook, the housemaid, and the help, do perfectly in your own comfortable London home. And these . . . are the pick of a family of some eighty or ninety. Twenty are too sick, or too old for work . . . twenty too clumsy; twenty are too young, and have to be watched and nursed by ten more." The elder Chesnuts' home place in South Carolina had "sixty or seventy people . . . to wait upon this household, two thirds of them too old or too young to be of any use." s The one sound reason for this multiplicity of persons was the system of informal apprenticeship, assigning to each slave specialist one or more young assistants to learn by doing, with much hullabaloo but some effectiveness.

Quantity, not quality, was the basis of the large Southern establishment. "The number of the servants rather than the elegance of the outfit advertised the wealth and dignity of the family." s By 1791 the wife of a Sea Island planter was complaining that the profits of local plantations were "mostly expended in the purchase of Negroes, as nothing is so much coveted as the pleasure of possessing many slaves." s Thirty years later another grand lady of South Carolina deplored for her son "the Majority of the People here, whose chief object is to make Rice to buy Negroes and Buy Negroes to make rice. . . ." [5] This is useful in accounting for the quasi-medieval slovenliness that seems to have permeated many—not all, mind you—large Southern houses. Mrs. Stowe's imaginative presentment of the jumbled filth in the St. Clare kitchen may well be the truest bit in her book. With a severity that reflects shock but is good evidence for all that, Miss Martineau wrote that "I never saw a clean room or bed but once within the boundaries of a slave state." She envied Southerners their ability to stay unruffled when "waiting half an hour for the second course, or [seeing] everthing done in the worst possible manner; their rooms dirty, their property wasted, their infants slighted; themselves deluded by artifices . . . every slaveholder's temper is subjected to a discipline which must either ruin or perfect it."

Nevertheless, when well handled, house slaves could be great credits to their ungrateful situation. Arriving at a Carolina plantation with letters to the absent master, Captain and Mrs. Hall were looked after cordially and deftly by a slave staff aware that this was what master would have wanted and knowing how to do it. In many slaves Miss Bremer discerned a quasi-feudal loyalty to master as chief in terms common to nonliterate tribesmen whether Highlanders or Ashanti. With great sincerity a rich South Carolina rice planter could put on a slave's gravestone: "In Memory of/My Servant Thomas/Carpenter/Honest and true/He died as for 40 years/He had lived/My faithful friend." Even field hands might feel a certain pride—the poor devils had little enough to be proud of otherwise—in the extent and fertility of the plantation and in the glittering glories of the Big House as they glimpsed it on holidays or in emergencies.

At the risk of churlishness we must get the Big House, basic symbol of what a reconstructed Southerner called "the Technicolor South," [5] in perspective down its avenue of live oaks or red cedars. In such gross respects as cubage or number of rooms it seldom exceeded the mansarded mansion that the town banker was to build in the North a generation later.

Even at the time the Yankee or York State merchant had built equivalent houses of as great, or greater, charm in Wiscasset or Dutchess County. One Southern-born historian calls the planter's Big House "a modest country house of ten or twelve rooms." ⁵ Another says: "Most of the plantation houses were . . . more commodious than elegant; and many had not even a rambling spaciousness." ⁵ George Mason's beautiful Gunston Hall, nucleus of a plantation of 5000 acres and 500 slaves, is, albeit roomy, only a story-and-a-half affair. Rosewell, rated by a recent authority as "in its day the lordliest mansion in Virginia," was "one of the few . . . as much as three stories in height." The main house had twenty-three rooms, a large but not staggering number that must have been highly unusual to judge from the awe with which the finest conceivable plantation house in Louisiana was described as having all of seventeen rooms. Even handsome Carter's Grove, rated finest surviving mansion in the Old Dominion, would have been no more than an adequate dower house for an eminent noble family in Britain.*

These discrepancies between American and transatlantic notions of magnificence naturally caused friction. It would have hurt the feelings of Mrs. Skirving to know how offhandedly Mrs. Basil Hall wrote down her plantation residence in the Carolinas as "small but very comfortable." Buckingham observed of Mt. Vernon: ". . . the mansion itself is not remarkable for size and elegance, but it is well arranged for domestic comfort," and Westover from the river reminded

---

* A potential exception was John Acklen's projected Gothic palace in cotton Louisiana, planned for fifty rooms plus bathrooms and closets, to cost $275,000, furnishings included. It did not get built. (Phillips, *American Negro Slavery;* 239.) With kitchen and sometimes office or library under separate roofs, the pretentious Southern house needed less cubage, of course, than its Northern opposite number. British travellers were nevertheless right; by the standards of the great world of the time, the typical Big House was pretty small potatoes.

him of "the old red-brick mansions seen about Camberwell, Clapham and Hampstead." Fetherstonhaugh, a young British geologist, dismissed The Hermitage as "built of brick . . . and tolerably large." Trollope saw Arlington as "picturesque, but neither large nor good." These witnesses were not always unkind or supercilious; rather, they were innocently unaware of saying "Nice little place you have here" about the pride of that whole end of the state.

Considered even grander than the neighboring Hermitage, Isaac Stephenson's Fairvue had a conservatory and icehouse but only four large rooms on each of two floors, plus a few small ones in the garret and one small wing. The core of many a Big House was the pioneer's "two-pens-and-a-passage" double log cabin boarded over, added to on the same level, buried under a second story, ending up with three times the original cubage but small title to be called palatial. The "Greek revival" * came in time to camouflage Cindy Lou's largish but commonplace dwelling. The same device—great wooden columns two stories high in a showy but strikingly useless portico—was fashionable at the same time in New England, New York State and New Jersey, but, thanks to stage sets and movies, we now associate these white "pillars" strictly with magnolias and mint. New-made cotton grandees especially loved the specious majesty of these façades for such Big Houses as the graciously beautiful Rosemount in the crotch of the Alabama and Tombigbee Rivers. These pillars were also distraction from slipshod service and maintenance.

---

* The "Greek revival" enraged Trollope: ". . . in front of a square brick house a wooden quasi-Greek portico, with a pediment and Ionic columns. . . . as a rule these are attached to houses which, without such ornamentation, would be simple, unpretentious, square, roomy residences. An Ionic or Corinthian capital stuck on to a log of wood called a column, and then fixed promiscuously to the outside of an ordinary house, is to my eye the vilest of architectural pretenses." (*North America;* 167.)

Fanny Kemble was not the only witness often reminded of
Castle Rackrent. Here is a Big House near Natchez in the
mid-1830's:

> A large colonnaded structure . . . with an imposing ef-
> fect . . . the abode of one of the wealthiest planters. . . .
> The grounds about this edifice were neglected; horses were
> grazing round the piazzas, over which were strewn saddles,
> whips, horse blankets. . . . In the front yard were several
> sheep, colts, calves, two or three saddle- and a fine pair of
> carriage-horses, negro children, and every variety of domestic
> fowl . . . A hammock, suspended between an iron hook
> driven into the side of the house and one of the slender col-
> umns . . . contained a nephew of the planter, fast locked
> in the arms of Morpheus. . . . many private residences in
> the vicinity of Natchez of an equally expensive character . . .
> whose elegant interiors, [contrast] with the neglected grounds
> about them suggest the idea of a handsome city residence,
> accidentally dropped upon a bleak hill. . . . Very few of the
> planters' villas, even within a few miles of Natchez, are
> adorned with surrounding ornamental shrubbery . . . ex-
> cept a few shade trees and a narrow, gravelled avenue from
> the gate to the house. 5

This was early in Natchez's glory, of course. But it is doubtful that many Southern establishments, whether in Mississippi
or the Virginia Tidewater, ever thoroughly fitted such summaries as Rackham Holt's picture of the South in 1860:
". . . physical labor on one side and physical well-being on
the other, brought about by good food, gracious surroundings
and perfect service." Yet how were slave-born Negroes to
know of Yankee standards of cleanly neatness and British
standards of luxury? For house servants as well as field hands
the Big House, with its five bedrooms, balustraded stair and
luster chandelier, was the finest dwelling in the world, even
if the paint was peeling off the volutes of the Ionic capitals.
Among slaves it was socially important to have been born in

its prestige-heavy shadow, and those so privileged looked
down on any "bought 'oman" imported from off the plantation.

These were the classical circumstances, the convict-cum-
trusty highest power of slavery—the framework in which,
given ever more land to ruin, slavery operated best, the economy that, by supporting the price of slaves, persuaded back-
going but slave-breeding sections to stand by the system. By
growing wheat with slave labor, Maryland and Virginia managed some recovery from the soil exhaustion due to tobacco.
A century before the New Deal Georgia was taking seriously
scientific advice about terraces and contours. But the very
cost of slaves discouraged agricultural reform:

> It did not pay to use an $800 slave in ditching, terracing or
> manuring $8 an acre land . . . when more could be bought
> whenever it was exhausted. . . . Many planters never built
> homes for themselves on their plantations, thus lessening
> their economic and sentimental stakes in their enterprises.
> To the absentee owner the plantation was . . . an open-air
> factory where land and slave labor were combined to produce
> cotton. Rich land was only a species of raw material. **s**

But the big gang plantation was not typical. The majority
of slaves served their life sentences elsewhere than in the great
establishments that dominated the psychology of rice, cotton
and sugar culture. In 1850 only 2300 Southerners owned
more than 100 slaves each. In 1852-1853, the year of *Uncle
Tom,* Macon and Greene Counties in Georgia, rich cotton
areas, showed only 177 landowners with 1000 acres or more.
Even in such big-plantation country typical holdings were
under 500 acres, many of them obviously not justifying over-

seers. A shrewd student of slavery finds a natural verbal cleavage in ante bellum Mississippi between the farmer, whose fewer than thirty slaves he could manage in person, and the planter, whose more than thirty slaves needed a deputy supervisor. [5] Though historians vary on details, none would quarrel seriously with Dodd's estimate that three to four Southern families "lived on the best lands and received three-fourths of the returns of yearly exports [of Southern-grown staples]. . . . Two-thirds of the white people of the South had no connection with slavery. . . . A thousand families received over $50,000,000 a year [from export of staples] while all the remaining 600,000 received only about $60,000,000." [5]

The typical slaveowner of the census of 1860 actually owned fewer than ten Negroes of all ages.* His upland farm produced sustenance for his family and his slaves, with tobacco, cotton or grain for cash crops. He usually worked along with his slaves, as the sons of smaller Virginia planters had done a hundred years earlier, and would have thought an overseer

---

* Hart's estimate (*Slavery and Abolition;* 66) was larger but still in the same order of effect: "Out of 9,000,000 whites . . . not more than 500,000 persons made a substantial profit out of slavekeeping. . . . about ten thousand families were the ruling South in economic, social and political life." Rhodes (*History of the United States,* I; 349) wrote of "a little aristocracy, whose nucleus was less than eight thousand large slaveholders." The leverage exerted by these few thousand families can be and has been exaggerated but it must have been immense all the same. Dodd's money estimates, be it understood, are gross returns from Southern export. Net to the planter, however wide his acres, however numerous his slaves, was far less. Even in the happy times before the Civil War all but the most thrifty depended upon the services of, and paid heavy commissions or interest to, the factor, a sort of combination banker-merchant-sales-agent located in the central market for the planter's principal staple. The man behind those Magnolia County white columns lived well according to his undemanding lights, but he had no such liquid resources as better management, particularly better financing, might have obtained him. Still, that has always been the colonial farmer's principal trouble—in Hawaii and the Gold Coast as well as the Gulf Coast.

as much of a luxury as college schooling for his young'uns. With luck, as King Cotton's realm spread and small men of this sort moved south or west to exploit these royal opportunities, he might rise to the land-rich and cash-poor affluence of the big-plantation owner and hope that he, or his sons at any rate, might be taken for gentlemen. Joseph Davis managed that for himself and his able young brother Jefferson. N. B. Forrest rose from hillbilly to cattle and slave dealer to master of large plantations and great soldier. "The charmed circle of Southern aristocracy, like that of England, was not rigidly closed," Dodd observed, "and aristocracy here as in England was therefore popular." [5]

Smaller establishments often worked out better for slaves. This farmer class "came closer into touch with the slave and in a hundred ways softened the harshness of an institution which no one knew how to modify in law." [5] The son of a North Carolina Baptist preacher* described his father's forty-slave cotton operation as not too intolerable:

> He never overworked his slaves, for I was a number of years foreman. . . . They started to work when I started; when I got a holiday they got one. . . . When any of the slave children were very sick they were brought into the house of the white family and there attended as one of the white children. He always provided for them to go to church on Sunday, allowing them to use the farm teams when necessary. . . . I

---

* The Southern clergy, whether one-horse like Rev. Phelps, or local grandee like Bishop Polk, saw nothing unfitting about owning Negroes. Apparently this was true of Catholics as well as of Protestants: St. Inigoe's Manor, founded by the Jesuits in Maryland in 1702, owned slaves up to 1838 without known misgivings. Then came instructions from Rome to get rid of this un-Christian scandal. So the Manor, retaining only two families of slaves for domestic uses, sold the rest to slave-dealers accustomed to supply planters in the dread Georgia rice swamps and Louisiana cane fields. There was a good deal of well-justified row about it. For this I rely on *The Manner Is Ordinary* by the Rev. John La Farge, S.J.

state the above on my honor as a Christian minister. P.S. He never allowed his sons to whip any of the field hands. **s**

Many small slaveholders were ignorant and, by our standards, must often have been barbarous, for the South kept up the ways of a permanent frontier. But the master did not have to be a preacher to be about as decent a person as his opposite number who was making an arduous living at the same period in Iowa or Michigan. Working so few Negroes, he did not develop the impersonal approach that underlay many of the evils of slavery. "My master was the best in the country," a former slave asserted. "He didn't had many niggers, but he sure took care of them he had. He didn't 'low nobody to hit 'em a lick." **N** And with tasks more widely varied in sustenance farming, and interracial contacts likelier, stimulus for the slave was often higher. Outside observers noted that, as they moved into the Southern upcountry where holdings were smaller, slaves looked more like people. On such hand-to-mouth operations as the Rev. Silas Phelps's place, the Negroes were isolated, often chuckleheaded and sometimes got bullied. But in comparison with the big-plantation field hand, they had dazzling opportunities to learn some adjustment to the white man's world.

In the upcountry white and Negro children were seen playing together on what looked like equal footing,* and a Negro occasionally ate at master's table, a thing unthinkable nearer tidewater—or anywhere in the South today, for that matter. The situation seems thus to have retained a tinge, however dim, of the redemptioner-white's status—a hired man working willy-nilly for his bare keep but not altogether a congenital convict. Olmsted found a pleasant example in northern Mississippi. Seven hands were working a newly cleared place.

---

* In this age of conflict over segregation in Southern schools, it is strange to read of "thirty children, of whom ten were negroes," taught in the same schoolroom in Rockbridge County, Virginia, in 1820. (Ballagh, *History of Slavery in Virginia;* 110.)

They lived in wretched cabins, true, but under an easy master who said that he had not "licked a nigger in five years," believed his slaves took as much interest in good crops as he did, and was proud of the fact that, taught by a literate comrade, they could all read and bought their own books, mostly pious, with their own hard-earned cash.

On such farms the cleavage between master's and slave's standards of living was less invidious. The slave's clothes were hardly rougher, his pork, corn, molasses and green stuff in season were about what master and missis had six days a week. By and large, Olmsted considered, free Negroes in the North lived better than the majority of Southern slaveholders, a striking conclusion but tenable when set against the authentic data. The farmer's house improved on the slave's "quarter" only in having somewhat greater cubage, flooring, perhaps two stories and, occasionally, the luxury of a few panes of glass. A certain planter operating 640 acres in Yallobusha County, Mississippi, lived in a two-pens-and-a-passage log-house apparently with no sense of incongruity. So did Colonel Grangerford, for all that he owned "a lot of farms and over a hundred niggers," wore white linen and was indubitable "quality," the aristocrat-magnate of his neighborhood. And nine tenths of his slaveowning neighbors probably wore hickory shirts and jean breeches and lived pretty much on the three M's. Mrs. Stowe briefed her reader hardly at all in either the field hand or the small-farmer's slaves. Legree's working force are stage extras, with neither personality nor substance. Of his slaves she took pains to develop only drivers, house servants and town-trained Negroes. Yet the bulk of Negroes for whom she was arousing such specious sympathy consisted of just the very field hands and farm slaves whom she neglected.

In the South's few sizable towns—Richmond, Wilmington, Charleston, Savannah, Mobile, Natchez, presently Atlanta*— the slave's world expanded. His pickings were rich in the households of masters able to afford town life and of the lawyers, doctors, parsons and middlemen who catered to the slave economy and skimmed much of its profit. Many a runaway from Richmond or Norfolk proved able to pay up to $100 for a seat on the Underground Railroad—a sum that no field hand could have raked together in three lifetimes.

To you and me these towns, except New Orleans and possibly Charleston, would have seemed inconsequential, sleepy, crude, as they did then to European and Northern visitors alike. But their impact on the slave, or on the up-country white of any but the "quality" class must have been like that of the shopwindows of Gopher Prairie on the servant girl in *Main Street*. Here before the slave's rolling eyes were steamboats, ships, high-steepled churches, pillared courthouses, occasional Yankees, political and military parades— some towns had to pass special ordinances forbidding Negroes to follow military bands—street vendors, hotels, saloons, carriages with liveried servants, and so on. He might not be privileged to the use of these things but he could whet his wits with the look of them and the uses that whites made of them. Against the advantage of stimulus, of course, stood the trauma of dislocation and the urge toward brittle opportunism that often goes with it. After rough adjustment to the plantation field gang or the house-servant's bucolic chores,

---

* I probably should have included Baltimore and Washington among Southern population centers, but their geographical positions were eccentric and their experience with outside influences unusual. The same applies to Louisville and St. Louis as they grew into importance.

the Negro was now asked again to adjust. It often worked out well, but it also led inevitably to town slaves' learning to live overcynically by the very wits that they were sharpening. Modern Harlem and the South side of Chicago are full of examples.

Master perhaps kept the hotel and worked slaves as waiters or porters, to the despair of visitors,* who found them dirty and slow though good-natured, but much to the broadening of their own horizons. Or master might own a steamboat and send his "boy" up and down the Mississippi, Alabama or Tennessee as cook or fireman or roustabout loading firewood and wrangling freight, in any case learning to gamble and sing new songs and cut a dash with the girls from St. Louis to Orleans or Columbus to Mobile. Russell found "a tall, neatly dressed" woman slave collecting tickets and handling passage money on a Baltimore-Norfolk steamer. John Mc-Donogh, of New Orleans, used some of his educated slaves as rent collectors. s

In town, in spite of ill-enforced laws against teaching Negroes, the slave's chances to learn to read, write and cipher greatly increased. His instruction might come from an eccentric master like McDonogh or from a literate fellow slave willing to risk a whipping, or it could be dogged self-improvement, as in Frederick Douglass's learning to write by piecing together the alphabetical markings on timbers in a shipyard. N Good Alabamans seeking a qualified missionary for Liberia actually turned up a slave with the rudiments of Latin, Greek and Hebrew; hastily they bought him for $2500—an order of price that one hears of otherwise only on beautiful quadroon girls—and sent him on his learned way. s

A field hand could go from year's end to year's end without even seeing print or writing to puzzle over. Nor, when lifting

---

* Combe (*Notes on the United States*, II; 293) on Kentucky inns: "The slaves run about with a wonderful display of muscular activity, but there is a sad lack of mind in it; they are active in body to avoid vituperation."

his eyes from the hoe blade, did he see much but the stump-
ugly fringe of woods with a buzzard tilting high over it. If
sold to a municipality to do public chores, he could look up
from his shovel and observe the amazing sight of real strangers, people he had never seen before and might well never
see again, not just singly but by scores and dozens. His personal acquaintance was no longer limited to a hundred or so
plantation hands changed only by birth, death or sale. Now
his circle constantly shifted, might include the body servants
of visitors down from half-Northern Baltimore or Louisville,
and the slave crews of fishing vessels. A free Negro might
have a slave wife, or vice versa, and to some extent town
slaves' social life imitated and mingled with that of the urban
free Negroes, who were most numerous in Richmond,
Charleston, Mobile and New Orleans. N

This little subculture included burial societies for financing
and celebrating funerals, a tradition brought vigorous from
Africa, and much churchgoing in gaudy fine clothes. A Scottish workingman trying his luck in the South said that on
Sunday Negroes in Charleston looked as if they had all been
blindfolded and then dressed themselves in whatever came
first to hand in a wagonload of secondhand clothes, some still
in good condition. Buckingham found the same effect in
Richmond "a very agreeable sight. . . . the negroes of both
sexes seemed so happy in the enjoyment of their holiday and
their finery, that I wished from my heart I could secure them
two Sundays a week instead of one, or still better, have them
thus happy all the week through." Savannah had Negro units
in the local militia, as well as Negro volunteer fire companies. In raw, new Tuscaloosa the house servants of a family that the Lyells visited were in a position to give a great
party for their friends with generous provision of turkey, cake
and ice-cream. Like all other manifestations of high life be-
lowstairs, such affairs usually struck masters and their hangers-
on as irresistibly comical. No doubt they often were so. But
a kicking would be too good for anybody determined to see

in such fumbling imitations of others' ways nothing but minstrel-show travesty.*

The town slave was not Jim Crowed quite as abjectly as his post bellum descendant. Railroads in Virginia had theoretical segregation rules, but on a train that Olmsted traveled on, no one observed them. He saw Negro passengers admitted to Southern stage coaches without demur; so did the Honorable Miss Murray, who was quite taken aback on an Alabama River steamboat when "a black woman came and sat down by me. . . . From what we hear in England I imagined Negroes were kept at a distance. That is the case in the Northern States, but in the South they are at your elbow everywhere and always seek conversation. This was an old nurse or aunty, or mammy. . . ." As for the FEPC aspect, cot-

---

* New Orleans certainly offered the most extreme example of slave-urban society as well as the largest group of well-off and relatively unrestricted free Negroes. I shamelessly scamp New Orleans for reasons that seem sufficient, or anyway discreet. Daniels gave me the major cue in writing that Louisiana was always "a Caribbean republic . . . in spirit and character . . . not a true Southern State for all the Negroes and the heat." (*Southerner Discovers the South;* 231.) It had heavy French and Hispanic overtones in race relations as well as in the geography that made New Orleans headquarters for filibusters with their schemes for the West Indies and Central America. In all economic strata there was an unusually high proportion of white immigrants from Europe and the North. Some of this was also true of Natchez and Mobile, and Charleston had a trace of Barbadian influence, of which J. T. Adams made too much. But none were as alien to the rest of the South as the Crescent City. None developed to New Orleans's degree recognized concubinage for "mixed blood" women, often with quasi-formal recognition of the offspring. None went so far toward treating free Negroes not only as recognized entrepreneurs but as people with whom, in some circumstances, one might sit at table. For such reasons I see New Orleans as a study in itself and have no intention of wearying the reader and confusing myself by keeping on saying: "But in New Orleans . . . ." The genuine South was confusing enough anyway. It is bad enough to have to make sense of both James Pemberton and Miss Watson's Jim, without also mixing in Quadroon Balls and the free Negro troops who offered their services to the Confederacy in 1861.

ton mills in both Virginia and Georgia mingled white with black operatives at the same work of machine tending.

In towns too the slave could best use religion as salve for his troubles and pretext for frequent "socializing." He had always leaned that way. On the plantation, if master or overseer was indulgent or considered religion a proper "opiate of the people"—on which opinions differed sharply—some slave with the gift of gab and smatterings of Bible lore, usually the simpler and less edifying tales from the Old Testament, might set up as local preacher. The extraordinary idiom of his homilies has been worked for authentic fun by Roark Bradford, for authentic power and dignity by James Weldon Johnson. A master might even countenance a slovenly little chapel. On Barnwell Island "One particularly dirty little hut was described to me as 'the church' . . . about fifteen feet square, begrimed with dirt and smoke, and windowless. A few benches were placed across it and the 'preacher,' a slave from another plantation, was expected next week." That very Negro church still exists in many parts of the South, standing lonesome and awry in a bare patch among the pines.

Certain Episcopalian-minded plantations of South Carolina, of the same stripe as those affording formal marriages to slaves, and some Mississippi planters provided decent chapels and self-respecting white ministry. Understandably "Servants, obey your masters," was a favorite text before slave congregations. Presentable hands were often allowed to sit in a separate gallery or behind a rail toward the rear of the white folks' church, likelier Methodist or Baptist than Presbyterian or Episcopalian. At the Methodist church in Abingdon, Virginia, all heard the same service but "the coloured class of communicants" was held separate from that for whites.

By Mrs. Stowe's time many slaveholders had lost their glibness about slavery as an indispensable means to Christianizing black heathen. Here and there zealots and decent people, particularly Methodists, continued to fan the embers of what amounted to home-missionary work among slaves. But the trend was contrary. A great cotton planter of Louisiana called preaching to slaves "the greatest piece of foolishness anyone was ever guilty of." **s** It was increasingly thought inadvisable to put anything whatever, even the Lord's Prayer, the Ten Commandments or the Beatitudes, into slaves' heads.

But it was too late. Missionary zeal and the social side of camp meetings had thoroughly impregnated slaves' ways of doing with an often spurious Christianity. Where master frowned on preachings, the hands held clandestine prayer meetings in remote shacks or the margins of swamps, relying on their superstitious conviction that to turn a big iron kettle upside down at the scene would keep hymns—or, on other occasions, fiddles—from being heard at a distance. **N** Privately and publicly they imitated—some think that their West African traditions helped to originate*—the orgiastic ecstacies of speaking in tongues, jerks and flops that accompanied the revivals of the period and still survive in white and Negro splinter sects. A Negro scholar has described these "manifestations of the spirit" as "resembling paroxysms that could hardly be expected outside of an insane asylum." **N** From the whites' camp-meeting hymns the slaves made their own, the lyrics dwelling with limpid eloquence on how the children of Israel were freed and the glories to come on the other side of Jordan where God blesses all alike, regardless of color or nappy hair:

> Nebbah yo' min' about strait'nin' it,
> God said He'd strait'n it better d'an you.

> They taken my blessed Jesus
>   and whipped him up the hill

---

* Accounts of Haitian *voudun* certainly imply resemblance to Pentecosters' or Holy Rollers' doings, and much of *voudun* came straight from West Africa. It nevertheless does not necessarily follow that parallel manifestations in North America came from the same source. Such things were not unknown in medieval Europe.

> With a knotty whip and a ragged thorn
> and He never said a mumbling word.
> Shout brother!
> He never said a mumbling word. . . .

The whole world now knows the poignancy of these "spirituals" and lesser slave hymns. They are not as "African" as is often asserted, being in most respects syncopated and sublimated redactions of evangelical white hymns or traditional Scottish or Irish airs.* But, except as this again shows the cultural orphanhood of the slave, I cannot imagine anything mattering less.

This religious music was usually far better than the preachers and services that occasioned it. It was not unknown for slave churches to be steadying influences on their members. The tradition of being one's brother's keeper and subjecting him to public discipline when he erred was strong among evangelical sects, and Negroes were known to imitate it. Mrs. Chesnut was impressed by how the Negro circuit rider "looks into everything, and if commandments are not kept, he turns out church-members. They dislike to be up before the church and excommunicated more than aught else in the world, so it is a wholesome discipline." 5 There was probably much, however, in Olmsted's conclusion that the slaves' "preachings" were too often only a "cloak for immorality," which was also true of many white camp meetings, the phrase "a camp-meeting baby" being well understood in the backwoods. A

---

* I rely heavily here on the analysis in Woofter, *Black Yeomanry;* 65-73, of the antecedents of the Sea Island spirituals, since, other things being equal, one would expect stronger African influences surviving in this area than anywhere else in the South, with the possible exception of New Orleans. Woofter notes syncopation itself as likely a "survival from Africa." His following summary recommends a middle course between two statements: one, that spirituals are "largely borrowed directly from white folk music"; the other, that they are "selections from white music" merely "influenced by the Negro's African musical heritage." But both leave the African influence relatively minor.

hundred years later, only a generation ago, Woodson described the "occasional visits of the underdeveloped [Negro] pastor" to Negro congregations in the South as likely to be followed by "an increase rather than a decrease in sexual indulgence." **N**

There were other anomalies: In town the Negroes might have regular, well-attended churches in imitation of white congregations. At least one such had bought, and had paid for in installments, its own slave-preacher. What quality of article they got is uncertain. The ante bellum slave preacher's prototypes were usually the ranting, ignorant, Methodist or Baptist exhorters who infected the run of white Southerners with a crackjawed Fundamentalism still regrettably vigorous and given to jackleg Fascism. The powerful and eloquent Negro preacher of whom one reads, a man clothed with the dignity of underprivileged and collective passion, did appear, but the average slave exhorter must have been a sort of cheer leader, a mere mechanical detonator for glorious singing and eventual mass hysteria. Both activities were, if you like, good socialized escapes from reality and so probably healthy for slaves.

Uncle Remus's "Sis Cow" and "Br'er Rabbit" in imitation of white usage show how important to Negroes was the evangelical notion of fellowship among the saved. Nothing known about Negroes prevents their Christianity from reaching validity as often as that of whites, or vice versa, in spite of Mrs. Stowe's curious theories about a special religious genius in the "African race." Of the six or seven people I have known who might well deserve the label "Christian," at least two were Negroes, a high proportion in view of the relatively few Negroes in my acquaintance. Yet the impact of churchgoing and Bible talk on the typical town slave, who got most of those influences, can hardly have been stronger than on town whites, that is, nothing startling.

Perhaps the slave especially needed a religion of redemption; so he may have felt a redemptionist religion a little more deeply. But it was not essential that he should, for he had another string to his bow in the satisfactions of superstition, much of it the dregs of West African animism. Puckett, the white scholar who actually got himself accepted as an adept colleague by Deep South Negro "root-doctors," found the African tinge strongest in folk beliefs about the pleasures of life, one in particular, and weakest in practical matters where whites predominate. The slave usually failed in efforts to find an apparatus of powders and roots that would keep master from punishing delinquents. N He sometimes did better in other departments of the "cunjur-talk" and "cunjur-doings" that had been endemic among field hands ever since "administering medicines" (that is, herbal poisons) had been the subject of special laws in colonial Virginia. But this relative effectiveness depended not as much on the potency of the natural alkaloids that slaves found in the South as on the victims' readiness to believe in them,* which they obligingly did. Only round New Orleans, however, did American Negroes evolve Africa-style cults on the order of West Indian *obeah* or Haitian *voudun,* descriptions of which clearly indicate syncretion of Catholicism, African animism and the inevitable psychopathology.*

Most of the hundreds or thousands of the slaves' superstitious techniques, notions and objects were unrelated. Touches straight from Devonshire or Clydeside would turn up cheek by jowl with those straight from Guinea. Thus Woodson concluded that "the Negroes have taken over so many [supersti-

---

* Hundley (*Social Relations in Our Southern States;* 332) was puzzled by the readiness with which a slave with a minor grudge would try to poison another in contrast with the rarity of slave efforts to poison whites whom they violently hated. It is a well-known magical principle, founded in clinical fact, that "hoodoo" poison works best when the object knows it has been administered and devoutly believes in its efficacy.

* Among the many shrewd things that Joyce Cary has said about Negroes and Africa, one of the shrewdest is ". . . morbid psychology and primitive religion—which are nearly the same thing." (*African Witch;* 209.)

tions] from the whites that it is difficult to draw a line between European and African influences."  Miss Watson's Jim's hairball was straight conjur, pure fetish; whereas the American Negro belief that, if you hear a screech owl call, somebody near you will die unless you turn your shoes upside down is probably just a case of North America naturalizing the Gaelic banshee, come over with Irish or Scottish redemptioners. The Negro's insistence that a murdered corpse will bleed afresh if the murderer touches it comes intact from a medieval European ordeal. The general point, however, the emotionally important part, is the way the slave lived in a climate of superstitions trailing off from his awe of intense old black women with witchy reputations. And to this day the Negro is the principal American consumer of what might be called superstition goods: luck-powders, charms, dreambooks and various preparations of High John the Conquer root. You could read all the works of Mrs. Stowe and never learn that any Negro slave, except Legree's sinister drivers under his hag-ridden influence, was ever superstitious about anything.

A slave did not necessarily belong to the man for whom he worked. Many farmers, professional men and manufacturers hired slaves' services from their owners. Such contracts usually ran from New Year's to the new hiring season during Christmas week, and the master furnished only what a shipman would call "bare charter," the hirer supplying quarters, clothes, food and doctoring as if he were actual owner. In rural parts Christmas week saw regular hiring fairs, like those of rural old England, where whites picked and chose among candidates on display. In both town and country slave craftsmen were often allowed to go seek their own employers, at which point things verged toward informal preparation for freedom.

One motive for hiring was that "if one neither owned nor hired a slave, one might be called a poor white." Or say a lackadaisical Virginia gentleman inherited a moribund to-bacco plantation and thirty-odd slaves with normal appetites whom, perhaps because he had scruples, he did not care to sell. He might keep the pick of the slaves for house servants and rent out the rest to a Richmond tobacco factory at $100 apiece paid him yearly. Manhandling the crude old tobacco presses was grueling work, the whole process was as little lightened by machinery as sluggishness could arrange. But this assured the owner—or perhaps the trustee of an estate including slaves whom it was not expedient to sell—cash in-come with small risk and less trouble.

Brokers made a living out of arranging such hirings out of slaves. Some considered these arrangements economically use-ful, others deplored them as tending to make slaves uppity. Slave hiring flourished in the North Carolina pinewoods when a boom in naval stores enabled smart operators to make $300 profit a year per hired-out slave working as hacker or dipper. Both Kentucky and Virginia had church congregations invest-ing in slaves for hire to pay the minister's salary. In the Vir-ginia case the original investment was in two Negro women bought in 1767, whose successive generations of descendants, fathered nobody cared how, were retained until a liquidation in 1835 when the total was some seventy head of human live-stock.

Though backward, the South made sporadic efforts at mech-anized industry and wherever enterprise thus intruded, the slave was usually involved, often on hire. The inchoate South-ern textile industry used slaves of both sexes, sometimes slave children. Slave labor was the backbone of the operation in Tennessee iron mills, Kentucky and Virginia salt works, Vir-ginia coal mines. In 1858 the Memphis & New Orleans line of steamboats was offering $40 a month, a high rate in those times, for hired-slave firemen and deckhands.

Southern railroads, developing rapidly in the decade before the Civil War, might own their own section hands. The Raleigh & Gaston, for example, counted on "the increase of the women" (I suppose their work was cleaning cars between trips) to "exceed any depreciation in the value of the property." The South Carolina Rail Road and the Mississippi Railroad were other such owners. Contractors building railroads might advertise for likely slaves to hire under good conditions but oftener they, like Southern canal builders, preferred imported Irish laborers. These were turbulent but also industrious and cost less per cubic yard of earth moved. Besides, when one died on the job, you did not owe his owner something between $800 and $1000 in damages. s It was widely recognized, of course, that slaves thus worked by people who did not own them got rather worse treatment, as any livery-stable horse could have predicted.

Owners of especially trusty Negroes might leave to them the job finding and even the payments. There was precedent in the pre-Revolutionary custom of letting skilled redemptioners pay master during their obligated time for the privilege of plying their trades. Furnished with a proper pass, the slave would go to town and fend for himself, sending back a specified sum each month to his owner. Negroes thus "hiring their time" were cooks, dressmakers, whores, nurses, midwives, laundresses, milliners, tailors, blacksmiths, silversmiths, gunsmiths, draymen, stevedores, barbers, bartenders, pilots, deckhands, fishermen, carpenters, cabinetmakers, printers, engravers, sailmakers—hardly a trade in the ante bellum South but a slave paid institutional blackmail for working in it. Some revived the West African's passion for petty trade and became street vendors of fish, baked stuff, fruit, their habit of carrying their wares on their heads and their specialized cries adding much to the picturesqueness of Charleston. And, for all the Negro's alleged shiftlessness, incapacity and lack of initiative, many of them did well.

So long as master or missis had no change of mind and those few dollars a month—the amount varied with skill and individual value from, say, \$120 to \$500 a year—were duly paid, these time hirers were almost as free as they would be after Emancipation, except that they could not shift base without permission. To save money to buy themselves free was often their motive in asking leave to "hire their time." But surprisingly few took advantage of their obvious opportunities for absconding. Many a roustabout on a steamboat touching free river ports was a time hirer and had only to walk ashore to stand a good chance of freedom, but few bothered. For twenty years a well-known slave blacksmith tramped the length and breadth of Georgia doing odd hire-time work for small planters. **N**

The slave lumberjacks of the Great Dismal were the most advanced of these parolees. Olmsted heard of them as leased year after year from their masters at round \$100 annually to spend ten months under loose control cutting timber and splitting shingles in the big swamp. They were paid the proceeds of their output less their hire and cost of supplies consumed on the job and lived "measurably as a free man; hunts, fishes, eats, drinks, smokes and sleeps, plays and works, each when and as much as he pleases. . . . No 'driving' at his work is attempted or needed. No force is used to overcome the indolence peculiar to the negro. . . ." These Great Dismal shingle splitters were in fact the base of a considerable industry in a country that always told the world how little Negroes would accomplish unless whites stood over them with whips. Nor were they George Harrises presumably moved to self-reliance by large admixture of "white blood." Other circumstances would have made them prime field hands sold to Texas to lead the life of a blind horse in a treadmill. With a fine instinct for the wrong emphasis, Mrs. Stowe's novel set in the Great Dismal completely omitted them, though she unquestionably knew of them from Olmsted's book.

Slavery had alleviations, amenities, even some decencies, but each of them made a fool of one or more of the slaveholder's excuses for himself. Perhaps realization of this lay behind the opposition to time hiring that soon developed. A Southern student of slavery has truly described it as "admission that the slave could produce more in self-direction than when under routine control, a virtual admission that for him slavery had no industrial justification." [5] White craftsmen in the towns were sulky about competing with black rivals, and the masters, deploring the hazards of this similitude of freedom, outlawed the practice again and again. But, the South being slipshod as she was, it went on nevertheless.

Legal or not, it was a sort of decompression chamber preparing the Negro to be his own man. Deliberate schemes to that end were however, not always successful. A well-meaning Georgia planter, for instance, gave a small gang of superior slaves a certain tract to be worked in their Saturday spare time on their own for their own profit. They got nowhere with it. Perhaps they lacked firm internal leadership. Lyell, hearing the story, attributed their failure to the numbing effect of their "holding the property in common," a Victorian verdict from an honest and intelligent source, but a mere guess all the same.

The Couper plantation—fifteen miles up the Altamaha River, managed personally by the son of the owner, succeeding with sugar in an area committed to rice—was the best that Lyell saw. What he said of and for it is about all that could ever have been said for American slavery. He commended

> ... an hereditary regard and often attachment on both sides. . . . The slaves identify themselves with their master, and their sense of importance rises with his success in life. . . . To one . . . direct from Europe, with a vivid impression on his mind of the state of the peasantry there in many populous regions, their ignorance, intemperance, and improvidence, the difficulty of obtaining sustenance, and the small chance they have of bettering their lot, the condition of the black laborers on such a property as Hopeton will afford but

small ground for lamentation or despondency . . . 500 negroes . . . a great many of whom are children and some old
and superannuated. The latter class, who would be supported
in a poor-house in England, enjoy here, to the end of their
days, the society of their neighbors and kinsfolk, and live at
large in separate houses assigned to them. . . . If a mistress
should lay on any young woman here the injunction so common in English newspaper advertisements for a maid of all
work, "no followers allowed," it would be considered an extraordinary act of tyranny. . . .

. . . the hospital consists of three separate wards, all perfectly clean and well-ventilated. . . . lying-in women . . .
are always allowed a month's rest after their confinement, an
advantage rarely enjoyed by hard-working English peasants.
. . . In general they refuse to take medicine from any other
hands but those of their master and mistress. . . . If the
mistress pays a visit to Savannah . . . she is overwhelmed
with commissions, so many of the slaves wishing to lay out
their small gains in various indulgences. . . . the sight of the
whip was painful to me as a mark of degradation, reminding
me that the lower order of slaves are kept to their work by
mere bodily fear, and that their treatment must depend on
the individual character of the owner or overseer. . . . the
negroes are often taught to read, and they learn much in
Sunday Schools, and for the most part are desirous of instruction. . . . The female slave is proud of her connection
with a white man, and thinks it an honor to have a mulatto
child. . . . Yet the mixed offspring is not very numerous.
. . . The coloured women who become the mistresses of
white men are neither rendered miserable nor degraded, as
are the white women who are seduced in Europe . . .*

---

* *Second Visit to the United States,* I; 352-367. Southern critics of Fanny
Kemble, specially Phillips, make much of Lyell's not unfavorable impressions of the plantations on St. Simon's and Butler's Islands that she
described so dismally. The point must be qualified by the fact that in
the seven-year interval both plantations had seen change of management.

"My nigger had a monstrous easy time, because I warn't used to having anybody do anything for me, but Buck's was on the jump most of the time."   —Huckleberry Finn

I have quoted Lyell at such length as responsible antidote for, and topical review of, much that has gone before. It would not displease me if readers should stop at this point and turn to reading Lyell, Olmsted, Fanny Kemble, Mrs. Smedes, William Johnson, *et al.*, in order to make up their own minds. Even witnesses of such high quality as that list by no means agree, of course. But on at least one point the sober geologist and the mercurial actress saw eye to eye: "To the dominant race," Lyell wrote, "one of the most serious evils of slavery is its tendency to blight domestic happiness, and the anxiety of parents for their sons, and a constant fear of their licentious intercourse with slaves, is painfully great."

Lyell might also have included daughters, as Fanny Kemble found. Not that the virtue of Southern white girls was often threatened in the same sense.* But what appalled Pierce

---

The lady's keen anti-slavery feelings did not keep her from being honestly well impressed—as she was not on her husband's plantations—by the way the Coupers did things at Hopeton.

* The Rev. John Rankin who, though an Abolitionist, was a born Southerner and no liar, said he could mention "several instances of slaves actually seducing the daughters of their masters . . . in the most respectable slaveholding families." (*Letters on Slavery;* 69.) Such couplings seem actually to have been very rare indeed after the middle of the eighteenth century. Rape of white women by Negroes was also infrequent but not, as professional Southerners often assert, unknown before Emancipation. Hundley, an ante bellum Southern witness, mentions such rapes as often the work of "spoiled and petted blacks belonging to owners who gave them too much latitude." (*Social Relations in Our Southern States;* 353.)

Butler's difficult wife was the effect on little Sally Butler of "the universal eagerness with which slaves sprang to obey her little gestures of command. She said something about a swing, and in less than five minutes headman Frank had erected it for her, a dozen young slaves were ready to swing 'little missis' —think of learning to rule despotically your fellow-creatures before the first lesson of self-government has been well spelt over!" Captain Hall had already written that "the slaves themselves delight in encouraging 'young master' or even 'young mistress' to play the tyrant over them. What at first is mere sport, becomes in time serious earnest." Earlier still Jefferson told a French inquirer:

> The whole commerce between master and slave is a perpetual exercise of the most boisterous passions, the most unremitting despotism on one part, and degrading submission on the other. The children see this, and learn to imitate it. . . . The parent storms, the child . . . puts on the same airs in the circle of smaller slaves, gives a loose to the worst of passions, and thus nursed, educated, and daily exercised in tyranny, cannot but be stamped with odious peculiarities. 5

Consider also the custom of giving each planter's child a slightly older slave boy or girl (according to sex) as lifetime body servant subject to the child's whims and any incidental juvenile experiments in sadism. Thus in 1779 Richard Taliaferro of Virginia left each of his grandchildren "a negro Boy and Girl apiece, as near their own age as conveniently may be out of my own stock of Slaves." No doubt this originated in the eighteenth-century fashion of making servile pets of small Negroes.* Under ideal conditions this lifetime assignment meant immense loyalty from the slave and genuine af-

---

* The West Indian French offer parallels here too: That will of the Empress Josephine's mother bequeathed to a small nephew-godson "a little Negro named André, aged 4, son of the slave called Marthe" and a two-and-a-half-year-old colt. (Fermor, *Traveller's Tree;* 97.)

fection from the master. But the fact that it sometimes turned out better than it deserved is no recommendation. To some degree the effect on the white child must always have been pernicious. No wonder planters so often told Captain Hall that slavery had necessarily "had a deleterious effect . . . on their own character."

The best conceivable slaveholder was actually like a conscientious officer seeking discipline without the moral support of proper articles of war;* with no courts-martial meting out responsible justice; no superiors on inspections to correct individual mistakes; no parliamentary questions asked; no relatives to demand redress for the rank and file on occasion. "I have seen something of the world," said Sir Arthur Helps, a man of incisive intelligence, "and . . . I think I know about *five* persons who might be entrusted with the supreme authority over their fellow creatures which is given by law to the slaveholder, indiscriminately in many a slave state." The cumulative effect after several generations helps to explain the traveling Southerner's—and the back-country redneck's—unsavory reputation in the ante bellum North for savage rages and physical violence. Mark Twain localized Old Man Boggs and Colonel Sherburne and Buck Harkness in Arkansas, but they would have fitted just as well into long-established, high-prestige Natchez. In the North such of their ways as came of pioneering circumstances tended to fade as settlements matured. In the South certain fixatives—slavery probably the most mordant of them—kept all sharp and clear. Jefferson had good reason to assert, "The man must be a prodigy who can retain his manners and morals undepraved by such circumstances." † s

---

* True, all slave states had some sort of laws against cruel and unusual punishment of slaves, separating mothers and children, and so on. But the evidence is scandalously plain that such laws were so laxly enforced as to have no general effect on treatment of slaves.

† *Notes on Virginia;* 160. This can be too definite. Vestigial influence from Scottish and Scots-Irish ways probably underlay the pioneer's

Over and over the decent planter told the visitor that, to keep his children halfway civilized, he had to send them North to school; that the whole iniquitous system was more deleterious to white masters than to black chattels. Unwary outsiders of good will, often including temperate and intelligent Northerners who disliked slavery, sometimes took such talk to mean that the South might gradually lose her addiction to slavery. If so many responsible Southerners felt as they said they did over drinks, why should they continue to insist on not only maintaining but spreading slavery?

This question underlay the successive compromises over slave territory and the Republican position set forth by Lincoln. Mrs. Stowe contributed greatly to it by making Mrs. Shelby and St. Clare such explicit antislavery Southerners. Unfortunately the astute minds of that time, when thinking was mechanistic, optimistic, utilitarian, lacked the intellectual tools for seeing that by 1850 slavery was primarily an emotional habit of the South, a fetish obsession. The position of these candid Southerners was basically false, a glib rationalizing, a passing of the buck, a responsibility-dodging whine: "Slavery is not our fault. Why blame us for what previous generations saddled us with? We've got a bear by the tail and don't know how to let go. Nor can Northerners suggest anything to the purpose because they don't know niggers. We do. And anything that we are forced to do in order to keep our grip on the bear's tail always hurts us worse than it does the niggers. They're better off than we are." The ready rebuttal

---

taste for prolonged feuds and physical redress of personal grievances. The brutalizing effect of slavery does not account for the Hatfield-McCoy sort of thing in neighborhoods where slavery had never effectually penetrated. The specially brutal terms of Southern-cum-frontier fighting— eye gouging, ear chewing, mouth ripping—may well have been partly a heritage from the transported convicts. Henry Adams saw the germ of it in the Yorkshire rough-and-tumble school of fighting. (*Formative Years,* I; 28.) But it remains true that even in long-settled states such as South Carolina slavery—or something—kept nudging young men toward exhibitionistic bad temper and physical outrage.

was seldom made: "Have you ever been a nigger and a slave? Go black up and try it before you dare say that."

In spite of Jefferson's bitterness the Southern slaveholding class went on creating numbers of civilized gentlemen—congenital patricians such as Thomas Dabney and Robert E. Lee, self-made ones such as Jefferson Davis. Honor the old North Carolina planter who summoned his slaves to his deathbed to tell them: "I have treated you all right; if I have wronged you, I beg your pardons." **N** And the South Carolina planter who paid $1200 for Phoebe, "daughter of my old and faithful man, Thomas . . . who has no child belonging to me. Hence my willingness to gratify him in his declining years." That any such masters could appear by 1850 speaks well for their own and their parents' moral stamina and emotional stability.

Jefferson Davis, a very decent man, carried *noblesse oblige* to extremes in handling slaves. He eschewed white overseers, making his body servant from the Army, James Pemberton, head overseer of Briarfield, his large cotton plantation. Master and James worked side by side on the log house that was the first building there. With his prim courtesy master always asked James to sit down when he came on plantation business and, at the end of the conference, invited him to choose a cigar just as if he had been entertaining General Quitman. Briarfield tolerated no slave nicknames. Few had the dignity of surnames, as James did, but as far as possible field hands were prevented from calling one another Abe and Andy. It was Abraham and Andrew.

After James Pemberton died in 1852, the Davises had great difficulty in finding overseers. The reason was plain: Their policies were bound to strike any white overseer as a subversive mixture of sacrilege, sabotage and criminal lunacy. Joseph Davis's axiom, zealously applied by the younger brother too, was that "the less the negroes were disciplined by force, the better they could conduct themselves." * They

---

* Heavy reliance here on Fleming's fine monograph, "Jefferson Davis, the Negroes . . . ," *Sewanee Review,* October, 1908. When taken to

were encouraged to hire their time, save money, set up for themselves, as did Ben T. Montgomery* who operated Davis Bend for a while after the Civil War. They were shielded from arbitrary punishment by their own courts, in which slave judges charged slave juries drawn from special panels of "settled individuals" among them and in which slave witnesses testified on oath. Master's reserved power to mitigate sentence was often used, since the slave juries tended to impose heavier penalties than he thought condign.† The system took root, and the newly freed slaves kept it up among themselves after the Yankees occupied the Davis plantations. A Federal officer made a fool of himself by adducing it to show how spontaneously Negro freedmen could create self-government. But none of this means that the Davises ever saw potential equals in their black chattels or that it ever occurred to them that James could be referred to as Mr. Pemberton. It all seems to have been merely manifestation of their own grave decency combined with effort to fit their slaves to do the best that in them lay, as if they had been hopelessly retarded children.

Richmond as master's body servant in 1861, James Pemberton's son took the first opportunity to run away and become a "contraband" at Ft. Monroe.

* Eventually Montgomery and other Negroes, backed by the Yazoo & Mississippi Railroad, which wanted to develop its area, founded the all-Negro community of Mound Bayou, Mississippi, inland and up the river from Greenville. The place has had its troubles but also intervals of doing well and remains a valued local center of Negro medicine and cooperative associations. Physically it looks just about like any straggly, white-dominated Delta town of comparable size.

† I have found no other plantations giving Negroes as much latitude as did the Davis operations. The slave-court idea alone was tried, however, and shown capable of success elsewhere by the elder Couper on St. Simon's Island (Bremer, *Homes of the New World,* II; 189) and A. S. Morehead of Copiah County, Mississippi. (Sydnor, *Slavery in Mississippi;* 76.)

4 *Darling Nellie Gray*

If Davis Bend or Hopeton or Olmsted's easygoing farmer was
slavery at its best, what was its worst? The auction block and
the leg irons, and the blubbering at the sale of slaves to settle
the estate of the late Peter Wilks. Even worse than any work-
'em-up-and-buy-more sugar plantation was the slave coffle—
the very word coming from the wicked old African trade—
of bought-and-sold exiles marching down the big road, shuffle
and clank, stare dully at the strange countryside, squat and
feed. It was just like what Mungo Park saw in West Africa in
the 1780's, except that women and children usually walked
loose under guard, only the men being ironed "like a string
of fish on a trotline," as young Lincoln observed. Sometimes,
however, both sexes and all ages were in chains. [5]

This coffle may include young Isom Cole, whom Colonel
Edmondson of Halifax Courthouse, Virginia, sold in 1837 to
James Williamson, a "speculator," as the South euphemized
the slave dealer. At the same sale another dealer bought Isom's
sister. Isom never saw her again, never even knew to what part

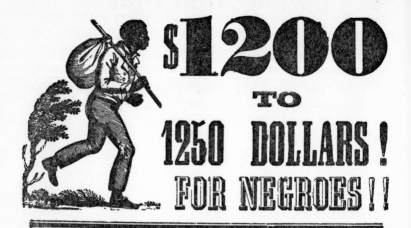

$1200

TO

1250 DOLLARS!

FOR NEGROES!!

THE undersigned wishes to purchase a large lot of NEGROES for the New Orleans market. I will pay $1200 to $1250 for No. 1 young men, and $850 to $1000 for No. 1 young women. In fact I will pay more for likely

NEGROES,

Than any other trader in Kentucky. My office is adjoining the Broadway Hotel, on Broadway, Lexington, Ky., where I or my Agent can always be found.

WM. F. TALBOTT.

LEXINGTON, JULY 2, 1853.

of the slavery world she was taken. Isom himself was exported southward in a coffle of ninety-nine slaves and twenty-nine horses for all of which Williamson found a market in the booming Black Belt of Alabama. Colonel Price, of Union-town, paid $600 for Isom, though he was only twelve years old. Five years later the Colonel refused $2000 for him, or so Isom boasted when, in 1914, they asked him about the old day. . . .

The coffle plods along, heads down and shoulders drooping. The dealer rides up the line and orders a song. The stock in trade sing. With the same purpose a Kentucky dealer used to head his coffles with a pair of fiddlers and an American flag. Slaves in transit on steamboats were often relieved of their irons so that they could dance and keep in good condition, a trick going back to the Guinea slave ships. Dancing often warmed them to a vacantly diverted burst of foot patting and hand clapping while the white passengers leaned over the rail, nodding in time and wishing that the Abolitionists could see what contented animals niggers really were. The dealer valued such "showing a good spirit," since his prospective customers mistrusted gloomy-looking and very possibly sulky specimens of slave.

Whether traveling afoot or sleeping in the sun on a steamboat, these exiles were at least better off than if shipped in the *Tribune* or the *Uncas*, Isaac Franklin's steam slaver brigs that made regular trips between Alexandria, Virginia, and the mouth of the Mississippi. Eighty women forward and 100 men aft were stowed Guinea-style, lying "as close as they can" on decks half a man's height apart. Perhaps because they were usually allowed on deck all day in good weather, perhaps because the voyage was shorter than the dread middle passage, they usually landed in fair shape in New Orleans or Natchez. Washed, got into neat new clothes,* they were fed to plumpness in the dealer's camp or the town slave-jail—equivalents of a stockyard. Then singly or in small lots, no doubt with some initial effort to keep families or at least mothers and children together, they were taken to the house flying a red flag, or to the local slave market with sheltering roof and open loggia or to the traditional spot under the big tree on the courthouse square. Printed broadsides have informed all and

---

* The outfit, according to Ingraham (*South-West By a Yankee,* II; 194) consisted for men of a black fur hat, corduroy roundabout and trousers, a white shirt and good strong shoes. He says that newly bought slaves soon discarded these easily identifiable clothes, since they did not wish it to be so plain that, through either their own fault or their master's troubles, they had been sold away from home.

sundry of the details. The slaves of John Carter, of Lewis County, Kentucky, are to be sold at public auction "On account of his removal to Indiana, a Free State":

3 BUCKS, Aged from 20 to 26, Strong Ablebodied
1 WENCH, Sallie, Aged 42, Excellent Cook
1 WENCH, Lize, Aged 23 with 6 Mo. old Picininny
One Buck Aged 52, good Kennel Man
17 BUCKS Aged from twelve to twenty, Excellent.

Auctioning off a slave-baby as conceived by an Abolitionist artist. Note the chains on the right and the whip on the left.

Since public opinion at the South put breaking up families out of the question, the teen-age bucks mentioned must all have been orphans.

"Buy me, massa, I got plenty work left in me, I ain't like these young whippersnappers got no gumption. . . ."

"There's a likely wench, major, but 'pears like she don't breed. Three years grown and no young 'uns yet. . . . Hold up your head, gal, how'd you come to lose them teeth?"

"Now, Mr. Peterson, I'm looking for a big buck nigger for a man for my cook. She's wall-eyed and rising thirty but I guess she's still frolicsome, anyway she told my old woman she's bleeged to have a man."

A slave auction rated with Daniel Webster, Trenton Falls, Auburn Prison and Girard College as one of the principal objectives of the alien sightseer. The prospective bidders' examination of the stock, male and female, was a titillating feature, though to them, as an authority on the domestic slave trade points out, "it was probably only a matter of plain business. Purchasers and spectators were about as indifferent to the nudity and sex of ordinary slaves as everybody is to those of small children. To be otherwise indicated pruriency or hypocrisy rather than virtue; the inspection was one of the least painful features of the sale. But many visitors liked to report how dreadfully they were shocked." Sensitive Southerners were nevertheless harassedly ashamed of these occasions. Mrs. Chesnut felt "faint, seasick" when she saw a bedizened mulatto girl up for sale in Richmond. A few days later, walking with an Englishwoman who was determined to see nothing bad in the South, she passed the same auction again in action: "If you can stand that," she told her companion, "no other Southern thing need choke you."

Southerners often made a squeamish point of despising the speculator as something between usurer and hangman. It was a major complaint against *Uncle Tom* that it showed Mr. Shelby, the Southern gentleman, drinking hob and nob with Haley, the slave trader, a thing allegedly unthinkable. Francis Scott Key, known now as author of "The Star Spangled Banner," then as a lawyer and pillar of the American Colonization Society, said that churches would not accept slave traders as "professors of religion." Presbyterian congregations sometimes did censure members guilty of slave trading. Planters moving by sea to the Southwest might write on the manifests covering passage: ". . . the owner of these slaves . . . is not a dealer in human flesh." It was said that even decent men entering this trade were soon corrupted by having to deal "with the most refractory and brutal of the slave population, since good and honest slaves were rarely permitted to fall into the unscrupulous hands of the speculator." That is a flat lie. True, recalcitrant slaves were often threatened with being "sold South," and the threat might be carried out.* But debt and death also gave many a dealer ample access to many a well-behaved slave at forced sale.

Nor should much stock be put in the alleged ostracism of such dealers. No doubt the "quality" looked down on the run of them, but so did they on horse traders. Let a slave dealer turn wealthy benefactor of the community, like John Mc-Donogh, of New Orleans, or prosperous hero, like N. B. Forrest, and much was forgiven. At one period Andrew Jackson stained his hands with slave dealing. Having been a slave trader may have kept Isaac Franklin from entering politics as a man of his wealth and prestige might otherwise have done, but "He was not a social outcast . . . he moved in a social circle which befitted his wealth" and married the daughter of a Presbyterian minister who had been a law partner of Senator Thomas H. Benton. [5] A warm apologist for slavery wrote that, in Mississippi in the 1830's, "Planters associate with [slave traders] freely enough in the way of business, but notice them no further." [5] Henry Laurens of South Carolina, a great Revolutionary leader, wealthiest Charleston merchant of his day, got much of his capital from slave trading, even though he did deplore slavery. Charleston brokers dealing in slaves as readily as in rice or land often carried the proudest

---

* Thus R. F. W. Allston to his wife in 1863 (*South Carolina Rice Plantation;* 194) about his slave Brass: "I sent him up to split Rails and told him upon his repeated failure that he must go to the vendue table . . . send him to Robertson Blacklock and Co. to be turned into money forthwith. It is the best thing to be done with Brass. There must be no fuss about it, no noise, or notice." On p. 426 it appears that Brass fetched $1600, a price probably reflecting inflation due to the war, since that would have been a high price for even a docile, prime field hand anywhere in 1860.

names of the Palmetto State: de Saussure, Gadsden, Heyward.
It is another case of whipping boy. Feeling that slave trading
was a nasty business, the slaveowner unloaded the onus on
the other party.

SLAVES WAITING FOR SALE, VIRGINIA.

Sketched in Richmond by Eyre Crowe, travelling as secretary with Thackeray.

A Southern historian soundly surmises that slave traders
"cannot have been full of the milk of human kindness, or
they would never have entered upon their callings." But there
were exceptions even among speculators who never rose to
eminence. The bestially named Mr. Bruin of the slave-trading
firm of Bruin & Hill, of Alexandria, sounds like a kindly man
in Abolitionists' accounts of his eager help in arranging to
have unfortunate slave girls bought free. An upcountry Caro-

lina refugee secretly besought a local slave trader to buy him
from a mean master "as he runs," that is, to buy title to a
runaway, catch-him-if-you-can, a common arrangement. When
master surlily refused this solution, the dealer fired up, said,
"I hope you never get your nigger back, sir," and supplied
the runaway with clothes, money and opportunity to get away
scatheless to Ohio. And a strange picture of the callous, brutal
dealer comes from an abolitionist emissary describing a Baltimore speculator:

> . . . one is ready to conceive that . . . the unfortunate slaves
> will instinctively shrink from him as from a demon. And yet
> . . . this man is reported, to be a most mild and indulgent
> master, and an upright and scrupulously honest man. . . .
> His word is implicitly relied on by all who know him. When
> he makes his appearance among his slaves, they gather round
> him with every demonstration of affection; and even the
> little children manifest the most eager solicitude to share in
> his attentions.

Whatever was thought of the trade and the traders, those
red flags kept flying, come one, come all, at Richmond and
the Charleston Exchange and the Forks of the Road. Demand
in the new lands of the Southwest was largely for prime field
hands, so the goal of the dealer exploiting this rising market
was to make up his lots principally from robust young men,
healthy young women and likely adolescents. It was often out
of the question to keep families together. The master might
do his best—John Cheesborough, of Charleston, offered his
man York to a local lady for several hundred dollars less than
could be got for him if sold West, "so that he may be with
his family." **5** But such sacrifice of values could not be expected of executors of estates or sheriffs selling assets by court
order. Businessmen disapproved of wills softheartedly direct-
ing that slave families be kept together, for such terms meant
fewer dollars per capita. **5** Hence, though gentlemen in the

crowd might frown, though the auctioneer might maneuver to keep close relatives in the same "lots," couples were frequently parted and mothers sold away from children. Couples were, in fact, sometimes listed in different lots in the dealer's prospectus. 5

It would have been a loathsome business even without the slaves' vague but lively and well-founded dread of being "sold South" or "down the river," a phrase now embedded in the American language. It was shortsighted of the South, poor public relations, so long to block abolition of the slave trade in the District of Columbia where, until 1850, dealers flourished and kept slave coffles slouching through the streets of Freedom's capital under the noses of Northern and European visitors and issue-seeking Yankee politicians.

Sale or threat of it occasioned many of the runaways that kept nudging Northern conscience and reddening Southern temper. Northerners could not see the Yankee schooners loading human freight at Norfolk for New Orleans. But many Northern towns saw runaways coming out of the Border States, the slave-exporting states, in a troubling trickle of which Abolition made the most, lacing its propaganda with grisly advertisements from Southern newspapers, all of them genuine, since faking was unhappily needless:

> "Ran away, a negro woman and two children. A few days before she went off, I burned her with a hot iron . . . tried to make the letter M."
> "Ran away, a negro man named Henry; his left eye out, some scars from a dirk on and under his left arm, and much scarred with the whip."
> "Ran away, Sam . . . shot a short time since through the hand. . . ." *

---

* These are culled from the selection in Dickens's *American Notes.* Almost invariably the source of such texts is from among the hundreds of examples supplied in Weld, *American Slavery As It Is,* the great Abolitionist's handbook.

The reader now knows a little of what lay behind these runaways. It is thirdhand, wordy knowledge, but all that is now left of slavery except the slave market shown to tourists, a few irons, some unusually durable quarters—and the festerings that it occasioned.

Since runaways were Mrs. Stowe's left bower, we now need a closer look at them, at the prototypes of Eliza and George Harris and the originals of the heartwarming people who helped them.

THE NORTH STAR

"As one reads . . . visions rise of the roads from the South congested with escaping blacks, jostled by long lines of United States marshals dragging their shrieking victims back to bondage." —HIBBEN, Henry Ward Beecher

193
63
130

Pa was away, on law business likely. Nobody home but mom, bub and sis, and here came word to shift them runaways quick—slave catchers only a few hours off and moving fast. Pa was Judge Thomas Lee, of Jefferson County, Ohio, an experienced Underground Railroad "conductor" for whom the emergency would have been nothing out of the way. In his absence they had to send the boy. Only ten years old, he was to drive three passengers eighteen miles at night over bad roads to the station in the next county run by a family named Work.

As the wagon gritted and creaked along and the Negroes under the bagged oats ceased to whisper and rustle and the equivocal silhouettes of trees against the starlight grew less familiar, the boy's eyes must have grown very round and the leather "lines" in his hands ever wetter and smellier. Toward morning, though he had faithfully followed what directions he had, the party was pretty well lost, the human part of it anyway. The old mare on the near side, Fly her name was, had been on many of these expeditions, however, and knew the Works's gate as well as she did her own stall. On reaching it in the dark she stopped dead with elderly conclusiveness. The boy was most unsure. What he could make out in the gloom was no help. He probably flapped the lines on Fly's fat old back, flicked her rump with the whip, perhaps even ventured "Giddap! G'long!" Having no good reason to obey, she continued to nuzzle the gate, and the boy gave in. The wagon creaked up the lane. He got down and rapped the prearranged signal on a window—*suppose it was the wrong place.* . . . It wasn't. The old mare had safely delivered another Underground "excursion."

The UGRR had such fourfooted heroes, even martyrs. After a long career of speeding fugitives out of danger in Illinois, White Lightning, Dr. Richard Eells's beautiful harness mare was killed by slave catchers in the shafts of the pilot buggy of an excursion. James Wagg, of Ripley County, Indiana, called his old white horse King William the Emancipator* because he had led so many slaves to freedom. When John Hogue, of Greenville, Pennsylvania, refused entrance to a yellow dog accompanying runaways from Virginia, a woman among them said: "Sir, if you only knew how he gave us the Alarm in the Woods in the Night you wood let him in. The Only dog—" Hogue wrote, obviously still wondering at his own softheartedness after fifty years—"the Only dog that ever slept in my House. . . ." †

The bulk of legends about the Underground Railroad were founded on fact. This time Mrs. Stowe's sins were not so much of direct misrepresentation as of misplaced emphasis

---

*This refers to William IV, king of England when the Negroes of the British West Indies were freed. The UGRR often used white horses as particularly easy for fugitives to follow in the dark.

† From a letter in the magnificent Siebert Collection in the Harvard College Library. Most of the data in this section are from the Siebert papers.

and implied exaggerations of scale. But that is a pity again, for the real UGRR was much more stirring and informative than any melodrama that she could create from exceptional data.

The Mende, a sturdy West African people who both bred and purveyed slaves for America, knew how to keep them from absconding. A new one, whether a war captive or bought from a dealer, was made to wash his feet and eat rice cooked in the water used. After that, for magical reasons in which both he and his owner believed, he was assumed unable to run away.‡ It probably also helped that he was more or less the same color as his enslavers and his half-acknowledged privileges of dalliance with the girls soon mingled his offspring into the community. In any case, though West Africa was thoroughly committed to slavery, one seldom hears of runaways there. The likeliest reason is the same as that which kept the cotton South relatively free of this hazard: A West African UGRR would have had nowhere to go.

This same slave, however, sold to white men and shipped to the Americas, received no such prophylaxis against "drapetomania," the term solemnly concocted by Dr. Cartwright for what he diagnosed as an endemic neural disease causing slaves to run away. The sequellae of this curious ailment were sometimes permanent. Slave fugitives from the Dutch and British in Guiana formed quasi-African, self-ruling communities that flourish to this day, one understands, in the upriver jungles of Surinam. In Jamaica slaves from the Gold Coast, mostly the stiff-necked and turbulent Fanti, took to

‡ Little, *The Mende;* 36. Puckett (*Folk Beliefs of the Southern Negro;* 317) has a possible American cognate in the Negro belief that a cat got to lick her paws will settle down better in a new house.

the mountains and founded colonies of Maroons that held out against the British for a hundred years; some of their villages still survive. Dissatisfied Negro slaves early sifted through the Georgia swamps to Florida, where Spain tolerated them as a sort of buffer against Indians. In 1826 a few of them, settled round an abandoned fort on the Appalachicola River under a leader named Garçon, captured a U.S. Army supply convoy and burned one of its men. Red-hot shot from a consequent punitive expedition noisily wiped them out by exploding their magazine of a thousand barrels of gunpowder.

These were hostile to Indians and so, no doubt, was the tiny but doughty runaways' colony in the Belle Isle Swamps of Georgia, dislodged only after generous offers of blood-money made it worth while for the local Indians to exterminate them. But other fugitives fused with Creek renegades to establish the Seminole people—a mixture that helped to provoke the little wars that brought Florida into the Union as high-handed prize of Andrew Jackson.* Later the putative slave status of the wife of Osceola combined with his own part-Negro ancestry to bring about that foul disgrace, the seizure of his person and his death in captivity.

Barring such exceptions, stateside runaway colonies were fragile and small, like most little groups on islands in Chesapeake Bay that Admiral Sir George Cockburn armed and set ashore for nuisance value when he and General Ross were harrying the area in 1814; or the periodically decimated but never annihilated group of fugitives in the Cypress Swamp of Alabama. Most of our runaways either returned to duty or kept running until lost among the free Negroes in the North and in Canada.†

---

* Indians' relations with fugitive slaves outside the South were inconsistent. Siebert's material gives some cases of their generously helping runaways, others of their selling them to slave catchers.

† I mistrust estimates, e.g., Buckmaster, *Let My People Go;* 18, that the Great and adjacent "Dismals" contained 2000 runaways at one time.

Taken to a Tom-show late in life, Harriet Tubman, once the most redoubtable Negro conductor on the UGRR, thought Eliza's escape "ill managed" and apparently felt that *she* could have arranged it better, as no doubt she could have. " 'Bloodhounds,' she said disdainfully, eyeing the two disconsolate mastiffs who appeared in the roles, 'I nevah made no min' of bloodhounds.' " Actually, neither in fact nor in Mrs. Stowe's fiction did Eliza have dogs to contend with. For she was a real person and, much as enemies of *Uncle Tom* scoffed at her great feat, really did cross the Ohio River ice under circumstances of equal panic and great peril.

Ice played a part in many abscondings. A party of Kentucky slaves consigned to the Cincinnati UGRR crossed the Ohio in sleighs when it was frozen solid. Nine fugitives crossed Lake Erie on foot in the dead of winter—thirty miles of ice with no guide but a pocket compass and a blizzard threatening. One likely prototype of Eliza crossed the Ohio at Greenup, Kentucky, towing behind a ferryman's boat in weather so cold that her baby died of exposure and she was plagued with rheumatism the rest of her life. Another is said to have carried a rope and a plank and, instead of leaping from floe to floe, Eliza-style, bridged her way across. But the most dramatic ice work—anyway that with the most spectators—occurred when the ferry from Detroit to

---

Two hundred would stretch credulity. The Great Dismal, an unfrequented wilderness, could not have supplied fish and game for both its lumbermen and any substantial number of fugitives. On such subjects anything like accurate data is impossible anyway.

Canada put back one day in January, 1852, because the ice in the river was a little too thick for the engines to buck. On board was William Johnson, a slave run away from a mean Kentuckian and determined "to cross over or die," he said afterward. Seeing that the boat was giving up, he leaped overboard and started walking across the unbroken ice beyond her prow. "It seemed as though the ice waved as I walked, but I got across all right 'nough, and de people threw a heavin' line to me and helped me up."

The likeliest original for Eliza* came across the Ohio to Ripley when, though not actually broken into cakes, the ice was so rotten that nobody had dared venture on it for twenty-four hours and water was standing in pools on top of it. The only recorded spectator was an unidentified Ohioan. Mrs. Stowe fleshed the boniness of this incident with by-gosh dialogue in which Eliza recognizes him as a kind neighbor from Kentucky, opportune presence unexplained. Actually he was no such trite *deus ex machina*. Presumably he had observed her splashing progress with amazement that became pity as he successively identified her as a woman and a Negro and saw that she carried a child. The hand that he reached down to her must have been as warm and strong but fumbling as his own emotions.

He probably had no direct UGRR connections because he did not refer her to any of the several active Underground agents who lived in the prim little houses that still stand there on the river bank. But he had local knowledge enough for her purpose. She seems to have known only that a "good man" this side of the river helped fugitives. In reply to her gasping question, this opportune angel, who probably wore deplorable cowhide boots, chewed tobacco and hadn't bathed since the preceding September, pointed aloft to the house of

---

* This is just my own personal choice. The evidence is well reviewed in Nye, "Eliza Crossing the Ice . . . ," *Bulletin of the Historical and Philosophical Society of Ohio,* April, 1950.

the Rev. John Rankin, Abolitionist leader,* perched high on
the bluff above the town. "Eliza" made for it, the man turned
away into anonymous immortality. He should have a statue
there at the river's edge, reaching down, awkward, no doubt
half-diffident about it all, shaken off balance by the demands
of pathos, probably never mentioning it to his wife. He
could represent all the nondoctrinaire men and women
whose inability to resist the impulse to clothe the naked, feed
the hungry and succor the afflicted was the ballast of the
UGRR.

It was a powerful impulse; the occasion was often heart
wringing. Thus the Mattesons of Seville, Ohio, took in a
poor black devil who said he hadn't seen the inside of a house
since leaving Kentucky, some 200 miles away.

> The roads were rough, snow on the ground. . . . His shoes
> were so bad that it was hardly possible to keep them on . . .
> his feet so sore he could only walk with great pain. . . . The
> poor man was kept . . . two or three days. Mother gave him
> warm stockings, father took him to a shoemaker in Seville
> . . . who gave him some good stout shoes. The man was
> completely overcome and said he didn't know he had so many
> friends in the world.

Thousands were thus helped to freedom—not millions, as
the legends imply, but enough to make it clear that good
people are widespread. A few such passengers had been urged
to seek freedom by atypical workers on the UGRR. But
this was no underground as the world now thinks of these
things. It was kept deliberately shapeless, too tenuous to be
called an organization, designed not so much to alleviate the

---

* Mrs. Stowe seems first to have heard of "Eliza" from Rankin at a
Presbyterian synod. This Southern-born enemy of slavery ran a combined theological coaching school and UGRR station in a neat little
red-brick house that still stands on the bluff above Ripley as a historical
shrine. The students' lights in its upper windows are said to have been
known to Kentucky slaves as reliable guides for runaways.

lot of slaves by funneling them out of the South as to assuage conscience when a needy fugitive appeared on his own
initiative. Some links in the network, which pervaded practically all states north of slavery, attempted formal organization, including the use of tokens to identify passengers and
make certain that they were not planted spies.* And there
might be sewing circles to supply stout and well-mended
clothes for the use of ragged fugitives. But on the whole the
UGRR was as evanescent as lantern light, as insubstantial as
the thudding suck of hooves plodding through a muddy road
in bad weather, as informal as chicken stealing.†

"The best plan," said a UGRR agent in Illinois, "was not
to let the left hand know what the right hand was doing.
That made [Undergrounders] poor witnesses in court." A
Quaker Hoosier agent had a "rigid rule" that no slave could

---

* Coin-shaped tokens used for this purpose round Toledo, Ohio, are
said to have carried the old device of the Emancipationists of Britain:
a kneeling slave with the motto, "Am I Not a Man and a Brother?"
For women fugitives, the figure was made female and "Sister" replaced
"Brother."

† Coleman (*Slavery Times in Kentucky;* 220) calls the UGRR "a highly
organized and thoroughly developed transportation system . . . despite
the drastic laws which made the road illegal." Nobody who has been
through Siebert's accumulation of case material at Harvard could conceivably agree with this. The exceptions, as noted above, are very minor.
The most viable was the Knights of Liberty, an organization of Negroes,
aimed at eliminating slavery, set up by the Rev. Moses Dickson, a Cincinnati free Negro working on river boats, in the early 1840's. Their
scheme was for their eleven members to promulgate freedom propaganda
in the South. In 1856 they decided that the situation warranted their
active support of the UGRR. Washington wrote (*Story of the Negro,*
II; 159-160) that "it was claimed that they assisted yearly thousands of
slaves to escape. The methods by which the Knights of Liberty expected
to accomplish their great objective have never been definitely known if,
indeed, they were ever definitely formulated." This is obviously all very
vague and probably was of miniature effect. But after the Civil War the
Knights were the nucleus of the Knights and Daughters of Tabor, an
influential and valuable Negro fraternal organization.

give his name or origin, so his "conductors" could truthfully say that they did not know. Another reason for the looseness of Underground organization was to handicap infiltrators: "We did think of forming a society with grips and pass-words, but . . . it was not considered safe, as spies could get into a society and we might in that way be betrayed." Thus, often the stationmaster of an Underground depot knew only the name and location of his colleagues immediately above and below him in the chain of posts. But another reason probably was that grips and passwords and sworn pledges, all smacking dreadfully of Masonry, were anathema to Quakers and thus unthinkable in a movement so dependent on them.

It is heartening thus to know how often whites' good will complemented Negro pluck. Neither such whites nor such Negroes were typical of their day, place or situation, yet their highly temporary relations improve one's faith in the human race. In the whole sad, painful story of American slavery, the UGRR rather than the cult of Abolition is the reconciling light spot in the composition. Some Underground workers were poor types. None was superhuman. But their activities usually carried a strong savor of that good and scandalously rare thing, man's humanity to man. "I claim no credit for the part I took," wrote the postmaster of Red Oak, Iowa, when historians came round to ask questions. "I did not incite anyone to flee but . . . I did not have it in my heart to betray a frightened human helpless creature who had committed no wrong & so far as I know was as worthy of succor as I would have been had I been thus situated."

What good talk that is! These were often great people. Gorham, Maine, resented the local UGRR agent, but its citizens went ingeniously out of their way to shield him and his passengers from slave catchers. An Ohio farm wife, caught between her own pitying instincts and conscience about the Federal laws against abetting fugitives, would admit Negro runaways to her kitchen, gravely put money and food on the table and then leave the room. In another Ohio community the UGRR men were harassedly trying to discourage slave catchers by running their passengers from one farm to another in a circle. Then a previously unsympathetic local character named James Henry appeared, saying, looky here, bring them niggers over to be hid on my place; them slave catchers won't never look for them here, they're boarding with me. Nobody was paying any attention to the reward involved—$2000, a small fortune in those times.

The slave catchers, loosely organized for mutual cooperation between one small-town vulture and the next north from Mason and Dixon's line, were in business for those rewards. Less predatory citizens were not. One morning the small son of Judge Benjamin Ross of Waynesburg, Pennsylvania, a convinced Democrat and anything but an Abolitionist, ran to his father panting that we can make $1500, those niggers they advertised for are hid in that old empty house up the hill. The Judge said shut your mouth, boy, and go tell your mother to send any spare victuals up there to feed them . . . When J. B. Turner, of Jacksonville, Illinois, found that his reputation for UGRR work was imperilling a batch of fresh fugitives, he took them round to a pro-Southern Presbyterian elder and said, "Here they are, turn them over to the law or take care of them—it's up to you." The elder took care of them. I should like also to have shaken hands with Harvey Chase, proslavery Illinois settler, to whom came a misdirected runaway actually seeking his antislavery brother and neighbor, James Chase. Harvey gave the fugitive careful directions for getting to James's house because, as he said, "the stranger came . . . in good faith and I, as a gentleman, was honor bound to keep the faith." Honorable men thus whipsawed between conscience and compassion often resorted to casuistry. Thus a banker in Crawfordsville, Indiana, paid regular UGRR "stock assessments" with the proviso, "Here it is but I don't want to know what you're doing with it."

Such marginal sympathies were the actual origin of the

UGRR, an institution certainly older than any bits of evidence that research has yet turned up. Well before the Revolution, New York State was plagued by runaways trying to reach Canada. George Washington complained that certain runaway slaves, some his, some other people's, were unlikely ever to be recovered because certain Philadelphia Quakers made a practice of helping them. By 1798 the legislature of Maryland was taking official cognizance of Jerseymen and Pennsylvanians giving illicit shelter to slave fugitives. In this period John Stapler, Quaker, of Bucks County, Pennsylvania, already had a wide reputation as a "friend to colored people," meaning that he was good for food, shelter and often a temporary job to help fugitives on their way to safety farther north. By 1820 the gradual transformation of New Jersey, New York and Pennsylvania into "free soil" had many people who greatly disapproved of slavery looking out for runaways. Even in Ohio, Indiana and Illinois, where only the great Northwest Ordinance had kept out a slavery disguised as "voluntary servitude under indenture," such attitudes were convenient for absconders.

A Negro slave could stand on the left bank of the Ohio and see the light shimmer on the willow leaves on the other, but that did not necessarily move him to do much about it. A former slave interviewed in the 1930's had rowed a hundred runaways to freedom, he guessed, without having felt inspired to try it himself. A Kentucky slave who had thus ferried some thirty fugitives across the Ohio followed suit for himself only when the owner of his children broke her promise never to sell them out of the neighborhood. But the temperaments of slaves differed as widely as those of any other people and, as Yankees with antislavery principles infiltrated the trans-Ohio states and Quakers moved up from the Carolinas to get away from the moral scandal of slavery, a poor black devil on the run was ever likelier to find Middle Western friends and allies.

The Underground Railroad is said to have been named

apropos of Levi Coffin, the sly Quaker prominent in its Middle Western operations. Certain slave hunters who frequently lost track of their quarry near the Quaker-dominated town of Richmond, Indiana, where Coffin was settled, complained, he said, that "they could never get the slightest intelligence of their slaves after they reached my house . . . there must be an Underground Railroad of which I was president." Others rated "President" of the UGRR were Robert Purvis, free Negro of Philadelphia, and Peter Stewart of Joliet County, Illinois. Which best deserved the title would be hard to say.* The metaphor naturally led to an elaborate but seldom serious jargon of "switch-points," "junctions," "excursion-trains," "stationmasters," and so on, to amuse the strait-laced and usually solemn participants.

Under certain conditions almost anybody might get tangled up in UGRR work. Generally, however, its consistent personnel came from four groups: Quakers, usually of the Hicksite (liberal) group; Yankees; those Covenanter (or "Free" or "Seceder") Presbyterians who, like Southern Quakers, had freed their slaves and moved to the Middle West; and Northern Negroes, either legally free or successful fugitives themselves. The Yankees were rife in upper New York, northern Ohio, northern Illinois, as well as in New England, where, though it caused much commotion, the UGRR had little serious existence. Quakers were crucial to it in Ohio, Indiana and Iowa, as well as in their traditional stronghold, eastern Pennsylvania. Mrs. Stowe's emphasis on them in *Uncle Tom* is well taken. Many a fugitive had been made aware that the broad Quaker hat and the queer Quaker coat betokened safety

---

* Another legend originates the name round Columbia, Pennsylvania, key center for smuggling fugitives, and involves both Quakers and a redoubtable colony of free Negroes. A third, endorsed by W. H. Siebert, the great authority on the UGRR, hinges on the mysterious disappearance of one Tice Davids, a fugitive swimming the Ohio at Ripley, the same place where Eliza was immortalized.

and help. Many another, often male, was smuggled to freedom in the voluminous Quaker gown and deep Quaker bonnet.

The relation was not inevitable. Orthodox (conservative) Friends were often lukewarm or sniffily averse to the UGRR. Coffin's group of Undergrounders were "read out of meeting." In Montgomery County, Pennsylvania, "The Society of Friends . . . was as a body untrue to its righteous testimony against slavery . . . ministers . . . who persisted in introducing the obnoxious topic . . . were regarded as 'subjects of uneasiness,'" that is, in Quaker parlance, heretics. But few Quakers, not even those deploring the UGRR and Abolitionism, would actively betray or apprehend a fugitive. For a delightful illustration: An Iowa conductor named Connor, seeking food and daytime shelter for a wagonload of fugitives hidden in a cornfield, accosted a Quaker farmer at his early chores, assumed a swaggering air for precaution and asked if any stray niggers had been seen in that neck of the woods lately.

"Friend," said the Quaker, "I fear thee is in a bad business," quoted the Golden Rule and read the stranger a lecture. "You're just the man I'm looking for," said Conner and told of his charges and their needs. The glib Quaker was mightily taken aback, said he'd have to see his wife about this and popped back into the house, Conner following anxiously. After a pause, here was the Quaker's wife: "This man of mine's afraid of the law," she said. "But thee bring thy niggers right along and I'll soon have breakfast for them."

Not until after World War I did the Society of Friends have another such opportunity to help the needy without respect of persons—and to manifest the Quaker genius for casuistry and evasion. "Thee knows there are no slaves here," a Quaker wife told her husband most convincingly in the presence of slave catchers; the garret was full of runaways at the time but she was not quite lying because her principles forbade her to consider any human being a slave. Levi Coffin excelled in this ironical art. When a Richmond grand jury examined him about slave harboring in the neighborhood, he told the foreman:

> "Persons often . . . stopped at our house who *said* they were slaves but I knew nothing about it from their statements, for our law did not presume that such people could tell the truth. This made a laugh among the jury. . . . I went on to say that a few weeks before a company of seventeen fugitives had stopped at my house, hungry and destitute, two of them suffering from wounds inflicted by pursuers who claimed them as slaves, but I had no legal evidence that they were slaves; nothing but their own statements and the law . . . did not admit colored evidence. I had read in the Bible . . . that it was right to feed the hungry and clothe the naked and to minister to those who had fallen among thieves and were wounded, but that no distinction in regard to color was mentioned in the good Book, so in accordance with its teachings I had received these fugitives. . . . Was I right . . . in so doing?"

No wonder the foreman "evidently wished to change the subject."

This old slicker never underwent a legal penalty for his Undergroundings. Thomas Garrett, the leonine Quaker merchant of Wilmington, Delaware, was not so lucky. In consequence of helping some 2700 slaves to freedom, he met prosecution after prosecution, fine after fine, that finally reduced his comfortable means to bankruptcy. After the sheriff's sale that took his last asset, a pompous official said that he hoped this would cure him of law breaking. Said Thomas: "Friend, I haven't a dollar in the world, but if thee knows a fugitive who needs a breakfast, send him to me."

Women's role in the UGRR was important too. It could be deliberate, as when the Abolitionist ladies of Syracuse, New York, sent to a Federal attorney who zealously pursued fugitives a little purse—of thirty pieces of silver. Or im-

Abigail Goodwin of Salem, New Jersey.

Thomas Garrett of Wilmington, Delaware.

PROMINENT UNDERGROUND RAILROADERS

promptu: When a slave catcher seized on a girl fugitive working in a tavern in New Castle, Pennsylvania, the landlord's daughter, working upstairs, heard the girl cry out, rushed down and screamed and beat the intruder with her broom until the wagon maker next door could come and knock him cold. When the interloper regained consciousness, the fugitive was gone for good. This same virago, Alvira Lewis, once stunned a slave catcher with a well-aimed stone which she threw not from antislavery principle—she and her father were ardent "doughface" Democrats—but because she thought slave catchers were low types and fugitives pitiable, in which she was usually right on both counts.

Daniel Gibbons

Mrs. Affadilla Deaver, of Deaverstown, Ohio, got her wagon badly stuck in a mudhole while transporting a consignment of fugitives concealed under an old quilt and miscellaneous garden truck. The four gallant passers-by who stopped to pry the wagon out were all ardent proslavery men. Mrs. Deaver thanked them prettily and went on her way blessing God that they had not suggested unloading to lighten the job. On warm summer days Mrs. E. F. Platt, of Tabor, Iowa, found it a relief from a hot kitchen to drive to the next town with a load of the shingles that her husband split—and a fugitive or so hidden among the bundles. She carried a blacksnake whip with a loaded handle and was confident that she could lay out a slave catcher with one whack. There was little of the weaker sex here. When pursuers sought to search the Sisson cabin on Little Raccoon Creek in Gallia County, Ohio, two women met them at the door with shotguns. "Why, boys," said the disgusted leader, "these damn fools will shoot!" and called off the search. Mrs. Patsey McIntire, of Adams County, Ohio, stood off slave catchers with a kettle of boiling water until one of her children fetched a pitchfork, with which she charged bayonets and drove the enemy from the field.

Quakers, Covenanters and Yankees often combined "temperance" zeal with their Undergrounding, equating the Demon Rum with the "peculiar institution" as a scandalous evil. In this arid atmosphere it is refreshing to find Mrs. McIntire's husband just as famous for the quality of his eggnog as for his UGRR work. He was a Virginian who had freed his slaves and taken up land in the "Virginia Military District" of Ohio as a Revolutionary veteran—a vigorous six-footer fond of Patsey, fine horses and well-matched packs of dogs. Reading *Uncle Tom's Cabin* so deepened the McIntires' already low opinion of slavery that General McIntire joined the UGRR. With a fellow Virginian, James Caskey, he volunteered his services to an Underground agent and turned the rich McIntire farm into an active depot on the line up from the Bluegrass through central Ohio. The elder McIntire children—there were eleven—ran the farm while the General, obsessed by his new hobby, "did little else than care for runaways." Just in case, Patsey always kept water boiling on the stove, and at worst, I suppose, it came in handy for the General's toddy.

At the other end of the social scale were the Negro personnel of the UGRR—free barbers, farm hands, craftsmen active in Pennsylvania and the Middle West. Sometimes a militant UGRR group paid a free Negro to enter slave territory and guide a party of runaways into their hands. The free-born Stewarts, Negroes, had a little place at Poke Patch on Dirty Face Creek in Gallia County, Ohio—these place names are real, not Al Capp's—through which went a hundred or so runaways out of the Kanawha Valley. In Springfield, Massachusetts, Mary Sly, fugitive cook at the famous United States Hotel, secreted runaways in the back premises and fed them on what was said to be the best cooking in New England under tacit agreement with the owner that he should pay no heed and she should never take him into her confidence. Practically every clump of Negro settlers in the free states was an Underground depot by definition, for the runaway considered a black skin an even more reliable promise of help than a Quaker broadbrim. A highly active UGRR agent in Indiana was an elderly Crawfordsville Negro whose free wife had bought him out of slavery; she called him "my old pumpkin-headed nigger" and, when vexed with him, loudly threatened to take him South and sell him down the river.

Sometimes the Negro Underground went violent. A slave catcher named Isaac Brooks fell foul of the Negro colony of Columbia, Pennsylvania, was stripped, dragged into the woods through deep snow and savagely flogged with hickory withes. Slave catchers carrying off a Negro girl from Sadsbury, Pennsylvania, were ambushed by the local Negroes, who rescued her and beat up her captors. A Tennessean who blacked up and passed himself off as Negro to spy on UGRR operations round Pittsburgh was found out one night when drunk. They picked him up next morning drowned in the Ohio.* The Christiania "riot" in Southern

---

* In a few instances Negroes betrayed runaways: the most notable was a Negro fortune teller in Chester County, Pennsylvania, who charged fugitive Henry Harris $10 for magic to prevent his master's retrieving

Pennsylvania was an armed clash between a Negro colony active in the Underground and a party of slave catchers. Before it was over, two white men were dead, a detachment of U.S. Marines had been summoned from Washington, D.C., and Negro participants tried for treason had been acquitted.

"*I took my flight and ran away;*
  Fire the ringo, fire away!
All the way to Canaday;
  Fire the ringo, fire away! . . .*"
—Roustabouts' song from Alabama

Late summer into early autumn was the busy season on the UGRR. Apples and roasting ears then helped to feed the fugitives, sleeping outdoors was endurable, fording or swimming streams practical, and the corn high enough for good emergency cover. Means of escape depended on the kind of obstacles. Most Delawareans and Marylanders used their feet, since the line between them and freedom was a mere surveyor's abstraction. Virginians' situation was complicated by eastern-flowing rivers dauntingly wide below the fall line and far from negligible above it—hence the stolen boat, the floating log, the improvised raft, the heart-in-mouth dash across the occasional bridge. West of the mountains the Ohio was either formidable obstacle or highway. Young Wash Mc-Quarry and three cronies, run away from central Kentucky, stole a skiff and paddled up the big river with pieces of bark: "After getting into Ohio they travelled by night and lay concealed by day. One of them had two or three dollars

him; then, having thus learned the master's name and whereabouts, he sent him word where to come and get Henry.

with him, which were used to purchase food. They would watch until the men had left the farmhouses for their daily work, then go in and buy something to eat from the women." * Farm wives suddenly accosted by a strange, shabby Negro showing money and demanding food were probably only too eager to supply and get rid of him, pay or not.

In the amphibious tidewater region slaves often used water as avenue instead of barrier. There were steamers from Richmond to Philadelphia and a variety of craft in the garden-truck trade north from Norfolk. On such vessels Negro stewards, often slaves themselves, could conceal fugitives in those noisome crannies, coal bunker or paint locker, in which ships abound. One Richmond steamer was actually fitted with a false floor under the captain's cabin for concealing runaways from searching officers. Sometimes the police battened down everything and smoked the hull to run fugitives out like rats.

Such inspection was frequent in other ports, too, since deepwater ships out of New Orleans, Savannah, Charleston might carry slave stowaways. In Louisiana the penalty for knowingly aiding a fugitive was two to ten years in jail and masters of vessels took such statutes seriously—not least the skipper of the brig *Ottoman* of Boston who, to his dismay, found a runaway slave on board when homeward bound from New Orleans in 1846. After looking in vain for a New Orleans-bound ship to which he could transship his unexpected passenger, he left him on the Boston pilot boat, whence the owners of the *Ottoman* shipped him on the outward-bound *Niagara*. She went aground down the harbor; the slave, poor dogged devil, stole a boat and escaped again, only to be retaken and shipped out again on the *Vision*. On

* *Reminiscences of Levi Coffin;* 542-543. Wash got a job working on the canal at Troy, Ohio; his master presently traced and took him back to Kentucky in a famous court case. I do not know what happened to his three comrades.

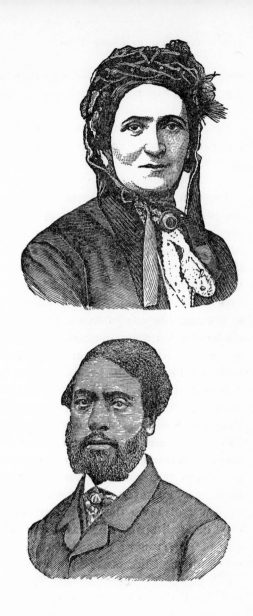

Ellen and William Craft, the most famous married couple ever to use the UGRR.

arrival the New Orleans authorities actually arrested the officers of the *Vision,* presumably for illicit possession of a runaway, but the grand jury had the common sense not to indict. The South's insistence on playing such agonized incidents to the bitter end helped greatly to keep Northerners agitated about the slavery that they might otherwise have preferred to forget.

Between improved inspection and well-publicized heavy penalties, Virginia had this floating division of the UGRR pretty well shut down by 1860. But it remained lively on the informally controlled "western waters." The stewards of Ohio River boats were clever about hiding fugitives. William Johnson, the free Negro barber of Natchez, was never sure whether his sulky slave Walker was stolen or ran away to get near his wife in Kentucky, but there was no doubt of his having got away somehow on a northbound steamboat. Tennessee River boats were equally handy for runaways. Lake steamers out of Sandusky, Cleveland, Ashtabula and Erie were famous in UGRR lore, and the *Illinois,* Captain Blake, from Chicago to Detroit, seems practically never to have sailed without a runaway or so on board. The captain had a histrionic habit of discovering his Negro just as the ship was nearing the southern end of Lake Huron, flying into a passion, putting in at Sarnia, Ontario, and indignantly kicking him ashore—a free man.

Now and again the eastern seaboard saw a saltwater escape in small boats. The slaves of a Norfolk oysterman stole one of the master's rugged little craft and sailed her 200 miles up the Chesapeake by guess and by God, landing beyond Baltimore. The rest was easy. Delaware slaves often stole boats to cross over to South Jersey, usually falling into friendly hands on landing. One such party, attacked offshore by a boatload of pursuers, fought them off with clubbed oars. On free soil they were required to shed their filthy rags and bathe, a hygienic measure often indicated for farm slaves unfamiliar with the personal significance of soap and

water. The squalid necessities of flight could also be the
cause. Slaves often came to the back door of the Rev.
Samuel J. May, Abolitionist and UGRR agent of Syracuse,
New York, "in clothes unfit to be worn and in some instances
too unclean and loathsome to be admitted." So parson and
runaway between them would carry a tub of hot water and
soap and towels out to the barn, where the Negro would
strip and throw his fetid rags on the manure pile. Once
bathed, he was outfitted with sound, clean clothes from a
store of mended and laundered garments that the ladies of
May's congregation maintained for just such purposes.

One party of seventeen seagoing runaways must have
caused the captain of their schooner bitterly to regret that he
had ever fitted up his ship for Negro smuggling. Because the
police were watching his usual berth for embarking fugitives, he had to stand off and on for hours, waiting for cover
of darkness, while they stood up to their discouraged chins
in water for concealment. Then two of the women in the
party proved too bulky for the narrow hatchway into the
prepared hidey-hole. They could be concealed among the
cargo only until the ship reached the regular check point at
which skilled inspectors came on board to sniff round for
fugitives. Then possible or impossible, they had to be got
below. The first was bullied through with immense difficulty. Protesting miserably the second and fatter was
stripped to her shirt and hauled on below by many hands
with others bearing down on her above, until she finally
popped in like a troublesome obstetrics case in reverse,
with much of the skin missing from her behindside. The
inspectors had obviously been alerted by telegraph to exert
special zeal. But they cut the job short when, asked how
things were back in Norfolk, the captain said cheerily everything was fine except yellow fever'd broken out again.

How much of it was funny for the runaways is another
matter. Flight must have been agony for the fugitive who
left Savannah on a projected voyage to freedom lashed be-

low the bowsprit of a deepwater steamer. The water was
cold and rough and he was dripping with bone-icy saltwater
most of the time. But he was plucky enough to go twenty-
four hours before breaking down and calling for help to
hands heaving the lead. The captain, humane if not merci-
ful, gave him dry clothes and ample food but turned him
over to the law at Newcastle, Delaware, all the same. With
the ferocious humor of the press at that time a Philadelphia
paper commented that at worst the shipowner could charge
only half-fare since the slave had "come half the way as a
fish."

A few slave women got away in men's clothes. The best
known was Ellen Craft, of cotton-belt Georgia, whose case
combined several typical features: She was white enough to
"pass"—just a little sallow, Miss Bremer noted, when they met
in Boston—and a lady's maid, of house-servant status. She
did not run away because of mistreatment. Her owners had
been kind but "they would not give me my rights as a human
being," particularly opportunity to learn to read and write.*
With her came her much darker husband William, a skilled
cabinetmaker hiring his time at $200 a year.

The initiative in the scheme had been hers. They planned
boldly to disguise Ellen as a gentleman-traveler, William to
play body servant. His semi-independence enabled him to
get together the money and elegant men's clothes required,
and Ellen's position in master's household had showed her

---

* Clarke (*Anti-Slavery Days;* 191) said that it was mistress's callousness
that moved Ellen to run away. She had insisted on Ellen's leaving her
baby at home to make a trip North; on her return, the baby had died.
This is possible enough, but in view of what Ellen told Miss Bremer,
as above, it is probably just one of these synthetic details with which
Abolitionists were so fond of embroidering the cases of fugitive slaves.
So far, by the way, I have yet to find any exact statement of where the
Crafts came from in Georgia. It must have been somewhere near the
railroad west of Milledgeville—that is all. Since speaking of exact locations often led informers to write to master as to runaways' whereabouts,
fugitives were usually shy of being specific on such points.

how white gentlemen did things. Though not ill-looking, she fortunately lacked any specifically female prettiness. The story was to be that young master was hastening to Philadelphia for special medical treatment for his rheumatism and other ailments, obviously much needed: his jaws were muffled in toothache-type swathings (to conceal Ellen's lack of beard), he wore green spectacles (for general disguise), he carried his right arm in a sling (to conceal inability to sign hotel registers), and, early in the trip, played deaf (to avoid having to converse in Ellen's highish voice). On the train to Savannah deafness also helped to discourage a chatty fellow passenger who had actually dined the day before at Ellen's master's house. But on the steamer from Savannah to Charleston she recovered her hearing and made bold to dine and chat with other passengers. William was much commended for his deftness and solicitude in cutting up young master's food, warming his blankets, and so forth.

From Charleston they went by rail to Wilmington, North Carolina, by steamer again from Wilmington to Fredericksburg, each hotel or ticket office presenting fresh hazards. At Wilmington, an awkward problem of permission for young master to import slaves, meaning William, was solved when the captain of the ship obligingly registered for Ellen. Baltimore had stiff and complicated regulations about Negroes boarding northbound trains, whether with their owners or not. Only William's voluble representations of how delicate master was and how, even with the utmost expedition, he might not live to see Philadelphia persuaded a kindly ticket agent to waive the rules just as the train was about to start.

This success in reaching freedom greatly tickled the whole antislavery world. The UGRR of Philadelphia sent the Crafts express to Boston to be lionized by the Abolitionists and, with great emphasis, to be legally married by the militant Rev. Theodore Parker. After the ceremony he gave the groom a revolver and dirk for use on possible slave catchers. The Crafts had fallen well. A lady upholstress of Abolitionist views was found to teach her trade to Ellen, already a clever needlewoman, and William was set up in a cabinetmaking shop of his own.

For a while Boston's deserved reputation as unsafe for slavecatchers kept those birds of ill omen away. But passage of the strengthened Fugitive Slave Act of 1850 brought a couple of them down on the Crafts, who went into hiding. These "hunters of men" probably never knew that the first Bostonian to offer Ellen a hiding place was the wife of a U.S. commissioner named Hilliard, the very official before whom they might find themselves swearing to their hoped-for captives. They tried to inveigle the Crafts to their hotel with clumsy offers to take letters home to Georgia for them. But they had no chance of success even had they been clever. They had hardly set foot in town when they were jailed on the curious charge of having criminally slandered one William Craft. When a local shipowner with Southern connections went their bail, the Boston Vigilance Committee—the Abolitionist emergency squad—sent Parker to tell them to get out of town or take severe and admittedly illegal consequences. Whatever this astringent and anomalous minister of the Gospel said to them, it must have been impressive. They left by the afternoon train.

Their attempt had been alarming, however, and the Crafts' sponsors sent them to unimpeachable safety in England.* There they were a sensation, much taken up by the

---

* On a presailing visit to Portland, Maine, Ellen is said to have met the Catholic bishop of the diocese who was a cousin of hers; his father, closely related to Ellen's master, had freed the bishop's slave mother and sent her and the boy to Canada, where he was educated to Catholicism. W. S. Siebert got this story off the record from S. T. Pickard, editor of the Portland *Transcript,* in 1893; in 1895 he repeated it in much the same terms. This seems good enough to be taken seriously. Pickard said that, though the bishop admitted the relationship readily enough to Ellen, he never did so in public, instead merely denying that he was "the son of a slave"—which was technically true, since his mother had been freed.

same do-good duchesses and high-minded M.P.'s who later smothered Mrs. Stowe with adulation. Several times they were taken to the Great Exhibition to loiter pointedly near the American exhibits as representing something of which the United States were not necessarily proud. They had three children (in slavery their union had been infertile) and seem to have done well in Britain, for, after the Civil War, they went back to Georgia and bought a farm near Savannah, settling down free where they had once been slaves.

A small, slightly made slave barber married to a free octoroon who readily passed for white reversed the Crafts' device by traveling North from Mobile in women's clothes as his wife's maid servant.

As railroads were extended, the UGRR often patronized its real namesakes, to the occasional chagrin of managements sued by owners of human runaway property. In 1855, for instance, the Pacific Railroad had to repay one John Best $500 for expenses that he had incurred in recapturing two slaves escaped "in the cars." The Crafts were not the only light-colored or heavily disguised fugitives to slip by the close watch kept on the Philadelphia, Wilmington & Baltimore, and one owner's suit in consequence cost the road $1000. Once on free soil, runaways found railroad transport, usually at UGRR expense, invaluable for speedy access to Canada or at least to American points remote enough for reasonable safety. A mulatto girl making the last leg of her flight by rail from Crawfordsville, Indiana, to Detroit, heavily veiled and equipped with a free Negro maid carrying a white baby borrowed for the occasion, found her pursuing owner on the same train in the same car. But the first he knew of her disguise was when, safe on board the ferry from Detroit to Windsor, with the baby left in the maid's arms on the dock and the moorings cast off, she leaned over the rail, dropped her veil and gave him what I hope was an impudent smirk.

Train crews on the Chicago, Burlington & Quincy actually

looked after runaways personally. The proslavery manager of the Sandusky, Mansfield & Newark never knew how many fugitives his conductors slipped into Sandusky to take the boat to Ontario. The Mad River & Lake Erie was highly fugitive-minded; so was the Providence & Worcester. The Grand Trunk gave free tickets to runaways arriving in Portland by sea. At the height of this runaway-by-rail tradition, U.S. marshals in Syracuse, New York, received a tip that a runaway was to be sent to Oswego and the boats across Lake Ontario on a regular passenger train of the Syracuse & Oswego. They carefully searched the cars standing in the station waiting for the locomotive—no fugitive. At the last second the locomotive backed in, coupled up and pulled out before it could be searched. At the first stop the marshals ran ahead to search, but the engineer waved a hammer at them and said nobody boarded his engine without a pass from the master mechanic. They let it go at determining to watch very sharp when the train reached Oswego. But the engineer had wired ahead for a "running switch," which would uncouple the locomotive in motion and divert it to a spur track while the cars coasted past on the main line at a point where a branch line ran down to the Oswego docks. It worked prettily. The switchman's split-second timing sent the locomotive through the tunnel to the waterfront while the cars continued into the passenger station. By the time the marshals had reached the dock in a hired cab, the fugitive was already on a Canada-bound boat—soaking wet; he had been in the locomotive's water tank all the way.

The most striking use of the rails was the technique of getting nailed up in a packing box to be sent by express. Henry Brown, who afterwards adopted "Box" as his middle name, survived twenty-five hours in a packing case 3 feet by 2½ feet by 2 feet. A young woman was nailed up by her sweetheart and sent to a Philadelphia consignee, who was so apprehensive about what might be found when the lid came off that he had an undertaker standing by; the shipment was groggy but still alive. Another such reached Rochester, New York, dead of suffocation. But it is wonderful what the human body will stand. A young man, nailed up in a coffin, survived being stood on his head for some hours. Personally I should rather have been headed up in a barrel, as was once done on the Illinois division of the UGRR.

Perhaps it was terror of having to go home and face punishment that enabled Charles Gilbert, waiting for his northbound schooner to arrive, to live for months under the built-up structure of an Old Point Comfort hotel, feeding off garbage and barking like a vicious dog when people came too near. But one can read only courage into the slave who started for freedom—and thanks to the UGRR, Ohio division, he got there—walking on the stumps of his ankles, his feet having been amputated after they were frozen when he was a boy. The records show at least one one-legged passenger and numerous pregnant women near term. When luck was bad or information scanty, runaways' hardships were pitiful. Said Levi Coffin, "Sometimes the poor hunted creatures had been out so long, living in woods and thickets, that they were almost wild when they came in, and so fearful of being betrayed, that it was some time before their confidence could be gained and the true state of their case learned." This was apropos of two young men fugitives who came under his charge with their feet frozen so clinking stiff in their boots that the leather had to be cut away. In Vermilion County, Illinois, the UGRR once found a sort of runaway Robinson Crusoe armed with an ancient musket and a knife made of the end of a broken scythe,* dressed in tatters patched and held together by the pelts of rabbits that he had been living on.

Many a slave catcher failed in his purpose because he had

---

* Runaways often carried such knives, which seem to have been made originally as a thrifty way to salvage use from a broken corn knife.

been tricked into seeking assistance from UGRR men expert in sabotage. Having searched and found nothing suspicious in the house of a Negro in Findlay, Ohio, the hunters hired him to help them at $2 a day, good pay for those times. Being an agent of the UGRR, he kept them running in circles until they had to leave for Kentucky empty-handed; then used their money for railroad fare to Sandusky for the fugitives whom they had been seeking. All the time they had been secreted under the puncheon floor of his dining room. The captain of a Wabash River steamboat which lost two slave roustabouts at Lafayette, Indiana, never knew that the local citizen whom he hired to help him pursue was the local UGRR stationmaster. A constable in the Pennsylvania backcountry was noted for the zeal with which he offered his local knowledge in aid of slave catchers, and for the care with which he then bustled them off in diametrically wrong directions. Nor was it even necessary for such obstructors of justice, as the South saw justice, to be connected with the UGRR. The clerk of Randolph County, Indiana, always warned the Quakers of Richmond whenever slave catchers appeared seeking local search warrants. He despised Abolitionists, he said, and strongly favored Southern slavery, but, when it was a matter of runaways, "he was not satisfied to have [them] captured and sent back in bonds."

Others were more businesslike about it. Sea captains regularly smuggling slaves to freedom charged from $30 to $125 per capita. Stewards and deck hands stowed fugitives away without the officers' knowledge at much the same prices, a steamer passage naturally costing more than one on a slow and irregularly scheduled schooner. A free Negro in Baltimore got $15 a head as agent for such arrangements; caught at it, he was sold South for thirty years. The celebrated case of the schooner *Pearl*, captured at sea in 1848 with seventy-seven runaways from Washington, D.C., was a virtual charter, if use of such a term suits so strikingly illegal a transaction, arranged by a local free Negro. Had the *Pearl* actually landed her cargo in a free state, this would have been the largest single party ever to travel the UGRR. The scheme miscarried through betrayal by a Negro, a boatman angered because a fugitive whom he had rowed out to join the ship could not pay the demanded fare of twenty-five cents.

Flight by land too was often expedited by zealous or grasping opportunists, black or white, willing to turn an illicit dollar. Consider the two Alabama slaves who hired a "mean white" to take them north in the guise of his personal servants. The slave of a Lexington, Kentucky, horse trader paid $50 to have himself and wife guided into Ohio. Fishermen ostensibly supplying fresh fish to steamboats below Owensboro, Kentucky, made much of their living by ferrying runaways across the Ohio on dark nights. The standard charge for convoy from Baltimore to York, Pennsylvania, thence to Columbia, a famous gateway to freedom, was $40. John Fairfield, the strange, harsh adventurer whom Coffin evenhandedly described as both "devoid of moral principle" and "a true friend to the poor slave," mingled sentiment with profit, or at least money-mindness, in a long and highly hazardous career of helping slaves to freedom, often in elaborate disguises. On free soil runaways needed money much less. Levi Coffin insisted a little invidiously that "the Underground Railroad . . . had its origin in the Slave States. It was, however, conducted on quite a different principle south of Mason's and Dixon's line [where] money, in most cases, was the motive; north we generally worked on principle . . ."

The most cynical paid "feeder" for the UGRR proper may have been Wash Spradley, free Negro of Louisville, who assuaged the suspicions of the police by habitually betraying to them every fourth or fifth runaway who sought his aid; the others got good service for their money. In many cases high compensation may have been justified, for risks were heavy and penalties high. John Mahan, of Highland County, Ohio, and John van Zandt, the original of van Trompe in

Uncle Tom, were ruined by the legal consequences of helping fugitives. Captain Jonathan Walker, caught smuggling
runaways out of Pensacola, was branded in the hand "SS"
for "slave stealer," a medieval touch that made him a plat-
form attraction as Exhibit A for Abolition. A Norfolk seaman got twenty-five years for piloting a small-boat party of
fugitives northward. Calvin Fairbank, an unpleasant but
persistent Abolitionist emissary, spent sixteen years in Kentucky prisons for "inciting" and abetting runaways. Richard
Dillingham, an earnest Quaker, died of cholera while serving three years in Tennessee for the same crime. Seth
Concklin, a Yankee with Shaker leanings and any amount of
cold-drawn courage, was caught guiding Negroes to freedom
and fell—or was pushed—overboard from a river steamboat
with his hands manacled.

Such conspicuous cases gave Southerners multiple night-
mares about Abolitionists skulking round the quarters and
inveigling slaves into running away. It had the same effect
when an Abolitionist meeting at Gerrit Smith's house in
Peterboro, New York, in 1840 publicly pledged aid to encourage slaves to abscond. But actually only a few white
agents from the fanatic minority in the UGRR ever ventured into slave territory. Though Negro "enticers" were
somewhat more numerous—the famous Harriet Tubman
was the most conspicuous and effective—even they actually
accomplished little relative to the slave population involved.
Most responsible Undergrounders agreed with N. C. Han-
sell, of Tanner's Creek, Indiana: "Any attempt to induce
slaves to run away was condemned as making the lot of those
who were left more intolerable, and as delaying their final,
hoped-for, peaceable emancipation. But, when they were
making an effort to escape, it was held to be a moral and
religious duty to render any assistance."

So the typical UGRR conductor waited for refugees to appear on the free side of the line. His problem was not to
persuade them to abscond but to baffle slave catchers and

keep their intended quarry in good traveling shape. The operations of Underground branch lines were as homey as they were ingenious. Agents hid their passengers in hollow trees, cornshocks, coal banks, the tall grass of the prairies, hazel thickets, brick kilns, sail lofts, haystacks, church belfries, under mill wheels and in wood piles specially constructed to conceal tiny rooms—hence, presumably, the proverbial "nigger in the woodpile." As Undergrounders prospered and built better houses, they might include a secret room for fugitives, some so cleverly concealed that succeeding tenants went for years without knowing that they existed. Under certain conditions, runaways traveled between stations on foot with simple directions or followed just within earshot or eyeshot of a horseman who would sing loudly or make the horse "act up" if anybody approached, thus warning the slave to dive into the bushes. When risks were higher, false-bottomed carts and farm wagons were used or market wagons with seats for eight or ten runaways within their black waterproof side curtains. The best-known piece of UGRR rolling stock in Ohio was such a wagon called "The Liberator" by its Quaker owner because it had freed so many slaves. Hard-pushed Undergrounders would resort to mock funeral processions or dress a black man in bonnet and pelisse and drive him through in daylight seated between the local UGRR agent's daughters. These were unavoidably family activities. You could not keep even the children out of them. Having ferreted out her father's UGRR activities, a little girl in Ohio was told that she must *never* mention anything whatever about them. She spent the next six months freezing her parents' blood by hailing every fresh visitor with "I know something! I know something! but I'm not supposed to tell!"

The whole thing, resourceful, truly rural and easygoing, is summed up in the recollection of his first UGRR experience preserved by Arthur Coiner, of Davis County, Iowa: Some local people named Elliott had been asked to guide a family of slaves trying to escape from over the Missouri border:

> . . . it was arranged that on a certain night they were to meet [the slaves' first relay of guides] at a certain fork in the road. . . . So on the evening of March the eight, I had been to Church and as I came out of the house some one I do not now remember who told me I was wanted to go out to Uncle John Elliotts that night as there was Nigers in the air. After taking my girl home I met Abdell Pruitt who was in the secret. He and I went to Mr. Elliotts house and was told they expected them some time in the night. So we was shown to bed and was soon asleep dreaming nigger hunters dogs and suthern shivalry when all at once one of Uncle Johns Girls nearly broke the doore in and said get up quick they have come. We were not long making our toilet. You may think we were in a hurry when I tell you it was about eight o'clock when I found I had on Pruitt's pants, and I was ten miles from him. We went out . . . Elliott and Hardy were in the wagon & Coiner was on horseback. That was the way they had went to the place of meeting where they had waited until about two o'clock when they were startled by a noise down the road sounded like a team running away. Coiner jumped on his horse and started towards them had only gone a short distance when he met a fellow riding a mule. Then we started for Eddyville . . . where there was a tole bridge over the Des Moines River the only place we could cross on a bridge in the country . . . We road on to the bridge found the tole keeper at the other end so we road on as independent as a couple of Cowboys asked him the bill he said ten cts apiece for us just then the wagon showed up it looked as though it had just got in from the planes. Elliott said take your pay out for that wagon also. He got five cents out of the half Dollar he was then going into his little shanty I think he was asleep before the wagon with its load got through the bridge . . . went to Alpha Englishes some three miles south

Mr. Coiner took out his white handkerchief and blew his
nose The other fellow says stranger we are a little late but
are all right (that was the signal). The wagon came up in a
minute and there was a man & woman and 4 children. They
were very light molatoes . . . [Their owner] was like many
others who owned slaves in those days. If they did hate the
Nigger they loved the Lord or said they did . . . the reason
our folks was so late the folks had gone to Church with the
wagon team and our people had to wait till they came home
and got to sleep before they could borrow the outfit for the
little excursion they had planned . . . but they got there
all the same. One of the fellows . . . watched the house so
as to give the alarm . . . but having been to church they
slept the sleep of the just.

Doubtless a limber young fellow with a narrow blue eye
and much fair hair on the backs of his big hands.

"Nothing new that I Know of Except that some people on
the other side of the River Caught One of those Runaway
Slaves that helped Kill a man by the name of Todd Living
near Red River—They Burned Him up soon after he was
taken. . . ."
—Diary of William Johnson [free Negro barber of Natchez]

The UGRR railheads were so remote from the Deep
South that few Black Belt slaves were ever passengers. A
given field hand's chances of ever meeting an Abolitionist
"enticer" were practically nil. But for personal motives,
sometimes little more than reflex, "Virtually all the plantations whose records are available suffered more or less from
truancy," wrote Phillips, best single authority. ". . . a fugi-

tive slave was the natural product of any friction in plantation management," wrote Sydnor, expert on Mississippi
slavery. To William Johnson, the gossipy Natchez barber,
runaways were as normal incidents of local life as gougings,
floods and yellow fever: "Four or 5 of the Runaways that
was in Jail Broke out Last [night] and run off. . . . Mr.
Dillon was Shot today and hurt by a runaway belonging to
Mr. Stanton whilst Dillon was in pursuit of him. . . .
Young Jno Gaines shot a Black man that had runaway from
Mr. Hutcheons this morning and killed him Dead. . . ."

Mr. Hutcheon's runaway can hardly have been aware that
he had run away because he desired an abstract freedom, as
Mrs. Stowe assumed. The Deep South's runaways were usually not seeking liberty but using an impulsive or calculated
truancy as tactics in the everlasting war between slave and
master. This truancy was a quasi-permanent institution with
its own ancillary trappings: special laws, special equipment,
special conventions between master and slave, no less real
for lack of formulation.

Lack of long-range purpose is its most striking aspect.
Very seldom did the Deep South fugitive manage to get by
sea to Europe or New England or to join his cousins among
the Seminoles or survive through arid Texas into Mexico.
Since it is difficult to exaggerate the ignorance of cotton-
chopping field hands, few of them can even have known that
to cross an international boundary—what was that?—meant
freedom. Nineteen times in twenty when the slave lit out
from the old place, he had in mind only an indefinite and
precarious vacation in the swamps or the wooded highlands.

In itself this was not impractical. The half-settled, often
waterlogged condition of the South was as well suited to hiding out as was medieval England, mostly forest and swamp,
for Robin Hoodish outlaws. Give the truant slave a dry ele-
vation among the cypresses, a trotline for fish, a few snares
for rabbits, an occasional foray to the old plantation, or to
another, to steal corn or beg meal and fatback from friends,

an occasional Negro girl to be raped or persuaded in a fence corner . . . and life could be tolerated a good while in spite of snakes, malaria and terrors born of lonesomeness. Come frost and the fugitive might well return from his impromptu holiday, take his whipping and realign himself with the plantation, or find a refuge with riverside Yankees cutting firewood for steamboats and willing to feed and conceal him in a sort of peonage in return for his labor.* In the rare cases where he made contact with the UGRR, he might also find himself at work again. The Underground usually sped Border State fugitives through as quickly as possible, since they were likeliest to be pursued. But those from the cotton states, hundreds of expensive miles from their masters, were seldom pursued very far, and a farmer needing hands could risk working them for a season at cutting wood or husking corn, their meager wages accumulating to give them a small traveling fund when they finally resumed their northward progress.†

The Deep South truant, however, seldom fled more than a day's journey from home, and for hiding out one swamp was about as good as another. Going far afield put him out of touch with potential supplies from allies on the old place, and the old neighborhood had its own magnetism of familiarity. Besides, these cotton-states runaways weren't going anywhere; they were just getting away from something—a nagging wife, or a whipping for stealing a shoat or for letting a team of mules run away. Some were chronic absconders of

---

* These woodcutters may have been likelier to take in runaways because they were often Northerners from Michigan or Wisconsin, unsympathetic to slavery, who stayed a few years, making $50 a month or so cash apiece and saving it to go home and buy farms. (Power, *Impressions of America*, II; 107.)

† Cynics sometimes alleged that UGRR agents worked fugitives for months without pay and then deliberately alarmed them about slave catchers to get rid of them in a hurry before pay could be mentioned. It may have happened, but I suspect such behavior was rare.

a sort known to penologists. On a big Mississippi plantation a certain field hand was called "Swamp" because he spent so much time there.

"Never threaten a nigger or he'll run" was a recognized plantation maxim implying that the decision was often quickly made. But truancy could also be a practical protest. "Why don't you stay home?" young Joe Harris asked Mink, the Georgia hide-out. "Dey don't treat me right, suh," said Mink with convincing dignity. Let the overseer select the wrong slave for driver and persist in his error and some morning all the best hands might disappear simultaneously, not to reappear until master came down from Wilmington or Savannah to straighten things out. Rarely but actually, such informal strikers might negotiate with the master as to terms on which they would return through slave intermediaries chosen from a nearby plantation.

One reason why individual runaways seldom stayed out long was a prevalent opinion that it was better to come in and take your licking than to be captured mutinously at large some morning when the overseer cared to make a special effort. There appears to have been agreement, however tenuous and unreliable, between masters and slaves that a one-time fugitive who voluntarily returned after learning his lesson out among the cottonmouths and screech owls would not be flogged too outrageously and could then sink back into normal servitude. But a stubborn fugitive who occasioned the trouble and expense of hiring dogs and men might, if the master were feeling nasty, be very badly cut up after capture and then sold for whatever a dealer was fool enough to offer for a man with a back so eloquent of trouble-making. One even hears of staking a flogged runaway out in the sun to see if dehydration and flies on the flayed back could show him the error of his ways.

The occasional slave who chopped down master or overseer with axe or hoe and then took to the swamp was probably a gone goose. I know of only one case of such a killer reaching freedom. Nor was the articulate mutineer much better off. Faced with a flogging, an Alabama field hand told his overseer that "he had taken the last whipping he would take from a white man. He wouldn't mind being shot; he had been shot twice already. But he would not be whipped. Having delivered his ultimatum, he turned and ran . . . the driver, overtaking him after a run of 150 yards, was severely stabbed. . . . To save his driver, the overseer shot and killed the slave. . . ." In *Dred* Mrs. Stowe justifiably made much of Southern laws that provided formal outlawry to legalize killing runaways on sight. Yet, except as protection against possible damage suits from litigious owners, these were probably the most pointless statutes ever passed. The odds were a hundred to one against indictment of a white man for killing a known runaway, outlaw or not, anywhere in the South.

Mrs. Stowe, as already indicated, was not directly responsible for the dog complex that haunts the *Uncle Tom* legend. The facts of fugitive-chasing "bloodhounds" are, as usual in connection with slavery, varied and confusing. There certainly were slave-hunting specialists with specially trained dogs who charged say $5 a day and expenses for pack and owner, a bonus of $10 per capture and $10 each for any unexpected captures on the side. Negro folklore furnished elaborate precautions against such trailing: graveyard dirt on your feet or in your shoes, or a mixture of cow-manure, snuff, turpentine and some hairs from the end of a dog's tail well rubbed into the soles, or Jimson weed rubbed over the whole body. . . . No doubt the dogs concerned were usually formidable, but Bill Locke took the field after Mink with only two scrawny hounds that were "the terror of the negroes, not because they were fierce or dangerous but because of their sagacity. Sound was a small brown hound . . . regarded with superstitious awe . . . could follow a scent thirty-six hours old."

An even-tempered owner or overseer would probably consider that a slave all cut up by savage dogs and then whipped into half-insane cringing was hardly worth tracking down. Yet here again one cannot rely on economic logic as between an owner and his human tools. To be run down by several big mongrel hounds with their blood up would be dangerous to begin with, and the men behind sometimes cheered the dogs on instead of whipping them off, particularly if the runaway showed fight. In those circumstances, Southerners told Olmsted, ". . . let 'em tear him a spell . . . runaways ain't much account nohow and it makes the rest more afraid to run away when they see how they are sarved." Bennett Barrow, the Louisiana cotton planter, was an intelligent and humane master, yet his diary shows some appalling entries about runaways: ". . . treed him, made the dogs pull him out of the tree. Bit him very badly, think he will stay home a while"; ". . . dogs soon tore him naked, took him Home . . . & made the dogs give him another overhauling." This cannot have been just for calculated effect on his fellow slaves. It must mean snarling anger with any slave daring to be defiant, the sort of thing that explains this description of runaway Bill in an Alabama newspaper: ". . . says he belongs to a trader by the name of George Grimes . . . a large fellow, very black, shows the whites of his eyes more than usual, has a scar on his right cheek bone, several on his breast, one on his arm, occasioned by the bite of a dog—his back very badly scarred with the whip."

Yet a typical pursuit had for purpose neither mayhem nor murder, and Whittier, that uncharitable Quaker, was just weaving disingenuous rhetoric in "The Hunters of Men" when he likened a slave chase to a fox hunt with the "politic statesman," "the priest with his cassock," and "woman, kind woman" all exulting to spur after the dogs with the black man as quarry. This was not "The Most Dangerous Game." It was just an expensive, disquieting, revenge-flavored search after the escaped convict. In Barbados runaways were already a problem in 1657 and elicited the same measures:

". . . in the night [runaway slaves] range abroad the Coun-
trey, and steal Pigs, Plantins, Pottatoes . . . and feast all
day upon what they stole the night before; and the nights
being dark and their bodies black, they escape undiscern'd,"
so they were hunted down by dogs specially trained for the
purpose. Barbados, however, presenting no long distances,
was probably little plagued by the most appealing type of
runaway—the slave moved by homesickness or affection, no
doubt often the two combined, to sneak back to the neighborhood whence he had been sold South. Hints of this are
rife in advertisements for fugitives. McMaster, the great
historian, thought it the most prevalent motivation for absconding. Certainly it was important. Thus an elderly slave
woman named Rachel would not let Levi Coffin ship her to
Canada on the UGRR until she had failed in several stubborn efforts to get herself bought by somebody near her old
home in Lexington, Kentucky.

Yet these motives must often have been unclear to the
runaways themselves. I suspect that many and many a slave
found himself making for the swamp as impulsively as Mark
Twain's Roxy, whom overwork and special brutalizing had
put into a frame of mind where "I didn't care no mo', nuther
—life war'n't wuth noth'n to me, if I got to go on like dat."
So in sudden rage she felled the overseer with his own stick,
jumped on his horse and galloped for the river, considering
drowning herself but willing to drift away in a canoe that
she found when it was most needed. "I had a pow'ful good
start, 'ca'se de big house 'uz three mile back f'om de river en
on'y de wok-mules to ride dah on, en on'y niggers to ride
'em, en *dey* war'n't gwine to hurry—dey'd gimme all de
chance dey could." The general impression is that of many
one-man mutinies, singlehanded demonstrations against brutal whites or poor working conditions, reactions highly understandable but making as little long-run sense as a small
boy's running away from a bad stepmother. And in some
cases, not necessarily numerous, there was probably a tinge

of psychopathology present. Consider this advertisement for
Sarah, who ran away from Bourbon County, Kentucky, in
1822:

> $50.00 REWARD . . . a negro woman named Sarah, about
> 6 feet high, and very slim; a very long face, with black gums,
> long teeth, white eyes and platted hair. Had on a white linsey
> dress and took with her a red changeable silk, and black dress,
> also a white robe and striped gingham dress. Sarah is the big-
> gest devil that ever lived, having poisoned a stud horse and
> set a stable on fire, also burned Gen. R. Williams stable and
> stack yard with seven horses and other property to value of
> $1500. She was handcuffed and got away at Ruddles Mills on
> her way down the river, which is the fifth time she escaped
> when about to be sent out of the country. . . .

God help Sarah if they did catch up with her this time.
The puzzle here is why on earth anybody wanted her back.

> *"Four million men cannot run away, until God sends ten
> Egyptian plagues to help them."*
>
> —HENRY WARD BEECHER

The statement quoted above gives much the same false impression as *Uncle Tom:* namely, that slavery seethed with
the impulse to run away, that absconding and the UGRR
were major phenomena. Actually disinterested observers
often marveled at the passive refusal of the Maryland, Kentucky or Missouri slave to take advantage of his opportunities. Slaves working on steamboats that touched at landing
after landing in free states seldom bothered to step ashore
and disappear. Reliable slaves sent to market vegetables in
free Cincinnati or Alton dutifully returned to master in the

evening with the proceeds. The UGRR of Chicago arranged for a Canadian-born Negro to get a job as porter on an Illinois Central sleeping car from Chicago to Cairo, Illinois (where numbers of Kentucky slaves could readily be approached), so he could smuggle runaways northward on the railroad. It took him all day to find one slave willing to accept his offer of overnight transportation to freedom in the bedding box.

Nor were many fugitives recaptured in spite of all the shoddy detectives who advertised themselves along the border of slavery as experienced slave catchers with impressive networks of connections all the way to Canada. Undergrounders' reminiscences are full of assertions that "There never was a 'wreck' on our line that I heard of." This is even stranger because the advertised rewards were often nonsensically high. A runaway, being by definition unruly, lost value at once, so it was mostly emotion, not economics, that caused a master to offer rewards of $100 or $200 for him. But one gets the other impression too—that many another owner said to the overseer, "Well, guess Yellow Pete's skipped out. See if you can get track of him, but if it looks like he's crossed the river, don't waste no time on him. Let him run."

The scale of the exodus was certainly nothing like what Mrs. Stowe's public assumed in consequence of the uproar over the new Fugitive Slave Law. Posterity has retained the error: Asked to guess the total of slaves running away to seek freedom in the decade 1851-1860, my questionnaire respondents' answers averaged 270,000, meaning 27,000 a year. Several went to a million. Close estimates of the actual passenger load of the UGRR would naturally be hard to come by. Few of the otherwise staid citizens involved kept records that might become evidence in court. But Southern estimates of the day were certainly not minimized, since the South wished the problem to sound very serious in order to justify Federal severity, and they are astonishingly low.

John A. Quitman, the Northern-born Mississippi filibuster, hottest of proslavery politicians, claimed only 100,000 slaves lost to the South by flight between 1810 and 1850, an average of a mere 2500 a year. Southern Congressmen denouncing the UGRR in Washington for the edification of the folks back home in Buncombe County never set the value of runaways above a million dollars a year. True, that sum meant far more in 1850 than it does now, but it is scarcely noticeable in relation to the assessed value of all slaves at the time, which was on the order of two billion dollars.

Set $500 as average slave value, which is more than fair,* and loss of a million dollars a year means only 2000 slaves escaping annually, a figure close to McMaster's estimate from other considerations.† Rhodes interpreted the U.S. Census to indicate about a thousand runaways escaping per year between 1850 and 1860. ". . . in Maryland and Delaware," says Nevins, historian of the ante bellum period, "many slaveholders thought themselves well rid of runaways. . . . But many Southerners, relying on wild guesses, convinced themselves that . . . the losses ran into tens of millions." For correction they needed only to study their own newspapers. In those of Huntsville, Alabama, for instance, just about on the margin of the sphere of attraction of free soil, only 562 fugitives were advertised between 1820 and 1860.

---

* An 1850 inventory of Isaac Franklin's slaves on his Louisiana cotton plantations shows average estimated value of $540 per capita, including all ages and both sexes. (Stephenson, *Isaac Franklin;* 165-169.) Coleman (*Slavery Times in Kentucky;* 244 *fn.*) quotes the New Orleans *Commercial Bulletin,* December 19, 1860: ". . . 1500 slaves have escaped annually for the last fifty years, a loss to the South of at least $40,000,000," which gives an average of $530 per capita.

† *History of the People of the United States,* VII; 248. Siebert, the authority on the UGRR, tried frequently to make the total of absconders more impressive. But nothing that he adduces can overcome the minimizing effect of the estimates that Southerners themselves put forward as proof of the seriousness of the problem.

For realism about runaways and the UGRR, the numerous surviving personal accounts are not ideal. Their authors were usually truthful, I assume, but their data suffer from overselection. They remembered the striking, not the usual, as people often do. A sounder picture is contained in a massive book, *Underground Railroad Records,* compiled by William Still, the free-born Negro superintendent of the UGRR in Philadelphia. As a sort of office manager for the Philadelphia Vigilance Committee, which cared for transient fugitives, he interviewed runaways from pretty well all over the Maryland-Delaware-Virginia area east of the Blue Ridge and secreted notes about them in a shed at a cemetery where he knew the watchman. His purpose in this risky proceeding was imaginative and touching—to enable relatives to trace runaways if the day should come when open freedom was possible for former slaves.

As a reporter this sober, plucky black man was exasperating. He practically never recorded the same range of data about two successive cases. Sex and home state are the only invariable categories. Resulting omissions are very likely much at random, however, so a good deal can be learned from this run-of-mine record. These are not just the picturesque cases that stayed in grandpa's head to be dredged up, perhaps with heightened coloring, for a posterity that valued his yarns. Week in and week out Still included all who came seeking help: the scarred repeater, the self-respecting craftsman, the fine lady's maid, the husky fisherman, the numbers of confused farm hands. No summary figures are dry when you know what lies behind them. In these summaries*

---

* My analysis of Still's data is crude, partly because I am no statistician, partly because they do not readily lend themselves to cross-analysis. Nevertheless, given the assumptions that these are pretty much random cases, and that the gaps in records of individuals are also random, which they probably are, the size of the sample (694) may allow considerable validity in these simple findings. At worst, they are the only such data available, and it would be a pity not to see what they can disclose

every check of the pencil once meant rebellion or terror or hunger, sometimes all those things together in one quick-breathing human being.

The most obvious generalization is of locality: Of Still's 694 recorded fugitives, only thirty-five came from the cotton South, land of the gang plantation and minimum stimulus. All the others were from the Border States of Delaware, Maryland and Virginia and the District of Columbia. Apparently few slaves risked striking for free soil from below a line 150 miles south of Mason and Dixon's; a 100-mile limit would almost be justified. Similarly, available facts show that runaways who crossed the Ohio and used the Middle Western UGRR to have come mostly from western Virginia, Kentucky and Missouri. Of 148 runaways noted in Levi Coffin's *Reminiscences,* 112 were Kentuckians.

This makes sense. Slaves living near free soil were subject to the suggestion of vicinity and were in better position to know where freedom was and how to reach it. Thus an up-standing slave hired out near Lexington, Kentucky, learned from talk among his fellows that a man named Coffin in Cincinnati helped runaways to a free country called Canada and that to reach Cincinnati one followed the railroad right-of-way northward and then crossed a big river. The towpath of the Wabash & Erie Canal was such another guide from Evansville, on the Ohio, to Toledo, with Canada just the other side of Lake Erie. Slaves on a Virginia farm visited by Ohio drovers learned which was the North Star—the slave's traditional beacon for escape—from a drover eager to do the master an ill turn. Farther south the slaves had a song about

---

checked against common sense and known factors. For instance, Still recorded degree of skin color in only 379 cases. But there is value in knowing how many of the 379 were obviously tinged with "white blood" and proceeding on the common-sense assumption that, of those un-recorded, most were inconspicuous because they were about as dark as was expected of slaves.

following "the drinking gourd" to freedom—this being their
designation of the Dipper with its pointers identifying the
North Star. A Yankee passenger on an Ohio steamboat gave
a slave fireman not only the identity of the star but sailing
directions: Go ashore at Pittsburgh, head north till you
reach water that you can't see across, then follow the shore to
the right till you see land on the other side with houses on
it—"and that's Canada." You could follow those directions
without knowing even the meaning of the word "map."

Many Delaware slaves were only one night's travel from
the boundary of freedom. Maryland slaves, even well down
the Eastern Sho' were almost as well off in comparison with
their kinsmen in Alabama, say. Thus it can be assumed that
the UGRR agent and the solicitous Abolitionist practically
never saw typical Deep South field hands to unsettle their
preconceptions of what kind of human raw material slaves
were. Even black farm hands from the small plantations of
Virginia and Maryland would be several cuts above the characteristic cotton chopper. Here Mrs. Stowe betrayed her
reader by the very fact that she did have firsthand acquaintance with runaways—of the superior Kentucky type. Her
book necessarily reflected and deepened for her public the
illusions that would underlie the errors of Reconstruction.
Here is an eminent Abolitionist parson-educator on his personal observations of the Ohio Underground:

> In general, the slaves that were contented and well cared
> for, and knew little of the positive cruelties of slavery, would
> not expose themselves to the risks involved in an effort to
> escape. Those that undertook the perilous enterprise . . .
> had their tale of horrors, and their scars and stripes to show.
> . . . The people of the North . . . knew little more of
> slavery than they gathered from such signs as these. . . .
> Now and then an honest planter from some rural district
> would appear upon the scene as claimant of his slave. But

oftener such a man would sell his claim to a specializing hunter who would conduct the business without scruple or delicacy . . . whose natural utensils were the bull-whip, the pistol, and the Bowie-knife; and . . . language and bearing corresponded with those weapons. Such a concept of the slaveholder was propagated by this business of slave-hunting, even in the country places of Ohio and Indiana.

A sound point: The very fact of running away was selective, hence bound somehow to intensify misconceptions. The considerable expense often necessary in escaping must have further weighted the mass of runaways toward an undue proportion of active and enterprising individuals; 15 per cent of Still's cases had come by water, almost all with some cash cost implied. Then assume that, even in the Border States, the farm slave was underdeveloped as compared with the town slave, and it is significant that so large a proportion of Still's runaways came from town situations: 30 per cent lived in town, or were hired out, or hired their own time, or were assigned to housework or to a special craft—in any case were somehow outside the standard vegetative status of farm hand. This must have been greatly out of proportion to the total number of slaves in the agricultural, meagerly industrialized regions involved.

So to some extent intellectual stimulus and decision to run away may have "gone together." Beyond that, what sort of automatic selection occurred is difficult to say. From the Negro point of view Miss Buckmaster called the UGRR "the safety valve for the South, running off the natural leaders who might have raised a vast insurrection. . . ." Southerners told Lyell that most runaways were chronic bad actors who, in free country, would always have been in jail for something and that the scars on them betokened not their masters' sadism but their own recalcitrance. As we have seen, there could have been some fact in this, supposing it confined strictly to the situation on gang plantations. But it can easily be overstated.*

In all common sense the Buckmaster position, if gingerly used, is likelier. Other things being equal, it was the brighter or anyway the less sluggish who would deliberately determine to run away, whether from restlessness or orneriness or to avoid being sold South. Among farm hands runaways must have been particularly notable, either more intelligent or more dynamically resentful. Hence the passengers on the UGRR were something of an automatically picked group, like Gideon's raiders, not at all to be taken—as doctrinaire Northerners did take them—as typifying the Negro slave's capabilities and personality. Whether they were potential organizers and leaders is not certain.† Of 100,000 or so probably escaping between 1800 and 1860, few enough showed marked abilities of that sort, certainly no more than could have been expected of an utterly random sample of whites. No doubt their average intelligence and initiative was a touch higher than that of American Negro slaves as a whole, both actual and potential. But the collec-

---

* Sellers (*Slavery in Alabama;* 268) says: "One must remember as one notes descriptions [of badly scarred backs] that many of the slaves described were probably habitual rogues and truants, the most unmanageable of the lot on the plantation . . . harsh punishments may have been provoked, though not justified, by their own recalcitrance." This neglects the fact that floggings might come of any one of several divergent kinds of attitude: pride, self-respect *or* pathological aggressiveness. Frazier (*Negro Family in the United States;* 130) rightly says that "The man who showed enough character to revolt against those in authority was often the very man most capable of self-direction as a freeman," and quotes a post bellum planter, "The man on this plantation who, as a slave, gave most trouble . . . was almost beyond control of the overseer . . . has grown honest, quiet, and industrious. . . ."
† Still's cases include eight runaway drivers or overseers, men who should theoretically have been especially content with their lives. That these, running away from favored status, were potential "natural leaders" is likely enough. I do not know what became of any of them.

tive "feel" of Still's cases suggests no high incidence of either delinquents or natural leaders. These were just underprivileged human beings of various degrees of simplicity or maturity, taking unusual risks because of special threat.

Mrs. Stowe helped greatly to bolster our notions of the superiority of "white blood" by making her principal runaways mulattoes or quadroons. Her brother Henry stated the theory: "The more enlightened and liberty-loving among the Southern slaves bear too much of their masters' blood not to avail themselves of any opening to escape." To judge from Still's records, admixture of Caucasoid ancestry had little to do with whatever it took to run away. Skin color, though not an infallible index of degree of miscegenation in a given individual, does mean something in large groupings; that is, if you divide a group of American Negroes into two, one *dark-to-black* and the other *saddle-colored-to-practically-white,* you can be confident that 300 years back the ancestors of the second group would show many more Caucasoids than those of the first group; and that "white" psychological traits, if such things exist, should be much more manifest in the second group. Here Still's data use a maddeningly confusing and overlapping terminology: without definition he sets down "black," "dark," "dark mulatto," "bright mulatto," "mulatto," "ginger," "copper," "dark brown," "chestnut," "dark chestnut," "dark orange," "orange." Yet a rough compilation, after all allowances are made, shows a strikingly high proportion of male runaways to have been solid Negro or close to it; 60 per cent were rated "dark" or "black." Obviously they owed little of their impulse toward freedom to their proud Caucasoid ancestry. Or put it the other way: Of male runaways fewer than 20 per cent were in the mulatto-to-almost-white category obviously dominated by Caucasoid genes.

These ratios do not hold for runaway women. Of sixty-eight of them whose skin color Still noted, only one in three was dark-to-black; the mulatto-to-almost-white group is slightly larger than the dark-to-black.* In the Siebert material too it is notable that instances of white-enough-to-pass fugitives are mostly women. Still mentions only two or three cases in which the wife persuaded the husband to run away with her. But it could be that light-skinned wives, probably more inclined to think slavery incongruous, had often worked on their husbands to take the risks necessary if the pair of them were to get away from the system.

On the other hand women slaves in general seem to have been less likely than men to abscond. Still's runaways are only 19 per cent female, a most reliable figure, since sex is invariably noted.† Three in four married-women runaways were with their husbands; only one in eight had left a husband behind. Married-men runaways were nothing like so devoted; 75 per cent of them had set off without their wives. In view of the tenuous nature of slave marriages, this is no surprise. It needs small comment in a world accustomed to refugees' leaving wives behind the Iron Curtain. The unexpected and gratifying thing is the fair number of men fugitives who, once established in a free state or Canada, risked coming South again to fetch wives and children or brothers and sisters. A fugitive named Charlie, very black

---

* Here is much room for speculation. Perhaps Still recorded female color oftener when it was lighter, hence attractively conspicuous? No; he noted color on women less often than on men. Perhaps light-colored women slaves were likelier to get into more stimulating circumstances? There might be something here. These women runaways also came from town situations oftener than did men. But does this fit with another datum—that most of these women runaways were with their "husbands," which would give the absurdity that men slaves married to lighter women were likelier to run away? Or is that absurd? Many slaves shared the master's belief that "white blood" carried innate prestige; hence it was occasion for personal pride, and perhaps particular resentment of the degrading circumstances of slavery.

† This is prettily confirmed by Seller's finding that 18 per cent of runaways advertised in the Huntsville, Alabama, papers between 1820 and 1860 were women. (*Slavery in Alabama;* 292.)

and very plucky, made a career of such repeated trips on the UGRR in Illinois, several times running off a party of slave friends from Missouri when it again proved impractical to abduct his wife. Henry Bibb, a Kentucky slave, came back twice from Michigan and managed to bring off his wife the second time. But the slave catchers caught them and sold them South, where resale separated them. Henry escaped again, and again started for his wife, only to hear reliably that she was living contentedly as her new master's mistress and probably would refuse to try another hazardous escape. The typical attitude of the married male runaway was more like that of James Massey, writing home from St. Catherine's, Ontario:

> Dear Wife—I . . . find myself on free ground and wish that you was here with me But you are not here, when we parted I did not know that I should come away so soon . . . I hope that you will try to come . . . Don't be Desscuredged I was sory to leave you . . . start and keep trying, if you are afread fitch your two sister for company and I will take care of you and treat you like a lady so long as you live. The talk of cold in this place is all a humbug, it is warmer here than it was there when I left . . . yours in Body and mind, and if we no meet on Earth I hope that we shall meet in heaven. Your husbern. Good night.

"Typical attitudes" are unreliable, of course, when persons of widely varying dispositions are under discussion. In 1855 a young man slave upset all precedent by running away with his baby daughter—master had given the mother away and her new owner, moving elsewhere would allow the new servant no encumbrances. Mrs. Stowe could have used that effectively. My own favorite among fugitive husbands is smart Jim, who got free from Kentucky to Canada, learning the ins and outs of escape en route, then returned to his master professing penitence and dislike of the cold up yonder and of mean Abolitionists he had met. He was restored

to favor without flogging and no doubt was encouraged to tell the whole neighborhood how little it paid to run away.*
Months passed; the weather again grew favorable—and one night Jim and his whole family, wife, children, and his brothers and sisters, disappeared, never to be seen south of the Ohio again. Years later in Canada he told Levi Coffin that he hoped God would forgive him all the lies he had told master, but he could find in his heart little yearning for his Old Kentucky Home. Just close your eyes and listen to the escaped slave and the Jesuitical old Quaker cackling over it.

Some twenty-five women, with or without their husbands, entered Still's UGRR depot accompanied by children ranging from babyhood to working age. Whatever was true of slave women in general, these must have been greatly attached to their offspring. Ann Maria Jackson astounded antislavery circles by singlehandedly bringing off seven children, and there would have been nine if her owner had not precipitated her flight by selling off the two likeliest. Her free husband had died and she was hiring her time from Joseph Brown of Milford, Delaware, a well-to-do widower "with a smooth face, bald head, light hair, long and sharp nose, swears very hard, and drinks." So far as I know this is the record. Runner-up was Rachel Moore, free Negro of Elkton, Maryland, who stole all her six children from her former master at one maternal swoop.

Both sexes escaped young. The men whose ages Still noted averaged twenty-eight years and the women twenty-seven,†

---

* In a few instances, of small significance, runaways voluntarily returned from free soil to resume slavery; for instance, see Coleman, *Slavery Times in Kentucky;* 54-56. Olmsted (*Cotton Kingdom;* 77-78) tells of a slave thus returning after buying his freedom and trying his luck in the North.

† These ages cannot be too reliable, for few slaves knew their ages exactly. Yet in most cases what Still noted cannot have been more than a year or two off; in a sample of well over 500, errors would pretty well cancel.

just the ages when slaves were most valuable—not too old to be prolific, mature enough to be steady, still at the peak of muscular and metabolic vigor. Loss of an elderly slave might inconvenience a master, especially if he were a long-trained servant, but it was not the economic blow felt when the absconder was a brawny young man worth upwards of $800 in Richmond or Alexandria, perhaps $1200 in Vicksburg. The shock might be even greater if the master had just been dickering to raise cash by selling him. Suspicion that such a deal was making was a frequent cause of running away. A mere glimpse of a speculator calling on the master and looking hard at Mandy's Bob as he took the visitor's horse might start Bob for the North Star that night, often taking along a crony of the same age and value for company and mutual protection.

Recognized procedure preserved all possible secrecy when master and trader were dealing. The first the slave knew of it all was when the trader suddenly came up, seized him and put him in irons for safekeeping en route to the slave jail where he amassed his stock in trade. Exactly that happened to young Alfred Thornton of Loudoun County, Virginia. He broke away from the dealer and the hired constable who had grabbed him and outran them to find his master, frantically demanding to know if he really had been sold as these white folks said. Master said, "Yes." "Why couldn't you sold me to some of the neighbors?" asked Alfred wildly and took to his heels again. Until nightfall he hid up to his nose in water in the millpond, then struck for freedom, only fifty miles away.

His protest is significant. Aside from the idea of being sold South, the slave was also often aghast at the notion of being exiled from such home as he had. Sordid as the little cabin was, little good as the Maryland or Kentucky fields and woods had ever done him, they were the only home he knew, the place where he was born, where the names of the mules and the dogs and the shape of the leaves on the trees and the rattle of the master's old spring wagon were achingly familiar. It was poor logic, but often the prospect of forcible separation from all this goaded him into seeking to carry out occasional previous daydreamings about freedom. Running away northward in response to threats to shift one westward or southward merely substituted one exile for another, but as a mutinous gesture it felt good. Many whom Still queried said that imminence of sale to settle an estate or pay a debt was their reason for leaving. The master of John Evans, Kentucky body servant, defrauded his creditors when he went bankrupt by writing John a pass to go to Detroit, thence to Canada. "He said if I was sold and had to work as a field hand I'd get strung up and whupped or killed sure thing because I didn't know how to work out of doors."

So Mrs. Stowe was sound in showing that even good masters could not always protect even favorite slaves from the speculator and shattering dislocation. But a master had only himself to blame when bad treatment was what moved a slave to take his "foot in his hand." Though the Border States were not so overseer-ridden as the cotton states, a certain amount of whipping went along with being a slave, or a convict, or, for that matter then, a child. It was one of the terms of the slave's existence, just as was the obligation to take off the remains of your hat when a white man asked you a question. But the tougher-minded slave had his own undefined standards of how much was enough. Beyond that point pain, anger and an outraged sense of fitness would start him northward, particularly if he knew how near freedom actually was in miles. So no doubt cruelty too had a selective effect on runaways. Of fifty former farm hands hired out to be more or less brutalized in tobacco factories, the one or two who gritted their teeth, swore they would take it no more and ran away to prove it must have been, on the whole, the more upstanding specimens.

Sometimes the cause was neither threat of sale nor cruelty. A score or so of Still's cases, usually from town situations, professed that their white folks had been fine, they had no complaints; they had just got tired of being slaves. Mrs. Elizabeth Scott Key of Braceville, Maryland, had been kind to her pretty mulatto girl Amerian, had taught her to read and write and play the piano and hired her out to nice people in Westminster where she was "used very well . . . had it good all my life." But at the age of twenty-one the accomplished and well-treated Amerian ran away just the same. Ebenezer Allison prospered as a hired-out barber in Richmond, Virginia, and "unhesitatingly declared that [his master, John Tilghman Foster] was a first-rate man. 'I had no right to leave him in the world, but I loved freedom better than slavery.'"

So those eloquent and explicit sentiments that made George Harris abscond even before he knew of the threat to his son were not impossible. They were merely atypical, a thing that would doubtless have puzzled Mrs. Stowe, who had obviously soaked herself in the abjectly false autobiographies that Abolitionists ghosted for *protégé*-runaways. What would have puzzled her still more would have been the evidence in Still's cases that practically none of his women runaways adduced unwelcome advances from white men as their reasons for running away; the *motif* is also rare in cases cited by Levi Coffin. Only mulatto Nancy Grantham of Richmond, Virginia, nineteen and pretty, told Still how her old goat of a master had threatened to come and take her on her pallet some night. She said that he had previously sold her sister South for resisting him, so she had borrowed men's clothes and arranged to be stowed away on a northbound steamer. The story was probably true enough. Perhaps the lack of other such tales was due to reticence, but if so, this delicacy was astonishingly consistent. It can hardly be that 133 of Still's 134 women passengers, so many young, so many light-colored, had never known molestation from white men. The impression persists that the matter was not actually taken as so important as Mrs. Stowe made it seem to Cassie and Emmeline.

In developing an alias for safety or in assuming the dignity of a surname for the first time, runaways chose the name Brown oftener than any other. One gets a good average feel of them by running down the list of Browns in Still's unalphabetized index:

Mulatto Louisa Brown ran away at sixteen from a Baltimore mistress; no further details.

Harriet Brown ran away from a Baltimore master named Stewart; no further details.

Chaskey Brown, coal-black farm hand, ran away from a foul-mouthed North Carolina planter, leaving wife and child behind.

Charles Brown, black farm hand, ran away from a hard-handed master of Sandy Hook, Maryland.

Young Solomon Brown, hiring his time from a Richmond mistress for $10 a month, suspected that she was going to sell him South and absconded as a stowaway on the *City of Richmond*.

John Brown, runaway with a fateful name, no details.

George and Angelina Brown, brother and sister, with four others, stole master's horse and carriage one night near Hagerstown, Maryland. The patrol challenged them. The horses panicked in the ensuing fracas and smashed the carriage. The fugitives beat off the patrol, unhitched the horses and proceeded on horseback, three to a horse.

Anthony and Albert Brown got away in a Norfolk oyster-boat.

William Brown of Prince George's County, Maryland, ran away because, when he resisted a flogging, master said, "No, I won't sell you South, boy, I'll keep you to make an example of."

Charles Henry Brown of Cambridge, Maryland; no details.

Stepney Brown, thirty-four, dark, slender, pious Baptist, ran away from a devout and close-fisted Richmond mistress because "I believed I had a right to be free."

Another John Brown, this one small, dark and ugly, ran away for no stated reason from a Baltimore shoe clerk from whom he hired his time.

Still another John Brown ran away from the farmer-son of his Baltimore owner.

Jacob Brown, black and husky, hired out in North Carolina by a Washington, D.C. owner, left as paying stowaway in a schooner.

William Brown ran away from a Maryland farmer with the ominous name of Lynchum who never flogged but seems to have had other ways (darkly unspecified) of putting the fear of God into slaves. . . .*

None of them sound much like characters in Mrs. Stowe's novel, let alone those in the play as it eventually developed.

With all this knowledge of the ascertainable facts of slavery to back us, we can now properly gauge the extent of the special perversions in the Tom-show. For, like *Ben Hur* and *The Clansman,* Mrs. Stowe's work was a three-stage rocket. Having gained all the altitude conceivable to a long book, it then received a second and even stronger impetus by translation to the stage and later, though less explosively, to the screen.† In the process some few of Mrs. Stowe's errors were smothered or omitted. But on the whole matters were wors-

---

* These names are relatively pedestrian. Others of Still's cases had or assumed more striking ones, such as Charles Congo and William Henry Washington. A number of them could be minor characters from a Smollett novel: Anthony Blow, Jim Bowlegs, Richard Booze, Isaac Fidget, Thomas Jervis Gooseberry, Sauney Pry, and so on.

† I have not traced down all the movie versions of *Uncle Tom.* The wonder is not that they were numerous but that, on the whole, they were so inconspicuous, in effect if not always in intention. I leave it to better heads than mine to understand why the most successful movies treating of slavery should have been *The Birth of a Nation* and *Gone with the Wind.*

ened because other errors were retained and accentuated. Low- and then lower-grade showmanship kept stamping into public consciousness, beginning with the semi-illiterates of the Bowery in the 1850's, a degenerate version of Mrs. Stowe's picture of the Negro as second-rate human being, a large, dark animal but sometimes worthy and probably with some sort of soul. In every whistle stop outside the South proper, grass-roots audiences came to Tom-shows primarily, no doubt, because they liked to laugh at Topsy and Lawyer Marks, hate Legree, weep for Little Eva and agonize as the dogs leaped snarling for the beef scraps hidden in Eliza's neckerchief. But they necessarily absorbed the derogatory implications of the Negro roles and went away still further confirmed in a destructive racism.

ORDEAL BY FOOTLIGHTS

> *"He beat poor Uncle Tom to death*
> *Who prayed for Legree with his last breath,*
> *Then Uncle Tom to Eva flew,*
> *To the high sanctoriums bright and new*
> *And Simon Legree stared up beneath*
> *And cracked his heels and ground his teeth*
> And went down to the devil."
>
> —VACHEL LINDSAY, "Simon Legree,
> A Negro Sermon"

I have seen only one true Tom-show—not a self-conscious revival but the traditional "kid-and-rube show" of commerce played straight. This was in Port Huron, Michigan, in summer, 1924. I now recall only the smallness of stage and audience and the dreariness of the performance, not under canvas but in some ramshackle hall. The company apparently lacked the skills for the usual specialty turns between the acts. Even the gaunt dogs seemed tired and were, of course, not bloodhounds but mastiffs more or less, since bloodhounds are rare and expensive and cannot look ferocious. The ice floes, unashamed cardboard cartons wrapped in white paper, obviously had become, like the symbols of astrology or the Oriental theater, mere arbitrary conventions. It was all heavy with the dead hand of it's-always-been-done-this-way, going in loose, ancient grooves, the reasons for which might not readily be recalled but no longer mattered anyway.

This phenomenon in a droopy Lake town did not surprise me thirty years ago. The idea of Tom-shows was familiar to my childhood, though, since Tommers did not thrive in bright lights, they seldom visited our sizable Middle Western city. Of my questionnaire respondents who had seen the play, a great majority had encountered it in places on the order of Crawfordsville, Indiana; Alfred, New York; Liberty, Missouri. Diligent search has found me no Tommers still operating. The last discoverable serious staging was that of the Slout Players of Vermontville, Michigan, touring central and southern Missouri under canvas in the summer of 1950. But this extinction is astonishingly recent. In 1927 Wesley W. Stout found a dozen troupes surviving. It is almost literally incredible that, until so few years ago, persistent people could still make some kind of living out of Eliza, Topsy, Legree and Lawyer Marks; that ninety-eight years after Thespis first blacked up to play Uncle Tom, he was still getting called on stage in that character. This bedraggled little fact calls for closer acquaintance with the nature and scope of the stage tradition that gave Mrs. Stowe her second means of inadvertent damage.

It was doubly inadvertent because she had not wanted her book to be dramatized. When Asa Hutchinson, of the Hutchinson Family of Temperance Singers (all militant Abolitionists*), sought her permission to stage *Uncle Tom,* she refused because

> . . . with the present state of theatrical performances in this country . . . any attempt on the part of Christians to identify themselves with them will be productive of danger to the individual character and to the general cause. If the bar-

---

* A typical Hutchinson song featured at an abolitionist rally at Faneuil Hall, Boston:

"Fleecy locks and black complexions cannot forfeit nature's claim;
Skins may differ but affections dwell in black and white the same."

rier which keeps young people of Christian families from
theatrical entertainment is once broken down by the introduction of respectable and moral plays they will then be open
to all the temptations of those which are not such . . . there
will be . . . five bad plays to one good . . . the idea of
reforming dramatic entertainments is . . . wholly impractical.

This stand, however consistent with her pious rearing,
would have had better grace if she had ever witnessed one
of these reprehended performances. But her biographers
assert (and I have no counter-evidence) that prudish scruples had kept her from visiting a theater until a friend took
her to see *Uncle Tom*, probably in 1857.*

In view of what happened to her story behind footlights,
her refusal, however stuffy, was well advised.† It was also
futile. Hutchinson took "No" for an answer, but others with
the same scheme did not even bother to ask permission,
which was then legally unnecessary for dramatization of published fictions. The fashion of doing such dramatizations was
stronger then than it is now. These days, though there are
sporadic exceptions, it is the screen—a better medium for
the purpose—that usually provides conspicuous novels with
moving, speaking, and often distorting illustrations. But
early Victorian standards of dramaturgy were looser than
ours; Victorian audiences loved elaborate sets and mechanical effects that no producer in his right mind would attempt

---

* In one story Francis Underwood takes her to the Aiken version. (Wilson, *Crusader in Crinoline;* 439.) In the other Charles Dudley Warner
takes her to the Conway version; she leaves in disgust at the lines and
character of Penetrate Partyside. (Birdoff, *World's Greatest Hit;* 190.)
Whatever the facts, they led to slanderous rumors in Andover that
Mrs. Stowe "actually visited the theatre in Boston when she felt like
it." (Phelps, *Chapters from a Life;* 132-133.)

† Mrs. Stowe later did a play version, *The Christian Slave,* sometimes
read at Abolition rallies by Mary E. Webb, a part-Negro actress. The
title shows what the author took to be the principal theme of the book.

today; so authors of novels of melodramatic content always risked seeing them staged and deriving mere courtesy revenues or none from the productions. For Mrs. Stowe it was none.

The first attempt to exploit *Uncle Tom* at the box office gave little hint of the gold rush to come. But it did show trends that would soon ruin what poor validity the novel had possessed. Within five months of publication of the book, the National Theatre, a low Bowery house specializing in cheap melodrama, riding acts and women in men's clothes, staged a dramatization by C. W. Taylor, an actor well known as a play cobbler. He himself created the role of Uncle Tom and was to become a specialist in the part, though not as he wrote it. The rest of the bill—theaters then always offered a light afterpiece and often a ballet or conjurer or acrobats—consisted of a burlesque of *Othello*,* a rope dancer, and an imitator of bullfrogs.

The script jettisoned the whole Louisiana block of plot. A happy ending restored the Harrises (for some reason their names were changed to Edward and Morna Wilmot) and Uncle Tom to the old plantation, all free and healthy. The whole was crammed with the standard claptrap of the period: "Cave of Crazy Meg . . . Maniac's Protection . . ." as well as an ice-scene for "Morna." And—this was ominous —it had interpolated numbers billed as "Chorus (Nigga in de Cornfield) Kentucky Breakdown Dances," probably led by T. D. ("Daddy") Rice, whose "Jump Jim Crow" song and dance had founded the nigger-minstrel tradition that was already vigorous on the American and British stages. Here began the infiltration of *Uncle Tom* with impertinent

---

* Such pieces were the origin of burlesque à la Minsky, but remotely so. In 1850 "burlesque" really did travesty classics or recent hits. The connection between this and bargain-rate sex came through the burlesquers' device of casting women as men titillatingly dressed in breeches, which gradually led to more and more exposure; and through the developing coarseness of the gags and business used.

tricks. The Victorian stage was all cluttered up with incidental songs and dances anyway, but in this case such numbers were soon acting like the camel in the tent.

Though it lasted almost two weeks—not bad for that house
in summer—the Taylor adaptation had no further future. In
view of the ingredients of its successor, the cause may have
been that it had thrown out the wrong plot: It had Eliza
and the ice, very good so far, but no Topsy, no Eva, no
Simon Legree.

That same autumn of 1852 a repertory troupe operating
the Museum Theatre in Troy, New York, created both
Topsy and Eva as the world ever after knew them. The
actor-manager of this company was George C. Howard; its
soubrette, *née* Caroline Fox, was his wife; and practically all
the other members were somehow her relatives in a manner
highly reminiscent of the Crummles family in *Nicholas Nickleby*. Their Infant Phenomenon was four-year-old Cordelia
Howard, billed as "The Child of Nature" or "The Little
Wonder," who, unlike her prototype, was really a child,
much too young, in fact, for her great role as Mrs. Stowe developed it. Their Nicholas was George L. Aiken, a cousin of
the Foxes, and a juvenile who, in odd moments, cobbled up
scripts to put novelty into the playbills.

The company were a cut above out-and-out barnstormers
but well below the best-established troupes. Small Cordelia
was looking more and more like the family meal ticket. So,
though Taylor's version was known to have been less than
enthusiastically received, Howard assigned Aiken to prepare
a stage-version of *Uncle Tom*. There is small reason to believe that either manager or writer cared one way or the
other about slavery.* But the company had recently done

* Possible correction: In 1932, when she was eighty-four years old, the
Little Wonder told the Boston *Advertiser* (October 30, 1932) that
Howard had produced *Uncle Tom* because "he desired the abolition of
slavery." She sounds like a very nice old lady but, for lack of any previous suggestion to this effect, I prefer to conclude what the text says.

well with *The Drunkard* in Boston, so they thought well of plays-with-a-purpose, and Howard was eager to set his amazing little daughter to lisping and tripping through that Eva role even if she was half the age of Mrs. Stowe's heroine.

He was building better than he knew, at least for the adults. At the age of thirteen Cordelia left the stage,* finished schooling, married happily and never put on make-up again. But the actor named Germon who at first balked at playing a Negro because it would be undignified wound up playing Uncle Tom the rest of his life. For similar reasons Mrs. Germon refused to do Topsy. Mrs. Howard took it up and in 1886, thirty-four years after they first rang up on *Uncle Tom* in Troy, Caroline Fox Howard was still doing Topsy and her husband was still doing St. Clare. Aiken's published memoirs fail to mention his having begotten the fundamental version of the world's most successful play, for which his only reward beyond regular walkings of the ghost was a gold watch from the company.

Committed to plenty of Eva, Aiken played exactly the opposite of Taylor's game—emphasized the New Orleans material and made the child's death the last curtain of the standard four-acter that was his first trial. He played George Shelby himself. Brought out on September 28, 1852, this ran four weeks—astounding for Troy. As its momentum fell off, Aiken glued together a four-act sequel covering the Red River episodes under the title *The Death of Uncle Tom: or, The Religion of the Lowly*. This did another brilliant four weeks. Already Aiken was under orders to boil the two successes down into one. No doubt swearing hard, he managed it—a six-act, twenty-nine-scene behemoth of a script that became a classic among half a dozen adaptations and furnished the mine whence the Tommers drew their raw material.

---

* So far as I can discover her last role was that of little Mary Morgan, the drunkard's child, in *Ten Nights in a Bar-Room*.

"There are a great many things here that make me sad"
Uncle Toms Cabin, Chapter XXIV.

LITTLE CORDELIA HOWARD

THE CHILD OF NATURE, AGED 5 YEARS.

In the Character of

EVA.

The Original personator of the part.

J. Frank Davis, who claimed to have seen at least twenty-five productions of *Uncle Tom,* said that no script short of fifty scenes could have been coherent. This one certainly was not, but then few melodramas of that day were so or needed to be. The company had to double parts to handle it even so, but that fitted their Crummles-like flavor: Aiken took both George Harris and Shelby; Mrs. Howard did both Aunt Chloe and Topsy; Mrs. Germon was both Cassie and Eliza. The death-of-Eva version left time for the usual afterpiece, building up G. K. Fox, Mrs. Howard's funny-man brother; so did the death-of-Tom version. But, even though they rang up at 7:45, this new colossus put the inclusion of any other items on the bill out of the question. So *Uncle Tom,* according to Odell, historian of the New York stage, first showed managers that, if popular enough, a single play could fill a house. The demonstration was impressive. When, after immense success in Troy, the Howards brought Aiken's dinosaur to the National Theatre, the same Bowery house that had tried Taylor's version, it ran over 300 consecutive performances—then just about inconceivable. Later the Howard child would charm audiences as Ida May, the Kidnapped Child; Oliver Twist; a Polish waif in *A Page of History;* Tom-Tit, the comic slave boy in a dramatization of *Dred;* and Little Katy in a stage version of Solon Robinson's *Hot Corn.** But it was her Eva teamed with her mother's tem-

---

* *Ida May* was a novel by Mary Langdon about a white child kidnapped and sold into slavery, dramatized in 1855. *Hot Corn* as a book was a compilation of sketches done by Robinson for the New York *Tribune* as part fiction, part fact about slums, fallen women and the perils of barrooms (all plentiful in New York at the time) avowedly aimed "to promote temperance and virtue." The title comes from its Dickensish description of the girl-children selling hot roasting ears on street corners, which seem to have been a contemporary institution. The title page gives the flavor: "HOT CORN/Life Scenes in New York/Illustrated/ Including/The Story of Katy/Madalina, The Rag-Picker's Daughter/ Wild Maggie &c. . . ." Little Cordelia Howard's repertory can readily be made to sound ridiculous and no doubt ridiculous it was. But no

pestuously impish Topsy that made the difference and gave the world the all-time pattern of a cheap theatrical hit.

In terms of the day Aiken was not a bad workman. The trouble lay in the assignment and in the day. The English-speaking theater was then precisely at its lowest ebb, in tone, not in profit. Its best playwrights—say Tom Taylor and Dion Boucicault—were only journeymen. Its best performers, who must often have been far better than their material, stuffed their repertories with dreary pseudo-Jacobean stuff like *Fazio* and *Virginius* and the absurdities of Kotzebue, which their public received as if they had been *King Lear* and *Macbeth*. Like the screen of today this theater relied abjectly on personal followings and flashy spectacle. Its traditions called for shifts in emphasis and heightenings of mawkish-ness that trebled the worst of such sins in the original book. Heaven knows Mrs. Stowe had had sickly intervals, particu-larly in handling Eva. But the stage deliberately retained and accentuated the sickliness, leached out much of the com-mon sense, and grafted on new elements that gradually grew into travesty of what she had meant to convey.

For example, Aiken equipped each of his original Troy versions with a by-gosh comedian's role, perhaps because G. K. Fox, the boss's wife's brother, was well known in such business but certainly because audiences expected low com-edy as periodic relief in melodrama. Its original *raison d'être* was to supply material that could be played downstage be-fore a drop curtain to give time to shift and assemble elabo-rate scenery and effects. In the 1850's every well-rounded company had a specialist in Yankee roles, a stereotype cre-ated as Sam Slick in the previous generation. So in the death-of-Eva script Aiken telescoped the Quaker conductor of the UGRR with a couple of minor figures and expanded the results into a stock Yankee funnyman with his finger in

---

doubt also she was a trouper of considerable parts and so, for that matter, were her ingenious parents and uncles and cousins.

every pie and strange language on his lips. A pretty Quaker-ess has cajoled this Phineas Fletcher into freeing his slaves: "I'm a teetotal victim to a pair of black eyes. Chaw me up to feed hogs if I'm not in a ruinatious state!" He ensnares the slave catchers who are pursuing George Harris by means of the indispensable stage trapdoor of the period and drives them down into it by flourishing a chair: "Down with you or I'll smash you into apple fritters!" Tableau! Gales of laugh-ter and applause! Curtain!

For the same sort of assignment in the death-of-Tom script Aiken supplied Fox with a role with the telltale name of Gumption Cute, manufactured out of whole cloth. He is a swindling cousin of Miss Ophelia's strayed to New Orleans and hired as slave catcher by Lawyer Marks. Then he turns up in New Hampshire where another comic Yan-kee, Deacon Perry (a mere name in the book) is courting Miss Ophelia while Topsy cuts monkeyshines all over the place.* No doubt one reason for thus expanding Topsy's time on stage was that this was the boss's wife's role. Mrs. How-ard's nightly business of "butting the Yankee" (played by her own brother) got special billing. (It is strange to reflect that, if the talents of the Howards and their relatives had not been just what they were, this might never have been "The World's Greatest Hit" or anything near it.) Working hard for laughs, Cute apostrophizes Topsy as "Charcoal! . . . Ex-tract of Japan! . . . Stove polish! . . . Ebony angel!" and proposes to tour her as a wild Whatisit. She flogs him into submission with a broom. In the end Marks and Cute learn that Legree is the very barroom rough who killed St. Clare and try to blackmail him. When he resists, they shoot him—

---

* The cut-down version that A. E. Thomas did for The Players' revival in 1933 dropped these New England scenes. Topsy's future was ac-counted for by Miss Ophelia's buying her at the sale of St. Clare's slaves. Thomas added dogs to the ice scene, as Aiken had not, and wrote in new buffooneries for Lawyer Marks, doubtless to commemorate the traditional importance of this role in later Tom-shows.

as part of Uncle Tom's death scene, utterly spoiling Mrs. Stowe's most devoted effort.

When combining the two pieces, Aiken retained both Phineas and Cute as specialty roles for Fox to double. The playwright left out no device for keeping his audience that the resources of his pen and the company could suggest. Harriet's Eliza fled weeping inarticulately. Aiken's must soliloquize: "They press upon my footsteps—the river is my only hope! . . . Courage, my child!—we will be free—or perish!" Interpolated songs included "Uncle Tom's Religion," Tom's rendition of "Old Folks at Home," recently popularized by the Christy Minstrels, and a number that Howard wrote for Topsy, "I'se So Wicked!" which Mrs. Howard made a high spot of the show.

The finale of the death-of-Eva version had been what Huckleberry Finn would have called "soul-butter and hogwash" but was actually billed as "A Grand Allegorical View of the Realms of Bliss." The stage directions read: "Gorgeous clouds tinted with sunlight. Eva, robed in white, is discovered on the back of a milk-white dove, with expanded wings, as if just soaring upward. Her hands are extended in benediction over St. Clare and Tom, who are kneeling and gazing up at her. Expressive music—slow curtain." In the combination script the harassed playwright, apparently fearful lest Tom's death be too grim a curtain, followed it with this spun-sugar tableau. All out of logical order, of course. Eva had been dead for months, and the audience received no explanation of why she was only now ascending to the Heaven that she had so confidently promised herself. But the scene became indispensable, and the Tommers insisted on one or another version of it for three generations.

Mrs. Howard usually hired a double to ride the dove at the ungodly hour to which the play ran; the "Child of Nature" had gone hygienically home to bed two hours before. But many and many an eventually famous actress, including Maude Adams and Minnie Maddern Fiske, was less solicitously guarded. They knew what it was like to balance on a moth-eaten prop the size of a he-ostrich while the professor bowed his fiddle through "Nearer, My God, to Thee" and the sweat started through Uncle Tom's smudging make-up. So did some male performers. A Tom-troupe needing an inexpensive Eva and lacking a girl of the right age and size scrupled not to put a long fair wig on the manager's small son and cause him to deck Uncle Tom with blossoms and prattle artlessly of "the new Jerusalem and bright angels and the land of Canaan." One veteran actor still complains of having had to play Little Eva, as the role soon became known, alleging that his soul never really healed from the psychic strain. Others seem to have taken it well in stride.

By November, 1853, the Aiken version had also triumphed in Philadelphia, acted by such distinguished figures as Joseph Jefferson and Mr. and Mrs. John Gilbert, and a doughty rival had appeared from Boston. Even as Aiken had been struggling with Uncle Tom in Troy, a fellow craftsman, Henry J. Conway (author also of *The Orphan's Dream, The Last Nail*, and *The New York Patriot: or, The Battle of Saratoga*) was trying his hand at a version for the use of the repertory company of the Boston Museum. Their chief attraction was William Warren, a famous comic actor, for whom Conway naturally wrote in a Yankee part, Penetrate Partyside.* Their ingenue, Helen Western, would soon be a "draw" in her own right, along with her sister Lucille, in "leg roles" in Bowery theaters. Just now she played Eva in Conway's *Uncle Tom*, which ran a stunning eighty-three performances in Boston. Then P. T. Barnum brought it to New York to oppose the Howard-Aiken version, and very well it did under the circumstances, running six weeks and getting revived profitably twice in the spring of 1855.

I know of no script of this version. To judge by the play-

---

* This comic Yankee trick was inescapable. The Bowery Theatre version of 1854 included both a Jerusha Jenkins and an Everlasting Peabody.

bills it left out the ice scene and muffed the whole religious point of the plot by having George Shelby rescue Tom in the nick of time and presumably restore him to Kentucky and Aunt Chloe. Obviously it did much to nudge competing productions toward the techniques of the minstrel show and the spectacle and so on and down to the Tom-show as such. It had a "Grand Panorama of a Portion of the Mississippi River Down to New Orleans" that should alone have been worth twenty-five cents admission, and many song-and-dance numbers: Its slave-auction scene, for instance, included a "Plantation Jig . . . Mr. Gray/Banjo Accompaniment . . . Mr. Brown," obviously a straight minstrel turn. "The Quadroon Lady's Maid's Burlesque Pas de Trois" supplemented Topsy's eccentric dances, the growing conspicuousness of which had already made the Topsy role a principal prop of any kind of *Uncle Tom*. There were plenty of variations. In February, 1863, New York had *four* rival productions of *Uncle Tom's Cabin* competing at once, all stuck full of banjos, cakewalks and tin-pan-alley coon songs with no relation to either the action or the character singing. All insisted more and more on the minstrel-show picture of the Negro as simian buffoon, agile, tuneful, rhythmic, but all the funnier for being imperfectly human. In working up the antics of the Shelby slave boys, Mrs. Stowe had sinned somewhat in that direction herself, but nothing like what was now happening to Topsy.*

The cleverest and, I suspect, the soundest-acting stage version of *Uncle Tom* was put together for London's Adelphi Theatre by two eminent playwrights, Mark Lemon and Tom Taylor. Showing either queasiness or great courage, they omitted Eva altogether and otherwise solved the difficulties of Mrs. Stowe's glut of characters by fusing similar types: Topsy remained herself alone, so did Tom and Cassy, but everybody else had to climb inside somebody else's skin. The

---

* See Rourke, "Harriet Beecher Stowe," *Encyclopedia of the Social Sciences.* Mrs. Stowe certainly never attended a minstrel show, but the minstrel stereotypes were lively in the national mind of her time.

action proceeds taut and trig, with some well-manipulated scenes, in the hands of Mrs. Shelby-Aunt Ophelia, Eliza-Emmeline, George Harris-Shelby, St. Clare-Shelby, and a tremendous villain combining the worst features of Haley, Loker and Legree. French adaptors lovingly cherished Eva. One of them even had Tom's prayers secure her a miraculous recovery and, in a miracle of his own, moved Canada to the northern bank of the Ohio. Another French adaptor made cotton a staple crop in Kentucky. The Eva-gets-well version was adapted for the London stage in 1878 with "a mate for Topsy . . . a fancy darkey named Julius . . . the two dance breakdowns together and sing comic duets and talk comic trash in a mixture of Irish, Cockney and Scotch which the . . . actors imagine is . . . the genuine cane-brake lingo," wrote Augustin Daly.

The British alone, however, were responsible for the version concentrating most invidiously on what these Americans did to slaves: It excludes St. Clare the kind master, Miss Ophelia the well-wisher, and Eva the consolation of the slave in favor of a completely gratuitous scene of Legree and dogs hunting a runaway, with horrible offstage noises as the pack run down their quarry and Legree shoots him as too mangled for further usefulness.* (This was the first use of dogs in *Uncle Tom*. The first such use in the United States was in an "Equestrian Uncle Tom's Cabin" at the Old Bowery Theatre in New York in 1862, with "real horses, dogs and mules.") A minor figure at the slave auction is engagingly named Mr. Yahoo. The slaves' gibberish: "Mas'r Haley take wrong road—Miss Lizzy 'scapy!" is worse than Mrs. Stowe's worst. An Ohio farmer and conductor on the UGRR tells the runaways: "Stay, tarry till the dawn, and I will with my sons conduct you hence. . . ." But again the greatest perversion is the insistence on horseplay and song

---

* This version was first produced at the Theatre Royal, Manchester, in early 1853. The printed version carries no author's credit.

and dance regardless of context. On both sides of the water these stage productions must have looked like what would happen if one sandwiched Weber & Fields in between scenes from Buchenwald.

The opening of this version is fantastic. Curtain rises on Shelby's slaves singing:

> Our work is done—our toil is o'er,
> Massa say we work no more,
>   While de moon is peeping;
> Sing and prance, let us dance,
>   While de world is sleeping;
> Uncle Tom, Uncle Tom, Aunty Chloe and Joe,
> Come along, join the song, and hear the merry banjo.

Enter Shelby, promises to free Uncle Tom and George and Eliza Harris. Enter Haley, spoils all by threatening to sell Shelby up, whereupon all hands, with a really lunatic jollity, break into a rollicking "Negro ballet." *

---

* This adaptor had trouble with Americanese: Mrs. Stowe's landlady told Eliza: "There's a man a piece down here that's going over [the river] with some truck this evening." To Britons "truck" then meant only a heavy wagon. This Briton assumed a copy error and made it "a man . . . going over with a truck." The superior Lemon-Taylor version did not altogether avoid queer details. Its landlord is named Skunk and the song of its slaves must surely have been written by the same genius who produced Marmaduke Ruggles's favorite "raccoon ballad" of "Away Down South in Michigan": "I wish I was in ole Verginny/Wid Dinah and de Pickaninny/Just sittin' down to dinner off Gumbo/For dat's de berry ting for Jumbo. . . ."

"WANTED!   WANTED!
Pair of Trained Bloodhounds
for Uncle Tom's Cabin
at Forepaugh's Theatre and Museum ...
Persons having such dogs to rent will
please communicate at once naming
amount of hire expected ..."
—*Advertisement in New York* Clipper,
January 9, 1886

After the Civil War the example of the Fisk Jubilee Singers combined with curiosity about the "freedmen" to swathe *Uncle Tom* in even stranger trappings. By 1878 the Howards, playing it at the Brooklyn Academy of Music, had alleged "Jubilee Singers" harmonizing "The Sweet Bye and Bye" and "Shall We Gather at the River?" while Eva died in the person of Little Gracie Wade. A fresh New York version offered the "Virginia Jubilee Singers," cotton fields in bloom, the race between the *Natchez* and the *Robert E. Lee,* and a Mississippi flatboat full of "Congo Melodists," a term straight out of minstrel ballyhoo.* The same season American producers sent to London, then relapsing into *oncle-tomerie* with *five* versions running at once, a large *Uncle Tom* company built round choruses of "genuine freed slaves." Such choirs and choruses probably amounted to the Negro's first substantial opportunity to earn a living behind footlights. There had been sporadic figures like Ira Eldridge, "the African Roscius," who often did Othello to Edmund Kean's Iago in Britain. Sometimes, not often, Topsy or Uncle Tom had been played by an actual Negro, of whom Sam Lucas seems to have been best known. But this new tradition

---

* This style of production soon leaked over into other traditional vehicles about slaves, notably *The Octoroon* and *The White Slave.* Perhaps *Uncle Tom* showed the way. *Cf.* Gaines, *Southern Plantation;* 104.

CARD TO THE PUBLIC.

This Company was organized with the express view to the proper production of the

GREATEST WORK OF THE CENTURY

MRS. HARRIET BEECHER STOWE'S

Uncle Tom's Cabin

OR, THE PIOUS SLAVE.

A work universally Read and Admired by All Classes, including the Clergy and Christian People of all Creeds and in its Dramatic Form has received the endorsement of all, as being a True Picture of Life in the South 35 years ago. Wherever we have presented it for the last 4 years in New England, the houses have been Packed to Overflowing, and in many Places People Turned Away.

One week in Providence, one week in Springfield, one week in New Bedford, Fall River, Newport, Boston, Cambridge, Lynn, Salem, Worcester, Hartford, Portland, Brunswick, Bath, Rockland, Eastport, Calais, Bangor and almost every New England Town.

The People and Press have given us their Support and Pronounced Our Version and Performance the Best they have ever witnessed.

It points to a moral Bold and True, and leaves an impressive beauty and nobility upon the mind of man.

SPECIAL FEATURES.

The Wild Flight and Escape of Eliza with her baby in her arms, across the river.

The fierce fight at the Rocky Pass, aided by natural surroundings.

The Home and House of St. Clair and Eva, to present Eva's life at home.

Eva's Death, with Angels gathering around.

Topsy in her native mischief element upon St. Clair's plantation.

The exciting Steamboat Race on the Mississippi.

The genuine Auction Sale of Slaves upon the plantation.

Lawyer Marks upon his donkey, "Tobey," at the auction.

Uncle Tom tied and beaten at the cruel whipping post.

Cotton hoeing and picking by slaves.

The death of Legree.

Uncle Tom's Work Done at Last, and the Victory won.

The Beautiful Allegory.

EVA IN HEAVENLY REALMS

Also, the Famous and Original Company of

KENTUCKY JUBILEE SINGERS,

Worth alone the price of admission. — A whole show in themselves. — Acknowledged everywhere the finest singers ever heard. Don't fail to hear their famous Plantation Melodies.

of Negro ensembles must have helped greatly to train a group of professional singers and dancers for at least off-and-on careers. Here may have been the germs of *Shuffle Along* and *The Green Pastures.*

These spangled *Uncle Toms* curiously anticipated the musical-show-with-a-moral in which Rodgers & Hammerstein today so skillfully fuse *schmalz,* sex and social significance. The Tommers at least left out the sex. Topsy was as unattractive as burnt cork and a fright wig could make her. Miss Ophelia dressed as a bony old maid, Mrs. Shelby was just a matronly walk-on, Eva a virginal juvenile; only Eliza had much scope for come-hithering. Earlier audiences seem to have been better prepared than ours to do without erotic spicing.

Dramatizations of *Uncle Tom* had already appeared from Berlin to Budapest and reached the antipodes; presently the overloaded flash productions followed. The piece became a stock repertory item for minor troupes on tour or leasing theaters in Chicago or San Francisco. Soon practically every actor in the American Theater had played in it at some-time or other. Eventually in Cooktown, away off at the top of beyond in Australia, an American company besought by local patrons to give them *Uncle Tom* could muster enough actors experienced in it to stage it *without a script.* That was the point of no return, the moment when the Aiken version began to sublimate into what Birdoff calls a "true folk-play." After a while a performance of *Uncle Tom* had no more need than Punch and Judy for a script.

Marginal repertory troupes began to find that, if they kept moving, they could get along with *Uncle Tom* and nothing else. Harassedly pursuing coffee and cakes, they cut this scene, expanded that, introduced new props and new business, built up minor characters with what became traditional business when applauded. Half the United States became conscious of Lawyer Marks's signature lines: "My name is Marks; I'm a lawyer; special attention given to runaway niggers and divorce cases; have a card!"; and of the similarly evolved vaunt of Phineas Fletcher, the Quaker rough diamond: "This right hand is sudden death, and this left hand is six weeks in the hospital—yeaaaaaaaaa verileeeeeeee!" Marks counted on winning an extra hand from the audience by instructing Sambo and Quimbo to feed Legree's corpse to the hogs. As these roles hypertrophied, others dwindled. Tom sank to a white-haired dodderer, a symbol of pitiful good nature, a mere quavering occasion for Legree's rasping and ranting. Miss Ophelia dwindled to a mere foil for Topsy. And year after year Marks grew in stature with the aid of a trick donkey ridden on stage and invariable, eagerly anticipated props such as a mammoth wallet and a huge umbrella to be opened as a burlesque shield against bullets in the battle-among-the-rocks scene.

These productions had a flavor of *commedia dell'arte*, a reference not necessarily flattering. Much as though they were Harlequin, Pantaloon and Columbine, the performers came to be thought of as Evas, Markses and Topsys instead of as generally competent soubrettes, ingenues or knockabout comedians. Tomming became a verb and a theatrical subindustry, a way of life somewhere between ragpicking and lighthouse-keeping in prestige and economic reward. People were born into, grew up and died in it. A girl child would do Eva as soon as she could learn lines and stay at it until shifted to Topsy, perhaps thence, as years passed, to Eliza, thence to Miss Ophelia or Mrs. Shelby, possibly with her own daughters succeeding her as Eva, as in the pleasant John Golden-Kenyon Nicholson comedy *Eva the Fifth*. Marked talent might begin with Tomming because born into it or forced to it, but at the first shadow of better opportunity talent usually went elsewhere.* The best that could be said for it all was that it was usually a living.

---

* Erstwhile Tommers listed in a Universal Pictures promotion poster for a movie version of *Uncle Tom* included: Fay Templeton, Hobart

Late eighteenth-century slaves having a frolic on a Virginia plantation. Note the Big House and quarters in the background; the headties, the banjo, the sticks knocked together for percussion—and the obvious portrait quality of the heads. Courtesy of Abby Aldrich Rockefeller Folk Art Collection.

Harriet Beecher Stowe

Slaves of the plantation.

The Big House. Architecturally it could just about as well be in Kennebunk, Maine.

The "quarters."

Closeup of slaves and a "quarter."

Slave auction at Charleston, South Carolina, 1856, as drawn from life by Eyre Crowe, Thackeray's secretary, during his American trip.

Rosemont, the ante-bellum mansion at Forkland, Alabama.

Hampton Plantation between Georgetown and Charleston, South Carolina, owned by Archibald Rutledge.

The Underground Railroad as envisioned by C. T. Webber, Cincinnati artist. The man in the wagon and the hooded woman are said to be portraits of Levi and Catharine Coffin, of whom Webber is known to have done formal portraits. Courtesy of Cincinnati Art Museum.

Undated French colored lithograph of Eliza crossing the ice. The general composition and the anomalous narrowness of the Ohio River make it likely that this was taken from a stage set. Courtesy of the New-York Historical Society, New York City.

Stationery, the original in very gay colors, of a standard Tommers'
troupe in the 1870's. A tableau of Lincoln freeing the slaves (as shown
here below UNCLE in the headline) was often included in the finale
after the Civil War. In the procession note Eva in the pony carriage,
the cabin on wheels, and the dogs (just ahead of the tail band). Courtesy
of the Theatre Collection, Houghton Library, Harvard University.

Left: Carrie Wyatt (Eva) and Maggie Moore (Topsy) in a West Coast *Uncle Tom's Cabin* production probably in the 1890's. Theoretically Miss Wyatt should have been in a blond wig. Courtesy of Museum of the City of New York.

Right: One-sheet of Peck & Forsman's "Mammoth Spectacular" Tom-show playing up the Two-Marks device. They were often billed as Marks Sr. and Marks Jr. and made up, as here, one younger than the other. Courtesy of Theatre Collection, Houghton Library, Harvard University.

Tommers were bent on making their show entertaining if it killed them and the play too. I readily understood when a questionnaire respondent wrote that yes, at the age of fourteen he had seen *Uncle Tom* in a small town, but neither at the time nor on thinking it over later had he been able to make any sense whatever out of what he had seen. The effect must often have been as though the personnel of a one-ring circus, animals and all, had taken over. Like circus people, instead of operating from New York or Chicago, where actors somewhat in the swim of the profession sought openings and the society of their kind, Tommers might work out of Syracuse, Peoria, or White Haven, Pennsylvania. They billed the dogs as big as the actors. Equally big type went to "Primo, the Great Trick Donkey Imported from St. Helena. Expressly for the Stage," and to "THE ONLY TRICK ALLIGATOR EVER INTRODUCED ON ANY STAGE." I do not know how alligators got into the act—perhaps as local detail in some sort of swamp scene in the Harrises' escape? The three-sheets also shouted about Little Eva's white ponies, which drew her basket carriage onstage—if the stage of Odd Fellows' Hall was big enough—and were featured, with the little angel blowing kisses from behind them, in the grand parade announcing arrival of the troupe in town.

Into the parade a big outfit would pour—or at least advertise—"FEROCIOUS MAN-EATING SIBERIAN BLOODHOUNDS," a calliope, Eva in her carriage, Marks on his educated donkey, Legree curbing a wickedly rearing horse and cracking a cowhide snarlingly at the public, a tallyho-coach heaped with the staider members of the company, a Silver Cornet Band (white), a Creole Girls' Fife and Drum Corps and a Negro ditto —total personnel of eighty, thumping and banging down

Bosworth, Eva Tanguay, Mary Pickford, David Belasco, Pearl White, Laurette Taylor, Theodore Roberts, Rose Melville (Sis Hopkins), Wilton Lackaye, Tom Wise, Effie Shannon, Fred Stone (did Topsy), Henrietta Crossman, Lotta Crabtree, Mabel Taliaferro, Denman Thompson.

Main Street. Such hippodroming culminated in "double companies" in which two Topsys, two Markses,* two Evas and so forth alternated in the indicated roles on the same evening. From any conceivable point of view this was showmanship gone mad, theatrical suicide. But it was not only tried, it was most successful and widely imitated seventy years ago. Everybody in the audiences must have been halfwitted. (The minstrel-show industry was contracting the same sort of senseless dropsy at the same time; here again, no doubt, Mr. Bones showed Uncle Tom the way to more and greater vulgarities.) V. S. Draper's Double Tom-Show also had a Beethoven Quartet and the Magnolia Jubilee Singers, doing very good business. In such competition, so very far from Mrs. Stowe's book, the S. R. Allen company could only advertise megalomaniacally "The Largest Uncle Tom's Cabin on Earth!"

Simultaneously mangey little troupes licked up marginal crumbs with two skinny dogs and seven or eight malnourished performers whisking in and out of costume to double and triple parts and enliven the intervals with soft-shoe routines and sacred selections. One salary might be saved by exploiting local vanity—a local child would be recruited and rehearsed as Eva, in the hope that the neighbors would come to see the little Mudge girl trying to be an actress. The height of economical use of personnel was the John Huftie company, Tomming through the West Virginia coal country with only five actors, including a boy-Eva, for the twelve fundamental roles. The effect must have been extremely strange. But consider Davis's sage comment on Tom-shows: ". . . nothing that was supposed to be serious got a laugh out of these audiences." It was abysmally low-grade.

The looks of a big-time Tom-show in the days when the tradition still prospered are still visible in tableaux and bits

---

* The two Markses were often brought on as Marks Senior and his brash son, Marks Junior, dressed just like him. For the others there can have been no attempt whatever at coherence.

of crucial action filmed from a performance of 1903 and preserved at the Museum of Modern Art. The sped-up film
prevents much gauging of the quality of the acting. A fine
sense of timelessness dresses the characters in the style of
1900—white ladies wear pompadours and high-boned collars,
the small Negroes in the levee scene wear "Russian suits," if
you remember what they were. Legree, however, is in a sort
of Buffalo Bill outfit with a widawake hat. (I have seen
photographs of Caruso so dressed for *The Girl of the Golden
West*.) The camera makes the levee set and the vanishing-
point perspective of the cotton-field backdrop even less plausible than they may have been under the lamplight in a
county-seat Opera House. But there is lively, uncued dancing; much Topsy, jerking and mugging; and a death-bed
scene for Eva obviously staged by the National Association of
Funeral Directors. The most notable single figure is Aunt
Chloe who, roused up at night to take counsel with Eliza,
comes on stage in a sunbonnet and a man's nightshirt—a
doughty effort for laughs at any cost.*

Minor Tommers had no enviable life out there on the
margin of show business: one-night stands, venal town marshals, distemper among the dogs, when there were enough
dogs for the preposition "among," and all the woes of the
itinerant cheapjack. They did bring low-cost excitement and
massed laughter to places where it occasioned several hours
of intense discussion when a stranger drove past the feed-
store. The vanishing small circus, the almost vanished tent
show, the medicine show and the traveling carnival still per-
form that function here and there. But in the days before
movies, radio and television Tommers probably reached
more amusement-starved people than any of these other en-
terprises because pious folk, for whom other kinds of shows
were sinful, could be persuaded that *Uncle Tom* was differ-

---

* I owe Mr. Harry Birdoff the idea that this film was probably made
not for exhibition but as copyright protection of certain production
details.

ent. "The most exacting Christian people," says a Tommers' flier of the 1890's, "never hesitate to visit this great Moral Show, which they always do with great pleasure and delight. All the characters are lifelike and no doubling. . . . High Class Specialties Between Acts. It is Delightful, Wonderful, Instructive and Strictly Moral."

This deceived the more readily because Mrs. Stowe's book still lay on the marble-topped table along with the Bible and the family album. Whatever mountebankery had done to it, an odor of respectability clung to her creation, just as it did to the stock statue in the courthouse square of the Union soldier leaning on his rifle. Though Mrs. Stowe lived well into the Tommers' heyday, she certainly never saw any of their galvanic but broken-backed performances. I wonder if she knew, or even had a hint, that straitlaced people were thus being deceived by her name into paltering with sin.

Movies, automobiles and punitive taxes on traveling shows killed Tomming. It is gone with "ten-twent'-thirt' " melodrama, the cakewalk, Sis Hopkins and the summer trolley car. Only a self-conscious antiquarian could think this an aesthetic loss. The Tommers did supply something that, at the time, many apparently wanted. But that could apply to a number of other kinds of enterprise, some vicious. In this case showmen had infected God's novel with the same order of traditional vulgarity as the female leg and the stage Irishman.

"Vicious," harsh as it sounds, probably applies. Tommers can seldom have given their social accountability much thought, except when considering how far they might safely venture into the Border States. But their influence on strata least liable to correction from other influences was inevitably morbid. Far and wide, year after year, generation after generation, they tempted the isolated and the ignorant to come and see the Negro as Topsy the mischievous, simian imp; as Uncle Tom, the subservient victim "with his aureole of cotton-wool hair . . . bobbing and bowing . . . Yes, Massa; no,

Massa"; as the vaudeville "coon," that subhuman, juba-patting, bones-knocking, banjo-strumming caterer to the white man's need for patronizing amusement, as seen by that rhetorical brute, Thomas Carlyle: "Do I then hate the Negro? No . . . I decidedly like poor Quashee; and find him a pretty kind of man . . . a swift, supple fellow; a merry-hearted, grinning, dancing, singing, affectionate kind of creature, with a great deal of melody and amiability in his constitution." The historian of what Britons called "nigger-minstrels" found it no accident that "Dixie" started life as a minstrels' walkaround and that minstrel shows always did best in the ante bellum South.

Tommers also helped the North to accept the South's necrophilic notion of what she had been like "befo' de wa'." As impressively as their credit with scene painters allowed, they overwhelmed the yokels with white-pillared mansions and aristocratic graces. They sowed one of Mrs. Stowe's errors broadcast by so juicily contrasting St. Clare, the solicitously benevolent Southern aristocrat, with Legree the plebeian monster. They improved on her by expunging her illusions about the practicality of colonization for Negroes but more than compensated for that minor service by also dropping her one solid contribution—that excellent sermon on the Pharisaism of the North's scolding the South for slavery while shrinking personally from Negroes. Neither Aiken's script nor any successor included St. Clare's advice to Miss Ophelia about the laying on of hands. Tom-shows even accentuated Mrs. Stowe's notions of the superiority of "white blood" by playing Eliza, George Harris and Cassie—the slave characters of energy and enterprise—with white actors using little if any dark make-up and eschewing Negro dialect. Only Tom, Topsy and the chuckleheaded minor characters were played as identifiable Negroes. A Tom-show made it unmistakable that a freedom-seeking Negro must, by definition, have a great deal of "white blood."

No wonder the American Negro hates the words "Uncle

Tom" and uses them to denounce what he sees as truckling treason to his people. But he should be better aware that it was the show that carried the name, rather than Mrs. Stowe's book, that most deserved his hatred. Book and woman were merely blundering and overweening, meaning well but ill informed and insufficiently intelligent for handling such materials. The show was cold-blooded exploitation, flogging a dead horse for gain, a cynicism as monstrous as the decision to produce *The Birth of a Nation.**

Nothing ever seen on the Tommers' rickety stages led the hayseeds of back-country Pennsylvania or way-out-yonder Iowa to question race segregation as the separate blackface and white bands blared past in the parade. To these audiences and their parents slavery had always been far away, and, as time passed after Appomattox, it was fast becoming long ago as well. Grandpa had been holier-than-thou about slavery at the same time that he hated niggers. Illinois Methodists who could square it with their consciences to go and see a Tom-show but not *East Lynne* would have walked out if a Negro had entered their church. Maybe the Tommers had good reason to omit Mrs. Stowe's best sermon. The troupe had a living to earn and could not risk anything that the customers might take personally. Besides, the time necessary to make St. Clare's point—if indeed the Tommers were aware that the book had any such moral—was better applied to building up Lawyer Marks and his donkey.

---

* In the fall of 1945 the American Civil Liberties Union protested when Negro leaders in Bridgeport, Connecticut, with support from the local pastors' association, the Communist Party and the CIO, secured the suppression of a projected musical version of *Uncle Tom's Cabin.* The Union's point—and sound, of course—was that antiracists have no more business than anyone else to ask for or countenance censorship.

"NEGROES ARE..."

1   *Cursed be Canaan*

"It's no disgrace to be a Negro but sometimes it's very inconvenient."   —BERT WILLIAMS

"White man in starched shirt settin' in shade,
Laziest man dat God ever made."   —Negro folksong

In her *Key,* Mrs. Stowe set down what is certainly one of history's most forlorn conditional statements: ". . . when the white race shall regard their superiority over the colored one only as a talent intrusted for the advantage of their weaker brother, *then* will the prejudice of caste melt away in the light of Christianity." It was sound thus to suggest a tinge of "caste" in prejudice against the American Negro. The term helps one to grasp the essential arbitrariness of such prejudice and we shall use it freely as we proceed. But otherwise the remark is in the same class as Engels's picture of the dictatorship of the proletariat leading to the classless society and so to the withering away of government.

Instead of jeering at the lady, however, consider the calmness of her assumption of the superiority of the white race. In her time she had everybody on her side, or at any rate most of those who mattered. The *reductio ad absurdum* is, as always, our old acquaintance, Dr. Cartwright of Louisiana, who described a new disease, "dysaesthesia ethiopica," brought on by ill-advised efforts of the whites to get hard work out of Negroes. In them he found "an innate love to act as body-servant" and "a natural fondness for alcoholic drinks and tobacco." * Though pertinent laboratory tests did not yet exist, he grandly anticipated modern biochemistry in ascribing their alleged "want of muscular and mental activity" to their consuming less oxygen than whites do. His evidence was "their motions being proverbially much slower"—as, one supposes, in the case of sluggish Jesse Owens, king of sprinters in the 1930's. Hear the good doctor roll on in a lecture before the faculty of the University of Mississippi: ". . . this defective hematosis, or atmospherization of the blood conjoined with a deficiency of cerebral matter in the cranium and an excess of nervous matter distributed to the organs of sensation and assimilation . . . has rendered the people of Africa unable to take care of themselves." This occasion is significant, for others took this bearded irresponsible's shirt-tail opinions just as seriously as he did himself. He was the quasi-official scientific authority and consultant for the pro-Slavery South.

Above Mason and Dixon's line non-Southerners also took

---

* The persistence of many Southern communities in maintaining nominal prohibition ties in, of course, with local belief that to allow Negroes access to alcohol would be disastrous. The position was once respectable: Edward Sheldon's *The Nigger* says: ". . . we're not in the habit of pouring liquor down the throats of our infants," hence the white man with the good of the Negroes at heart will desire prohibition. In West Africa I took pains to get the impressions of local police authorities as to how Gold Coasters, Sierra Leoneans and Liberians took their drink, to which they have as much access as they can pay for. Everywhere I was assured that, though these racial cousins of American Negroes are often enough police problems, drunkenness seldom has anything to do with it. Nor is it altogether a matter of cash for liquor. The West African knows a good deal about moonshining and does not hesitate to practice the art when he feels it worth his own or somebody else's while.

Mrs. Stowe's position as much for granted as she did herself. Horace Mann, the most influential American educationist before John Dewey, was a plucky Abolitionist but firmly believed Negroes naturally inferior to whites. The historian Rhodes, a boy in Mrs. Stowe's day but soon the post bellum spokesman for the North, damned the Negro with praise almost as faint as hers: "So long as Southern reasoners maintained that the Negro race was inferior to the Caucasian, their basis was scientific truth. . . . But the assertion that the Negro does not partake of the nature of mankind is as repugnant to science as it is to common sense. The chimpanzee is not so near in intellect to the blackest Congo as is this negro to Daniel Webster."

Even so free and quick a mind as Jefferson's was unreliable in these matters and not just because he was Southern. With whatever show of reluctance, he clung to his "suspicion," admittedly unproved, that those whom he called "blacks" and discussed in terms appropriate to the stockyards were innate inferiors of their white masters. Earlier, the even finer mind of David Hume, Lucifer of metaphysicians, was

> . . . apt to suspect the negroes and in general all other species of men . . . to be naturally inferior to the whites. There never was a civilized nation of any other complexion than white. . . . there are negro slaves disperst all over Europe of which none ever discovered any symptoms of ingenuity; though low people without education, will start up amongst us and distinguish themselves in every profession. In Jamaica indeed they talk of one negro as a man of parts and learning; but 'tis likely he is admired for slender accomplishments, like a parrot who speaks a few words plainly.*

---

* From "Of National Character," in *Essays and Treatises* . . . 277 (London, 1753). This anticipates Dr. Johnson's comparison of a woman preacher to a dancing dog. The Jamaican was probably Francis Williams, protégé at Cambridge of the Earl of Montagu. See Phillips, *American Negro Slavery;* 432.

All this is a more or less—usually less—polite way of stating the familiar point that the Negro is "nearer the animal." Here Dr. Cartwright not only adduced the Negro's prognathous (underthrust) jaw but even asserted that he "approaches the lower animals in his sense of smell." * Actually this issue of "animal" versus "human" traits is not intelligible. Anthropologists considering the whole organism find neither whites nor Negroes monopolizing traits showing evolutionary nearness to the subhuman primates of the fossil past.† Thus the Negro's long legs and thick ("everted") lips may set him off as *farther* than whites from the anthropoid apes. Some consider that lack of prognathism, as seen in puppies, kittens and some small monkeys, as well as in adult whites, indicates a sort of stunting when prolonged into the mature phase. But too little is known about this to make discussion worth while. Better wash it all out with a sweeping anthropolgical dictum of La Barre's: "A Nordic is no more 'higher' than a Melanesian than a Buff Orpington is 'higher' than a Rhode Island Red."

Freethinkers like Hume and Jefferson supported their prejudice with subjective hunches. The pious had better backing —the messy old story in Genesis of how Noah got drunk and exposed himself indecently and son Ham was less solicitous of the old man's dignity than were sons Shem and Japheth; so, on sobering up, Noah cursed Canaan, Ham's son, condemning him and his descendants forever to subjection to his cousins and their descendants. To account for Noah's disproportionate wrath, tradition gives dark hints that Ham took advantage of the opportunity to emasculate the old gentle-

---

* "Slavery in the Light of Ethnology," in Elliott, Ed., *Cotton Is King. . . .* The doctor does not deserve the possibility that there is a *little* something in this. Darker olfactory areas are associated with keener sense of smell, and Negroes' olfactory areas are darker to correspond with heavier skin-pigmentation.

† See the good concise statement in Boas, "Race," *Encyclopedia of the Social Sciences.*

man, a Freudian touch with no further explanation. The
story is obviously an effort after the fact to justify the He-
brews' ruthless enslaving of those Canaanites whom they
did not kill when invading the Promised Land. It gives no
hint that either Ham or Canaan was Negro. But it was
somehow generally understood that the accursed father and
son were black, hence the term "Hamite" still applied to
certain racial groups in northeastern Africa. This touch seems
to have come out of Talmudic legend, presumably familiar
to theologians, that Ham and all his progeny were turned
black as penalty for having violated the tabu against sexual
intercourse in the Ark. But, though this reiterated emphasis
on sex would doubtless have interested him, the average
Southerner neither knew of nor needed these edifying details.
He was already willing enough to let his preacher assure him
that the Good Book condemned all blacks to serve lighter-
skinned people, world without end. Amen.

You and I can hardly believe that such data, not to speak
lightly of such authority, could seriously affect grave issues.
Nevertheless they did. Mrs. Trollope, for her day an enlightened woman, felt no absurdity in causing a touched-with-the-
tarbrush heroine to write in a suicide note: "This dreadful
will was stamped upon my wretched race thousands of years
ago." Darwin had not yet published his theories; "higher
criticism" had hardly begun. The Bible was still God's Word
unchallenged on any topic that it chose to treat, and church-
goers were not inclined to question the parson's authority
for identifying the seed of Canaan with the field hands of
Georgia.

Nor was Mrs. Stowe so inclined. The last quarter of her
Key ably rebutted the proslavery divines' contention that
slavery squared with the new dispensations of Christianity.
But she did not touch on "Cursed be Canaan. . . ." Known
interpretations of that text fitted with her own notions of the
relative qualities of "white blood" and "black blood." Even
though cursed in patriarchal times, Canaan and his seed

could have souls for Christ to save, even as all the seed of
Adam, earlier and more thoroughly cursed, could be saved
by grace and faith—or faith and grace, depending on one's
theological inclination. (To many readers this may be gibberish now but it was intelligible and important then.) Lyman Beecher's daughter was unlikely to be as concerned
about justice in this world, or about her own responsibility
to stirred-up readers, as about the professional questions
whether a given subhuman entity had (a) a soul to be saved
and (b) adequate opportunity to seek such salvation.

Even without religious backing, racist ideas die hard. In
1921 an eminent historian from a noted antislavery family
was still writing: "It is about as hard for the Ethiop to
change his institutions and racial conceptions as it is for him
to change the color of his skin. Both his institutions and his
skin are a matter of heredity." In the year of Pearl Harbor
a most reconstructed Southerner unabashedly called the
South's "chief blood-strain . . . likely to be Celtic—of all
Western strains the most susceptible to suggestions of the
supernatural. . . ." Myrdal, the austere authority on the
American tangle of race, uses such unscientific language as
"Everybody having a *known* trace of Negro blood in his
veins" in defining the current meaning of "Negro" in the
United States. Even American Negroes have their own troubles of this sort. Du Bois, scholar-spokesman for his people,
arrogated to West Indian Negroes the occult distinction of
being "European in speech and outlook but largely African
in their unconscious memories and survivals." * Such pseudo-
scientific romancing stakes out a Negro claim to the best

---

* *Black Folk Then and Now;* 180. Such talk obviously is akin to Jung's
doctrine of the "collective unconscious," perhaps somewhat misinter-
preted. Or the debt may be the other way round. Long before Freud
and Jung used such ideas as framework for their speculative gropings,
ethnologists were muttering pretentiously about "basic myths" and
"racial memory," and among laymen the Jack London type of mind was
most impressed.

of both worlds, and why not? The intellectual sharp practice is no more marked than that of the slave-owning Southerner's belief both that Negroes loved to work in a hot sun and that only a whip could ever make them stir.

The field hand's understimulated mind was certainly unlikely to question master's major premise that he was Cuffee's born superior and his conclusion, by means of numerous minor premises, that he was therefore privileged to push Cuffee around for the poor soul's own good and master's pleasure and profit. West Africa had no tradition that one black man was as good as another, so the slave had small basis for dreaming of equality with whites obviously wealthier, more powerful and technologically farther advanced. Some of his owners might draw up theories of "inalienable rights" and have fits of conscience leading to manumission, might wonder whether Negroes were not fully human, then put the notion away as after all, a little too outrageous. Abolitionists might proclaim that, fully human or not, the Negro slave's situation was repugnant to whites' sense of right and wrong. But few slaves were aware of these goings-on. Their rebellions, at least those in North America, were not strokes for supraracial self-respect but mere sporadic explosions of caste pressure. In the early 1930's a WPA interviewer found a former slave still using Noah's curse to explain the Negro's subordination to whites, going on: "So . . . there we are, and that is the way God meant us to be."

Such ignorance and good will are a little pitiful. Nothing so cordial can be said of the rank rationalizations that go with notions of "white supremacy." What people said to excuse their exploitation of Pompey and Chloe fitted damningly well with their need to live off them and theirs unto infinite generations. With Mrs. Stowe, that alleged best friend of the Negro, actually concurring on many points, Dr. Cartwright "scientifically" described the Negro as needing bondage because he had a "servile mind . . . almost void of reflective faculties . . . unable to provide for and take care of himself." Or because Negroes were cowards deserving exploitation, lucky that it was often humane; or because they were completely immune to the climates and diseases that unfitted whites for heavy work in the South; or because hewing wood and drawing water, and chopping cotton, cutting cane, planting rice and cleaning spittoons were proper functions for creatures that smelled to heaven and were ineducable past a certain point; or because, oh, my brethren and sistern, see what says the 'Postle Paul, that valiant man of God, about the runaway slave Onesimus. . . .

Occasionally men using their own eyes and wits spoke out. James Habersham, owner of 200 slaves in pioneer Georgia, thought the opinion of "ignorant people" that Negroes are "scarcely reasonable creatures . . . an absurdity too obvious to deserve refutation. . . . as far as they have had the opportunity of being instructed, [they] have discovered as good abilities as are usually found among the people of our Colony." Acutely generous for a Tennessean, Sam Houston told de Tocqueville that apparent mental differences among Negroes, Indians and whites came "solely from the different educations they have received." Even Dr. Cartwright maintained that schooling made Negroes more useful and more trustworthy. Such enlightened common sense is an excellent tool, if sometimes clumsy or unreliable, and it is a pity our forebears, who were just as clever as we are, did not make more use of it on these matters. If they had, Mrs. Stowe could never have been so foolishly lyrical about small and large differences between white master and black slave. But better hindsight than never. It is still essential to assemble the wrongheaded body of beliefs about Negroes summarized above, immerse them in objectivity, introduce a strong current of common sense, and see what collects on the positive pole after the old ideas have come apart.

"*It warn't the grounding—that didn't keep us back but a little. We blowed out a cylinder-head.*"

"*Good gracious! Anybody hurt?*"

"*No'm. Killed a nigger.*"

—Huckleberry Finn

In all this confused folly the nearest-to-tenable excuse for Negro slavery was the matter of immunity, and overstatement came near to ruining that. Louisiana doctors gave Lyell to understand that the merest touch of "Negro blood" lent immunity to yellow fever. The contention would astound French government doctors now devotedly innoculating West Africans against this very disease. But it was understandably popular among well-off Southerners able to visit Saratoga in the blazing Southern summer. Even Henry Adams took seriously Southern talk about "deadly fevers sure to kill the white man who should pass a night on one bank of the Ashley River."

True, Southern cities were periodically ravaged by Yellow Jack; but so were Philadelphia and New York. True, life in unscreened dwellings in the Sea Islands a hundred years ago did entail high risk of malaria. But many a white overseer survived these hazards while his employer was telling his fellow passengers on the ship to Europe of parts of the South where "a few hours stay would mean almost certain death to any white person." American Negroes, whose West African forebears had long been harried by mosquitoes carrying the organisms of both these diseases probably did have relative immunity to them; at least the symptoms were often less acute. But for both ailments *relative* is the key word. "It is probably true," says high recent authority, "that the case fatality is lower among them. Nevertheless Negroes do develop severe and even fatal yellow fever." The same holds true for malaria. Georgia overseers often reported serious numbers of slaves put out of action by "chills and fever," that is, malaria.

Macmillan, shrewd observer of both Africa and the West Indies, is scornful of such "vulgar errors about tropical diseases and black immunity." The Negro's advantage, such as it was, lay in the same sort of relative insusceptibility, likely arrived at by the same early, continued exposure, that makes Europeans-per-million less liable than Polynesians-per-million to tuberculosis. The difference is real, but it does not keep tuberculosis from being a grave problem among whites. In parallel, Negro slaves suffered much from the traditional tropical scourges. "The number of deaths among the Allston slaves," says the historian of a great Carolina rice plantation, "does not support the general belief that Negroes enjoyed almost complete immunity from the diseases of the Rice Coast." As for hookworm, "it may be the [Negroes] suffered as much as the whites."

At best a master calling Negro labor indispensable because white labor could not survive in the Sea Islands or the Black Belt used half-truth to excuse full measure of injustice. Similarly the generalized plea of white-killing heat was not totally invalid. Booker T. Washington, familiar with cotton-belt weather, inclined to think there was something in it. Recent experiment with white and Negro sharecroppers in the Yazoo Delta revealed that Negroes working under hot summer conditions showed certain minor physiological advantages. Similar research in the California desert has shown confirmation. But the differences are too small to mean much practical contrast between a given Negro and a given white in a given cotton patch.

This notion of "too hot for white men" almost certainly arose from the early European settler's indignation over what struck him—child of a really temperate climate—as in-

fernally hot New World summers. Scottish and German settlers in early Georgia resisted Negro slavery partly on moral
grounds—all honor to them—but partly because they thought
whites better workers than Negroes thereabouts; what they
wanted was more solid, industrious Scots and Rhinelanders.
A wry Southern historian observes that small farmers in the
cotton belt working with "a few slaves or alone with their
families . . . did not know that white people could not en-
dure the Southern sun, and that the slave system had placed
a stigma upon manual labor." A post bellum Carolinian once
cited Texas and Southern Florida to dispel "the old nonsense
about our climate and the inability of the white man to toil
under the blazing summer sun." In all common sense: if
temperatures often above 90°F. in the shade coupled with
high humidity barred whites from long and effective labor
in full sun, the Pennsylvania Dutch would never have become our best farmers.* The South really deserved a Yankee
historian's gibe: "It was almost an axiom of slavery that cotton could not be raised with white labor, partly because to
admit the possibility was to lose one of the reasons for slavery."

All right, said the planter, the nigger is a natural-born
slave. Long after Appomattox a great Southern scholar
echoed him: "Impulsive and inconstant, voluble, dilatory,
and negligent, but robust, amiable, obedient, and contented,

---

* Master would have had better pretext for skulking in the shade while
Sambo hoed had he known of modern theories as to the relation between sunburn and cancer of the skin. In any but high latitudes this
hazard is real for all but swarthier skins, increasing with fairness of
complexion, apparently worst for white-skinned redheads. See my "The
Truth about Suntan," *Saturday Evening Post,* July 31, 1948. Professor
F. R. Wulsin, of Tufts University, questions the assumed direct relation
between sunburn trauma and skin cancer; he feels that, as far as current knowledge goes, the advantages of stripping for activity in hot
climates outweigh this risk. At this point, while thanking him heartily
for his answer to my query, I leave him and the dermatologists to have
it out between them.

[Negroes] have been the world's premium slaves. Prehistoric Pharaohs, mediaeval Pashas, and the grandees of Elizabethan England esteemed them as such." The Negro's ready adjustment to slavery is often invidiously contrasted with an alleged freedom-mindedness of the American Indian pining away or fighting to the death when Spanish and British colonists tried to enslave him. True, Negroes were first brought to the New World (at the instance of a Catholic missionary) to lessen pressure on the disappearing aborigines. Beyond this the data are not all one could wish. Only in a very wide biological sense is there a generalized Red Indian. Some Indians stood pretty stiff slavery under fellow Indians in the Pacific Northwest* and under whites in New England and French Canada. They performed the forced labor that mined all that silver and built those colossal churches in Mexico and yet survived as principal ingredient of the present Mexican population. The dying out of the West Indian Arawak is the sort of thing that can happen, and often does, without actual slavery as well as with it when Western man moves in on an isolated, nonliterate population. The causes of the tragedy are probably lack of immunity to exotic diseases plus a general shattering of culture that leads to psychogenic troubles. Abstract craving for freedom or innate courage may have little to do with it.

The likelier reason why Negroes replaced the Arawak is that they were more efficient; Spaniards rated one Negro as doing the work of four Indians. They were more familiar with intensive agriculture, an art widespread in West Africa, where some chiefs had even worked out a sort of big-plantation, slave-powered economy. The Negro was also far

---

* The "Civilized Tribes" of the South took readily to enslaving Negroes. Greenwood LeFlore, a Choctaw chief who stayed behind when his people went West in 1830, died owning 400 slaves, including a fancy New Orleans maid purchased for his wife for $1800. (Sydnor, *Slavery in Mississippi;* 131.) Maybe this adaptability explains the epithet "Civilized" as well as their ready skill at white-style farming.

from home, as the Arawak was not; and it was axiomatic among "blackbirders" in the South Pacific that the same "native" who was useless on plantations on his own island did far better in a strange island where he had no relatives to hide him if he ran away, no tactical familiarity with the country and its resources and sometimes few cultural ties with the local population. On the same principle New Englanders capturing Pequods often shipped them to the West Indies for sale or exchange for Negro slaves instead of trying to work them in the Bay Colony. Such considerations must have applied to West African importees to some extent, but whatever docility they encouraged was hardly innate.

In the Civil War both sides marveled at the lack of opportunistic mutiny among slaves back of the Southern lines where, with so many men gone to war, supervision was even looser than usual. The wife of Senator Wigfall of Texas was sure that "with Yankees in front and Negroes in the rear . . . slave-owners must expect a servile insurrection." Clever Mrs. Chesnut found it sinister when no such thing occurred: "Are they stolidly stupid, or wiser than we are, biding their time? . . . why don't they all march over the border, where they would be received with open arms? . . . these creatures are to me inscrutable in their ways and past finding out." Though South Carolina-born and -bred the lady was not among those Southerners confident of understanding Negroes because they have long lived among them. The bloody stench of San Domingo did not argue great tractability in the full-blooded Negroes. Their failure to rise between 1861 and 1865 may have come partly of lack of sense of solidarity, partly of loyalty, of a simple, tribal sort, to the white folks associated with all that their lives had been, what there was of them—sentiment akin to the slave's already described dread of being sold away from the old place, prison though it was.*

---

* Mrs. Stowe's son Charles took this absence of slave-rebellions during the Civil War to mean that slavery was not too bad: "If slavery were

In the teeth of occasional slave bravery in emergencies, such as fires, a spokesman for the South like the Rev. Dr. Ingraham found it reassuring to call the Negro "wholly destitute of courage . . . cowardice is a principle of his soul, as instinctive as courage is in the white man." This had already been challenged in a famous letter from Commodore Isaac Chauncey, USN, to Commodore O. H. Perry, USN, during the War of 1812, in which he said, "I have yet to learn that the color of the skin . . . can affect a man's qualifications or usefulness" and asserted that numerous Negro seamen were among the best in his Lake Ontario squadron. A generation later a lieutenant in USS *Brandywine,* a crack frigate, described the forty-odd Negroes on her muster roll as "not at all inferior to the whites either in . . . skill, readiness or courage. Nor did the white seamen evince the least reluctance to be associated with them on terms of the most perfect equality." Brutal as were the days of wooden ships and iron men and the cat-o'-nine-tails, the U.S. Navy had something here to which it has reverted only within the last few years.*

As organized fighter on land the American Negro's record is inconsistent. In the Revolution, thinks a recent expert, the Negro slave, "inured to fatigue and hardened and disciplined by slavery, made a better soldier than his master.

---

unutterably evil . . . how can we account for the fact that when the Confederate soldiers were at the front . . . the Negroes took care of the women and children . . . and nothing like an act of violence was ever known among them?" (Letter quoted in the Charleston *News and Courier,* February 4, 1954.)

* Cooper's sea novels, written by a former U.S. Navy officer, provide confirmation of this throughout. So, from another service, does the testimony of Captain Basil Hall, RN, who was a less-than-harsh critic of American slavery as he saw it: ". . . precisely as the Negro has a fair chance given him [in the Royal Navy], so he proves himself equal in capacity to the white man." It should be noted, however, that in the U.S. Navy (and in the Royal Navy, too, so far as I know) no Negro could hope for a commission.

No observer ever went on record that the blacks broke in panic any quicker than the whites." Jefferson grudgingly put the shoe on the other foot, calling Negroes "at least as brave [as whites] and more adventuresome. But this may proceed from a want of forethought, which prevents their seeing a danger till it be present. . . . they do not go through with it with more coolness and steadiness than the whites." Rhode Island even took the risk of raising and arming all-Negro units with white officers—notably Colonel Christopher Greene's regiment that showed such "desperate valor" covering Sullivan's withdrawal from Newport. (When, one wonders, will the Daughters of the American Revolution elect a member offering one of those black Rhode Island wildcats as qualifying ancestor? *) Washington's forces usually averaged fifty Negroes per battalion, many of them freed by master on condition of enlisting, which amounted to buying exemption with some £80 worth of slave.

It goes without saying that the battalions in question came from states north of Mason and Dixon's line. When, in the black winter before Appomattox, the Confederacy finally decided to enlist Negro troops, fiery Howell Cobb of Georgia summarized the social argument against the Negro soldier: "The day you make soldiers of them is the beginning of the revolution. If slaves will make good soldiers our whole theory of slavery is wrong. But they won't make soldiers." The Federals had already proved him wrong to some extent. By 1865 more than 200,000 Negroes, mostly freemen, had worn the

---

* Maryland got round to raising Negro troops at the end of the war; Virginia had a few Negroes earning freedom with honorable discharge; there were some, but few, further exceptions in the South. The President-General of the national DAR says I am correct in stating: "So far as the National Society Daughters of the American Revolution are aware, no descendant of a Negro veteran of the American Revolution has ever been a member." She adds that DAR applications do not ask for race or religion. I am confident that if any applicant had ever offered a Negro ancestor, the national officers would know about it.

blue uniform in all-black regiments with white officers above company grade and usually below as well. Their record was spotty, but so was that of white units as a whole. Forrest's command butchered one Negro outfit at Ft. Pillow, probably after surrender; another was decimated in the bungled attack through the crater at Petersburg; but another tore itself determinedly to pieces in its maiden action trying to storm Ft. Wagner, and a fourth was publicly thanked for gallantry by a Federal general who had been a slaveholder.

The performance of such segregated units in World War I remains to this day a matter of fogbound dispute. Recently, however, controversy as to the innate courage and fighting capacity of the racial comrades of Joe Louis and the French Army's redoubtable Senegalese regiments has been largely resolved by "integration" of whites and Negroes in the U.S. Armed Forces. The success of this revival and extension of the traditions of the Continental Line and the Navy of Preble and Farragut has startled even the American Negro's friends. My own hindsight—that of a civilian knowing military matters only as a reporter occasionally observing them—is that the issue was always false. The equivocal past of the American Negro soldier is readily referred to likely causes that are scarcely related to his innate qualities, whatever they may be: his usually subsocialized background—I-told-you-so attitudes among the brass studying his record—the effect on morale of persistence in military segregation after the nation's general attitude had begun to shift against segregation—and the lively possibility that white officers assigned to Negro outfits were not always, to put it mildly, the cream of the crop.* It is usually true of the U.S. Army as of others that there are no poor battalions, only poor officers. An astute Southerner attached to the 92d Division

---

* Poor morale is not inevitable under segregation. Consider Greene's Rhode Islanders; Robert Gould Shaw's 54th Massachusetts; the Negro regulars before Santiago de Cuba; and the World War II records of the 99th Pursuit Squadron and 332d Fighter Group, both all-Negro.

(Negro) in World War I distinguished between capable
Negro officers who had been sergeants in "the old army"
and those "lazy, undevoted and without pride . . . come
from civilian life by way of training camps." Two "able devoted" Negro officers told him that their men would fail in
combat because "a Negro won't follow a Negro"—a generalization that would interest the ghost of Toussaint l'Ouver-
ture. The implications of these observations are somewhat
confusing. But at worst they mean that nothing ails Negro
soldiers that proper screening and reorientation can't cure.

> *"The whole affair simply proved what the white village had
> known all along: you can't educate a nigger. Hooker's Bend
> warmed with pleasure that half of its population was in-
> educable."* —STRIBLING, Birthright

Mrs. Stowe agreed with the observation of her time that, beyond a certain age, usually the early teens, Negro children
ceased to advance under schooling. Bostonians told Lyell in
1847 that they segregated Negro pupils because they could
not keep pace with whites after the age of fourteen. An eminent Virginian scholar once candidly attributed this alleged
fact to "the advent of puberty and sexual development"; it
was well known in North Africa and the Middle East, he
said, that "the negro eunuch was a vast improvement in
shrewdness and general intelligence on the unaltered black."
Mrs. Stowe may well never have met this indecorous theory
of selective education, but she glibly chimed in: "In conducting the education of negro, mulatto and quadroon children, the writer has often observed . . . that . . . up to a
certain age, they were . . . often superior to the white children . . . but that there came a time when they became

indifferent to learning, and made no further progress." *
Her explanation of such lagging was that they had become
aware that meager futures awaited people labeled "niggers."
A social researcher in the 1930's found this confirmed by
Negroes themselves: ". . . they saw no reason to stay on [in
school] since they would never be permitted to do the kind
of work for which a more advanced education would fit
them."

In any case this is not a problem solely of Negroes. One
hears the same complaint from Western teachers of both
Melanesians (probably distant biological cousins of Negroes) and Polynesians (probably more "white" and Mongoloid than anything else). I once heard one such teacher
ascribe this lack—and plausibly, I thought—to lack of abstract words and ideas in these children's early backgrounds.
Nonliterate peoples are usually poor in equivalents for our
words ending in *-ity* and *-ness* and in corresponding traditions of abstract thought. So, as subject matter tends to approach abstraction, "native" pupils flounder for lack of the
appropriate intellectual habits, not necessarily for lack of
basic wits.

I once saw what may have been a demonstration of this
sort of thing. A West African girl of full Congo descent,
meagerly educated at a Protestant mission, was eager to
study maternity nursing in the United States in order to
bring modern obstetrics to her people. Her zeal finally
landed her in a stateside school to prepare for nursing training. Zeal or not, she was a tearful, inept failure and made
appallingly low scores in the nursing-school's aptitude and
intelligence tests. Her tears and the pleas of a Negro missionary who believed in her secured her further preparation

---

* There is some evidence that psychologically Negro babies develop
somewhat faster than white babies on the average. (See letter from
Prof. Henry E. Garrett in *Time*, September 17, 1951.) But the differential levels out long before puberty; so, though indicating difference
between white and Negro, it has little to do with the above issue.

and a second chance. She failed again, but the nursing school mercifully waived its rules. Thus admitted, she gradually gained intellectual momentum and turned into an outstanding graduate going on to do brilliant work in postgraduate training. She is now back in West Africa saving lives right and left with small resources in money and equipment and showing initiative, tact and organizing skills that would have seemed incredible to her early instructors. Obviously nothing was wrong with her *potential* capacities. But it is quite a trick to get the hang of Western approaches to things, abstractions included, when you are not born among them.

Substitute "white-American-educated" for "Western" and the same may hold for many American-reared Negroes. A recent report of the National Scholarship Fund for Negro Students showed less than half of the top 10 per cent of Southern Negro high-school seniors making "at least the minimum qualifying score" in scholastic aptitude tests for probable ability to do college work. From that the report concludes, not that Negroes are incurably stupid, but that Southern schools for Negroes are mostly poor, which is incontrovertible, and further that it is a "serious handicap" for "students from the lower socio-economic brackets" to have to "acquire elsewhere the cultural background necessary for college, when it is not found at home." This succinctly states a most useful truth.

It is curious to note that Mrs. Stowe, who really had taught a few Negroes and whites together in Cincinnati and to that extent knew whereof she spoke, virtually denied her own notions of white superiority by including *all degrees of admixture of white blood* in her generality. With the pellucid honesty of inadvertence she alleged no differences in postpuberty intellectual blight as between children all-black and those three-quarters white; whereas, if "white blood" does carry mental superiority with it, as she usually assumed, the quadroons should have gone longest unstultified and the all-blacks flunked out first. This time it is accidentally a credit to her that she tended to be right for the wrong reasons—as right as the buyers at Mississippi slave auctions who bid about the same, sex for sex, age for age, for mulattoes and coal-black Negroes indifferently.

> *"Non-anthropologists, who do not have to worry about scientific proof, will tell you that Negroes have the gift of laughter, a keen sense of rhythm, and a love of dancing."*
> —COON, The Story of Man

Acquaintance with contemporary as well as archaic attitudes toward alleged Negro traits makes one almost despair of finding common sense winning anywhere. To account for the mixture of slut and lady in the octoroon heroine of his *Birthright* (an otherwise valuable white man's novel of race contacts) Stribling's mulatto hero suggests that "the morals of black folk" are incongruent with those of whites because of the blacks' "more exuberant vitality"; whereas "white blood in Cissie . . . kept her struggling . . . to gather around her the delicate atmosphere and charm of a gentlewoman." That great Virginia gentleman, George Washington, was courteous about the verses of little Phyllis Wheatley, the African-born, Yankee-sponsored Negro bluestocking, but Thomas Jefferson, a man of much higher formal cultivation than Washington, went out of his learned way unnecessarily to sneer at her and at them.*

---

* *Notes on Virginia;* 146. Her heroic couplets are actually as good as those of several Britons whose lives Dr. Johnson wrote as those of accredited poets. Griswold justly called Miss Wheatley's work "equal to much of the contemporary verse that is admitted to be poetry. . . . it would be difficult to find in the productions of American women [as of 1849] . . . anything superior in sentiment, fancy, or diction." (*Fe-*

At that, neither of these statesmen was a literary critic. For the same reason many modern students of race issues fail to perceive how significant it is that many American Negro writers are not very good. That is, the average quality of American Negro writers is not far below what one would expect of a group of American white writers of similar numbers in a given period. For example, sort out current American white novelists of some serious reputation; do the same for American Negro writers ditto; and you find the same range of skill and emotional content, only one assortment is much smaller than the other.

In my day James Weldon Johnson, Countee Cullen, Langston Hughes, J. Saunders Redding show the limberness of born writers. Ralph Ellison and George Lamming (from another quondam slave culture) have qualified as able, real writers no more handicapped by derivative self-consciousness than their white confreres of equal validity. Willard Motley and Richard Wright share with many whites of the same professional stratum an effect as if they were writing earnest travesty of Farrell or Dos Passos. Frank Yerby stirs up a bosom-bed-and-brandy bestseller as handily as anybody with a fair skin and an equally fugitive purpose. The cultural stimulus of the vast American environment is evident in the fact that, though the white population of Canada is about the same as the Negro population of the United States and the average level of education among Canadians is far higher than that among American Negroes, the number of significant Negro writers is far higher than that of significant Canadian writers. But it means something else that present-day Negro writers average three times as able as those represented in Calverton's *Anthology of Negro Literature* of thirty years ago. Since the average quality of white Americans' writing has shown no such rise in the same pe-

male Poets of America; 36.) It is too bad for Negro writers so frequently and unjustifiably to condescend to this tragic little figure of genuine talent.

riod—has certainly done no better than remain at the same level—this must mean that recently widening educational and cultural opportunities have been catching up with potential Negro talent previously obscured. Hence this range of Negro writing skill and maturity of attitude from as-good-as-any to as-poor-as-any, even to as-vulgar-as-any.

So it actually does look as if, as writers, Negroes are nothing special mentally or aesthetically, not especially uncreative, not especially talented. This should not lead to jumping to conclusions about other congruencies between white and Negroes. As sprinters persons with prevalently West African ancestry do seem to show a specifically racial innate excellence. As settlers in Finland they might not do quite so well as Nordics over ten millennia—though Peary's companion in his final dash to the Pole was Matt Henson, American Negro. But, given a reasonable chance at literacy, they write about as well as everybody else. Their intellectual sensibilities, sensitivities, knack of narrative, skill in marshaling data, the emotional subtleties that they develop—all are of much the same excellence or limpness. Set a bright young Negro of reasonable education to reading Thomas Wolfe and the inevitable consequences on paper will be just as unfortunate as if he were white.

This observation may distress some Negroes as well as certain whites of the sort that used to rhapsodize into the gin-gingerale about the primitive *verve* of *Shuffle Along* and weave patronizing theories about a generalized vitality lacking in whites but rampant in Negroes, Red Indians, Polynesians, Russians and, no doubt, Eskimos. (This marriage of romantics to irresponsible ethnology is seen at its worst, I suppose, in D. H. Lawrence's murky mutterings about "blood.") Du Bois endorses a statement that "presumably no other people" than Negroes would have developed a new folk music out of the slaves' contact with white man's instruments and musical conventions. This is ethnologically naïve: no other people except the Hawaiians,

European gypsies, Fijians, Canadian Indians and, no doubt, a dozen others of whom I do not happen to know. Music is often the first thing to burgeon into something new and rich when a complex culture impinges on a simpler one. Mrs. Stowe's notions—and ours—about special Negro aptitude for music are particularly treacherous because there is some scientific reason to see musical talent as heritable in families. But aptitude tests presumably gauging musical ability give conflicting results on Negroes; one such showed them *inferior* in this respect to Red Indians.* Such talk tempts the unwary into claims of racial virtue as ill founded as Ku Klux talk about racial vices. Thus Du Bois: "In disposition the Negro is among the most lovable of men." How nice for him! Rackham Holt attributed to him "an indescribable sweetness and charm . . . seldom found so universally in any other race." And in September, 1954, a special issue of the London *Times* Literary Supplement devoted to American literature pontificated about "what is innate in the Negro: his sense of life, his joy, his inspiring gift of song. . . ."

American whites working with Negroes and Negro problems sometimes get so committed to their audiences, patients or colleagues that they act like doting mothers of juvenile delinquents. Study of these wrongheaded zealots helps one to imagine what the worst of the old Abolitionists were like. They tempt otherwise valid Negroes to sound like Irishmen on St. Patrick's Day, which, though understandable, warps them as much as professional Hibernianism warps people named Kelly. The Negro's quest for status as full human being will never succeed until he hears much less from any lips, thin or thick, of how "American Negroes are . . ." and much more of how "Most Americans classed as Negro do . . ." thus and so. My own impression from working alongside Negroes where their jobs were better than mine

---

* Klineberg, *Race Differences;* 206-207. See also Lowie, *Cultural Anthropology,* 207-208, on the lack of ethnological significance in what are thought of as peculiarly Negro musical instruments, etc.

and from meeting Negroes on three continents is that they include some of the brightest and some of the stupidest, some of the nicest and some of the meanest people with whom I have ever dealt.

This versatility in both temperament and ways of doing is clear in Liberia, where certain local attitudes have evolved well away from those of its American Negro founders. Its special flavor sometimes recalls the British West Indies, sometimes seems unique, in any case as unfamiliar as most definitely foreign places. Now, whether aware of it or not, we Stateside whites are reared to think of American Negroes as a caste apart, members of a consistent subculture, and to regard them almost wholly as Negroes, hardly at all as Americans. The remedy for that is to meet an American Negro teacher or technician in Liberia. He is like a letter from home, from right next door, not from some racial Darktown ghetto. His ways of talking, joking, dressing, taking hold of a job are all subtly or grossly different from Liberian ways and, whether better or worse, welcome because familiar. Unconsciously recognizing as much, American whites in Monrovia say of a given Mary Smith that she is "American" and may never make it clear that she is not white. Then you begin to hear from Liberians of the ruling class that Negro GI's stationed there during World War II had thrown their money around to the inconvenience of local people, monopolized all the girls, talked incessantly of how the United States did things bigger, better, faster. I had last heard that same range of complaints about white GI's station in New Zealand. In Liberia much of the Stateside distinction between white and Negro is readily seen as that proverbial stupidity, a distinction without a difference.

Long ago one shift in biological theory cleared off an old error about the Negro: the notion that he has degenerated from abler and more attractive ancestors and that careful rehabilitation over many generations can restore him to his original qualities. At least one Negro historian once accepted this idea. More generously a proslavery white parson of the 1850's taught that "The African intellect has never been developed" and that schooling to quicken the wits of promising Negroes, an improvement passed on biologically to their progeny, would eventually permit the Negro mind to "bear comparison with that of the white man . . . a few generations will dispose of those mental shackles which, like chains loaded upon the body, have so long borne [the Negro] down to the level of the brute."

Unless modern biology is dead wrong, this was benevolent nonsense. Scientists now agree—outside the Soviet Union, that is—that traits acquired through outside influences, such as sun tan, the ability to speak English and skill at lacrosse, do not reappear spontaneously in the offspring as do ability to breathe and tendency to grow a certain color of hair. What is inherited is the potentiality of tanning and of learning to speak and play games, but only as generalized possibilities to match certain growth patterns of nerves and muscles and requiring development after birth in particular social contexts known as "cultures." (I, too, dislike this sort of language; but from here on we must resort to it now and again for accuracy and clarity.) That is, in generation after generation you can cut the tails off rats, breed the resulting tailless she-rats to the resulting tailless he-rats, and the baby rats that are the pledges of their love will be born with tails regardless. The same expectation probably applies to the heritable aspects of human intelligence, though these matters are less well explored. So, even supposing that the parson's Negroes had been potentially as low grade as he obviously thought them, centuries of schooling would have done little for them.

In a way that was a pity. This theory of how to sharpen Negro wits might have secured them schooling and social and economic privileges that, faulty as the notion was, might have had the same effect on individuals as if it had been sound. But, as Lamarckian teachings about biological transmission of acquired traits lost ground, and it became clearer that outside manipulation could not breed higher intelligence into Negroes or any others, at least the basic issue could be intelligibly stated for the first time: Opportunity for opportunity, are Negroes the intellectual and moral equivalents of whites?

Vociferous votes of "No" often rely on the obvious backwardness of Negro cultures in West Africa: ". . . after long, elaborate, and ample trial," wrote Thomas Nelson Page, a kindly and literate Southern racist, "the Negro race has failed to discover the qualities which have inhered in every race of which history gives the record, which has advanced civilization or has shown capacity to be itself greatly advanced." Few such judges had ever seen West Africa, but some knew the more or less reliable accounts of explorers, missionaries and officials whose low opinions of the cultural achievements of the area were not too ill justified. West Africa is not now and probably never was an ingratiating part of the world, and the conditions of its being, as Portuguese and later investigators found them, could boast little but great virtuosity in carving and metalwork.* The devices and intellectual techniques that have gone round the world did not originate in that Guinea coast which is Africa for the purposes of students of *Uncle Tom*. It was a cultural

---

* The possibility that Africans invented the smelting and forging of iron is now discounted. (Coon, *Story of Man;* 319.) Many Negro and some white scholars harp on the dead glories of the medieval Negro kingdoms of the Western Sudan, also of the kingdoms of Dahomey and Benin and the Ashanti "empire." The Sudan kingdoms did whatever flourishing they managed well to the north of the true West African "Guinea," and in any case little is known about them to judge by. It does not obviate the meagerness of San Blas Indian culture, say, to point out that the Maya, racial cousins of the San Blas people, developed civilizations in the same grand division of the same continent. Benin and Dahomey were well, if most bloodily, organized Negro states highly skilled in metallurgy. But they never developed writing, and only museums would be the poorer if they had never existed.

backwater before the slave trade damaged it and still is one, though the slave trade has long ceased to harass it.

The significance of this, however, is not what racists think it is. Negro backwardness in Guinea need not mean innate low Negro potential in ingenuity, initiative or whatever. If it did, whites also would look bad, as of a few thousand years ago. Suppose a dark-skinned Egyptian of 2000 B.C. enabled to visit the Germanic folk already settled on the Baltic shore in cultures much less advanced than those of the Ashanti or Ybo of A.D. 1400. He would have described your and my not-so-remote forebears, presumedly carrying whatever innate potential of civilization we possess, as sordidly and dishearteningly savage, obviously unable to cope, else why hadn't they accomplished more? This is a splendid anti-racist gambit. Aristotle's opinion of the Northern Europeans of his day was that, though "full of spirit," they were "wanting in intelligence and skill . . . keep their freedom but have no political organization, and are incapable of ruling others." This, mark you, of the ancestors of the very people who organized and for centuries administered the British, Dutch and French colonial empires. Some day a great genius will form a tenable theory of what suddenly starts a people achieving much in a given place at a given time without having previously shown marked enterprise in the same environment. Until he appears, it is vain to draw scornful conclusions from the fact that the Indians in the admirable climate of California lived the lives of vegetables while, on the energy-sapping Mexican plateau, their racial kinsmen exerted both the enterprise and the brute physical energy to build great cities.

This is about as far as common sense alone can take us. Great men, such as Goethe, Mill and Darwin, who postulated extremely close kinship among all sorts of human beings were just making informed guesses, of little greater weight than that of ancient Greeks similarly guessing at theories of evolution. Only in our lifetime has a new branch of biology called "genetics" opened up promising study of these "white" and "black" races that our grandparents—and too many of their grandchildren—made occasion for group libel and group narcissism.

Promising approaches is about all that genetics yet offers. An immense amount of involved experiment, delicate mathematics and very hard thinking must be got through before geneticists can say much to the laymen who endow them. But some of the consequences are already impressive. As often happens with chimeras, many venerable notions just disappear when the man in the white coat applies the right lens. But the right lens it must be. You can peer for a lifetime through a very powerful regular microscope, which here stands for common sense, and never see the fluffy spheres of influenza virus. They unveil only for the electronic microscope, which here stands for the statistical-biochemical approach of genetics. That is, you can ponder Nature and Nurture as ingeniously as you please, but without the basic concepts of genetics you will never make head or tail of what actually goes on.

There is such a thing as race, make no mistake about it. In fact, depending on definition, there are a dozen things with some title to be called "race." Certainly there are innate differences between individuals of one race and those of another—between individual members of the same race, of the same nation, the same family. But the genesis of these inborn differences, and the meanings thereof, can no longer be seen in terms that would be at all familiar to Jefferson, or Marcus Garvey, or Adolf Hitler, or Thaddeus Stevens, or Francis Galton—or Harriet Beecher Stowe.

2   *Aren't we all?*

"For we must rid ourselves of that incubus of 'immutable race characters.' . . . What has the Englishman of today in common with that rather lovable fop, drunkard and bully who would faint with ecstacy over Byron's Parisina *after pistolling his best friend in a duel about a wench or a lap-dog? Such differences as exist between races of men, exist only at a given moment."*

—NORMAN DOUGLAS, Old Calabria

On the eve of the Civil War a bewildered spokesman for the South described

> . . . a very singular fallacy . . . belief in the absolute non-superiority of races . . . absolute equality of all men, of every creed and color. A new sect of philosophers . . . refusing to acknowledge the notorious superiority in all climates and all lands of the pure white races, have the impudence and temerity to declare that this superiority is only apparent, and does not indicate any inherent superiority of blood.

Today this sounds like clumsy travesty written for a left-wing weekly. It was in dead earnest then. You and I, however, have small reason to plume ourselves on having ceased so emphatically to jabber this kind of nonsense, for we are still tempted to accept other kinds. We may just be inarticulately, imperceptibly accepting what Mrs. Stowe taught our forebears; or we may be showing our overcorrection as people of good will seeking to replace old wives' tales with new ones opposite in direction and, we hope, equal in force. Thus, following a current ethnological cult, modern schools drum it into pupils that race stops inside the skin, is not important in any case, could not conceivably be significant. While drafting this chapter I found in a 1955 almanac, of all unlikely places, the following attributed to "Unknown":

I am the person who was born to live in a skin with a different color from yours.

I could not choose my parents, nor you yours.

Thus, the color pigments imbedded by the unchangeable hands of nature in your skin are perchance white, while mine are black, or brown, or yellow.

But, underneath I am just like you.

My muscles ripple in the same waves of power, and thrill to the same throb of joyous action.

My mind has the same function as yours.

I love and hate, hope and despair, rejoice and suffer, along with you.

When my children lose their fair chance of life, and become aware of the bitter road of prejudice that they must tread, then I know what my color has cost.

I offer you my hand in rebuilding an unjust world, that you and I can make better than we have found it.

I am the person in a different skin.

The intent throughout this is decent and constructive. But is it wholly "perchance" that skin pigmentations differ? Is it true all the way that the speaker is "underneath . . . just like you?" Generally, to what extent can responsible science now stand behind such well-meant antiracist propaganda? What are chances that, as knowledge advances, it can continue to do so? Soberly seeking to learn and formulate what he himself should think about "race" and "created equal," a lay observer will now try to dissect the valid away from the specious. He will need all the cooperation a reader can give him in trying to get the hang of what he says—and does not say.

"Mr. Madison told me that if he could work a miracle . . . he would make all the blacks white; and then he could do away with slavery in twenty-four hours."
—MARTINEAU, Society in America

It is maintained—the doctrine was of Marxist origin but long since escaped that icy clutch—that invidious race feelings, particularly those reflecting skin color, are relatively new. The rising class of merchants and then of industrialists was supposed to have invented and fostered race prejudice as a pretext for the colonialism that secured them raw materials and marginal markets. The current version, self-righteously deploring prejudice, is conveyed by the lyric in *South Pacific:* "You've got to be taught to hate . . ." This is essentially the smug old doctrine of the essential goodness of man. Fortunately there are many reasons more substantial than that for heartily renouncing color prejudice.

Where and when color prejudice began I do not know. The lady of *The Song of Songs* was black *but* comely, which at least implies a significant attitude in the translators of the King James Version decades before a British colonialism had arisen. At about the same time Iago used *black* as literally denigrating epithet in the classic spirit of would-you-let-your-daughter-marry-a-nigger: "Even now, very now," he taunts Brabantio, "an old blacke Ram/Is tupping your white Ewe." A certain color feeling in his audience is evidently taken for granted. An earlier Shakespeare postulated such feeling even more confidently in developing Aaron in *Titus Andronicus*. Seeking to dissuade John Rolfe from marrying Pocahontas, Sir Thomas Dale described her as "of a different and despised color . . . a hated race, not one of whom has ever looked above the meanest of the colonists." A Virginia statute of 1690 called the potential offspring of white indentured women servants and Negroes "an abominable mixture," which hardly sounds like generous color acceptance. But then generations before Watt and Arkwright conspired to proletarianize the masses, laws reflecting race prejudice in the lumping of Negroes and Indians together in various disabilities were steadily strengthened year after year. Decades before any of this, medieval-minded Spanish historians called the aborigines of the West Indies "not human in the same sense as were the Spaniards."

By 1738 biology had chimed in. Linnaeus, father of taxonomy, described the various kinds of human beings as of different species, not just varieties, and described them in terms unfavorable to black men: The American Indian was at least "tenacious, free, contented" and the European Caucasoid "lively, light, inventive"; but the Negro was "cunning, slow, negligent." Nor are color and race prejudices confined to white men, as the antiracist with a bad conscience so often implies. Samoans sneered at Fijians as "black things" long before white men infected them with intolerance and gonorrhea. And the Chinese, says a realistic anthropologist, regarded themselves as "superior to all foreigners, whom they looked upon with disgust and contempt. Race prejudice touched a peak in China. . . . The Chinese and the Hindus were the racial snobs [of the period 1600-1800]."

Nobody yet knows whether color prejudice itself is, as alleged, biologically artificial, appearing in man only as a cultural, "learned" trait. (Logically, of course, no line can be drawn between "natural" and "artificial." It is nevertheless useful to know whether a certain kind of behavior appears in nonhuman animals, as do jealousy and sense of property, for instance, for, if it does, it can be presumed to have deeper emotional and biological meaning.) Hostility from members of an ingroup of mutually adjusted organisms toward a newcomer or an out-group is dismally familiar in both sociology and zoology. Consider, for example, the current hostility of big-city American Negroes toward Puerto Rican newcomers who, though often just as much Negro, look, speak and act differently. Can color as such set off this sort of reaction among animals that can distinguish colors or color values? What about tales of albino robins driven from mating grounds? A highly responsible biologist has seen an albino grackle badly mauled by a flock of normal grackles. . . .

With such odd bits in my head I assumed, when launching on this book, that these matters had been looked into to the point of useful conclusions. After all, popularizers of anthropology had been preaching so confidently that race prejudice in general and color prejudice in particular must be acquired, like a taste for olives. But actually the more I sought, the less I learned. Numbers of busy scientists took time courteously to tell me that they knew of no such extended body of research, but I might go to such-and-such a next-door neighbor, and so I repeatedly did, without ever finding much to get my teeth into.

It is at least known that color antagonisms can appear in children well below kindergarten age, hardening and intensifying as age increases. Perhaps Western insistence on removing grime from light skins tempts Caucasoid children to associate dark skin with lowness or badness; hence, says Goodman's study of the subject, "a child could conceivably wind up strongly inclined to reject Negroes . . . having evolved the whole attitude by himself . . . starting from a strong negative attitude toward dirtiness. He could, but he rarely if ever does . . ." because his early environment of home, school, street contains, as things now are, ample suggestions of color prejudice to account for his developing the attitude outside this possibility.*

And that is about it, which is extraordinary in view of the great importance of the matter. It has not had a thousandth part of the attention repetitiously devoted to the relative degree of Negro IQ. Psychology has long had techniques for determining animals' ability to distinguish colors and for studying their social attitudes. Color is known to affect some biological relationships. Yet, so far as I can find, nobody has properly explored whether the hostile reactions of an in-group of animals to a newly introduced outsider are altered, accentuated or prolonged when he is of a different color that they can distinguish as such. A week after this is published, no doubt, several readers will send me reprints of valuable research along these lines that I have missed. They will be good news. But whatever such work may exist is too obscure; certainly it is not known widely enough among the sociologists, anthropologists and psychologists who should have it at their clever fingertips.

A layman's guess would be that, when such research is properly carried out, the eventual conclusion will be: No—color as such makes no significant difference among animals studied. That will valuably instruct antiracists, since, if color prejudice is altogether learned, a mere "cultural trait," it will probably not require what a psychiatrist would call "deep therapy." However, suppose the conclusion to be:

---

* Or it is possible—I throw this in merely to show how involved the issues are—that in human beings the impulse toward race prejudice appears at a certain biological age well after birth, as a normal development like the closing of the fontanel or the descent of the testicles, in such a manner that it looks as though it were being learned. The late Sir Arthur Keith, an august figure, taught that race prejudice, with color as a principal occasion, was biologically useful in helping to keep races from "mongrelizing." But then he was a very old man, dying in 1954 at the age of eighty-eight, and his training had long preceded modern geneticists' revisions of scientific attitudes toward miscegenation.

Yes—we do find that, of numerous sorts of animals checked, lemurs, say, raccoons and canaries persecute odd-colored newcomers significantly longer than normal. This would in no way *justify* race prejudice, a force necessarily destructive in a world such as ours is now. But it would *warn* projectors of antiracist schemes that they are dealing with something inconveniently close to emotional fundamentals and their means should be correspondingly subtler. Rape, murder and theft are other sorts of destructive behavior the control of which requires awareness that the impulses behind them are not artificially pumped up in one culture and missing in another. Yes or No, here is a crucial item in "the unfinished business of science," and it is a scandal that it should be unfinished.

The Ku Klux-cum-Nazi type of agitator has so viciously exploited and warped "race" that some anthropologists wish altogether to abandon the word as a moral booby trap. It is probably futile thus to expurgate the dictionary. Hitler and Streicher could have roused the same emotions without even knowing the word *Rasse*. In fact, I once knew a creature who leeringly used "Eskimo" for "Jew" when babbling anti-Semitisms. The biological and statistical meanings of race would still exist if the label used were something like "group-entity of order III." In order that science may deal with them at all, things must be grouped according to common resemblances or circumstances. Hence the biologist's tidy pyramid—much tidier than the component facts—of genus, species, variety. And as it happens the anthropologist —a specialized biologist dealing with a single species of animal, *Homo sapiens,* whose biology domestication has thrown all out of shape—needs several other group distinctions, among them this hard-to-define and easily perverted notion of "race."

The word has led a hard life. People have talked of "the white race," "the Nordic race," "the Anglo-Saxon race," "the Jewish race," "the Aryan race," "the Hapsburg race," no two of which are of the same order of grouping. In that list the word applies to (1) a grand division of mankind; (2) a subdivision of that grand division; (3) a national group seeking an illusion of biological coherence; (4) a religious-social caste ditto; (5) a paranoid glorification of a linguistic grouping; and (6) a family line showing one or more readily discernible innate traits. You can't do that. A term cannot be used six ways at once and mean much in any single context. "Race" may apply to either the white-black-yellow-red kind of classification of mankind or to the Hatfield-McCoy kind, but not to both.

The best approach is through traits that "run in families," such as fingerprint patterns, baldness, red hair, turning up generation after generation in significant relations. Say the Hatfields show a consistent cropping up of redheads; the McCoys do not, but the thick upper "McCoy lip" appears again and again down the years.* Let a Hatfield espouse a McCoy, if that can be arranged without setting off the shooting again, and both the red hair and the thick lip *may*—it isn't certain—appear in a certain number of their descendants, though not necessarily in the same individual. (Postpone the why of this until after we meet genetic theory in a later section.) Not only physical but also "mental" traits, such as those assumed to affect "intelligence" (however defined), may run in such "strains." Some kinds of feeblemindedness certainly do; schizophrenia and musical talent almost certainly do.

Now set ashore on a rich, empty continent a dozen married

---

* These attributes of Hatfields and McCoys are purely fictitious. To my knowledge I have never met any members of either family and have no wish whatever to offend either.

couples, all members of which show the same striking and unusual family traits under heavy genetic influence—say six-toed feet, blue eyes and Dante-style aquiline nose. Let them be fruitful and multiply for 10,000 years without outside dilution. In the interval certain "mutations" * of feet, eyes or nose may occur in certain family strains. In most traits normally dominated by heredity, such as hair color, skin color and tendencies to given diseases, variations will have occurred freely. But the bulk of the resulting millions will show twelve toes, blue eyes and Dantesque beaks, a striking if senseless cluster of traits making most of them readily identifiable as—call them Danteans from their single striking nose trait as Negroes are so called from a single striking skin trait.

This would be a new "race." The specific traits in the cluster, mind you, need have no intelligible relation. They may be just packaged together like an auctioneer's "lot" of a kettle, a tire iron and an alarm clock. Some racial traits, such as the Negro's dark skin—which protects him against tropical sunshine—show usefulness. Others may be only consistent freaks, such as the spots on a coach-dog, neither helping nor hindering biological survival. The racishness consists of this identifying consistency, this prevalence of the same trait or set of traits within a national or geographical or social group.

Try definition: A race is a multiple-to-very-large group of families related to some extent, however distantly, but

---

* A "mutation" is a sudden shift in the results of gene influences on an organism due to a change in relations between genes and organism and resulting in a new trait that thenceforth "breeds true" in recognized genetic patterns. Most mutations are poor ideas, which handicap survival, so they usually disappear soon. Those surviving to leave persistent marks on successive generations are sometimes improvements biologically, thus strengthening the organism's chance of survival, or they can be without positive survival value, just going along for the ride, so to speak, but doing neither good nor harm to the organism showing them.

enough for most of the individuals within the families to show a certain cluster of traits expected of most of the families. Or call a race a sort of genetic eddy in marginal contact with other race eddies; mingling occurs between eddies but always far more intensively within than without the rather vague eddy limits. For professional definitions take La Barre, a psychiatry-minded anthropologist: "Races are statistical inferences based upon genetic facts." Or Anastasi, a research psychologist: "Race . . . is a biological unit based upon hereditary community." Or Coon, Garn & Birdsell, from the point of view of the physical anthropologist: "When one group has become sufficiently distinct from another group so that the majority of its members are easily identifiable, we call it a *race*." But even this blazed trail of authority will not get us out of the woods. Beyond "What is race?" lies "What degree of resemblance in how many traits qualifies a group of related families to be called a race within the meaning of the statute?"

There was a happy if specious time when anthropology cut mankind up into five segments allowed somewhat to mingle at the edges but nevertheless offering ample occasion for prattle about the "racial qualities" of white, black, yellow, brown and red. It was soon embarrassingly clear, however, that the stated colors failed to suit in too many cases: Sicilians were seldom notably white, or Caribs red, or Hottentots black, or Japanese yellow. So science renamed each segment after its allegedly typical representative: Caucasian, Mongolian, Negro, American Indian, Malay. But then it seemed absurd to label "Caucasian" a Shetland Islander who had never heard of the Caucasus and to apply the name of Inner Asiatic nomads to patent-medicine millionaires in Singapore. The terms were revised to Caucasoid (that is, Caucasian-like), Negroid, Mongoloid, and so on, with a minor "Australoid" slot for the Australian aborigine and his odd cousins in India and Japan. Then it was objected that "Negroid" had to bend all out of shape to fit both Hotten-

tots and Melanesians; that this nomenclature left no room
for the rather consistent genetic cocktail that Polynesians
have developed from a mixture (largely assumed) of Caucasoid, Mongoloid and Negro ancestries; that Australian
aborigines actually seemed to be two or three different kinds
of people. . . .

These issues may well never be definitively closed. Fresh
systems of classifying mankind will keep appearing until the
end of civilization as we know it. But the current shift is
toward a new realism regarding new biological facts. After
sifting the accumulation of a century of checking the appearance and dimensions of various groups of human beings,
Coon, Garn & Birdsell recently revised the old five-ply
framework to six-ply: Mongoloid, Caucasoid, Negroid, Australoid, American Indian (once only a branch of Mongoloid) and Polynesian. Even more recently Boyd, a crack geneticist, boiled down many findings on the relative incidence
of blood groups—probably the most closely identifiable and
most distinctly heritable of all human traits—and on this
thoroughly biological basis constructed six "grand divisions"
of mankind: European, Asiatic, American [Indian], African, Australian, and "Early European" to allow for a little
enclave of special blood-group patterns among the Basques
of northern Spain and southwestern France. Those, say the
blood groups, could well be the basic ancestor groups out of
which current human beings have been variously stirred together, understandably showing fairly definite geographical
distribution. The quota of European, African and so forth
in each of us is a matter of history/geography/morals/fecun-
dity.

Boyd calls these six grand divisions "races." They fit with
small difficulty into any definition given above, even though,
unlike skin or eye color, one's blood-group classification is
not grossly visible. But many ethnic problems call for a vocabulary narrower than this. Boyd's "Africans," that is, a
significant prevalence in Africa of individuals with certain

blood groupings, takes in an unhandily wide range of peoples. A Kru from Liberia may have enough ancestry in common with a Masai from East Africa to put both into this African category of blood group, but they look about as much alike as a bulldog and a Borzoi. The Kru, however, probably shares not only blood group but skin color, eye color, nose shape, hair type with most West Africans, that is, the Guinea peoples who made up the bulk of the slaver's stock in trade. So it may serve our purposes better to use the clumsy phrase "grand divisions of mankind" for Boyd's six-way classification and reserve the term "race" for the next range of subdivisions under them.

Of such races Coon, Garn & Birdsell distinguish thirty-odd by appearance and measurement. Most of them sort pretty well into one or another of Boyd's six major heaps. Specifically, the race that these students call "Forest Negro" is the very West African whom we have been discussing so much. Another race grouping that they call "North American Colored" is the result of varying mixtures of this Forest Negro with Boyd's Europeans (more or less what used to be called Caucasoids) and his Americans (more or less what used to be called Red Indian). To make the most sense in this lay book, however, we should use our own terms, carefully defined:

"Race" will mean not a "grand division of mankind," such as Boyd's Asiatics or previous students' Caucasoids, but a subdivision of the same, such as "Nordic" or "Forest Negro" as above.

"Caucasoid," though an old term, meaning most Europeans, will do us better than Boyd's "European" grand division, since we shall be talking principally about "white" people settled in America, not in Europe.

"Negro" will apply to the Forest Negro mentioned above as a sample race—the group entity of West Africans whom Herskovits, another anthropological pursuer of these matters, has designated the "True Negro."

"American Negro" will mean the "North American Colored" race mentioned above. Socially this group tends to be extended by Myrdal's all too well grounded definition of the American usage of "Negro" as meaning anybody "with a *known* trace of Negro blood." Here the notion of "race" tends to merge dangerously into the notion of "caste."

It is most important to mark that Boyd's "grand divisions" are mere genetic spot maps, as it were. They carry no implications except those of biological cousinship about the groups or individuals involved. There never was anything like the order of "African race"—consistent in appearance and spirit—of which Mrs. Stowe and St. Clare spoke so brashly. Though isolated, Africa has been washed over by frequent waves of strikingly varied immigrants in both historic and prehistoric times. Exploring whites found limber yellow Hottentots in South Africa; two kinds of pygmies (one yellow, one dark); slender, dark "Nilotic" people in Egypt; darker and still more attenuated "Hamites" elsewhere in the northeast; dark and highly varied "Bantu" peoples south of the Sudan; and the "Negroes" aforesaid. Even though it shows meaningful patterns of blood groups, Africa is little more of an ethnic than a political or climatic unit, something not always clear to outsiders or to African leaders either.

Such illusions about Africa and an "African race" in the old sense begot the curious "colonization movement" aimed somehow to solve the problem of the American Negro. Mrs. Stowe, remember, sent George Harris off to Liberia in a burst of racial patriotism, yearning for more "African blood" to match his feelings. Spelling out her moral in the finale of *Uncle Tom*, she urged Christians to educate runaways for independent usefulness and then ship them to Liberia, the American Colonization Society's settlement in West Africa, to prepare the way for more and more.

Colonizationist reasoning ran thus: We are grieved and incommoded by a mass of members of "the African race" forcibly fetched here from Africa, their original home. That must be the best place for them. Hence, the fair and wise way to redress the ancient wrong of slavery is to send these Africans back where they came from—namely, Africa. Every use of "African," as in the title *The African Repository* of the colonizationists' magazine, fended off common-sense realization that this was like assuming that a white man adopted and reared by Red Indians—a thing sometimes happening—would fit well into London or Cologne simply because his ancestors had happened to be European. Neither the Northern free American Negro nor the Southern field hand was any more an "African" in such a sense than for all his Teutonic-Scandinavian forebears, Harold Stassen is now a Viking pirate. Yet as late as *Dred*, Mrs. Stowe still toyed with such delusions. Lyman Beecher, of course, had always contrived to be simultaneously a nominal friend of the Negro, a colonizationist, and a holder-forth in high places on the moral beauty of slaveholding.* He and his daughter were both earnest exponents of the principle laid down by Walt Whitman: "Do I contradict myself? Very well, then, I contradict myself!"

> *"La plus stupide des noblesses—l'aristocratie de la peau."*
> —*Review of* DE BEAUMONT, Marie

"Miscegenation" is not itself a dirty word. But I felt a slight mental start when it first came to me that its Latin roots imply only "mixed descent." Like the lady in the pet shop who had never heard "bitch" applied to a dog, I had never

---

* Barnes, *Anti-Slavery Impulse*, nicely analyzes Beecher's position on slavery, if "analysis" can be applied to discussion of such a welter of contradictions.

heard or thought of "miscegenation" in any but a most specific context.

This prefix *mis*- has shaming overtones: *mis*carry, *mis*call, *mis*apply, *mis*creant, *mis*guide; whereas in *miscegenation* it is no prefix at all, merely the first syllable of the verb *miscere*, to mix, no heinousness implied. Yet this meaningless coincidence has long endeared the word to the racist, making it a better bridge to the shame idea of "mongrelization." It could apply to the breeding of a wirehair to a Dachshund in hopes of a new breed of dog or to fertile union between a Chinese and a Papuan. But actually it is used only of unions of Caucasoids with non-Caucasoids, often with connotations of unnatural vice, the sort of thing that gets cases heard in chambers. Thirty of the United States have laws against it. There is reason, particularly evidence from blood groups, to believe that much crossing and recrossing has gone on among various races of *Homo sapiens,* not to mention his once-existent and not quite so *sapiens* cousins. Such crossing of strains—that is, miscegenation—may even step up persistent biological vigor in some of the offspring. Certainly it must have been thousands of years since a notion like "mongrelization," with its implications of feckless degeneracy, ceased to apply in human genetics. But beware of these topics at your next dinner party; your hostess may dislike hearing that she is necessarily a mongrel.

This nip of back-of-the-corn-crib spice has often tempted the Caucasoid fictioneer handling race problems into concentrating ill-advisedly on miscegenation, particularly on the crypto-Negro: the hero reared to think of himself as white suddenly learning that he had a Negro ancestor, the "passing" character living a life of harried lies, the presumed Negro suddenly learning that he is white-as-you-are; the dreadfully facile plot angles: blackmail, divorce, renunciations; the messy dialogue about had-I-but-known, oh-mother-how-you-must-have-suffered, cannot-we-go-away-just-you-and-I, . . .

This story line seems first to have tempted obscure novelists in Restoration France, a land in which, one has always been given to understand, the color bar has never been known. De Tocqueville's comrade Gustave de Beaumont followed with a watery novel, *Marie,* laid in Baltimore and the Michigan backwoods. Outside France, Hildreth played the *motif* to a fare-ye-well in *Archy Moore: or, The White Slave,* a story that obviously influenced Mrs. Stowe's views on "white blood." Mrs. Trollope, Cooper, Charles Kingsley variously had at it. Mayne Reid cobbled it up again in *The Quadroon.* William Wells Brown, a valuable fugitive witness about the UGGR let them put his name on *Clotelle,* a novel ghosted by an Abolitionist hack, in which the handling of miscegenation is a veiled insult to American Negroes.* Then Dion Boucicault, the George M. Cohan of his day, doubled Reid's bid with *The Octoroon* (based on *The Quadroon*), a melodrama that, if *Uncle Tom* had never been staged, would have been the world's greatest hit about slavery.† The thing goes on and on. Mark Twain gave it a new and unkind twist in making a sniveling coward of the crypto-Negro in *Pudd'nhead Wilson.* Edward Sheldon handled it better than most in *The Nigger,* even though the at-

---

* The London *Times* Literary Supplement of September 17, 1954 (devoted to American literature) most naïvely took seriously both *Clotelle* (though misspelling the title) and its attribution to Brown. Quoting a few words should suffice: the quadroon heroine is described at one point as with "dark golden locks rolled back from her almost snow white forehead and rolling over her swelling bosom . . . in a sky-blue dress, with deep black lace flounces and bertha . . . hair . . . arranged . . . at the front in the French style (à la Imperatrice). . . ." This, if you please, presented as written by a male escaped slave!

† First seen at the Winter Garden, New York, in 1859, with a cast including A. H. Davenport, Agnes Robertson, Joe Jefferson. Boucicault himself played the sinister Indian. The plot involves use of photography to identify the villain, no doubt the first appearance of the device on any stage. Otherwise it is just a standard play of the period, rather better than any version of *Uncle Tom* that I have seen.

titudes of the play toward prohibition are now obviously absurd. Edna Ferber worked it hard in *Showboat,* and Sinclair Lewis mauled it in *Kingsblood Royal.* W. L. White gave it a "documentary" treatment in *Lost Boundaries,* and just the other day Robert Penn Warren trotted it out again.

The device substitutes the melodramatic for the meaningful, the teary for the tragic. It aims to discredit racism by *reductio ad absurdum,* but actually it distracts the reader from issues that he might otherwise be cajoled into facing but would really rather skip. It lets him dwell on the minor problem "What would it be like to know you're a nigger even if you look white?" in order to avoid having his nose rubbed in "What is it like always to be treated like a nigger because you look like one?" Usually, too, the novels named above and their many rivals implicitly misrepresent the meanings of racial mixture. Too often the residual impression is the old error of *Uncle Tom*—that cross-breeds owe their energy and acumen to "white blood." An astute American Negro critic wrote of such works: "Unmistakable again and again is the hypothesis that white-Negro hybrids have attractiveness because of their white ancestry, that . . . their . . . bitterness, defiance and ambition are traceable to their proud paternal forebears." Mark Twain gives no antidote as Roxy scolds her son for cowardice: "Thirty-one parts of you is white, en on'y one part nigger, en dat po' little part is yo' soul." This is the classic racist position: Any touch whatever of non-Caucasoid ancestry, however remote, clings and taints and makes a "nigger" ad infinitum.

Even the colonies in which the problem first arose did not go that far. In Virginia in 1705 mixed descent was legally degrading to only the second generation in case of Indian ancestry, to only the fourth in that of Negro ancestry. In 1830 North Carolina allowed the franchise to free Negroes past the octoroon generation. But there was also a counter trend with its own evil momentum. Forty years after Appomattox the best-selling novels of a Tarheel preacher, the

Reverend Doctor Thomas Dixon, Jr., building on a pseudo science about "racial mongrelization," dripped with this sort of thing: "One drop of Negro blood makes a Negro. It kinks the hair, flattens the nose, thickens the lip, puts out the light of intellect, and lights the fires of brutal passions. The beginning of Negro equality is . . . the beginning of the end of this nation's life." This completes the extreme of what a psychologist calls the "either-or" aspect of American attitudes about good-bad, right-wrong, clean-dirty, and so on. When Dixon's young Negro—represented as a son of Mrs. Stowe's George Harris—aspires to the beautiful Yankee girl, her philanthropic father thunders out: "I happen to know . . . that a man or woman of negro ancestry, though a century removed, will suddenly breed back to a pure negro child, thick-lipped, kinky-headed, flat-nosed, black-skinned. . . ."

Since dilution works both ways, it follows that, as St. Clare told his brother, miscegenation does "black blood" a moral and intellectual favor, altering its innate handicaps in the direction of fuller humanity and higher intelligence. Racists have usually assumed with Jefferson that "the improvement of the blacks in body and mind, in the first instance of their mixture with the whites . . . proves that their inferiority is not the effect merely of their condition of life." An Abolitionist propagandist, for whose book Mrs. Stowe wrote a preface, called mulattoes "the best specimens of manhood to be found in the South. The African mothers have given them a good physical system, and the Anglo-Saxon fathers a good mental constitution." But other racists, Southern and Northern, described Caucasoid-Negro crosses as innately vicious, infertile, short-lived examples of all the alleged evils of "mongrelization." Racists usually try to have it both ways and often succeed.

A century ago halfbreed Injun Joes were assumed vicious by definition, and few could make sense of racial issues, American Negroes no more than anyone else. Fanny Kemble noted how "the faintest admixture of white blood . . . appears at once, by common consent of their own race, to raise them in the scale of humanity." Helper, poor-white hater of both planter and Negro, was amused when a little slave-boy whom he had called "nigger" wept and blubbered out that mammy said only the devil was a real nigger (that is, incurably black); in the hereafter all Negroes would be white. Levi Coffin's solicitude for runaways did not keep him from deploring all "amalgamation." He exhibited a young slave mother and child of very light color to Cincinnatians from whom he sought help for the UGRR, noting their comments: "Can it be possible that they are slaves, liable to be bought and sold? It is a shame." But it did not occur to him to teach a lesson in the unity of mankind by asking whether buying and selling human beings was less shameful if they were coal black. He was just using a subtler form of Mrs. Stowe's concentration of sympathy for slave women on pretty, literate and able-to-pass-for-white Eliza and Cassie.

"Of the flood that feeds my heart, one drop in eight is black . . . that one drop poisons all the flood . . . I'm an unclean thing . . . an octoroon!"

—BOUCICAULT, The Octoroon

Able to pass for white. That is the prurient core of what keeps people writing such plays and novels. Actually we have far, far more reason for such interest than most of us dream of. It is quite conceivable that now, in 1956, something between one in five and one in ten nominal native-born American "whites" could truthfully be told, like the boy in *Lost Boundaries,* "You have colored blood in your veins." People are interested in the *Lost Boundaries—Pudd'nhead Wilson* sort of story because they think it a scandalous emergency.

As we learn more of the probable facts of our ancestry, miscegenation may lose its appeal because we come to take it more or less for granted.

Start with the fact that, among us American Caucasoids, it is a wise child indeed who knows all about the 8000-odd ancestors preceding him since Jamestown was settled. Exact data on the number of light-skinned American Negroes who have "passed" since 1619 will obviously never become available, but highly indicative cases are known: Thus in 1822 a Tennessee overseer ran away with "a remarkably likely bright Mulatto woman named POLLY, about twenty years old, light hair, inclined to curl a little . . . would . . . pass as a white woman. . . . They will undoubtedly try to reach the free states. . . ." No doubt they did, and the overseer's child with which Polly was pregnant was probably reared as white and his descendants down to the present day never knew the difference. That militant soldier-cum-parson T. W. Higginson knew of a light-skinned slave mother and children —her father had begotten them on her, it was noted in passing—who came north on the UGRR, married a white Northerner and never told him either that she was technically Negro or that her children were of incestuous origin. In the 1920's a detailed anthropological study of Caucasoid-American Negro families was thrown out of balance because "in many families one or more members had left home and were passing for white." The late Walter White wrote that practically every American Negro knows of and keeps silent about a case of "passing."

Then there is dead reckoning. Analysis of the U.S. Census of the decades when it had "Negro" and "mulatto" as separate categories indicates that every year some thousands of nominal American Negroes, mostly men, "pass" into the world of whites. Dr. Charles S. Johnson, originator of much of this work, now considers that his previous estimates of some 25,000 "passers" a year should be raised. Even after certain technical doubts receive due force, this number very likely remains far over 10,000.* In such populations as the United States has long supported, that is no great number. But it means at least a million—likelier two million, could be three—such episodes since Emancipation gave the American Negro greater physical and social mobility. If such "passers" have little more than reproduced themselves—and families run large in the social strata where most of them probably ended up—a million, likelier two million, could be three million, nominal American "whites" unwittingly carry some of that "black blood."

Nor can ante bellum whites have been free of Negro admixture to begin with. A little imagination plus arithmetic works wonders here. Suppose that each year from 1656 through 1805—six generations of twenty-five years each ending a century and a half ago—a single colonist with a single Negro forebear left his birthplace, "passed," married as a white man or otherwise begot on white women only two children surviving to reproduce, each of whom had two children surviving ditto, and so on down to now. Omit the possibility of ancestors in common which, though real, need not have bulked inhibitingly large among people so footloose as Americans, and those 150 "passers," only one a year, would by now have close to 200,000 descendants among us, people touched with the tar brush added to the offspring of Johnson's post bellum "passers."

Now suppose that each of the years 1656-1805 saw only 100 such "passings" or equivalent infiltration of Negro ancestry with such persistence of survival to reproduce in successive generations of offspring. That would mean an addition of almost 20,000,000 people now among us descended from Negroes but unaware of it. Leave out acknowledged

---

* Personal communication. These findings and the technical issues raised are discussed, pro and con, in Herskovits, *American Negro;* 62-65; Klineberg, ed., *Characteristics of the American Negro;* 305-314; Myrdal, *American Dilemma;* 1207-1208. Eckard, *American Journal of Sociology,* May, 1947; Burma, *American Journal of Sociology,* July, 1946.

Negroes, foreign-born Caucasoids and their progeny (who can so far have had little share in this unwitting miscegenation), and this is a good fifth of us Americans now taken to be "white." The above conditions are not fantastic, whatever the results may seem. The American population in the eighteenth century was fairly fluid, particularly south of New England, so "passing" need not have been prohibitively difficult. The total of "passing" ancestors here used, some 15,000 over 150 years, is probably less than the total of people annually "passing" today. A good deal of such colonial "passing" could have been unconscious. We know that at least in the earlier part of the period sexual congress between Negro men and white women (as well as between white men and Negro women) was by no means unknown, and an indentured servant mother might not see fit to tell her bastard son that his father was the quadroon driver on the next plantation, even if indeed she could be specific on the subject.

There is a technical hitch to all this: Nobody can say whether American fecundity was ever consistent enough to produce many such persistently fertile family lines.* But in

---

* For even more striking results consider the possibility that a few of these "passers" between 1656 and 1805 might have started chains of descendants surviving by threes instead of twos. Only *ten* such cases a year during that same five generations, a total of only 1500 such passers over a century and a half, would now have rather more than 100,000,000 descendants—again supposing the matter of common ancestors omitted.

The above text has been read by a mathematician-specialist in statistics and the theory of probability of unimpeachable qualifications. He noted that studies of the survival of family names show about an even chance that they will not survive the first generation; but also that the family name usually goes only with male children and that my concern is with survival of a lineage in both males and females. In any case, he allowed, such data are not necessarily relevant here because "they were gathered for a homogeneous white population where psychological blocks and racial prejudices were minimal . . . The whole problem is, I fear, rooted in inaccessible data." Then the gloom lifts somewhat: "It seems to me that you can use some such passage . . . provided that you make it quadruply clear that you are talking about what *could*

view of the numbers of unconscious as well as conscious passings that probably occurred, and of the relatively small numbers of such necessary to produce statistically striking consequences, given enough time, common sense makes that estimate of 20,000,000 current "white" Americans with at least one Negro ancestor look somewhat conservative. Nevertheless, cut it in half to allow for common ancestors and general caution, and the notion of 10,000,000 of us actually "tainted with black blood" is still something that "white" America is, to say the least of it, ill prepared to contemplate.* It makes more than a joke of the alleged comment of a Southern politician on a bill to stiffen the legal definition of "Negro": that its terms wouldn't leave enough statutory white voters in the state to pass it in a referendum. Consider also that, since those 10,000,000 "taint" carriers presumably marry freely, fresh unions spread the "taint" every day. If folklore and good Dr. Dixon were correct about that "one drop of black blood," the only sound precaution against unexpected black babies is never to beget children on an American woman unless she comes of known immigrant parents or grandparents from Northern Europe.†

---

happen if so and so . . . and so and so . . . and so on. You can at least point out how fast these descendants must die out in order to avoid the spread of the 'black blood' throughout the population."
* Glass and Li ("The Dynamics of Racial Intermixture," *American Journal of Human Genetics*, March, 1953) found strong evidence of miscegenation in the blood groupings of American Negroes but little if any in those of American Caucasoids. This does not necessarily rule out the above speculations, however. These researchers were investigating the current ingredients of the gene pool of a group, not their actual lineage. And numerous successive crosses always into a white spouse may often have "pinched out" Negro genes.
† My questionnaire asked respondents: "In your opinion how many generations of consistent interbreeding with non-Negroes are required to extinguish any possibility of an eventual child's showing Negro traits? Please make a serious guess if you do not have an informed opinion." The Dixonist faction was small: only one guessed a thousand generations, only eight said, "Never." Guesses from the others ranged

For the odds against "taint" are obviously highest among
the progeny of immigrants from northern and interior Europe, whose Polish, say, or Finnish ancestors had least opportunity to mate with Negroes or those of crypto-Negro ancestry. Since Southern Italy and Portugal were much infiltrated
from North Africa, many New Bedford mill hands and California truck gardeners may also be raising the proportion of
Negro genes in our "gene pool." But the "Old Americans"
of whom eugenists are so fond need not vaunt themselves
invidiously. This putatively widespread Negro ancestry probably concentrates among them, particularly among those
with ancestors from outside New England. Other things being equal, the longer your folks have been in this country,
the higher your chances of. . . . Well, if Negro genes were
radioactive particles, how many of us would already feel
nervous around Geiger counters! I have no definite reason
to assume that I personally would start one clicking. But my
forebears—those of whom I know anything at all—came to
America on an average of eleven generations ago, and so far
as I know none were ever Yankees. It would be a statistical

---

from two to ten generations. Actually the issue is so fouled up by
faulty notions of "Negro traits" and by the fact that Negro skin-color
(and probably many other Negro traits) involves multiple genes, some
dominant-recessive, some maybe not, that intelligible answers were
hardly possible. For expert opinion: Montagu (*Man's Most Dangerous
Myth;* 235): "When a colored infant is born from 'white' parents, it is
proof that the parents carry Negro genes." Dunn and Dobzhansky
(*Heredity, Race, and Society;* 32) call stories of "births of mulatto
children to white parents . . . unadulterated humbug," which would
be more help if the terms were better defined. Boyd (*Genetics and the
Races of Man;* 309-310) mentions a researcher's failure to find in
Jamaica "clear-cut cases of 'throwbacks' in mixed marriages in which
the parents are apparently white." See also Myrdal, *American Dilemma;*
1207-1208, and Wirth and Goldhamer in Klineberg, ed., *Characteristics
of the American Negro;* 305. The consensus certainly does not bolster
Dixonism. But, as in so many other issues treated in this book, inadequate knowledge produces a regrettable blurring at the edges of the
subject.

miracle if, among the 2000-odd ancestors implied, the tar-brush had not touched at least one. Five or six are likelier—sallow or swarthy men, I suppose, drifting west or north to marry among strangers, living quiet lives and letting their secrets die with them.

A 1939 *Fortune* survey found the percentage of us contemplating "amalgamation" as ultimate outcome of the race problem ranging by regions between 1.2 per cent and 3.9 per cent—negligible in all cases. On this subject we had better start changing our minds. Biologist Curt Stern of the University of California sees complete "amalgamation" as bound to come whether we approve or not, whether we know it or not, with average American skin color shifting to "light brunette" and only a few thousand definitely black people born in any given generation, most of whom will have thin lips and straight hair—for reasons that may be clearer after our upcoming wrestle with the science of genetics. Recent work on blood groups has led other researchers to set a thousand years more or less as the time necessary to complete this amalgamation. That is a good while. But they were considering only the ascertainable rise in Caucasoid gene content among persons acknowledgedly Negro. This less conspicuous rise in history-of-Negro-ancestry (actual Negro genes may well not accompany it, but you never know) is a secret force in the same direction. Awareness that this force exists might even speed up amalgamation by persuading people to stop taking intercaste marriage so big. In any case amalgamation is inevitable—or rather, only hydrogen bombs can stop it now.

To the layman it sometimes looks as though scientific investigation of these issues had so far only whittled away things that *don't* make sense. As a necessary preliminary to sense, however, that is progress of a sort. A conspicuous casualty is the notion of "colored blood in your veins"—for some moronic reason always veins, never arteries.

Whether taken literally or figuratively, this does not add up at all. The only ascertainable difference between normal Caucasoid blood and normal American Negro blood—or that of Tahitians, Patagonians or Kalmucks—lies in blood groupings. These inherited idiosyncrasies also may differ among individuals whom you think of as consistently Caucasoid, Negro or whatever. Otherwise, human blood is human blood through all the mysterious properties and quirks that make it the strangest organic entity in the world.

No blood is transferred from Him to Her in sexual congress. So no consequent child can have "his father's blood in his veins," except temporarily if he receives a transfusion from his father.

No blood is transferred from mother to child during conception, pregnancy or birth. The placenta blocks off the mother's system of blood vessels from the child's. Nourishment passes between them through cell walls, but blood does not. The growing embryo makes its own blood and, for genetic reasons, may be of a blood group different from its mother's, for the groups are heritable by genetic predestination, not by infection.

Blood cannot pass on heritable traits, such as red hair,

from parent to child. They are transmitted because the body cells of each child imitate the internal structure of the germ cells—egg and sperm—supplied by the parents in sexual congress.

Apparently one must go into such elementary details, else why would blood donated by Negroes have been so strangely mistrusted during World War II? Frank fear of "nigger blood in your veins" was accentuated by dread of its bringing about mulatto offspring. For that matter, Orthodox Jews have risked their lives by refusing blood transfusions from gentiles on such grounds. This stupid old idea readily extends to "good blood," "bad blood," "blue blood," "peasant blood," as devices to think with—if thinking it be.

Subtler errors admit such usage of "blood" to be figurative but find it handy to symbolize and formulate incorrect but enticing ideas of what occurs when races or strains mingle. The error consists in thinking of the result as a complicated cocktail wherein inherited traits blend with and modify one another, like the whiskey, vermouth and bitters in a Manhattan. Thus a man with an inherited bad temper marrying a woman of inherited meekness would have children of normal irritability. Or a breeder wanting a gray horse would serve a white mare with a black stallion. A horseman of any experience would know that was absurd. Actually, as we shall soon see, the effect is often that of a pousse-café, the various ingredients remaining distinct within the glass. But many a person who was asked what would come of a stubby man's mating with a tall girl would say: children of medium height, of course; whereas the likelier result in a prolific union would be, say, six children of heights ranging from His to Hers.

Subtlest of all are stubborn old notions about things being "in the blood," that is, specious association of kinds of behavior with physical traits. Kipling's story about the red-headed half-caste son of an Irish deserter and an Indian hill-woman whose turbulence made him lord of the village was meant to be amusing, but its basic premise was taken seriously by the author and most of his contemporaries. Many a promising colt must have been sold cheap because of the old rigmarole that ends, "Four white feet and a star on his nose —shoot him in the head and give him to the crows." Every other old woman in small towns still lards her talk with "That boy's got his grandfather's buck teeth and narrow-set eyes and he won't come to no good."

Applied to races, this sort of thing means that black skin and obtuseness "go together," one the outward and visible token of the other. Yet anthropologists, according to one of their most heredity-minded leaders, have yet to find "relationship between any physical criterion of race and mental capacity, whether in individuals or groups."

"*I will praise Thee; for I am fearfully and wonderfully made.*"   —Psalm cxxxix: *14*

The son of Jesse praised the Lord for making him so outrageously complicated. At this point my impulse is different. If genetics, the essence of what makes man what he is, were simpler, we should all be much better off for the next few pages. There should be—but there is not—some way of packing it all into a hypodermic syringe and injecting it into readers needing it, so they could get the drift of it all as quickly as the bloodstream circulates. I am pledged, however, not to try to tell my reader what to think but to give him— and me—the materials and approaches that, working from within his own mind, will exempt him from the wrongheadedness that Mrs. Stowe and *Uncle Tom* conveyed. So, since there is no other, this briefing must be done the hard way. A student of miscegenation once wrote that the idea that people inherit ways of behaving as they inherit long legs "arose and prevailed because it offered an explanation within the comprehension of the simple mind." In dealing with race problems, always to some extent problems in genetics, we can no longer afford the luxury of the simple mind. Instead we must plunge flounderingly into the gene pool.

Mention genetics to literate people and the train of association runs: "Mendel . . . monk . . . sweetpeas . . . monastery garden . . . recessive and dominant . . ." as if groping after a story from the *Decameron*. Actually the notion of recessive and dominant traits is only one aspect of what Mendel learned among his flowers. His basic work was the discovery that organisms reproducing sexually, that is, by collaboration between two organisms playing different parts, pass innate traits from parents to offspring *one by one and at random*.

Blood types are an example. Which type your blood shows is altogether a matter of how chance, impersonal as an honest roulette wheel, chose the genes in your ancestors' body cells all down the generations. The moment your parents' reproductive cells—sperm and egg—fused to begin you, you were committed to this or that blood type. Nothing you can do permanently alters the blood properties that show up as A, B, O or whatnot in the laboratory. Yet what blood type you show seems to bear no necessary relation to other traits of body or mind—how tall you are, how your eyelids are shaped or how quick you are on the uptake.

The physical plant of genetics is wheels within wheels. Each of your body cells contains a nucleus visible under a powerful microscope. Each nucleus contains numerous chromosomes—bodies often shaped like attenuated crullers, visible only at certain stages under a very powerful microscope. Each chromosome contains genes—entities exerting ancestral influences on you and visible as actual bumps on the chromosome only under an electronic microscope. Each bump consists of a highly individualized protein in a specially assigned area of a particular chromosome as if it were a color band on a croquet stake. What actually passes from redheaded parents to offspring is not red hair as such but a master set of genes on chromosomes that prescribe the gene pattern for all the cells of the offspring-to-be. If the appropriate genes in the parents prefer redheadedness, then in the offspring the special proteins of the corresponding genes will exert influences toward whatever it is that makes for redheadedness.

For most innate traits, that is, the structures and qualities that genes seek to create in organisms, it remains as simple as that. Nine tenths of the way people are is subject to pretty much the same biological destiny. The genes of practically all human beings agree in favor of two eyes, five toes on each foot, inability to hear sounds above a certain frequency, the details of brain tissue (whatever they are) enabling you to learn to talk. Without such run-of-the-mine gene influences you might just as likely have hooves instead of fingernails. Families showing six-toedness as a recessive trait are a good rule-proving exception. In general the innate traits that make us specifically "human" (however one defines that) are, for practical purposes, unanimously sought by the appropriate genes in us all. But a small proportion of gene-influenced features are not thus standardized. And that is where the trouble starts.

Each human cell has forty-eight pairs of chromosomes together carrying genes numbering maybe as high as 44,000-odd. They are arranged in identical order on both chromosomes of a given pair, like croquet stakes from the same set side by side. Under immense difficulties science has now started to "map" the relative positions of a few particular genes on certain chromosomes. But, though they occupy the same locations and influence the same kinds of traits, the kinds of influence that these opposite-slot genes exert is not necessarily the same. This must be made very clear: As between any two cells in the same organism, the gene patterns are exactly alike. They are alike both in their genes for standardized traits and in those for unstandardized traits. For those nonstandardized traits, however, these gene patterns are not like those of a fellow organism next door. They are, in fact, as individualized as a thumbprint, for all practical purposes unique. If this were not true, all human beings would be as much alike as identical twins—and for the same biological reason.

Now suppose that eye color, skin color, hair color, nose shape and blood group are each controlled by a single gene and that all five genes concerned are located on the human A-chromosome. (None of this is really true but we must begin somewhere; the real facts of genetics, where known, are seldom simple enough to make good elementary examples.) This means that the cells of a man with blue eyes, fair skin, red hair, a snub nose and M-type blood each carry A-chromosomes with genes favoring those traits. In ordinary body cells, remember, the chromosomes are paired, hence offer two genes for any given trait. But when the organism makes reproductive cells (sperm in this case) the paired chromosomes separate and the resulting sperm cells show only single sets of chromosomes—hence single sets of genes. The pattern of each set still covers all kinds of traits, but it is no longer present in duplicate.

Now suppose a girl with blue eyes, red hair, light skin, a snub nose and M-type blood. Her reproductive cells—eggs in this case—will also carry single strings of genes on chromosomes reflecting her traits. Now let him impregnate her. As his sperm cell fuses with her egg cell, the separate strings of chromosomes pair up A-to-A and so forth. (This is not precisely what happens, but near enough for now.) This starts the offspring with a new double pattern derived from both parents for his traits to follow. Since both parents' genes vote for the same traits, Junior too will have blue eyes, fair skin, red hair, and so on.

But parents are never identical in all traits. Suppose the

lady's nose gene votes for Roman shape. Now when the A-chromosomes range alongside to set up the new patterns, on the subject of noses they will disagree. One insists on a Roman nose, one on a snub. Genes resolve such conflicts most undemocratically—not by tossing coins or yet, in some cases, by compromising between snub and Roman, but by arbitrary biological custom called "dominance"; that is, in such a situation, Roman may be supposed always to win over snub, like scissors-cut-paper in the child's game. Roman is said to be "dominant over" snub; snub is said to be "recessive to" Roman.

So Junior's visible nose will be Roman. But this does not extinguish the snub gene. It was present in the original egg-sperm fusion that set the pattern for his cells-to-be. So it must also appear in one of the paired A-chromosomes in all his ordinary body cells. And so it does. The Roman gene, of course, will be in the corresponding slot in the other A-chromosome in each cell.

Now when Junior's chromosome pairs split to make sperm cells, every other one carries a Roman gene but also *every other one carries a snub gene.* So Junior's love life presents three possibilities: (1) When a Roman-carrying sperm of his happens to fertilize a Roman-carrying egg, the child will be Roman-nosed, for there is no conflict. (2) When a Roman-carrying sperm of his happens to fertilize a snub-carrying egg—or vice versa—"dominance" will see to it that the child is Roman-nosed. But (3) when a snub-carrying sperm of his happens to fertilize a snub-carrying egg, there is no conflict to invoke dominance and no Roman gene present; so the child will be snub-nosed even though both Junior and the lady are Roman-nosed, with a snub gene similarly buried in her ancestral past. Such contingencies sometimes worried people before they understood how family resemblances are transmitted. It has been a minor but gratifying result of Mendel's work to exonerate faithful brownhaired wives who bore anomalously redheaded babies to brownhaired spouses, red hair being somewhat complicatedly recessive.*

All this is thick with "happens to" because it is strictly chance which type of sperm of the thousands released at once happens to meet which type of egg. We have been using only five kinds of possibly disagreeing genes. Actually there are probably thousands operating under the dominance code, which means teeming millions of possible different combinations. That makes the odds against genetic identity between any two offspring even of the same parents staggeringly high. The rule-proving exception here is the uncommon case of identical twins, which come of the freak splitting of a single sperm-egg fusion to form two individuals obviously sharing the same genes-on-chromosomes pattern. Fraternal twins, on the other hand, are only conceived at about the same time from two separate sperm-egg fusions and are no likelier to be alike than any other two children of the same couple.

This is the *at random* part. The *one by one* part appears in the dominant code's creating or suppressing snub noses without regard to Junior's inheritance of blood groupings or skin color, the genes of which have all the while been playing their own unrelated games separately. Suppose musical talent to some extent innate, as it almost certainly is, and make Junior's father a great composer. It is quite in the cards for Junior to be his very image—blue eyes, red hair, snub nose and all—and yet be unable to tell the Doxology from "Turkey in the Straw" because the shuffle did not deal him some gene that made the difference in father as a musician.

So far this has been a sort of mock-up of genetics. Had the

---

* Because light eyes are somehow recessive to dark, it was once taken also to follow that blue-eyed spouses could not legitimately have a brown-eyed child. This sometimes embarrassed virtuous wives until it was learned that blue eyes come of several genes in combination, not just one; hence it is theoretically possible, though rare, for a brown-eyed child to come of a both-blue-eyed union.

science remained that simple, its implications would be such common knowledge that none of this would need writing. But actually it covers little more than what one needs in order to appreciate—I do not say understand—the complications. Later modifications do not destroy Mendel's approach. But exploration of the principle of *one by one and at random* has turned up material far more involved than what Mendel looked into. His two-choice, single-gene, straight dominant-code situations—as in his pea blossoms, some white, some purple, no color blends, no third hue intruding—do exist but are uncommon.* Actually most innate traits readily picked out and once thought to be single-shot affairs—such as red hair, hereditary baldness, the "Hapsburg lip"—are resultants of numerous genes exerting combined but not necessarily blending influences.

Thus a Negro's dark-brown-to-black skin involves at least three known genes and probably several more as yet only guessed at, some of them observing the dominance code, some maybe able to blend. This may account for a Caucasoid father and Negro mother often having children consistently "mulatto" in skin color, apparently halfway between the parents' differing pigmentations; whereas the offspring of these mulattoes mating with other mulattoes can range from beige to about as dark as grandmother. Perhaps in such cases various recessives buried under dominants in the first generation show up in certain individuals' gene patterns in various combinations in the second generation. Certainly the possibilities of variation are widened by inclusion of the individual

---

* Even in a two-alternative situation the degree of intensity of the gene influence may vary as a sort of subtrait genetically transmitted and, as seedsmen say, "breeding true" generation after generation. Though "hemophilia" (the very rare, easy-bleeding disease) may well be a two-choice, dominant-recessive affair, it shows a wide range of severity on sharply separated levels, each "breeding true." Such layered variations within a gene-influence are called "alleles"—a complication apparently put in by Nature just to make it hard.

gene patterns of another Caucasoid and another Negro in the persons of the grandparents on the other side of such mulatto-to-mulatto marriages.*

More confusingly still, genes are now known often to exert various degrees of influence on widely disparate traits. Experimental change of one gene in a certain breed of fruit fly means striking change not only in its legs but also in antennae, wing design, location of bristles. Yet crossing this strain with another would not necessarily see these new traits "going with" one another in the offspring, since genes from the other parent might dominate some or all of the novelties. *One by one and at random* tends still to persist under all the apparent confusion.

But not altogether scatheless. Genes are transmitted "particulate," as geneticists say, that is, are not diluted by associations. But this transmission may not always reflect strict chance modified by dominance. As data about innate traits accumulate, a genetic linkage begins to take shape. Red hair and fair skin, for example, hang together oftener than chance and dominance should seek to account for. There may be a significant relation between dark eyes and susceptibility to poliomyelitis. Genes from the same chromosomes are suspected of hunting in couples or packs either because of subtle intrachromosome influences or perhaps just because they are near neighbors during the process of fusion and development of new patterns. As another example consider that *male* cats with blue eyes are usually deaf. Sex is a matter of genes. So the sex chromosomes (usually labelled X) of cats at least are

---

* A last word on those Dixonist black babies: Nothing in genetic theory rules out rare occasions when, through mutation of a gene or genes affecting skin color, two spouses, *neither with any Negro ancestry at all,* might produce a child with skin-color matching that of the classic Forest or "True" Negro. Legends of such unexpected births may have arisen from such a case or cases, which would, however, obviously be very rare indeed. For the possibility in general, see Coon, Garn & Birdsell, *Race;* 12.

believed to carry genes affecting eye color and hearing. Since hemophilia in both dogs and mankind is a recessive trait that usually crops up only in males, the gene that controls it must also be on the sex chromosome. Such linkages are as yet little better explored than those "canals" on Mars. But they amount to good reason to suspect that genetic odds can sometimes be cooked, so one cannot be too categorical about *one by one and at random*.

The principle nevertheless tends to give tenable answers to perplexing old problems, which often means that a theory is valid. The old notion of innate traits merely blending in offspring could never account for those occasions, familiar to all, when anomalously stupid children are born to clever parents or a man like Lincoln suddenly springs from a low-grade couple. Some biographers have sought to account for Lincoln by assuming he was begotten the wrong side of the blanket by some amorous backwoods genius. Genetics does better, and less scandalously, along such lines as these: "Intelligence" is a vague term; but some such thing exists and there is no better single word for the contrast in acumen between a possum and a chimpanzee or between Puck and Bottom the Weaver. There is authority for believing that, whatever is true of relative average intelligence between groups such as races, intelligence is to some extent heritable in individuals and can be seen to "run in families." It may well be no single trait but a cluster of interacting traits influenced by many interacting genes and modified in use by the total physiology of the whole body.

All this means an astonishingly wide range of possible combinations of what goes into intelligence as chance and dominance shuffle and deal their interlocking games of solitaire. But it may help more to keep in mind the old, and no doubt apocryphal, story of how, when Isadora Duncan suggested to George Bernard Shaw that they two have a child gloriously to combine her body with his brains, he answered, "Ah, but suppose it had my body and your brains?" In a more complex situation, though neither Nancy nor Thomas Lincoln held a good tactical combination of cards in the game of intelligence, their pooled hands could readily afford the raw material of a grand slam for chance to pick out. Contrariwise, though Mr. and Mrs. Bright had good tactical combinations of cards, chance could still find a Yarborough for Junior. Neither eventuality is anything to count on. The good bet is still that high IQ in the parents means high IQ in a given child of theirs, and that low IQ makes a dull child likely. But fact and theory agree that the unexpected can happen, and the application of genetics to whatever makes for intelligence is so far the best way to account for it.*

At any rate the gene-pool idea is neither shaky nor vague. It consists of the total of individual genes affecting the structure and perhaps behavior of any group of organisms closely enough related for interbreeding to produce fertile offspring. This may be anything from a test lot of fruit flies in a laboratory through our Dantean race to the whole of mankind. If all human beings had genes agreeing on all traits, there would be no point in the idea. But mankind has probably never been in that situation ("homozygous" is the technical word) since some ominous mutation first laid our genetic foundations hundreds of thousands of years ago. And ever since mutations, most of them disappearing, some staying around as improvements or at worst harmless, have been gradually varying the content of mankind's gene pool.

Natural selection is assumed to steer variations in this or that direction by sifting mutations for "survival value," such as better resistance to this or that climate. Thus the Negro's dark skin, numerous sweat glands, dark eyes and, perhaps,

---

* Dunn and Dobzhansky (*Heredity, Race, and Society;* 22) attribute 65 to 80 per cent of "intelligence" to heredity. Klineberg (*Race Differences;* 154) sees genetic influence on intelligence marked "within individual family or germ plasmas." Montagu (*Man's Most Dangerous Myth;* 175) chimes in. Even the extreme caution of Boyd (*Genetics and the Races of Man;* 13-14) leaves plenty of room for the above discussion, since he admits "great differences in mental ability . . . between different individuals."

flat nose may be assumed to fit him better for the hot, sunny tropics. Carried far enough, this would make a given race's gene pool a sort of biological blueprint of the traits best suited to a given environment, passed on to all members of the race as an environment-tailored package. The "going together" of the various traits shown, as in Negroes, need imply no inter-gene linkage or affinity, merely adaptation for certain circumstances. But the sum of such speculation would be more impressive if it had got farther with accounting for such other traits in the Negro package as everted lips and pink palms. So far they are little more than occasion for an engrossing parlor game among scientists. Perhaps they have some pointless but intimate linkage with some Negro gene that does imply definite survival value . . .

Since this is no textbook, it can afford to say that genetics is an exasperating science in need of more money and logic and less emotional bias. Things were far more comfortable back in the old days when one could say knowingly that a certain type of behavior was "in the blood," conceive race mixture as mechanically blending low and high qualities and babble sagely of "racial heritage" along with Augustin St. Clare, Harriet Beecher Stowe and Thomas Carlyle. For the next generation or so—here is fair warning—the trend in genetics will probably be toward the very ideas that so far most geneticists spend their lives trying to denounce. There will develop a growingly impressive case for "mental" innate traits as well as "physical." This will probably mean a revival of eugenics. A cloud little larger than Francis Galton's hand is already visible on the horizon. It might do mankind some good if it confines itself to advocating, perhaps successfully, that intelligent people have more children. But now and forever it will still be inadvisable to keep on making those rule-of-thumb, wise-old-woman judgments about correlation between skin color and morals, sloping foreheads and intelligence, thick lips and talent for music, venery or religious ecstasy.

3 New wives' tales

"We are all the product of heredity and environment. The genes provide the blueprints and the carpenters, the environment the lumber."
— COON, GARN & BIRDSELL, Races

Such elements of genetics are obviously only the beginning of wisdom, the tools to find answers with but not answers in themselves. So, in the waxing and waning battle in men's minds between Nature and Nurture, one finds both the eugenics crank and the anthropological Pharisee appealing to the same Mendelian laws. Both are pseudo-scientific empire builders arrogating to themselves more than, in the present state of knowledge, either can fairly claim. All that genetics can yet say firmly is: "Men are like other organisms in that certain of their traits—rather, the biological quirks that favor those traits—are overtly or cryptically heritable."

Such statements lack maximum bite unless they go on to say *which* traits are thus heritable and what they imply. Interest in Nature-versus-Nurture is especially concerned with traits that not only vary widely among persons but carry social impact. Blood groups matter only in hospitals and in law suits over paternity. A family tendency toward twinning, also highly heritable, matters only when it runs wild, as with the Dionnes, or among certain nonliterate peoples who take twins as here a good omen, there a scandalous calamity. But if diabetes, epilepsy and certain severe mental illnesses "run in families," if, as racists believe, intelligence, erotic laxness, rhythmic agility and musical talent are "racial traits," we should know such things definitely enough to take social steps about them.

Note that "heritable" is not the same word as "racial." Redheads are not infrequent among some races; among others they are practically unknown—but there are no redheaded races. One can say intelligibly only that redheadedness "runs in families." Partly because the genes affecting many striking traits are recessive, partly because one usually sees what one is looking for, partly because it often takes skilled investigation to tell inborn from learned behavior, confusions throng about these issues like amateur doctors round a fainting woman. A given race may contain several family-transmitted traits perpetuating themselves, even widening their scope, without yet meaning much about the race itself. The progeny of the late Bill Robinson might show a striking number of persons adept in body rhythms, but that would mean nothing about a generalized Negro genius for dancing. After all, the man who brought "Negro dancing" to the professional stage with immense impact on both whites and Negroes was T. D. Rice, a white man. Races—this is another of those interlocking definitions—are the long-range results of the mutual dilutions and adjustments of ever more extended outbreedings. It follows that the nearer one gets to anything definable as a "race," the more one narrows the list of traits significantly prevalent among the population delimited.

Even a family-transmitted trait need not strongly affect most of the members. Only a minority of the existing individuals of a family may show heritable schizophrenia, for instance. For, as in the case of redheadedness, what passes from generation to generation is not the ailment itself but only a special biological situation encouraging it. Either environment or the organism itself may thwart the genes. Certain individuals in the family may be better able than others to compensate emotionally or physically for gene effect on brain tissue or metabolism or whatever it is. And this ability to compensate *might itself be a gene-developed difference between one family member and another*. For all this vagueness, however, both the tendency and the disease are real and over several generations the family will probably show an undue proportion of obvious psychotics. Family tendency to tuberculosis acts the same way. What is passed on is not tuberculosis itself but an immunological state less than normally unfavorable to the disease when it attacks. Within a family risk may vary from very low to tragically high, depending not only on recessives in the family gene pool but also on the varying effects on each individual of environment, general health and emotional strain.

So Nature and Nurture can team up or struggle as opponents. Certain genes may destine you to grow tallish, but diet and general health in childhood may make an inch or so difference just the same. Some scientists see close relation, within gene-determined limits, of course, between IQ and quality of nourishment for children. Or suppose that a child is born with high-intelligence genes but meets meager intellectual stimulus; then he will never be as clever as if he had been reared among clever and learned people. Or environment can prevent the consequences of genetic handicaps: A woman with a gene-narrowed pelvis almost certain to kill her in childbirth can live to old age if her genetically determined facial features so far outrage local ideas of beauty that she never marries.

Such considerations allow genetics *almost* to shirk involvement in the Nature-versus-Nurture contest. An eminent geneticist recently rejected any "hereditary-environment dichotomy" (a clotty way of saying Nature-versus-Nurture) in favor of "continuous gradation between defects in which heredity plays a small role and those in which it is the major determinant." But the bypass cannot be complete, because these relative influences differ in range much more than this implies. So far as anybody yet knows Nurture has no effect whatever on blood grouping. If the genes say blue eyes, Nurture can prevent blue eyes only by violence. At the other extreme, innate influences apparently have just about nothing to do with human choice of foods within the normal limits of mental health; there is no such thing, old wives' tales to the contrary notwithstanding, as innate liking for "long pig" or watermelon. Evidently Trait A can be .999999999 Nurture and only .000000001 Nature, and Trait B vice versa. So far genetics has only restated the problem as "In the control of a given trait does Nature or Nurture markedly predominate?" In the absence of knowledge much wider than is now available, Naturist and Nurturist can persist in struggling over that almost as bitterly as if they were still belaboring each other with absolutes; and in sounding off for the bewildered lay public almost as confidently as ever.

Present knowledge does at least indicate that traits so widely distributed, so consistent and so dominated by heredity as to warrant being called "racial" are usually passed on independent of one another. In case of highly consistent association, linkage *may* be involved. But the better bet is that common ancestry and prolonged similar environment are the agencies that have packaged these traits as a common heritage. Thus, the Mongoloid's sparse body hair, fat-embedded eyes and sallow skin, regardless of whatever survival value each may carry, are probably just a cluster of disconnected racial trade marks. The same holds for the Caucasoid's hairiness and light skin and for the Negro's long jaw, dark skin and frizzy hair.

This view of race as an arbitrary constellation of obvious but not necessarily linked traits allows for wide variation in other traits among members of a given race. It holds race-marking traits as very few among thousands in which all men

of whatever groups are alike. It implies that known intraracial resemblances are usually crude, the sort of thing that
makes all the East Indians on the streets of Port of Spain—
or all the Negroes—look alike to the newly landed European.
But it also allows that not all racial traits need be grossly
visible. A list of traits that might become racial by getting
more and more widely shared among intraracial family lines
might include, to name only a few, A-type blood, twinning,
musical ability.

Theoretically, if our Danteans had been further screened
for musical talent, they would have fused into a race notably
musical, as is often assumed of Negroes. But in this case
possibility is not demonstration. If it were, American Negro
musicians would lean notably toward darker skin and flatter
noses; whereas a glance at Negro dance-bands soon shows
that no such correlation exists. It fits observable fact better
to suppose that tone and rhythm bulk large in the lives of
the families and neighbors of American Negro children;
hence their musical potentials get especially high, full and
early development. Or consider a boy who, as his relatives
point out, has the same gait as his father: "Ah," they say, "a
chip off the old block!" The boy has not consciously imitated
father's walk, true. But even if he were an adopted orphan,
and in the same emotional frame of mind about his "father,"
the same resemblance in gait would develop. In these matters
it is best to attribute no trait to heredity unless there is very
solid evidence of genetic connection or unless it is very difficult indeed to see how cultural influences could have produced it.

The racist's error, often nasty, is to wield the idea "race" as though it covered much more than anything so far implied. He confounds it with the selectively and deliberately inbred blood lines of the animal breeder. He compounds error by denouncing interracial breeding of mankind as "mongrelizing." This neglects the fact that all present breeds of dog many of them vigorous both physically and mentally (in canine terms) came of crossing and recrossing the several basic dog varieties, once probably as far apart as the "grand divisions" of mankind ever were.

In the South he has often made a fool of himself by averring, in the teeth of copious evidence, that mulattoes, fruit of "mongrelization," hence necessarily degenerate, are less fertile than either Caucasoids or full Negroes. He never heard of Mendel's cautionary finding about *one by one and at random* and would in any case take no stock in its implications. Instead he takes the American Negro as an all-inclusive package of linked, single-shot, innate "racial traits"; dark skin, mental sluggishness, prognathous jaw, musical skill, sloping forehead, erotic prowess, pink palms, superstitiousness—all are proclaimed "in the blood." Knowing little of the difference between a largely innate and a largely cultural trait, he labels "racial" such a detail as the American Negro's typical skill in cooking. It makes one wish miraculously to whisk him off to West Africa and make him eat what Negroes cook in what pass for hotels in that most distressful country.

This is that primitive intellectual device of thinking in clots—like a fox-terrier I once owned who first met a tiled floor at the vet's and ever after refused to set paw on tile anywhere. Violently the racist resists the suggestion that lack of cultural privileges might account for many American Negroes' blurring of mental skills above certain levels. Sulkily he ignores the notion that, even in his own terms, heavy infiltration of Caucasoid ancestry should have made a marked difference in many persons whom he classes as niggers. His stubborn, stupid creed is that anybody with that "known Negro ancestor" is a "nigger . . . always would be that and nothing more . . . could not be expected to measure up to the white man's standards . . . by nature inclined to criminal behavior, partly because of his animal nature, and partly because of his irresponsibility and immorality . . . ," to compress the late Howard W. Odum's summary of the decent Southerner's belief. This is to maintain the untenable because to do so scratches one's own emotional sores—never a pretty picture, however familiar.

The racist's better-educated, though often half-educated, ally is the eugenist, overaware of the determinism in genetics and choosing to ignore its teachings about chance. His prophet is Galton who, long before Mendel published, became a genetic determinist by analyzing cases in which paupers had spawned paupers and bright, prosperous people had spawned bright, prosperous people. Galton cannot be sneered at. He set off exhaustive analysis of the histories of twins, a most fruitful thing in genetics, and stirred up issues that badly needed—and some day will get—resolution. But he and his less intelligent admirers proposed to protect mankind from innate defects by discouraging breeding among the unfit and encouraging it among the fit. Three generations ago such schemes were not so readily seen to be dubious. The in-the-blood theory, which took no account of chance in combination of innate factors, left small reason to doubt that silk purses offended against the future of mankind when mating with sows' ears. Such common-sense, post hoc judgments are often correct, else society would never have got as far as it has. But the basis for this one was about as sound—and as irresponsible—as that of the social worker's thesis that slums, low pay and ignorance are the sole causes of urban delinquency.

Fifty years ago the eugenists were making the Kallikaks, Jukeses and Edwardses intellectual household words. Sir Charles Galton Darwin, pillar of the British Eugenics Society, was recently candid about some of their troubles: "The breed of race horses has been improved to a remarkable degree. . . . We would like to do the same for humanity; but it is a very difficult business deciding what human beings have won the race of life." The rest is that genetics has flawed the basic assumptions of eugenics, so far as it applies to qualities valued in given individuals.

For when denying offspring to a Jukes, say, the eugenist may forestall an obscure mutation or chance combination of genes that would have produced another Edwin Booth. A thorough eugenics program in backwoods Kentucky would certainly have prevented the genesis of Abraham Lincoln. No doubt the average level of intelligence could be gradually raised in a given group if only those with IQ above 100 were allowed to breed. Scientists of the standing of Julian Huxley and the late E. A. Hooton have firmly stated their convictions that a eugenics responsibly based on modern genetics is both possible and most desirable. But to the layman eavesdropping on geneticists, their science does not yet feel ready boldly to blueprint mankind. Certainly it needs saying that the eugenist is too often an amateur. His voice is shrill, his purpose all too crudely to propagate people like himself and to extinguish those whose manners, ideas or skin colors he finds repugnant. Scratch a eugenist, that is, and three-to-one you find a cryptoracist.

". . . you can define any idea in such a way that it is discredited."

—ALLEN, Our Wildlife Legacy

The third man in this squabble is often more civilized and has small use for the other two. He may be a cultural anthropologist or trustingly take his lead from that school of ethnology that hankers after equalitarian talk and behavior. He believes, or at least preaches, that race is no more significant than blood groups; and that, barring pigmentation, eye color and a few other such indifferent details, all arbitrary groups of mankind are exactly alike. Differences in behavior between an Andaman Islander and an Andalusian he ascribes altogether to environmental-societal (that is, "cultural") influences. Rear an Andamanese baby in Andalusia, he says, and it will be as devout a Catholic and as handy with castanets as if its parents were Juan Lopez and Maria Garcia. He insists that all stocks, races, ethnic groups, whatever one calls them, bear the same moral and intellectual potentials, but that these are manifested in varying culture-contexts and with varying tools and materials. So a potential Toynbee or Confucius is just as likely to turn up among Tasmanians as among Chinese or Britons—only there is no use looking now because the Tasmanians have long since been exterminated. In aggressive moods he implies that, since human groups get more complexly interbred all the time, as blood groups show, it is racist minded even to admit such an ethnic entity as race, however disinfected by relabeling. There stands the *human race,* he says, with a certain generosity of eloquence. All members thereof are brothers and the bare mention of distinctions among them only fosters unnatural feelings, such as color prejudice.

At the top of his bent he even talks as if all men were not merely brothers and sisters but identical twins under the skin—call this the Judy O'Grady complex. It is a self-cocking *reductio ad absurdum,* but that need not obscure the great weight of much of such doctrine. In view of current knowledge, it is very likely that, just as physical traits must be some 95 per cent Nature, so social, aesthetic, moral, intellectual traits should be largely, *though by no means altogether,* Nurture. Only some such assumption can account for the wide cleavages between ways of feeling and doing even within the same races. Maori and Hawaiians, Polynesians both, are as different as Kru and Ashanti. The average French-Canadian is amazingly unlike his close cousin in Rouen or Cherbourg. And if Indian infiltration can be suspected there, consider further that many a Minnesotan comes of the same gene pool as born Swedes do, yet the American could not possibly be mistaken for a boy from the old country; his gait, the set of his face, the hang of his hands are all different. Culture—the sum of group notions as to what is done how and what means what—saturates us all as alcohol pervades the blood stream and nerve cells of a drunkard.

This is all Anthropology A, of course. Overdilution of it produces the dogmata about race relations that many American children are now taught outside the S-u-h. It may be rude to cavil at teacher's professionally acquired belief that little-Indian-Sioux-or-Crow and little-frosty-Eskimo live in terms that little-Junior-Jones would find just as jolly as the charming drawings in the book. It can be maintained, casuistry though it is, that thus to deceive the rising generation is socially proper; that the more people believe in the absolute equality and equivalence of men, race for race and so on, the better off the world will be. An eminent psychologist solidly opposed to hyperequalitarian notions of race once told me, "I can't swallow their assumptions. But I'd almost go along, scientific conscience or not, if I were sure it would make us treat Negroes better." I too wish that the equalitarians' posi-

tion were unimpeachably sound stem to stern. I like their
kind of talk. I know why it so attracts people properly
ashamed of the racist-minded past. But as the geneticists learn
more, we should make reservations, else we may eventually
overreact into some foolish kind of neoracism.

The definiteness of race, for instance, is now absurdly
soft-pedaled in conscientious quarters, where good will can
lead the unwary into endorsing both the stereotype complex
and the sounds-like-hell-to-strangers fallacy. It takes little
thought to explode the second, but even that minimum is
seldom applied. The current form of it is: We Americans
must renounce color segregation because our persistence in
it hampers our foreign policy in Asia and elsewhere.

This is both cynical and inordinate. It is like saying, "Stop
beating your wife because her screams give you a bad name
among the neighbors." We need the support of Asiatics and
Africans so—grudgingly, opportunistically—choke down your
loathing of the American Negro and outlaw Jim Crow purely
as heavy-handed public relations, international window dressing. This is assume-a-virtue-if-you-have-it-not with a vengeance. Merely to suggest it in print should go far to spoil
whatever incidental good effect the Supreme Court decision
on segregation may have had outside the United States.
Asiatic leaders are clever enough to draw their own conclusions that the Court's ruling was only an expedient, meaningless hypocrisy ordered by Wall Street without our thus encouraging such ideas. The subtler trouble, however, is the
oncletomerie involved. Even at face value this is a superior-
race–inferior-race approach, a condescending, *unilateral*
gesture, not exoneration and apology but a pardon. No
American Negro of sound instincts should countenance it.
Fortunately for the cause of desegregation the reasons for it,
even the selfish ones, are all better than this.

Misgivings about the stereotype complex are less crisply
stated. The well-meaning have long used the word *stereotype*
as a universal weapon against racism, as an epithet instead

of a useful technical metaphor. Its victims have been the Jewish comic, the stage Irishman, the Octavus Roy Cohen "darky" and the Indian, Chinaman and Mexican as villains-by-definition on radio and screen. Any entertainment showing a Tibetan as anything but a fine fellow now elicits hot protest from the Tibetan colony of Chicago and a formal telegram from the Tibetan consul-general in Los Angeles demanding apology and receiving it, plus posting a bond to sin no more. Hence such crude stupidities as banning a movie of *Oliver Twist* because of Fagin. A touch more and *Huckleberry Finn* ("I see it warn't no use wasting words—you can't learn a nigger to argue") will be banned from school libraries. Most of this has happened since 1930, when *The Green Pastures* came on, studded with traditional Negro stereotypes. Now how about that?

Intellectual footing is slippery here. Undeniably The Two Black Crows, Amos 'n' Andy and Florian Slappey have bolstered destructive American attitudes toward Negroes. Dr. Fu Manchu and Injun Joe have probably damaged good relations between Caucasoids and non-Caucasoids. But this censorship approach—and this is what antistereotypers verge on, whether they know it or not—assails the problem from the wrong end. The most constructive thing it can think of is to exterminate the old villainous Indians and create a substitute tribe of nobly good Indians just as false to reality. To replace Injun Joe with Straight Arrow only plants another stereotype in the same spot. It may quiet the Tibetan uproar to show Tibetans as only wise and brave friends of the hero, but it does not improve the audience's intellectual-emotional bad manners, wherein the real trouble lies.

The anonymous author of that "person in a different skin" bit previously quoted also meant well, but he cannot have looked closely into his subject. If he had, he would have learned that a significant proportion of Negroes differ from Caucasoids not only in skin color, but also in number of sweat glands, thickness of horny-skin layer, jaw length, slope of forehead, flatness of nose, twist of hair, eversion of lips, length of leg and size of brain. (The last, mind you, is too small a difference to mean anything about relative intelligence—Eskimo brains are *larger* than those of Caucasoids by about the same amount—but the trait is pretty consistent.) The Negro shows not only special incidence of blood groups but also a tendency to sickle-cell disease (a rare anemia) and those relatively higher immunities, probably with an innate aspect, to malaria and yellow fever. And his tissues, remember, are slightly better adapted than those of Caucasoids for hard work in very high temperatures.

By huddling away these aspects of Negroes as an identifiable group, the equalitarian actually plays into the hands of the caste-minded racist. Only when one knows why racial groupings are real can one distinguish properly between the West African Negro on the slave ship in 1705 and his American Negro descendant in 1955 with his Negro physical traits (and his Negro mental traits, if any such exist) modified by the new environment, by stray mutations, and most of all by heavy admixture of Caucasoid genes over the intervening 250 years. The man-of-good-will's objective should not be to over- or understate in the interests of decency and justice for the Negro. He should rather do his best to cease confounding race with caste in his own mind and teach his children—and other people's if he is a teacher—that skin color is a poor gauge of an individual's personal quality.

"I came to the opinion long ago in Africa . . . that . . . there is no original or congenital difference between [Negroes and whites] any more than there is between a black horse . . . and a white horse. . . . With the same chances and the same treatment, I believe that distinguished men would be produced equally from both races."
—FROUDE, English in the West Indies

To mention the possibility of innate mental traits sets the equalitarian and the racist to trying to palm off the burden of proof on each other—a sure sign that neither is confident of knowing what he is talking about. With some justification the racist says that it is up to the equalitarian, as the party challenging venerable beliefs, to produce clinching evidence that the world has been wrong in associating relative lack of acumen with Negro physical traits. After all, he says, genetics does recognize the possibility of "linked" traits. The equalitarian stands, owlish and uneasy, on the UNESCO statement of 1950: "The scientific material available to us at present does not justify the conclusion that inherited genetic differences are a major factor in producing the differences between the cultures and cultural achievements of different peoples or groups. . . . there is no proof that the groups of mankind differ in their innate mental characteristics whether in respect of intelligence or temperament." * This is the Scot-

---

* Press Release UNESCO/220/Add. 1 18 July, 1950; original draft by a committee of appropriate specialists, including members from New Zealand, Mexico, Brazil, the United States (Negro), Britain, India, France; revised by Professor Ashley Montagu of Rutgers University, "rapporteur" of the committee, after criticism from experts including Myrdal, Klineberg, Dunn, Dobzhansky, Julian Huxley, to all of whom this text so far has referred in one place or another. Dunn and Dobzhansky once wrote more succinctly: "The question of whether or not human races differ in hereditary psychological as well as physical traits

tish verdict of "not proven" on the other side of the fence.

In that state of knowledge debate can hardly be intelligible but it goes on anyway. The racist, it was assumed above, is so contentious because he likes his world to contain so many millions of people whom he can openly look down on and, in many cases, privately hate. The equalitarian zealot scolds on and on partly because he cannot stand the racist's blusterings—and who can blame him?—but also partly because he is usually committed to Rousseauist emotional postulates about fundamental human goodness and basic blame on society for everything that individuals do. Rousseau dredged these ideas up for his contemporaries from his own unstable, peevish soul and then adduced vanishing peoples whom he had never seen personally—very like Mrs. Stowe—as evidence of what he hoped was true.

This rigid openmindedness about all mankind is no less rewarding a cult for its affording the emotional luxury of Pharisaism. Thank God, one can say, I am not as other men, race-minded, hateful, wishful thinkers. This recalls the suffragette of fifty years ago who, because society persisted in certain unfairnesses to women, ramped up and down maintaining that there was no difference but unmentionable physical accident between men and women.

These antagonists' wrongheadednesses nicely complement one another. The racist exaggerates both physical and mental differences while refusing to admit that the only decent thing to do about such things is to try to reduce them where they are harmful and to let the individual make the best of them where they are harmless. The Southerner, probably wrong in

---

for the time being must be regarded as open." (*Heredity, Race, and Society;* 115.) Another considered statement by an eminent geneticist is Boyd, *Genetics and the Races of Man;* 317: ". . . present evidence . . . does not suggest that any existing human race differs materially from any other . . . in regard to any such important characteristics as intelligence, adaptability, or ability to survive in various climates with suitable artificial aids."

assuming innate mental inferiority in Negroes, is certainly
wrong in increasing the assumed handicap by scamping education for the Negro. In the other camp the equalitarian
comes as near as he dares to denying mental and even physical differences,* which creates a barrier of disillusion between
whites and some sorts of Negro and between some Negroes
and whites from whom they seek fair treatment.

The unsatisfactory nature of known "intelligence" tests
helps to promote unseemly squabbles. So far psychology has
been unable to devise extracultural tests not suspect of obscure unfairness to one or another cultural group.† As for the
standard IQ tests now familiar to most people, they are, as
Lord Hailey said long ago, useful tools for educators in
gauging relative potentials within a group but of little reliable help to the anthropologist studying man as such.

Yet that is no reason for not using them, with all indicated
discount. For almost forty years now scientists have been
raking over the elaborate studies of soldiers' IQ's made in
World War I. Data therein can be made to show that American Negroes from Northern states tested brighter as a group
than whites from several Southern states; that American
whites as a group tested brighter than Southern Negroes;

---

* There is no answering Hooton here (*Twilight of Man;* 129): "All
reputable anthropologists condemn the malignant nonsense about racial
psychology which is preached and published by those who try to justify
the oppression of ethnic minorities . . . this pseudo-scientific stuff ap-
peals to morons everywhere. For this reason anthropologists . . . who
oppose racial injustice have tended to go beyond the legitimate statement that racial psychological differences have not been demonstrated
and have alleged that they do not in fact exist. I doubt that the ex-
igencies of democratic principles . . . justify such statements. . . . we
must neither deny nor assert."

† The strongest skepticism about the validity of any intelligence tests
is Hooton's in *Why Men Behave Like Apes* . . . ; 107-108. Klineberg,
Characteristics of the American Negro; 65, is interesting on the factor
of motivation in such tests. For antidote see Porteus, *Primitive Intelligence and Environment; passim.*

that Northern Negroes as a group tested brighter than Southern Negroes,* but mainly they show that ingenious men, even when dealing honestly, can reach a wide range of conclusions from the same mass of facts. Subsequent research has shown that markedly better environment may improve a child's IQ to a degree implying great importance of Nurture in the growth of intellect. But to what extent this works through emotional-intellectual stimulus and to what extent through physiological factors, such as better nutrition, is not clear. Findings as to whether Negro IQ varies with apparent Caucasoid admixture are vague and confusing.†

One of the few solid findings is that the *range* of IQ in American Negro children is the same as that in Caucasoid children—that is, all the way from imbecility to the upper-limit IQ of 200 popularly hailed as "genius." The Negro girl who attained that score, also doing miraculously well in ancillary tests, shows no physical signs of Caucasoid ancestry; nor do her parents. Even more significantly the search that turned up her case also found a substantial number of American Negro pupils in Chicago public schools with IQ well above the 135 mark usually taken to betoken exceptional intelligence. There were, as psychologists have pointed out, fewer of them per thousand pupils than is usual among Caucasoids. But if IQ scores mean anything at all—and their worst enemies usually allow them some validity under responsible interpretation—these really do make fools of the large sample of Southerners who not so long ago expressed the opinion that *no* American Negro could be more intelligent than the average among whites. They cannot even plead that

* The bitter controversies in this area are well summarized by a participant in Garrett, "Negro-White Differences in Mental Ability in the United States," *Scientific Monthly,* October, 1947.

† See Garrett, "Comparison of Negro and White Recruits . . . ," *American Journal of Psychology,* October, 1945. Pasamanick, "Comparative Study of the Behavioral Development of Negro Infants," *Journal of Genetic Psychology,* 1946; 69, 3-44.

American Negro children with that order of IQ probably have some "white blood," because they have always maintained that any touch whatever of the tarbrush means "nigger" and inferiority.

The moment that a single Negro touches the highest reaches of the IQ scale, the classic racist's case collapses under him. The Rev. John Rankin, the "good man" whom Eliza was seeking, saw that with austere clarity five generations ago:

> . . . apparent want of talent in our Africans . . . is totally owing to the cruel hand of oppression. There is but one other source . . . a different organization from the rest of mankind. But such organization would be universal in its effects, and thus prohibit a single instance of prodigious genius; for if it admit of one, it may on the same principle admit of a thousand. Among the Africans . . . many . . . possess the strongest power of mind; this . . . none that are well informed will deny.

Nor anybody who ever met the abler upcountry chiefs of present-day West Africa, often redoubtable men as black as any slaves ever brought through the Middle Passage. One can debate the meaning, as to Nature and Nurture, of the fact that as a group American Negro automobile drivers in North Carolina are worse risks than male Caucasoid operators as a group. But debate should not obscure the other fact that, in daily observation, certain Negroes, actually a good many, are highly responsible drivers.

Equalitarians use such information to back their theory that the several grand divisions of mankind, and their subdivisions, show the same intelligence both on the average and in the aggregate. This is not justified. Once allow that intelligence (however defined) varies as between individuals and is to some extent determined genetically, which few geneticists would care to deny, and a race of relatively higher average or aggregate intelligence is readily conceivable.* Suppose those young couples founding our Dantean race were chosen for high IQ in addition to physical traits. Intelligence being so likely a matter of multiple genes, their eventual descendants might show wide variation in it after 10,000 years. But the original gene pool would have had an unusually high proportion of genes making for unusually high intelligence, which would unquestionably mean that each generation would contain far more clever people than it would have if their ancestors had ranged, as did ours, between imbecility and IQ 200. Outsiders eventually studying these Danteans might conclude—erroneously—that there is something about blue eyes and beaked noses that "goes with" intelligence.

A race distinctly stupider than another is just as conceivable. Nothing in genetic theory rules out the possibility that, when the slave trade began, the Negro gene pool was a touch inferior to the Caucasoid in intelligence genes and that this assumed lower level was still reflected in the average lower level of Negro IQ in World War I. Another possibility is that the poor devils of Negroes whom their own people sold into slavery averaged duller, as well as personally unluckier or more unpopular or slower afoot, than those left in West Africa.† Julian Huxley, a great geneticist, while pointing out that he lacks scientific demonstration for his views and duly insisting on the wide *range* of intelligence within races, nevertheless calls it "wholly probable that true Negroes have a

---

* Porteus makes this point unanswerably in *Primitive Intelligence and Environment;* 213.

† Herskovits (in Murchison, ed., *Handbook of Social Psychology;* 239-242) maintains the opposite, depicting the exported slaves as a social cross section of West Africa, with only a few exiled criminals possibly lowering the average quality. This too is mostly surmise. My doubts of such contentions come of the general meekness of slave cargoes, which does not look as if they were too well spiked with chiefs and priests fuming under indignities.

slightly lower average intelligence than the whites or the yellows." Perhaps something of that sort was trying to show up in those World War I IQ scores, particularly those from tests intended to put illiterates on the same footing as literates: In them the relative standing of Negroes markedly improved but was still definitely below that of whites.

Assume, for the sake of argument, that some of that gap is real, not wholly the result of understimulus. This would be a real "racial inferiority." But, however that may be, it obviously cannot be marked enough to make any common-sense difference in society's treatment of the lower-average group. At worst the gap cannot be greater than, say, that between the average level of skills in the American League and in the International League—real if you wish, but knife-edge thin. Rattling good baseball is played in the Little World Series, and both pennant winners could put up a good fight for first division standing in the big leagues. This is the *range* point again. Let Huxley apply it to the race problem for us:

> . . . it is to be presumed on general grounds, though it has not yet been proved, that some at least of the racial groups will, if proper techniques and methods can be devised, be found to differ in average level of intelligence . . . [but] any such average difference would be only moderate, and . . . populations of different racial origin would always be found to overlap in genetic intelligence except for a small segment at either extreme.

A group inferiority loses most of its apparent meaning when the variations within the group are wide. American Negroes with IQ's between 135 and 200 are obviously better able to profit from higher education than are the great majority of Caucasoids, and the profit must often be society's as well as theirs. For instance, nobody acquainted with the work in social sciences of Frazier, Woodson, Eric Williams and C. S. Johnson has further reason to doubt the educability, not to say intellectual prowess, of American Negroes. Only the psychology of caste, a thing that we profess to deplore in India, denies optimum schooling to individuals on account of arbitrary categories. Even baseball has stopped that sort of thing.

American attitudes about sharp cleavage of opportunity between the white and the American Negro castes seem sillier still in view of Herskovits's finding, a generation ago, that over three out of four American Negroes had some non-Negro ancestry, often Red Indian, oftener Caucasoid. Cut that to two out of three in view of possible defects in his method;* but a dilution of some such order unquestionably exists. The American first going ashore in the old West African slave country—at Dakar, in my case—is taken aback by the deep, deep darkness of skin color in these largely undiluted Negroes, for which seeing American Negroes all one's life is most inadequate preparation. It is like tasting straight whiskey for the first time after having always watered it.

After running a small sample to check Herskovits's results, Stern recently judged that "Probably by 1980 there will hardly be a single Negro in the United States who can claim a purely African descent." From Boyd's blood-grouping data he estimates that "about two thirds of the genetic building material of the United States Negro comes from Africa and about one third from Europe." † Whatever the ratio may be, the Negro gene pool that came piecemeal out of Guinea to

---

* He asked a large sample of American Negroes if they had non-Negro ancestry. Some who said Yes may well have claimed mixed ancestry out of desire to oblige or impress the researcher. This could have been particularly true of claims of Indian ancestry, for the Indian appears as often as the African king in Negro fantasy about lineage.

† "The Biology of the Negro," *Scientific American,* October, 1954. This must not be taken to mean that most American Negroes are one third Caucasoid. It concerns the ingredients of the *gene pool only,* within which the ingredient patterns of individuals would range widely at random.

the New World has obviously been massively diluted in the United States, hence much reoriented in any gene-influenced traits, intelligence included. Since intrusion of Caucasoid intelligence genes (if such exist) can hardly have lowered average quality, the level can only have been raised or stayed the same, depending on one's guess at original relative standing. At worst this race mixture must also have increased the range of possible variations.

Perhaps incidence of genius-level IQ among American Negroes may never equal that among American Caucasoids proper, though, in view of the abysmal lack of knowledge here, only a fool would rush into that one. On the other hand, Goodman's groups of New England nursery-school children from "mixed" neighborhoods showed Negro male IQ's ranging from 80 to 132; Caucasoid male, from 84 to 133; Negro female, from 93 to 137; white female, from 90 to 145. Chart that and you get something remarkably close to Huxley's informed guess previously quoted. This is an excellent illustration of the contention of the psychologist Anastasi: "When the distributions [of behavioral traits] of any two biologically or culturally differentiated groups, such as the sexes or 'racial' and national groups, are compared, the *overlapping* is so large as to render any difference between averages of doubtful significance."

This edges toward definite usefulness, as in Klineberg's dictum, "It is permitted to speak of group differences only when care is taken not to apply the results of group comparisons to individuals." Myrdal pinned it down firmly:

> . . . even if future research should be able to establish and measure certain innate psychic differences between American Negroes and whites . . . it is highly improbable that such differences would be so large, that—particularly when the overlapping is considered—they could justify a differential treatment in . . . education, suffrage and entrance to vari-

ous sections of the labor market. This is a practical conclusion of immense importance.

It is indeed. It means there is no tenable case against desegregation and FEPC.

As fool-rushing-in, I still judge Mrs. Stowe wrong in arrogating superior mental qualities to "mixed bloods." I have met too many very dark Negroes,* both American and African, of obviously great capacity to accept that idea. I have seen, too, the eloquent difference between the expressions on the dark, broad-nosed, thick-lipped faces of such able Negroes and the expressions on the similarly made faces of chuckle-headed and flatfooted American Negro loafers in Mississippi —who are much like the slack-jawed, vacant-eyed average villagers of the back country of Liberia or Sierra Leone. This is not a matter of prognathism but of firmness of cheek muscle and directness and shrewdness of glance, plus many other less identifiable facial habits reflecting differences in mental habit and emotional approach. Nevertheless, even a considerable "racial" inferiority of a sort that I take little stock in would still be good reason for ridding American life of the caste-system.

Obviously caste robs society of the full abilities of the few or many American Negroes with IQ above 135, the indispensable leaders in research and the arts, of whom no society ever has enough. Somewhat less obviously caste prevents getting the most output man-hour from inadequately trained and emotionally maladjusted American Negroes in the 90-to-135 range of IQ, which includes the people who do the everyday work of the world on various levels of skill and enterprise. And perhaps most damagingly it so neglects the

---

* This does not imply that darkness of skin accurately shows relative proportions of Negro and white ancestry in an individual. The multiplicity of skin-color genes rules that out. But when dark Negroes consistently crop up among the brightest, it means something.

below-90's that an unnecessarily large proportion of them are bound to fall by the wayside of technological advance and, in one way or another, become either public charges or clogs on the economy. In no category does the denial of full educational and economic opportunity to Negroes make sense. Suppose that a man had a white horse and a black one teamed together and found that the black one could not pull as hard as his teammate, which reduced efficiency in application of their combined power. He would hardly take that as reason to give the white horse a disproportionate share of oats, grooming and further training in how to get his shoulders into the collar. Nor would he devote time every day to teasing the black horse to render him jumpy and puzzled.

The social acids of caste restriction vary in strength but are secreted everywhere that the white world draws conclusions about individuals based on racial traits. These emotional acids eat into all three IQ classes among American Negroes. Perhaps they are worst for those of the 135-200's who cannot escape into the somewhat less color-barred worlds of science and the arts. I am Caucasoid and not only do not but cannot, thank God, know about these things—which is bad, which is worse. I have sometimes been shamed (and hoped I did not show it) by the game good will with which American Negroes discussed race relations with me, easing the topic skillfully with wry jokes and dry wit. I am not the Recording Angel to know what underlies this social pluck, or to gauge the exact ghastliness of the first time one of my color lashes a little black boy across the face with "Nigger!" But I need no laborious researcher's proof that, to the extent that the caste system hurts—which no Caucasoid has any business minimizing—it wantonly cripples the American Negro's potential, whether his work is diplomacy or writing novels or mopping up.

And the morals of it are atrocious. How can one make a

presumed lower average mentality excuse for perpetuating a pariah caste?* "I would hate to think," an anti-Rousseauist anthropologist told me, "that the treatment my grandchildren get will depend on their IQ's."

One good thing about World War II: it developed information on the educability of the American Negro that goes far to hearten the side of the angels—those believing that any gaps in averages between Caucasoids and Negroes are almost altogether of cultural origin. The U.S. Army set up Special Training Units for training illiterates (defined as those unable to meet fourth-grade school standards) in reading and writing by the most intensive modern techniques. Hopeless cases—those unable "to meet graduation standards in the prescribed period of time"—were discharged after a number of weeks deemed adequate to sort them out. These Units taught both American Negroes and Caucasoids in numbers adequate to statistical validity. Of Caucasoids enrolled 14 per cent were discharged as hopeless. Of American Negroes only 12.3 per cent were discharged as hopeless.

A Negro scholar justifiably calls this a "shattering blow at racists." The qualifications are easy: Yes, it takes less initiative for a Caucasoid civilian to learn reading and writing because his opportunities are usually readier and better; hence one would expect a somewhat higher level of potential but so far unexploited intelligence among illiterate American Negroes than among Caucasoids. But it is a stunner all the same and I love every word of it.

---

* Huxley supplies an ingenious addendum to this issue (in Dunn, ed., *Genetics in the 20th Century;* 619): "The geneticist who wants to apply his genetics in the form of eugenics, is bound to advocate the fullest possible equalization of opportunity, not only on moral or political grounds, but for technical genetic reasons . . . it is the simplest way of finding out the degree of genetic inequality present and therefore of insuring the rapidity and effectiveness of any eugenic measures that may be adopted."

". . . enlightened Americans among whom prejudice is as unfashionable as it is prevalent."
—GOODMAN, Race Attitudes in Young Children

The way we American Caucasoids spell out caste values would often be funny if the context were less brutal. My wife was once looking into a racial situation at a coeducational eastern college. A lady dean told her how, though Negroes of both sexes were freely admitted and often did well, the campus had its own spontaneous convention: No crossing of race-lines between the sexes. My wife mentioned in demurrer that she had just visited a hall where Negro boys and white girls were having a great time together putting up decorations for a student entertainment. The dean asked a question or two, and then her perplexity cleared: "Oh, those boys aren't Negroes," she said. "They're Haitians. They speak French."

American Negroes tell me that, in some parts of the country, a turban made of a bright scarf will get them restaurant service that would otherwise be denied. On the same principle some learn to jabber a little French or Spanish. A formidable and definitely dark-skinned lady whom I met in West Africa often visits the United States with her sons. They have little caste trouble, even in a certain former Border State still full of Jim Crow, because, at the first sign of hesitation in desk-clerk or headwaiter, they gabble among themselves in the tribal language of their home region. This staccato demonstration that they are exotics, hence exempt from the caste system, usually procures them rooms, table or service. Nor is this new. James Weldon Johnson noted exactly the same thing ironically as of forty or fifty years ago. Do not conclude that, in the American Caucasoid mind, discrimination stops at the three-mile limit, else Bermuda would not use American tourists as reason and, it may well be, pretext for keeping up discrimination. But at least we Statesiders are not committed to the ultimate absurdity of the three-layer caste system: white ruling class, mulatto-or-whiter bourgeoisie, Negro peasant-proletarian, after the example of the French and, to some extent, the British West Indies. This actually emphasizes white supremacy by making it socially unmistakable that half a loaf is better than no bread.

In Mrs. Stowe's day the caste system could not look quite so evil because the American Negro had not yet had reasonable opportunity to show what was in him. The racist's position as of 1850 had not yet been riddled by the examples of writers like James Weldon Johnson; statesmen like Ralph Bunche; judges like William L. Hastie; scientists like George Washington Carver; Negro organizers like Booker T. Washington and Lester Grainger. Note, too, that this list contains almost all degrees of American Negro pigmentation.

Nor in 1851 was there a science of genetics to curb the solemn maunderings of those who taught Mrs. Stowe that Negroes were something like superior apes with souls, whom enough "white blood" could upgrade to full humanity; who, perhaps because they are so little tempted to intellectual pride, are specially gifted with meekness and Christian lovingkindness; and who would really be better off by themselves, conducting their own worthy but doubtless second-rate affairs in some sort of African colony under pious white direction.

CLARITY BEGINS AT HOME

"This power of generalizing which gives man so much the superiority in mistake over dumb animals."
—GEORGE ELIOT, Middlemarch

This book promised de-confusion. Some readers may have fallen off as we rounded one or another of those hairpin digressions. But the view back from here is surely simpler than what loomed ahead as we clanked up that first steep incline. In some respects consciences may now be eased.

We Americans were no more to blame than any other sentimental mass public for the affliction visited on us in the shape of *Uncle Tom's Cabin*. We have even been specially penalized for admiring it by having had to live with the consequences of taking it seriously. But we are much at fault in having failed to outgrow Mrs. Stowe's puerilities as we have outgrown the naïvetés of the "temperance movement" and the use of the hickory in schools. And we owe a heavy and peculiar national penance for having inflicted the Tom-show on ourselves. There was really no need thus to quadruple the subversiveness of Mrs. Stowe's errors.

We are not uniquely to blame for our barbarities toward

American Negroes. Given human orneriness in such circumstances, such caste values are bound somehow to appear. England is showing the same reflex, in a form that sounds dismally familiar, as West Indian Negroes coagulate in Cardiff, Liverpool and London. But we have been and still are much at fault in persisting in exculpatory lies, of both Mrs. Stowe's and the Rev. Dr. Dixon's kinds, about slavery and the innate limitations of Negroes.

Even so, regret of our gullibility and presumption need not swindle us into guilt feelings about the original crime of slavery. Guilt feelings are notoriously noxious in all contexts. Like novels about "colored blood in your veins," they distract from the healthful duty of rubbing one's personal nose in the lunacies and anomalies of the caste system of 1955.

It was not I who bought the naked blacks from the barracoons of Goree and Old Calabar. Those who did that are long since dead and gone and doubtless frying in hell, though some of them may not have been such bad fellows. It was not the American Negro visible today in Harlem or Sunflower County who survived the middle passage chained 'tween decks in his own slippery filth. He too died long ago. His grandson was freed by an economic and political tangle and a war that, for a rare but possible exception, had some aspects of decency. Our continuing crime, however, which we do personally and daily commit, is countenance of the caste system that resulted. The Supreme Court's recent action, state and local FEPC and integration in the Armed Forces are all good omens. But the Caucasoid–American Negro "either-or" is not as near extinction as by now it should be. We did not invent it. But we middle-aged Americans are the first generation privileged to be sure that it is an emotional and moral stupidity. In just purely despising niggers Grandpa at least had the excuse of not knowing what psychology, hematology, genetics and the accumulating results of higher education for American Negroes now tell about their capacities and the place of Negro genes in the national gene pool. We have no such excuse. Little as science yet knows, it can already support this:

Suppose the equalitarian right. Then the caste system must be abandoned. Morally it is unfair and cruel. Economically it impairs the full usefulness of millions of more or less able people.

Suppose the racist right. Any conceivable "racial inferiority" is nevertheless too slight to justify the caste system. One does not tie tin cans to the tails of Dalmatians just because they are, on the average, not quite so clever as poodles.

Whichever is right, the only practicality and the only decency is to let the American Negro find his own level according to the luck and genes chance gave him, without caste pressures to keep him underdeveloped or overstrained. To do anything else amounts to that silliest of blasphemies, trying to play God.

As for the society-page sort of problem, I trust the reader also enjoys seeing the joke turned on us race-minded whites. Those estimates of annual "passings," the arithmetical necessities of the situation, sound better justified every time one thinks of them. Define a "nigger" as somebody with one or more Negro ancestors and. . . . As this aleatory scandal gains wider curency, some Balkan-born immigrant to Detroit may refuse to let his son espouse the daughter of an essembly-line worker from Southern Indiana because he won't have his boy marry where "tainted blood" is a considerable risk.

If only to save our faces, it is high time we "whites" learned not to care. Perhaps our descendants can manage that. For all its thraldom to the irrational, mankind also has a sporadic rational streak. As each succeeding generation learns a little more impressively through a growing body of research that a sizable and growing proportion of itself consists of crypto-Negroes, race feeling may pass less virulently to the next generation. If our progeny does manage this, it will be a very rare thing—intelligent popular use of a statistical generality.

So far we have little notion of how to use generalities intelligently. We derive them from scant instances, like Europeans judging Americans from busloads of tourists. We even base generalities on fictitious data, such as the characters of *Uncle Tom,* and those same Europeans assume that Americans are like the people in Hollywood movies and Dos Passos' novels. Now and again we make a generality of some validity, such as "Englishmen drink tea for breakfast." But too few of us feel the substantial difference between this and "All Englishmen drink tea for breakfast," an ironclad assertion about each and every individual in a large group. That sort of thing underlies the incisive bit in *The Invisible Man* when the white hostess graciously takes it for granted that her American Negro guest can and would like to sing spirituals. On a slightly lower cultural level she would have assumed that he carried a razor, a pair of dice and a policy slip.

On any level such assumptions are nonsense, even when the implied generalization may have something in it. No doubt a higher proportion of American Negroes than of Caucasoids in New York City play policy; the error lies in not allowing for the considerable possibility of subgroups of Negroes or individuals failing to correspond to formula. Thus stated, this sounds so simple that obviously only very stupid people could behave so. Yet this is the very flaw that underlies all details of caste segregation in the United States, so far as it has an even remotely rational basis.

To that extent the remedy for *oncletomerie* lies not in scolding about stereotypes one by one but in getting people out of the puerile habit of using any stereotypes, no matter whose, no matter whether liberally or reactionarily sponsored. Abolish the whole mental-emotional function now performed, according to the subject's taste and fancy, by the Bolshevik-with-the-bomb, the politician-with-the-paunch, the boss-with-the-blacklist, the hero-with-the-halo, and so on.

Or say that we must flout Gospel precedent and become "respecters of persons." Teach your children *not* that "Negroes are just like everybody else." That is untrue, thanks to the hangover from slavery, caste segregation and perhaps—barely possible, though very unlikely—to minor differences innate in most American Negroes. Teach them instead that there was just as much difference between George Washington Carver and the chuckleheaded, chicken-stealing original of the funny-paper stereotype—who really existed and still does—as there was between George Washington and the verminous English pimps transported to the Virginia plantations. Teach them to respect persons, not preconceived notions about them—not even preconceptions that feel generous.

So much for your and others' children. While you last, you yourself are more of a problem, because there is no knowing how superficial your reorientation has been. Your present confidence that you may be above race feeling can be deceptive. Middle-aged caste feelings rooted in irrationality that may not yield to widening knowledge, said the man talking to himself, may well persist under well-meaning lip service. If you once felt caste values to some extent—and reared as we were, most of us have done so—they probably went deep into the in-group/out-group feeling so prevalent among mankind. You probably acquired them before you knew how to wash your own face. Haul as you may on your spiritual and emotional bootstraps, you can hardly aspire altogether to win free.

This dismal truth has uses. You may well be an incurable case of the disease of caste feeling, if only as a sort of typhoid carrier mistaken about the fact of recovery. The procedure is not to lie to yourself about your suspicions of yourself, but to act as if you had lied and succeeded in believing yourself. Think of it as treating your embedded caste feeling like an irreducible deformity, which it actually is. Ignore it as far as possible, practice movements and attitudes that minimize its clog on your behavior and intensify the lip service. Be an outrageous hypocrite about it. Letting no caste-inspired word ever escape your lips keeps you from contributing to others' moral delinquency by encouraging their caste feelings. So at least you will no longer be a stumbling block to your brother. And you will pass on to younger persons, all the way down to small children, who pick such things up with ghastly alacrity, a minimum residue of such feelings.

Youngsters are bound to acquire some of it, perhaps some from you still. But it will be less than it would be if you were to act naturally. And such successive diminutions of caste-feeling are the only way in which, in this respect, people-to-be will ever be improvements on you. This is assume-a-virtue-if-you-have-it-not to some purpose. Perhaps—don't count on it—prolonged forcing yourself to make sense outside will help you to make sense inside, and your illusion of lacking caste-feeling will gradually come nearer actuality than you realize.

An obituary of the late Mary McLeod Bethune, a great American Negro leader, quoted her: "I want my people to prepare themselves bravely for life, not because they are Negroes, but because they are men." That would make her a good epitaph. If it were so used, perhaps the day might come when the inscription was found to have vanished, self-erased, because it had lost all meaning, because the cruel old distinction without a difference was gone.

Hasten that day! Amen.

References

In order to avoid peppering the text with index-numbers, always a trial to the eye and a distraction to the mind, specific sources not identified in footnotes are listed below in succession as they occur in successive chapters of the book. Surnames, initials of given names, initials of works are given in the appended check-list to the extent necessary to identify. A full listing means that the work had too little pertinence to the general subject of the book for inclusion in the check-list. Subdivisions within the following blocks of chapter-listings indicate corresponding subdivisions within the chapters as aids to locating the reference wanted.

Such location will not be difficult for those already acquainted with the various literatures involved. It will be awkward for others, but that evil is probably less than the alternative of the full panoply of a doctoral dissertation, which this book is not. There is no even fairly good solution of this problem of how to serve the interests of both the general and the specialist reader.

PROLOGUE

F. Wilson; 294-295.   Foster; 15.   Stowes; 471.   Myrdal; 24.

MRS. SCRIBBLE-IN-HASTE

George May, *Harper's,* June, 1953.

Stowes; 144-147.   Martineau, ROWT; 251.   Bremer, II; 108-109.
F. Wilson; 259-260.   Wendell; 354.   Allen, *Century,* October, 1887.
N. Adams; 158.   Fields, L&L; 173.   F. Wilson; 335.   Fields,
L&L; 222, 233.   Olmsted; 32, 111, 162, 190.   F. Wilson; 414.

Kemble; 199, 263, 95.   M. Armstrong; 343.   Fields, L&L; 271-272.

THE LITTLE LADY WHO . . .

Phelps; 138.

Stowe, *Key;* 39-40.   Stowe, MOOT; 326.   Seldes; 243.   Stowe,
PP; 519.   Barnes; 251.

Sellers; 309.   Odum, RAROR; 22.   Embree, *Brown Americans;* 13.
Rhodes, I; 364.

Field, L&L; 151-157.   Warner, *Atlantic Monthly,* September, 1896.
McLaren, *The Scots;* 39.   *Manchester Guardian* Weekly, December 23,
1954.   Letter in Siebert Collection.   Parsons; 291-293.   Still;
247-250.   Olmsted; 276-278, 269-270, 399.   Rhodes, I; 276.   Parsons; 291-293.   Chesnut; 199 *et passim.*   Johnston; 443.   Personal communication.

THE CRIME OF COLOR

E. A. Andrews; 141.   Jefferson; 147.   Little, *Negroes in Britain;*
171-172.   Ballagh; 41-42.   C. M. Andrews, CF; 187-189.   Mays;
3-5.   C. M. Andrews, CF; 187-189.   Jernegan; 49.   Gysin; 203-204.   Goodrich, "Indenture," *Encyclopedia of Social Sciences.*   Brackett; 175.   Ballagh; 7-8.   C. M. Andrews, CF; 187.   Spears; 9.
Brawley; 13.   *Writings of Benjamin Franklin* (Smith edition, New York,
1905), II; 66-67.   Wertenbaker, OS; 5.   Taylor; 20.   C. M. Andrews, CF; 188.   Jernegan; 56.   Cash; 21.   A. Mackay, II; 86.
Phillips, ANS; 395.   Cash; 61.   Mays; 46.   Sellers; 321.

Phillips, ANS; 333.   Greeley, *History of the Struggle for Slavery Extension;* 3-4.   Russell; 147.   Paulding; 203.   Rhodes, I; 26.   Mar-

tineau, SIA; 347; also Phillips, ANS; 162.   Bancroft; 11.   Rhodes, I;
315.   Dodd, CK; 26.   Phillips, ANS; 398.   Buckingham, SS, I;
162.   Ingraham, SWBAY, II; 235.   Dew; 359.   Clark, "The Slave
Trade. . . ."   Simkins; 153.

GOOD TO THEIR NIGGERS

N. Adams; 37.   Paulding; 203.   Sydnor, SIM; 42.   Sellers; 86.
Russell; 146-147.   Washington, UFS; 2-3.   Olmsted; 161.   Sydnor, SIM; 43.   Martineau, SIA, I; 224.   Buckingham, SS, I; 134.
Sydnor, SIM; 40.   Woodson, MOTN; 411.   Russell; 493.   Olmsted; 249.   Phillips, ANS; 298.

T. D. Weld; 18.   Kemble; 149.   E. A. Andrews; 173-4.   Thom-
son; 189.   Mrs. Hall; 218.   Cartwright, "Slavery in the Light
of Ethnology," in Elliott, ed., *Cotton Is King. . . .*   J. Campbell; 93.
Montagu; 221.   Klineberg, RD; 130.   Kemble; 23-4.   Ingraham,
SWBAY, II; 242-243.   Fisk University; 43, 115.   Blackford; 111.
Heyward; 182.   Flanders; 213.   Carter, LM; 207.   Fisk University; 254.

Rhodes, I; 315.   Russell; 274.   Ball; 28, 127-128.   N. Adams; 36.
Stephenson; 218-220.   Ingraham, SWBAY, II; 54-57.   Phillips, ANS;
305.   Buckingham, SS, II; 57.   Phillips, ANS; 305.   Olmsted;
407-408.   Bremer, I; 296.   *Ibid.*, I; 293.   Mrs. Hall; 220.
Phillips, L&L; 124.   Bassett; 86.   Phillips, L&L; 136.   Phillips,
ANS; 207.   Flanders; 213.   Sellers; 27.   Mays; 11.   Carter,
LM; 209.   Olmsted; 104-105.   Lyell, SVUS, II; 174.   Douglass,
L&T; 176.   Combe, NOTUS, II; 293-294.   Letter in Siebert Collec-
tion.   Taylor; 43.   Flanders; 222.

Jefferson; 145.   Matthews; 130.   Bremer, I; 369-370.   Russell;
140.   J. Campbell; 471.   Du Bois, SOBF; 156.   Botkin; 56, 148.
Fisk University; 295.   *Ibid.;* 255.   *Ibid.;* 300.   Washington,
SOTN, I; 166-167.   C. S. Johnson, SOTP; 20.   Washington, SOTN,
II; 35.

THE SUN SHINES BRIGHT

Becker, *Gallus;* 220.   Fermor, *Traveller's Tree;* 95.   Russell; 133.
Harris; 230.   Flanders; 139.   Harris; 35.   Phillips, ANS; 256.
Sellers; 270, 61.   Hundley; 188.   Bernard; 127-128.   Trent; 37.
Carter, LM; 208.   Phillips, ANS; 260.   Olmsted; 43.   Gaines;
189.   Heyward; 132, 203.   Sydnor, SIM; 108.   Chesnut; 169.
C. A. Murray; 163-164.   Olmsted; 454-456.   Phillips, L&L; 310-
312.   Bremer, I; 294.   Flanders; 160-165.   Carter, LM; 210.
Phillips, ANS; 387.   Ingraham, SWBAY, II; 121.   Stephenson; 113-

114.   Sydnor, SIM; 53.   Sellers; 114.   C. Davis; 89.   Sellers; 53.   Allston; 245.   Phillips, L&L; 323.   Mrs. Hall; 221. Lumpkin; 31.   O. K. Armstrong; 218-219.   Kemble; 89.   C. Davis; 48.   Ballagh; 78.   Sellers; 237-238.   *Diary of William Johnson;* 500.   Chesnut; 514-515.   Coleman, STIK; 255.   N. Adams; 93.   Polk; 163-164.   Sydnor, SIM; 88.   Stuart, II; 69, 72-73.   Mrs. Hall; 227-228.   Longstreet; 175-179.   Howe to Sumner, *Liberty Bell,* 1843.   A. Murray; 209.   B. Hall, II; 233-234. Sellers; 78-79.   C. Davis; 54, 60.   Sydnor, SIM; 62.   Flanders; 277.   Hundley; 204.   O. K. Armstrong; 146, 150.   E. A. Andrews; 101-102.

Polk; 170.   Dick; 92.   Ingraham, SWBAY, II; 128.   Woofter; 210.   Mrs. Hall; 223.   Dealer's letter book quoted in Siebert Collection.   Ingraham, SWBAY, II; 194.   Sydnor, GOTONR; 94. Smedes; 9.   E. A. Andrews; 148.   Frazier; 213.   O. K. Armstrong; 172-173.   Lyell, SVUS, I; 368.   Chesnut; 21.   Bassett; 86.   Odum and Johnson, *The Negro and His Songs;* 166.   C. S. Johnson, SOTP; 49.   Woofter; 207.   Martineau, ROWT, I; 191. *Time,* March 1, 1954.   "Slavery in the Light of Political Science," in Elliott, ed., *Cotton Is King. . . .*   *Narrative of Henry Box Brown;* 9. Cash; 95-96.   Coffin; 282.   *Ibid.;* 222.   Stuart, II; 64-65. Olmsted; 240.   Fraser, "Louisa C. McCord."   Dodd, CK; 55-56. Chesnut; 199.   Sydnor, SIM; 181.   Bancroft; 74.   *Ibid.;* 86. C. S. Johnson, SOTP; 58.   Kemble; 61.   *Ibid.;* 60.   Bassett; 86.   Lyell, TINA, I; 184.   Heyward; 102.   Frazier; 77.   Botkin; 61.   Russell; 141.   Miller; 508*fn.*   Russell; 126.   Martineau, SIA, I; 226.   Botkin; 154.   Stuart, II; 56.   Nicolay and Hay, eds., *Complete Works of Abraham Lincoln,* I; 178.   Olmsted; 596-597.   Rhodes, I; 332.   Horn; 157.

Fleming, "Jefferson Davis. . . ."   Sellers; 196-197.   *Ibid.;* 138.   Heyward; 100.   Sellers; 163.   Phillips, L&L; 248.   Parsons; 25-26. Buckingham, SS, I; 244.   Fisk University; 201.   Kemble; 68. Smedes; 33.   Dixon, TLS; 314.   Russell; 146.   "A Mississippi Bubble," *Roundabout Papers.*   Chesnut; 63.   Dodd, CK; 72. Woofter; 22.   Allston; 54.   Martineau, SIA, II; 109.   B. Hall, II; 209-211.   Bremer, I; 386.   Allston; 356.   Rice; 176.   Dodd, CK; 71.   Phillips, L&L; 332.   Kocher & Dearstyne, *Shadows in Silver;* 66-67.   Ingraham, SS; 318.   Mrs. Hall; 218-219.   Buckingham, SS, II; 438-439, 565.   Fetherstonhaugh, I; 189.   Ingraham, SWBAY, II; 97-100.   Holt; 124-125.   Matthews; 116.

Sydnor, SIM; 190.   Hart; 66.   Raper, PTP; 99-100.   Sydnor, SIM; 67.   Olmsted; 24.   Mays; 9.   Dodd, JD; 211.   Bassett;

47.   *Ibid.;* 87-88.   Botkin; 171.   Lyell, SVUS, II; 9, 82.   B.
Hall, II; 260.   Olmsted; 346-350.   Robinson; 458.

Russell; 80.   Nuhrah; 61.   Sellers; 393.   Frazier; 144-150.
Puckett; 87.   Thomson; 178-179.   Buckingham, SS, II; 427.   N.
Adams; 22.   Lyell, SVUS, II; 84.   Olmsted, *Seaboard Slave-States*, I;
18-19.   A. Murray; 193, 304.   Buckingham, SS, II; 112, 411.   Rus-
sell; 147.   Matthews, *passim.*   Sydnor, SIM; 59.   Buckingham,
SS, II; 275.   Flanders; 179.   Sellers; 311 *et seq.*   Carter, LM; 210.
Fisk University; 162 *et passim.*   Woodson, RN; 160.   Matthews; 26.
Fisk University; 79.   Chesnut; 170.   Olmsted; 460.   Woodson,
RN; 136.   Puckett; 78.   Bibb; 27-28.   Woodson, RN; 7*fn.*
Sydnor, SIM; 61.

Bancroft; 146.   Sellers; 209-210.   Bancroft; 175-176 *et passim.*   Taylor; 38-40.   Coleman, STIK; 123-124.   Bancroft; 87.   Sydnor,
SIM; 6-7.   Sellers; 196-197.   Bremer, II; 490.   Annual report
kindly supplied by Alvin F. Harlow.   Phillips, ANS; 376.   *Diary of
William Johnson;* 313.   Cotterill; 263.   Phillips, ANS; 378.   Coleman, STIK; 64.   *Ibid.;* 160.   C. M. Andrews, CF; 186-188.   Phillips, ANS; 403.   Sydnor, SIM; 174.   Frazier; 131.   Olmsted; 114-
115.   Phillips, L&L; 216.   Lyell, SVUS, I; 361.   A. Murray; 219.
Flanders; 101-102.

Lyell, SVUS, I; 366.   Kemble; 58.   B. Hall, II; 235.   Jefferson;
160.   Transcript in files of Colonial Williamsburg.   B. Hall, II; 235.
Helps, *A Letter on Uncle Tom's Cabin:* 5.   Frazier; 199.   Allston;
122*fn.*

DARLING NELLIE GRAY

Nicolay and Hay, eds., *Complete Works of Abraham Lincoln,* I; 178.
Blackford; 43, 107.   Matthews; 38.   Rankin; 45*fn.*   Stephenson;
38.   Bancroft; 279.   Coleman, STIK; opp. 147.   Bancroft; 106.
Chesnut; 10, 18.   Stearns; 146.   Combe, II; 363.   Phillips, ANS;
182.   Sellers; 330.   Hundley; 140.   James, *Life of Andrew Jackson;* 59, 104.   Ingraham, SWBAY, II; 245.   Stephenson; 4.   Bancroft; 175.   Phillips, L&L; 158.   Stowe, *Key;* 163 *et seq.*   Coffin;
135.   E. A. Andrews; 81.   Allston; 66.   Flanders; 188.   Sydnor, SIM; 139-141.   Taylor; 70.

THE NORTH STAR

The authority for much detail in this section comes from
materials in the Siebert Collection of Underground Rail-

roadiana in the Houghton Library, Harvard College Library. The following references are for details *not* somehow in the Siebert papers. Anything unkeyed can be assumed to be somehow there.

Olmsted; 95.   Daingerfield, *Era of Good Feeling;* 125.   James, *Life of Andrew Jackson;* 275-276.   Phillips, ANS; 509-510.   Stuart, II; 41.

S. H. Adams, *Grandfather Stories;* 275.   Coffin; 471.   Phillips, ANS; 110.   Brackett; 85.   Child, *Hopper;* 33-35.   Botkin; 185-189. Coffin; 190.   *Ibid.;* 192-193.   Still; 634.

McMaster, *History* . . . , VII; 261-262.   *Diary of William Johnson;* 185. Still; 528-530.   *Ibid.;* 559-563.   *Ibid.;* 242-243.   Bremer, I; 124. Coffin; 338-340.   Personal communication from Alvin F. Harlow. Brackett; 84.   Still; 609.   *Ibid.;* 235.   Coffin; 119-120.   Still; 693.   Brackett; 90.   Stowe, *Key;* 157-158.   Martineau, ROWT, I; 244.   Coffin; 448.   Still; 736.   Coffin; 448.   Coffin; 305.

Phillips; 305.   Sydnor, SIM; 107.   *Diary of William Johnson;* 619, 717, 746.   N. Adams; 87.   Sydnor, SIM; 107.   *Ibid.;* 102.   C. Davis; 60.   Harris; 29.   Phillips, ANS; 303-304.   L&L; 325   Botkin; 92.   Sellers; 248-249.   *Ibid.;* 286-287.   Puckett; 248.   Harris; 35.   Olmsted; 388.   Carter, LM; 211.   Sellers; 288.   Aspinall, *Pocket Guide to the West Indies;* 106-107.   McMaster, *History* . . . , VII; 243-245.   Coffin; 160 *et seq.*   *Pudd'nhead Wilson;* 228 *et seq.* Coleman, STIK; 233.

Siebert, "The Underground Railroad," *New England Magazine* (undated tearsheets in Siebert Collection)   Rhodes, I; 378*fn.*   Nevins OOTU, I; 383-384.   Sellers; 292.   Coffin; 392.   Fairchild; 94.   Buckmaster; 346.   Lyell, TINA, I; 189-190.   Barrows; 229.   Bibb; 188-189.   Still; 143-144.   Woodson, MOTN; 371.   Coffin; 139-144.   Still; 512-513.   *Ibid.;* 452-454.   Blackford; 2.   Still; 435.   *Ibid.;* 449.   *Ibid.;* 459-460.

ORDEAL BY FOOTLIGHTS

Stout, "Little Eva Is Seventy-Five."   Kaye, "Famous First Nights: Uncle Tom's Cabin," *Theatre Magazine*, August, 1929.   Odell, *Annals of the New York Stage*, VI; 228.   King, "The Great American Drama," *Metropolitan Magazine,* undated article in possession of Houghton Library, Harvard College Library.   Ames, "First Presentation of Uncle Tom's Cabin," unidentified magazine article in possession of Museum of the City of New York.   Davis, "Tom-Shows."   Odell, VI; 237.   Interview with

Mrs. Cordelia Howard Macdonald, *Christian Science Monitor*, October 11, 1933. Daly, *Life of Augustin Daly;* 277. Odell, VII; 402.

Isaacs; 27. De Angelis, "My Beginnings," *Theatre Magazine*, June, 1905. Davis, "Tom-Shows," *op. cit.* Theater Collection, Houghton Library, Harvard College Library. Gysin; 8. Carlyle; 311. Wittke; 82. I am also indebted throughout to the general guidance of Harry Birdoff, *The World's Greatest Hit.*

CURSED BE CANAAN . . .

Stowe, *Key;* 25, 33. "On the Caucasians and Africans," in Elliott, ed., *Cotton Is King.* . . . "Slavery in the Light of Ethnology," in *ibid.* Sydnor, SIM; 244. Woodson, MON; 282. Rhodes, I; 370. Jefferson; 148. *John Jefferson Whitlaw,* III; 29-30. Channing, V; 125. VI; 20-21, 102. Cash; 66, 108. Myrdal; 113. Botkin; 15. Appendix, van Evrie, DSD. Flanders; 47. Pierson; 613. van Evrie, DSD; Appendix.

Lyell, SVUS, II; 127. *Formative Years,* I; 77. McKinley; 112. Kerr, in Strode, ed., *Yellow Fever;* 399. Flanders; 163. Macmillan; 109. Allston; 30. Phillips, L&L; 347*fn.* Washington, I; 117-118. Thorndike, *Athletic Injuries;* 54. Coon, SOM; 212. Flanders; 14. Simkins; 137. McKinley; 145. Hart; 60. Phillips, ANS; 44. Brackett; 7. Murchison, ed. *Handbook of Social Psychology;* 240. Phillips, ANS; 101-102. Chesnut; 34, 38, 92-93. Ingraham, SWBAY, II; 259-260. Mackenzie, *Life of Perry,* I; 386-387. Buckingham, SS, II; 471-473. Ward, II; 509. Jefferson; 145. Ward, II; 592. Miller; 509. Cole; 403-404. Percy, *Lanterns on the Levee;* 198-200.

Lyell, SVUS, I; 129-130. Barringer; 17. Key; 50. Klineberg, RD; 94. Interim Report—Southern Project, 1953-1954. Sydnor, SIM; 137.

Stribling; 306-309, 98. BFT&N; 116, 118. Holt; 176. London *Times* Lit. Supp.; September 17, 1954. Williams, I; 47-48. Ingraham, SWBAY, II; 198-200. Page; 248. Aristotle, *Politics,* Jowett translation, I; 218.

AREN'T WE ALL?

Hundley; 311.

Simkins; 24. Ballagh; 44. Jernegan; 55. Klineberg, RD; 2. Dunn and Dobzhansky; 92. Coon, SOM; 327, 373. Goodman; 107-108.

La Barre; 133.   Anastasi; 482.   Coon, Garn and Birdsell; 79. Boyd, GATRM; 252-275.   Coon, Garn and Birdsell; 113-131.   "Social History of the Negro" in Murchison; 209-210.

Gloster; 17.   *Pudd'n'head Wilson,* 138-139.   Ballagh; 58-59.   Bassett; 42.   Dixon, *Leopard's Spots;* 198, 385.   Goodman; 107-108. Jefferson; 47.   Parsons; 65-66.   van Evrie, N&NS; *passim.*   Kemble; 194.   Helper, *Nojoque;* 99-100.   Coffin; 282-288.

James, *Life of Andrew Jackson;* 349.   Higginson to Siebert, in Siebert Collection.   Hooton, "The Anthropometry of Some Small Samples . . ." in Day; 42.   White, MCW; 3.   Klineberg, CAN; 301, 207.   Stern, "The Biology of the Negro."   Glass and Li, "The Dynamics of Social Intermixture."

Hooton, AM&M; 152.

Coon, Garn and Birdsell; 10.   La Barre; 97.   Dunn and Dobzhansky; 30.   *Ibid.;* 50.   David and Snyder, "Genetic Variability and Human Behavior," in Rohrer and Sherif; 56-57.   Coon, Garn and Birdsell; 79. *Science News-Letter,* July 10, 1954.   La Barre; 135.

NEW WIVES' TALES

John L. Fuller, paper read at Gaines Symposium, 1954.   Kugelmaas, Paull and Samuel, *"Nutritional Improvement . . ."*

Odum, RAROR; 19-20. *Time,* January 17, 1955.

Klineberg, COTAN; 91.   Witty and Jenkins.   Garrett, "Negro-White Differences. . . ."   Klineberg, COTAN; 201.   Rankin; 13. *Bulletin,* North Carolina Department of Motor Vehicles . . . , October, 1952. Huxley, MSA; 53.   Huxley, "Genetics, Evolution and Human Destiny." Derived from tables on pp. 224-245, Goodman.   Anastasi; 328.   Klineberg, RD; 19-20.   Myrdal; 149.   Davenport, "Implications of Military Selection. . . ."   Aptheker, *Journal of Negro Education,* Fall, 1946.

Works Consulted

Obviously this does not include everything read in preparation for this book nor is it intended to be an exhaustive bibliography of any of the topics discussed. It is merely a check list of the more pertinent books and articles that went into the compost. It omits a good deal of material on the slave trade, West Africa, the West Indies, Abolition, and so on, which will be more appropriately cited in a book that may follow this one.

In addition to special histories, some of which are here listed, I have also made considerable use of such general histories of the United States as those of Rhodes, McMaster, Wilson, Channing, Morison and the Beards.

Abbott, George. *Sweet River. An Adaptation of Harriet Beecher Stowe's "Uncle Tom's Cabin."* Carbon typescript in Theatre Collection, New York Public Library.

Adams, Henry. *John Randolph.* American Statesmen Series. Boston, Houghton Mifflin Company, 1882.

The Formative Years. Condensed and edited by Herbert Agar. London, Collins, 1948.

Adams, James Truslow. *America's Tragedy.* New York, Charles Scribner's Sons, 1934.

Adams, Nehemiah. *A South-Side View of Slavery: or, Three Months at the South.* Boston, T. R. Marvin, and B. B. Mussey & Co., 1854.

Adams, Samuel Hopkins. *Grandfather Stories.* New York, Random House, 1955.

Allen, James Lane. "Mrs. Stowe's Uncle Tom at Home in Kentucky," *Century,* October, 1887.

Allport, Gordon W., ed. *Controlling Group Prejudices.* Annals of the American Academy of Political and Social Science, Vol. 244, March, 1946.

Allport, Gordon W. *The Nature of Prejudice.* Cambridge, Addison-Wesly Publishing Co., 1954.

Allston, Robert F. W. *The South Carolina Rice Plantation: As Revealed in the Papers of . . .* Edited by J. H. Easterby. The American Historical Association.

Anastasi, Anne. *Differential Psychology: Individual and Group Differences in Behavior.* New York, The Macmillan Company, 1937.

Andrews, Charles M. *Colonial Folkways: A Chronicle of American Life in the Reign of the Georges.* The Chronicles of America, Vol. 9. New Haven, Yale University Press, 1919.
The Colonial Period of American History. New Haven, Yale University Press, 1934. . . .

Andrews, Ethan Allen. *Slavery and the Domestic Slave-Trade in the United States.* In a Series of Letters Addressed to the Executive Committee for the Relief and Improvement of the Colored Race. Boston, Light & Stearns, 1836.

Anonymous. *The Planter: or, Thirteen Years in the South.* Philadelphia, H. Hooker, 1853.

Aptheker, Herbert. "Literacy, the Negro and World War II," *Journal of Negro Education,* Fall, 1946.

Armstrong, Margaret. *Fanny Kemble. A Passionate Victorian.* New York, The Macmillan Company, 1939.

Armstrong, Orland Kay. *Old Massa's People. The Old Slaves Tell Their Story.* Indianapolis, The Bobbs-Merrill Company, 1931.

Ashmore, Harry S. *The Negro and the Schools.* Foreword by Owen J. Roberts, Former Associate Justice, Supreme Court of the United States. Chapel Hill, University of North Carolina Press, 1954.

[Baldwin, James.] *In My Youth.* From the Posthumous Papers of Robert Dudley. Indianapolis, The Bobbs-Merrill Company, 1914.

Baldwin, James. "Everybody's Protest Novel." *Partisan Review,* June, 1949.

Baldwin, Joseph G. *The Flush Times of Alabama and Mississippi. A Series of Sketches.* New York, D. Appleton, 1856.

Ball, Charles. *Slavery in the United States. A Narrative of the Life and Adventures of . . . A Black Man . . .* Lewistown, Pa., John W. Shugert, 1836.

Ballagh, James Curtis. *A History of Slavery in Virginia.* Johns Hopkins University Studies in Historical and Political Science. Extra Volume XXIV. Baltimore, The Johns Hopkins Press, 1902.

Bancroft, Frederic. *Slave-Trading in the Old South.* Baltimore, J. H. Furst Company, 1931.

Barnes, Gilbert Hobbs. *The Anti-Slavery Impulse. 1830-1844.* New York, D. Appleton-Century Company, 1933.

Barringer, P. B. *The American Negro: His Past and Future.* Raleigh, Edwards & Broughton, 1900.

Barrows, John Henry. *Henry Ward Beecher: The Shakespeare of the Pulpit.* American Reformers Series. New York, Funk & Wagnalls, 1893.

Bassett, John Spencer. *Slavery in the State of North Carolina.* Johns Hopkins University Studies in Historical and Political Science. Series XVII, Nos. 7-8. Baltimore, The Johns Hopkins Press, July-August 1899.

Beecher, Catharine Esther. *An Essay on Slavery and Abolitionism, with reference to the Duty of American Females.* 2d. ed. Philadelphia, Henry Perkins, 1837.

Beecher, Charles, ed. *Autobiographical Correspondence . . . of Lyman Beecher, D.D.* New York, Harper & Brothers, 1865.

Benedict, Ruth, and Gene Weltfish. *The Races of Mankind.* New York, Public Affairs Committee, 1943.

Bernard, John. *Retrospections of America.* Edited from the Manuscript by Mrs. Bayle Bernard with an Introduction, Notes, and Index by Lawrence Hutton and Brander Matthews. New York, Harper & Brothers, 1887.

Bibb, Henry. *Narrative of the Life and Adventures of . . . an American Slave. Written by Himself.* With an Introduction by Lucius F. Matlack. New York, Published by the Author, 1849.

Birdoff, Harry. *The World's Greatest Hit: Uncle Tom's Cabin.* New York, S. F. Vanni, 1947.

Blackford, L. Minor. *Mine Eyes Have Seen the Glory: The Story of a Virginia Lady, Mary Berkeley Minor Blackford, 1802-1896, who taught her sons to hate Slavery and to love the Union.* Cambridge, Harvard University Press, 1954.

Boas, Franz. "Race," *Encyclopedia of the Social Sciences.*

Bontemps, Arna. *Story of the Negro.* New York, Alfred A. Knopf, 1951.

Botkin, B. A., ed. *Lay My Burden Down. A Folk History of Slavery.* Chicago, University of Chicago Press, 1945.

A Treasury of Southern Folklore: Stories, Ballads, Traditions and Folkways of the People of the South. Edited with an Introduction by . . . With a Foreword by Douglas Southall Freeman. New York, Crown Publishers, 1949.

Boucicault, Dion. *The Octoroon.* In Arthur Hobson Quinn, ed., *Representative American Plays.* New York, D. Appleton-Century Company, n.d.

Boyd, Julian P. *The Murder of George Wythe.* Philadelphia, Privately Printed for the Philobiblon Club, 1949.

Boyd, William C. *Genetics and the Races of Man. An Introduction to Modern Physical Anthropology.* Boston, Little, Brown and Company, 1953.

"Rh and the Races of Man," *Scientific American,* November, 1951.

Brackett, Jeffrey R. *The Negro in Maryland: A Study of the Institution of Slavery.* Johns Hopkins University Studies in Historical and Political Science. Extra Volume VI. Baltimore, N. Murray, 1889.

Bradford, Gamaliel. *Portraits of American Women.* Boston, Houghton Mifflin Company, 1919.

Bremer, Fredrika. *The Homes of the New World. Impressions of America.* Translated by Mary Howitt. New York, Harper & Brothers, 1853.

Brooks, Van Wyck. *The Flowering of New England. 1815-1865.* New York, E. P. Dutton & Co., 1937.

Brown, Henry Box. *Narrative of the Life of . . . Written by Himself.* First English Edition. Manchester, Lee & Blynn, 1851.

Brown, Herbert Ross. *The Sentimental Novel in America 1789-1860.* Durham, Duke University Press, 1940.

Brown, William Wells. *The American Fugitive in Europe. Sketches of Places and People Abroad.* With a Memoir of the Author. Boston, John P. Jewett and Company, 1855.

The Black Man. His Antecedents, His Genius, and His Achievements. New York, Thomas Hamilton, 1863.

Clotelle: or, The Colored Heroine. A Tale of the Southern States. Boston, Lee & Shepard, 1867.

Narrative of . . . A Fugitive Slave. Written by Himself. Boston, Published at the Anti-Slavery Office, 1847.

Bryce, James. *The Relations of the Advanced and Backward Races of Mankind. . . .* Oxford, Clarendon Press, 1902.

Buckingham, J. S. *America, Historical, Statistic, and Descriptive.* London, Fisher, Son, & Co., n.d.
The Slave States of America. London, Fisher, Son, & Co., 1842.

Buckmaster, Henrietta, pseud. (Henrietta Henkle). *Let My People Go. The Story of the Underground Railroad and the Growth of the Abolition Movement.* New York, Harper & Brothers, 1941.

Bullard, F. Lauriston. "Abraham Lincoln and Harriet Beecher Stowe," *Lincoln Herald,* June, 1946.
"Uncle Tom on the Stage," *Lincoln Herald,* June, 1946.

Calverton, V. F., ed. *Anthology of American Negro Literature.* Edited, with an Introduction by . . . New York, The Modern Library, 1929.

Campbell, Byram. *American Race Theorists: A Critique of Their Thoughts and Methods.* Boston, Chapman and Grimes, 1952.

Campbell, John. *Negromania: Being an Examination of the Falsely Assumed Equality of the Races of Men* . . . Philadelphia, Campbell & Power, 1851.

Carlyle, Thomas. "Occasional Discourse on the Nigger Question," in *English and Other Critical Essays;* Everyman Edition. London, J. M. Dent & Sons, n.d.

Carmichael, Leonard. "Science and Social Conservatism." Fourteenth Annual Phi Beta Kappa Address Delivered before the American Association for the Advancement of Science, December 30, 1953.

Carter, Hodding. *Lower Mississippi.* The Rivers of America. New York, Farrar & Rinehart, 1942.
Where Main Street Meets the River. New York, Rinehart & Company, 1953.

Cash, W. J. *The Mind of the South.* Doubleday Anchor Books, Garden City, 1954.

Champion, Thomas E. "The Underground Railway and One of its Operators," *Canadian Magazine,* May, 1895.

Channing, William H. "A Day in Kentucky," in *The Liberty Bell,* by Friends of Freedom. Boston, Massachusetts Anti-Slavery Fair, 1843.

Chesnut, Mary Boykin. *A Diary From Dixie.* Edited by Ben Ames Williams. Boston, Houghton Mifflin Company, 1949.

Chesnutt, Charles W. *Frederick Douglass.* Boston, Small, Maynard & Company, 1896.

Child, Lydia Maria Child, ed. *Incidents in the Life of a Slave Girl Written by Herself.* Boston, Published for the Author, 1861.
Isaac T. Hopper: A True Life. Boston, John P. Jewett & Co., 1853.
"Slavery's Pleasant Homes," in *The Liberty Bell,* by Friends of Freedom. Boston, Massachusetts Anti-Slavery Fair, 1843.

Clark, Thomas D. "An Appraisal of Uncle Tom's Cabin," *Lincoln Herald,* June, 1946.
"The Slave Trade between Kentucky and the Cotton Kingdom," *Mississippi Valley Historical Review,* December, 1934.

Clarke, Lewis, and Milton Clarke. *Narratives of the Sufferings of . . . Dictated by Themselves,* Boston, Bela Marsh, 1846.

Cobbett, Elizabeth. "Uncle Tom Is Dead," *Theater Guild Magazine,* June, 1931.

Coffin, Addison. *Life and Travels of . . .* Cleveland, William G. Hubbard, 1897.

Coffin, Levi. *Reminiscences of . . . The Reputed President of the Underground Railroad . . .* 2d ed. with appendix. Cincinnati, Robert Clarke & Co., 1880.

Cole, Arthur Charles. *The Irrepressible Conflict.* A History of American Life, Vol. VII. New York, The Macmillan Company, 1934.

Coleman, J. Winston, Jr. "Mrs. Stowe, Kentucky, and Uncle Tom's Cabin," *Lincoln Herald,* June, 1946.
Slavery Times in Kentucky. Chapel Hill, The University of North Carolina Press, 1940.

Collins, Winfield H. *The Domestic Slave Trade of the Southern States.* New York, Broadway Publishing Company, 1904.

Combe, George. *Notes on the United States of North America during a Phrenological Visit in 1838-9-40.* Philadelphia, Carey & Hart, 1841.

Conrad, Earl. *Harriet Tubman.* Washington, D.C., The Associated Publishers, Inc., 1943.

Coon, Carleton S., Stanley M. Garn and Joseph E. Birdsell. *Races:* A Study of the Problems of Race Formation in Man. Springfield, Illinois, Charles C. Thomas, 1950.

Coon, Carleton S. *The Story of Man from the First Human to Primitive Culture and Beyond.* New York, Alfred A. Knopf, 1954.

Cotterill, R. S. *The Old South. The geographic, economic, social, political, and cultural expansion, institutions, and nationalism of the antebellum South.* Glendale, Calif., The Arthur H. Clark Company, 1936.

Corson, Hiram. "The Abolitionists of Montgomery County. . . ." Prepared for the Historical Society of Montgomery County, Pennsylvania. Vol. II. Norristown, Pennsylvania, [Published by] the Society, 1900.

Couch, W. T., ed. *Culture in the South.* Chapel Hill, University of North Carolina Press, 1934.

Crevecoeur, J. Hector St. John. *Letters From an American Farmer;* Everyman Edition. New York, E. P. Dutton & Co., 1925.

Criswell, Robert. *Uncle Tom's Cabin Contrasted with Buckingham Hall the Planter's Home.* New York, D. Fanshaw, 1852.

Cromwell, John W. *The Negro in American History. Men and Women Eminent in the Evolution of the American of African Descent.* Washington, D.C., The American Negro Academy, 1914.

Crowe, Eyre. *With Thackeray in America.* New York, Charles Scribner's Sons, 1893.

Curtis, Anna L. *Stories of the Underground Railroad.* Foreword by Rufus M. Jones. New York, The Island Workshop Press Co-Op, Inc., 1941.

Daniels, Jonathan. *A Southerner Discovers the South.* New York, The Macmillan Company, 1938.

Davenport, Roy K. "Implications of Military Selection and Classification in Relation to Universal Military Training," *Journal of Negro Education,* Fall, 1946.

Davis, Charles S. *The Cotton Kingdom in Alabama.* Montgomery, Alabama, State Department of Archives and History, 1939.

Davis, J. Frank. "Tom Shows," *Scribner's,* April, 1925.

Day, Caroline. *Study of Some Negro-White Families in the United States.* Cambridge, Peabody Museum of Harvard University, 1932.

Day, Katherine Seymour. "Harriet Beecher Stowe," *Lincoln Herald,* June, 1946.

de Beaumont, Gustave. *Marie: ou l'Esclavage aux Etats-Unis. Tableau de Moeurs Americaines.* Paris, Charles Gosselin, 1835.

de Forest, John William. *A Union Officer in the Reconstruction.* Edited, with an Introduction, by James H. Croushore and David Adams Potter. New Haven, Yale University Press, 1948.

de Tocqueville, Alexis. *Democracy in America.* Translation by Henry Reeve . . . New York, The Century Company, 1898.

Denman, Thomas, Lord Denman. *Uncle Tom's Cabin, Bleak House, Slavery and Slave Trade.* Six articles by . . . reprinted from the "Standard." . . . London, Longman, Brown, Green, and Longmans, 1853.

Dew, Thomas R. *Review of the Debate in the Virginia Legislature in 1831 and 1832.* In *Pro-Slavery Argument.* Philadelphia, Lippincott, Grambo & Co., 1853.

Dick, Everett. *The Dixie Frontier: A Social History of the Southern Frontier from the First Transmontal Beginnings to the Civil War.* New York, Alfred A. Knopf, 1948.

Dickens, Charles. *American Notes.* New York, Thomas Y. Crowell Co., n.d.

Martin Chuzzlewit. New York, Thomas Y. Crowell Co., n.d.

Dixon, Thomas, Jr. *The Clansman: An Historical Romance of the Ku Klux Klan.* New York, Doubleday, Page & Company, 1905.
The Leopard's Spots: A Romance of the White Man's Burden. New York, Doubleday, Page & Co., 1902.

Dodd, William E. *The Cotton Kingdom: A Chronicle of the Old South.* The Chronicles of America. Volume 27. New Haven, Yale University Press, 1919.
Jefferson Davis. American Crisis Biographies. Philadelphia, George W. Jacobs & Company, 1907.

Dollard, John. *Caste and Class in a Southern Town.* New Haven, Yale University Press, 1937.

Douglass, Frederick. *The Life and Times of . . .* Written by Himself. . . . With an Introduction by the Right Hon. John Bright, M.P. 3d ed. London, Christian Age Office, 1884.

Drake, Thomas E. *Quakers and Slavery in America.* New Haven, Yale University Press, 1950.

Drew, Benjamin. *A North-Side View of Slavery. The Refugees; or the Narrative of Fugitive Slaves in Canada. . . .* Boston, John P. Jewett and Company, 1856.

Du Bois, W. E. Burghardt. *Black Folk Then and Now. An Essay in the History and Sociology of the Negro Race.* New York, Henry Holt and Company, n.d.
Color and Democracy: Colonies and Peace. New York, Harcourt, Brace, and Company, n.d.
Darkwater: Voices from Within the Veil. London, Constable and Company, Ltd., 1920.
The Souls of Black Folk. Chicago, A. C. McClurg, 1904.
The Suppression of the African Slave-Trade in the United States of America. 1638-1870. New York, Longmans, Green, and Co., 1896.

Dunn, Leslie C., ed. *Genetics in the 20th Century.* New York, The Macmillan Company, 1951.

Dunn, Leslie C., and Th. Dobzhansky. *Heredity, Race, and Society.* New York, New American Library of World Literature, 1946.

Eastman, Mrs. Mary H. *Aunt Phillis's Cabin: or, Southern Life as It Is.* Philadelphia, Lippincott, Grambo & Co., 1852.

Elliott, E. N. ed. *Cotton Is King, and Pro-Slavery Arguments: . . .* Augusta, Ga., Pritchard, Abbott & Loomis, 1860.

Embree, Edwin R. *Brown America: The Story of a New Race.* New York, The Friendship Press, 1936.
Brown Americans: The Story of a Tenth of the Nation. New York, The Viking Press, 1943.

Erskine, John. *Leading American Novelists.* New York, Henry Holt and Company, 1910.

Fairbank, Calvin. *Rev . . . During Slavery Times. How He 'Fought the Good Fight' to 'Prepare the Way.'* Edited from His Manuscript. Chicago, R. H. McCabe & Co., 1890.

Fairchild, James H. *The Underground Railroad.* Tract No. 87 in Vol. IV, Western Reserve Historical Society.

Featherstonhaugh, G. W. *Excursion Through the Slave States, from Washington on the Potomac to the Frontier of Mexico. . . .* London, John Murray, 1844.

Fields, Annie. *Authors and Friends.* Boston, Houghton, Mifflin and Company, 1898.

Life and Letters of Harriet Beecher Stowe. Edited by . . . Boston, Houghton, Mifflin and Company, 1898.

Fisk University, Social Science Institute. *Unwritten History of Slavery. Autobiographical Accounts of Negro Ex-Slaves.* Social Science Source Document No. 1. (Duplicated typescript). Nashville, Social Science Institute, Fisk University, 1945.

Flanders, Ralph Betts. *Plantation Slavery in Georgia.* Chapel Hill, University of North Carolina Press, 1933.

Fleming, Walter L. "Jefferson Davis, the Negroes, and the Negro Problem," *Sewanee Review,* October, 1908.

Foner, Philip S. *The Life and Writings of Frederick Douglass.* New York, International Publishers, 1950.

Foster, Charles H. *The Rungless Ladder: Harriet Beecher Stowe and New England Puritanism.* Durham, Duke University Press, 1954.

Foster, Thomas Henry. *America's Most Famous Book: A Dissertation on Harriet Beecher Stowe, "Uncle Tom's Cabin,"* and Uncle Tom Shows. Privately Printed for the Friends of May and Harry Foster at the Torch Press, Christmas, 1947.

Franklin, John Hope. *From Slavery to Freedom.* A History of American Negroes. New York, Alfred A. Knopf, 1947.

Fraser, Jessie Melville. "Louisa C. McCord," *Bulletin of the University of South Carolina,* No. 91, October, 1920.

Frazier, E. Franklin. *The Negro Family in the United States.* Revised and Abridged Edition. New York, The Dryden Press, 1951.

Froude, James Anthony. *The English in the West Indies: or, The Bow of Ulysses.* New York, Charles Scribner's Sons, 1892.

Gaines, Francis Pendleton. *The Southern Plantation: A Study in the Development and Accuracy of a Tradition.* New York, Columbia University Press, 1924.

Garrett, Henry A. "Comparison of Negro and White Recruits on the Army Tests Given in 1917-1918," *American Journal of Psychology*, October, 1945.
"Negro-White Differences in Mental Ability in the United States," *Scientific American*, October, 1947.

Gilbertson, Catherine. *Harriet Beecher Stowe*. New York, D. Appleton-Century Company, 1937.

Gilman, Caroline. *Recollections of a Southern Matron, by* . . . Author of "Recollections of a New England Housekeeper." New York, Harper & Brothers, 1838.

Glass, Bentley, and C. C. Li. "The Dynamics of Racial Intermixture—an Analysis Based on the American Negro," *American Journal of Human Genetics*, March, 1953.

Gloster, Hugh M. *Negro Voices in American Fiction*. Chapel Hill, The University of North Carolina Press, 1948.

Goodman, Mary Ellen. *Race Awareness in Young Children*. Cambridge, Addison-Wesley Press, 1952.

Goodrich, Carter. "Indenture," *Encyclopedia of the Social Sciences*. New York, The Macmillan Company.

Gosse, Philip Henry. *Letters from Alabama, (U.S.) chiefly relating to Natural History*. London, Morgan and Chase, 1859.

Graham, Shirley. *The Story of Phyllis Wheatley*. New York, Julian Messner, Inc., n.d.
There Was Once A Slave . . . The Heroic Story of Frederick Douglass. New York, Julian Messner, Inc., 1947.

Grayson, William J. *The Hireling and the Slave*. 2d ed. Charleston, John Russell, 1855.

Greg, Percy. *History of the United States from the Foundation of Virginia to the Reconstruction of the Union*. London, W. H. Allen & Co., 1887.

Grégoire, H. *An Enquiry Concerning the Intellectual and Moral Faculties and Literature of Negroes*. Translated by D. B. Warden. Brooklyn, Printed by Thomas Kirk, 1810.

Grimes, William. *Life of . . . the Runaway Slave Brought Down to the Present Time. Written by Himself*. New Haven, Published by the Author, 1855.

Gysin, Byron. *To Master—A Long Goodnight. The Story of Uncle Tom, a Historical Narrative*. New York, Creative Age Press, n.d.

Hale, Sarah Josepha. *Northwood: or, Life North and South: Showing the True Character of Both*. 2d ed. New York, H. Long & Brother, 1852.

Hall, Basil. *Travels in North America in the Years 1827 and 1828.* Philadelphia, Carey, Lea, & Carey, 1829.

Hall, Mrs. Basil. *The Aristocratic Journey: Being the Outspoken Letters of . . . Written during a Fourteen Months' Sojourn in America 1827-1828.* Prefaced and Edited by Una Pope-Hennessy. New York, G. P. Putnam's Sons, 1931.

Hall, Francis. *Travels in Canada and the United States, in 1816 and 1817.* Boston, Wells and Lilly, 1818.

Halsey, Margaret. *Color Blind: A White Woman Looks at the Negro.* New York, Simon and Schuster, 1946.

Hand, John P. *Negro Slavery in Illinois.* Transactions of the Illinois State Historical Society for the Year 1910. . . . Springfield, Illinois State Journal Co., 1912.

Harris, Joel Chandler. *On the Plantation: A Story of a Georgia Boy's Adventures During the War.* New York, D. Appleton and Company, 1892.

Hart, Albert Bushnell. *Slavery & Abolition. 1831-1841.* The American Nation; A History, Vol. 16. New York, Harper & Brothers, 1906.

Haviland, Laura S. *A Woman's Life Work: including Thirty Years' Service on the Underground Railroad and in the War.* 5th ed. Grand Rapids, S. B. Shaw, 1881.

Hawkins, William G. *Lunsford Lane.* Boston, Crosby & Nichols, 1864.

Haynes, Elizabeth Ross. *Unsung Heroes.* New York, Dubois & Dill, 1921.

Helper, Hinton Rowan. *The Impending Crisis of the South: How to Meet It.* New York, Burdick Brothers, 1857.
Nojoque: A Question for a Continent. New York, George Wm. Carleton & Co., 1868.

Helps, Sir Arthur. *A Letter on "Uncle Tom's Cabin" by the Author of "Friends in Council."* Cambridge, John Bartlett, 1852.

Henson, Josiah. *Truth Stranger than Fiction: Father Henson's Story of His Own Life.* With an Introduction by Mrs. H. B. Stowe. Boston, John P. Jewett and Company, 1858.

Hentz, Caroline Lee. *The Planter's Northern Bride: or, Scenes in Mrs. Hentz's Childhood.* Philadelphia, T. B. Peterson & Brothers, n.d.

Herskovits, Melville J. *The American Negro: A Study in Racial Crossing.* New York, Alfred A. Knopf, 1928.
The Myth of the Negro Past. New York, Harper & Brothers, 1941.
"Social History of the Negro," in Murchison, ed., *Handbook of Social Psychology.* Worcester, Mass., Clark University Press, 1935.

Heyward, Duncan Clinch. *Seed From Madagascar.* Chapel Hill, University of North Carolina Press, 1937.

Hibben, Paxton. *Henry Ward Beecher: An American Portrait*. With a Foreword by Sinclair Lewis. New York, The Press of the Reader's Club, 1942.

Hildreth, Richard. *Despotism in America: An Inquiry into the Nature, Results, and Legal Basis of the Slave-Holding System in the United States*. Boston, John P. Jewett and Company, 1854.

The Slave: or, Memoirs of Archy Moore. Boston, Bela Marsh, 1848.

Hill, Helen. *George Mason, Constitutionalist*. Cambridge, Harvard University Press, 1948.

Hill, Walter B. "Uncle Tom without a Cabin," *Century*, April, 1884.

Holt, Rackham. *George Washington Carver: An American Biography*. Garden City, Doubleday, Doran and Company, Inc., 1943.

Hooton, Earnest Albert. *Apes, Men, and Morons*. New York, G. P. Putnam's Sons, 1937.

Twilight of Man. New York, G. P. Putnam's Sons, 1939.

Horowitz, Ruth E. "Racial Aspects of Self-Identification in Nursery School Children," *Journal of Psychology*, January, 1939.

Hundley, D. H. *Social Relations in Our Southern States*. New York, Henry B. Price, 1860.

Hungerford, James. *The Old Plantation, and What I Gathered There in an Autumn Month*. New York, Harper & Brothers, 1859.

Huxley, Julian Sorel. "Genetics, Evolution and Human Destiny," in Dunn, ed., *Genetics in the 20th Century*. New York, The Macmillan Company, 1951.

Heredity East and West. New York, Henry Schuman, 1949.

Man Stands Alone. New York, Harper & Brothers, 1941.

Ingraham, Joseph Holt. *The Quadroons: or, St. Michael's Day*. New York, Harper & Brothers, 1841.

The Southwest by a Yankee. New York, Harper & Brothers, 1835.

The Sunny South: or, The Southerner at Home, embracing Five Years' Experience of a Northern Governess . . . Philadelphia, G. G. Evans, 1860.

Isaacs, Edith J. R. *The Negro in the American Theatre*. New York, Theatre Arts, 1947.

Jefferson, Thomas. *Notes on Virginia*. In *Basic Writings of* . . . Garden City, Halcyon House, 1944.

Jernegan, Marcus Wilson. *Laboring and Dependent Classes in Colonial America*. Studies of the Economic, Educational, and Social Significances of Slaves, Servants, and Poor Folk. Chicago, University of Chicago Press, 1931.

Johnson, Charles Spurgeon. *The Negro in American Civilization: A*

Study of Negro Life and Race Relations in the Light of Social Research. New York, Henry Holt and Company, n.d.

Shadow of the Plantation. Chicago, University of Chicago Press, 1934.

Johnson, H. U. *From Dixie to Canada. Romances and Realities of the Underground Railroad.* Buffalo, Charles Wells Moulton, 1894.

Johnson, James Weldon. *Along This Way: the Autobiography of . . .* New York, The Viking Press, 1933.

The Autobiography of an Ex-Coloured Man. With an Introduction by Carl van Vechten. New York, Alfred A. Knopf, 1927.

Black Manhattan. New York, Alfred A. Knopf, 1930.

God's Trombones: Seven Negro Sermons in Verse. New York, The Viking Press, 1943.

Johnson, William. *William Johnson's Natchez. The Ante-Bellum Diary of a Free Negro.* Edited by William Ransom Hogan and Edwin Adams Davis. Louisiana State University Press, 1951.

Johnston, Sir Harry H. *The Negro in the New World.* London, Methuen & Co., n.d.

Johnston, Mary. *Pioneers of the Old South: A Chronicle of English Colonial Beginnings.* Chronicles of America, Vol. 5. New Haven, Yale University Press, 1918.

Jorgenson, Chester E., ed. *Uncle Tom's Cabin as Book and Legend.* Detroit, The Friends of the Detroit Public Library, 1952.

Kalmus, H. *Genetics.* In collaboration with Lettice M. Crump. Harmondsworth, Penguin Books, 1948.

Kaye, Joseph. "Famous First Nights: 'Uncle Tom's Cabin.' " *Theatre Magazine,* August, 1929.

Kellar, Herbert Anthony, ed. *Solon Robinson, Pioneer and Agriculturalist. Selected Writings. . . .* Indianapolis, Indiana Historical Bureau, 1936.

Kemble, Frances Anne (Butler). *Journal of a Residence on a Georgian Plantation in 1838-1839.* New York, Harper & Brothers, 1863.

Kennedy, John Pendleton. *Swallow Barn: or, A Sojourn in the Old Dominion.* Rev. ed. New York, George P. Putnam, 1852.

King, Everett C. "The Great American Drama," *Metropolitan Magazine.* . . . Tearsheets in Siebert Collection, Houghton Library, Harvard University.

Klineberg, Otto, ed. *Characteristics of the American Negro.* New York, Harper & Brothers, n.d.

Klineberg, Otto. "The Intelligence of Migrants," *American Sociological Review,* April, 1938.

Race Differences. New York, Harper & Brothers, 1935.

Kocher, A. Lawrence, and Howard Dearstyne. *Shadows in Silver: A Record of Virginia, 1850-1900.* Photographs Taken by George and Huestis Cook, with additions from the Cook Collection. New York, Charles Scribner's Sons, 1954.

La Barre, Weston. *The Human Animal.* Chicago, University of Chicago Press, n.d.

Laughlin, Clarence John. *Ghosts along the Mississippi.* New York, Charles Scribner's Sons, 1948.

Leiser, Ernest. "For Negroes, It's a New Army Now," *Saturday Evening Post,* December 13, 1952.

Logan, Rayford W., ed. *What the Negro Wants.* Chapel Hill, University of North Carolina Press, n.d.

Loguen, Jermain Wesley. *The Rev . . . as a Slave and as a Freeman. A Narrative of Real Life.* Syracuse, Office of the Daily Journal, 1859.

Longstreet, Augustus Baldwin. *Georgia Scenes: Characters, Incidents, etc. in the First Half-century of the Republic.* New York, Harper & Brothers, 1897.

Lowery, I. E. *Life on the Old Plantation in Ante-Bellum Days: or, A Story Based on Facts. . . .* Columbia, S.C., The State Co., 1911.

Lucas, E. *La Littérature Anti-Esclavagiste au Dix-Neuvième Siècle: Etude sur Madame Beecher Stowe et son influence en France.* Paris, E. de Boccard, 1920.

Lumpkin, Katharine Du Pre. *The Making of a Southerner.* New York, Alfred A. Knopf, 1947.

Lyell, Sir Charles. *A Second Visit to the United States of North America.* London, John Murray, 1849.
Travels in North America: with Geological Observations on the United States, Canada, and Nova Scotia. London, John Murray, 1845.

Mackay, Alexander. *The Western World: or, Travels in the United States in 1846-7: exhibiting them in their latest development, social, political, and industrial; including a chapter on California.* From the second London edition. Philadelphia, Lea & Blanchard, 1849.

Mackay, Charles. *Life and Liberty in America: or, Sketches of a Tour in the United States and Canada, in 1857-8.* London, Smith, Elder and Co., 1859.

MacLean, Grace Edith. *Uncle Tom's Cabin in Germany.* Publications of the University of Pennsylvania. New York, D. Appleton & Company, 1910.

Marryat, Frederick. *Second Series of a Diary in America, with Remarks on Its Institutions.* Philadelphia, T. K. & P. G. Collins, 1840.

Martin, Harold H. "How Do Our Negro Troops Measure Up?" *Saturday Evening Post,* June 16, 1951.

Martineau, Harriet. *Retrospect of Western Travel*. London, Saunders & Otley, 1838.

Society in America. London, Saunders & Otley, 1837.

Matthews, Essie Collins. *Aunt Phebe, Uncle Tom and Others: Character Studies Among the Slaves of the South, Fifty Years After*. Columbus, The Champlin Press, 1905.

Mays, John David. *Edmund Pendleton: 1721, 1803. A Biography*. Cambridge, Harvard University Press, 1952.

[McCord, Louisa C.] Review of *Uncle Tom's Cabin* [signed L. C. M.] *Southern Quarterly Review*, January, 1853.

McCray, Florine Thayer. *The Life-Work of the Author of Uncle Tom's Cabin*. New York, Funk & Wagnalls, 1889.

McDougall, Marion Gleason. *Fugitive Slaves (1619-1865)*. Publications of the Society for the Collegiate Education of Women. Fay House Monographs No. 3. Prepared Under the Direction of Albert Bushnell Hart, Ph.D. Boston, Ginn & Company, 1891.

McIlwaine, Shields. *The Southern Poor-White from Lubberland to Tobacco-Road*. Norman, University of Oklahoma Press, 1939.

McKinley, Carlyle. *An Appeal to Pharaoh: The Negro Problem, and Its Radical Solution*. 3d ed. Columbia, S.C., The State Company, 1907.

Miller, John C. *Triumph of Freedom: 1775-1783*. Boston, Little, Brown, and Company, 1948.

Montagu M. F. Ashley. *Man's Most Dangerous Myth: The Fallacy of Race*. 3d ed., revised and enlarged. Foreword by Aldous Huxley. New York, Harper & Brothers, 1952.

Moody, Richard. "Uncle Tom, The Theatre and Mrs. Stowe," *American Heritage*, October, 1955.

Mott, Frank Luther. *Golden Multitudes. The Story of Best Sellers in the United States*. New York, The Macmillan Company, 1947.

Murchison, Carl, ed. *A Handbook of Social Psychology*. Worcester, Mass., Clark University Press, 1935.

Murray, The Hon Amelia M. *Letters From the United States, Cuba and Canada*. New York, G. P. Putnam & Company, 1856.

Murray, Charles Augustus. *Travels in North America during the Years 1834, 1835, and 1836. Including a Summer Residence with the Pawnee Tribe of Indians, in the Remote Prairies of the Missouri, and a Visit to Cuba and the Azore Islands*. London, Richard Bentley, 1839.

Myrdal, Gunnar. *An American Dilemma: The Negro Problem and Modern Democracy*. New York, Harper & Brothers, 1944.

Nell, William C. *The Colored Patriots of the American Revolution with Sketches of Several Distinguished Colored Persons*. Boston, Robert F. Wallcut, 1855.

Nelson, John Herbert. *The Negro Character in American Literature.* Bulletin of the University of Kansas, XXVII, No. 15, September 1, 1926. Humanistic Studies, Vol. IV, No. 1. Lawrence, 1926.

Nevins, Allan. *The Emergence of Lincoln.* New York, Charles Scribner's Sons, 1950.
Ordeal of the Union. New York, Charles Scribner's Sons, 1947.

Nichols, Lee. *Breakthrough on the Color Front.* New York, Random House, 1954.

Nicholson, Kenyon, and John Golden. *Eva the Fifth: The Odyssey of a Tom Show in Three Acts.* New York, Samuel French, 1928.

Northup, Solomon. *Twelve Years a Slave. Narrative of . . . a Citizen of New York, Kidnapped in Washington City in 1841. . . .* Auburn, Derby and Miller, 1853.

Nye, Russel B. "Eliza Crossing the Ice—a Reappraisal of Sources," *Bulletin, Historical and Philosophical Society of Ohio,* April, 1950.
Fettered Freedom: Civil Liberties and the Slavery Controversy. East Lansing, Michigan State College Press, 1949.

Odum, Howard W., and Guy B. Johnson. *The Negro and His Songs: A Study of Typical Negro Songs in the South.* Chapel Hill, University of North Carolina Press, 1925.

Odum, Howard W. *Rainbow Round My Shoulder: The Blue Trail of Black Ulysses.* New York, Grosset & Dunlap, 1928.
Race and Rumors of Race: Challenge to American Crisis. Chapel Hill, University of North Carolina Press, 1943.

Olmsted, Frederick Law. *The Cotton Kingdom: A Traveller's Observations on Cotton and Slavery in the American Slave States, Based upon Three Former Volumes of Journeys and Investigations by the Same Author.* Edited, with an Introduction, by Arthur M. Schlesinger. New York, Alfred A. Knopf, 1953.

Ottley, Roi. "New World A-Coming." *Inside Black America.* Boston, Houghton Mifflin Company, 1943.

Page, Thomas Nelson. *The Negro: The Southerner's Problem.* New York, Young People's Missionary Movement of the United States and Canada, 1904.

Paine, Lewis W. *Six Years in a Georgia Prison. Narrative of . . . Written by Himself.* Boston, Bela Marsh, 1852.

Parsons, C. G. *Inside View of Slavery: or, A Tour among the Planters.* With an Introductory Note by Mrs. H. B. Stowe. Boston, John P. Jewett and Company, 1855.

Pasamanick, Benjamin. "A Comparative Study of the Behavioral Development of Negro Infants, *"Journal of Genetic Psychology,* 1946, vol. 69, 3-44.

Paskman, Dailey, and Sigmund Spaeth. *"Gentlemen, Be Seated!" A Parade of the Old-Time Minstrels.* With a Foreword by Daniel Frohman. Garden City, Doubleday, Doran & Company, 1928.

Pattee, Fred Lewis. *The Feminine Fifties.* New York, D. Appleton-Century Co., 1940.

Paulding, James K. *Slavery in the United States.* New York, Harper & Brothers, 1836.

Percy, William Alexander. *Lanterns on the Levee: Recollections of a Planter's Son.* New York, Alfred A. Knopf, 1941.

Phelps, Elizabeth Stuart. *Chapters From a Life.* Boston, Houghton, Mifflin and Company, 1900.

Phillips, Ulrich Bonnell. *American Negro Slavery: A Survey of the Supply, Employment and Control of Negro Labor as Determined by the Plantation Regime.* New York, D. Appleton-Century Company, 1940.
Life and Labor in the Old South. Boston, Little, Brown, and Company, 1929.
"Slavery: United States." *Encyclopedia of the Social Sciences.*

Pierson, George Wilson. *Tocqueville and Beaumont in America.* New York, Oxford University Press, 1938.

Polk, William M. *Leonidas Polk.* New York, Longmans, Green & Co., 1893.

Polk, William T. *Southern Accent: From Uncle Remus to Oak Ridge.* New York, William Morrow and Company, 1953.

Porteus, Stanley David. *Primitive Intelligence and Environment.* New York, The Macmillan Company, 1937.

Power, Tyrone. *Impressions of America, During the Years 1833, 1834, and 1835.* Philadelphia, Carey, Lea & Blanchard, 1836.

Puckett, Newbell Miles. *Folk Beliefs of the Southern Negro.* Chapel Hill, University of North Carolina Press, 1926.

Quarles, Benjamin. *Frederick Douglass.* Washington, D.C., The Associated Publisher, 1948.
The Negro in the Civil War. Boston, Little, Brown, and Company, 1953.

Rankin, John. *Letters on American Slavery. Addressed to Mr. Thomas Rankin, Merchant at Middlebrook, Augusta Co., Va.* Boston, Garrison & Knapp, 1833.

Raper, Arthur F. *Preface to Peasantry: A Tale of Two Black Belt Counties.* Chapel Hill, University of North Carolina Press, 1936.

Redding, J. Saunders. *On Being a Negro in America.* Indianapolis, The Bobbs-Merrill Company, 1951.

Reuter, Edward Byron. *Race Mixture: Studies in Intermarriage and Miscegenation.* New York, Whittlesey House, 1931.

Rice, John Andrew. *I Came Out of the Eighteenth Century.* New York, Harper & Brothers, 1942.

Richie, Andrew. *The Soldier, the Battle, and the Victory: Being a Brief Account of the Work of Rev. John Rankin in the Anti-Slavery Cause.* . . . Cincinnati, Western Tract and Book Society, n.d.

Richmond, Anthony H. *The Colour Problem. A Study of Racial Relations.* Penguin Books, 1955.

Robinson, Solon. . . . *Pioneer and Agriculturist.* Selected writings, edited by Herbert Anthony Kellar. Indianapolis, Indiana Historical Bureau, 1936.

Rohrer, John H., and Muzafer Sherif, eds. *Social Psychology at the Crossroads.* New York, Harper & Brothers, 1951.

Ross, Alexander Wilson. *Recollections and Experiences of an Abolitionist: From 1855 to 1865.* Toronto, Rowell & Hitchinson, 1876.

Rourke, Constance Mayfield. *Trumpets of Jubilee.* New York, Harcourt, Brace & Company, 1927.

[Rush, Caroline.] *The North and South: or, Slavery and Its Contrasts.* Published for the Author by Crissy & Markley, 1852.

Russell, William Howard. *My Diary North and South.* Boston, T. O.-H. P. Burnham, 1863.

Ryerson, Florence, and Colin Clements. *Harriet: A Drama in Three Acts: In The Best Plays of 1942-1943.* . . . Edited by Burns Mantle. New York, Dodd, Mead and Company, 1943.

Schmidt, Hubert. *Slavery and Attitudes on Slavery in Hunterdon County, New Jersey.* Flemington, Hunterdon County Historical Society, 1941.

Seldes, Gilbert. *The Stammering Century.* New York, The John Day Company, 1928.

Sellers, James Benson. *Slavery in Alabama.* University, University of Alabama Press, 1950.

Shewmake, Oscar L. *The Honorable George Wythe: Teacher, Lawyer, Jurist, Statesman.* An Address by. . . . December 18, 1921. N.P., n.d.

Shuttleworth, Frank K. "The Nature *Versus* Nurture Problem." *Journal of Educational Psychology,* November, 1935.

Siebert, Wilbur H. "Ohio's Aid to Fugitive Slaves as a Contributing Cause of the Civil War." Typescript in Siebert Collection, Houghton Library, Harvard University.

"The Underground Railroad," *New England Magazine* . . . Tearsheets in Siebert Collection, Houghton Library, Harvard University. *The Underground Railroad for the Liberation of Fugitive Slaves.* Washington, American Historical Association, 1896.

"The Underground Railroad in Ohio," *Archeologist,* February, 1895. Ohio State Archeological and Historical Society.

Simkins, Francis Butler. *A History of the South.* [Originally Published as The South Old and New: A History 1820-1947.] New York, Alfred A. Knopf, 1953.

Smedes, Susan Dabney. *A Southern Planter.* London, John Murray, 1889.

Smedley, R. C., *History of the Underground Railroad in Chester and the Neighboring Counties of Pennsylvania.* Lancaster, Pa., Printed at the Office of the Journal, 1883.

Smith, Abbot Emerson. *Colonists in Bondage: White Servitude and Convict Labor in America. 1607-1776.* Chapel Hill, University of North Carolina Press, 1947.

Smith, Frank E. *The Yazoo River.* Rivers of America. New York, Rinehart & Company, Inc., n.d.

Smith, Lillian, *Now Is the Time.* A Dell First Edition, 1953.

Spears, John R. *The American Slave-Trade:* An Account of Its Origin, Growth and Suppression. New York, Charles Scribner's Sons, 1900.

Starkey, Marion L. *The Cherokee Nation.* New York, Alfred A. Knopf, 1946.

Stearns, E. J. *Notes on Uncle Tom's Cabin: Being a Logical Answer to Its Allegations and Inferences against Slavery as an Institution.* With a supplementary Note on the Key and an Appendix of authorities. Philadelphia, Lippincott, Grambo & Co., 1853.

Stephenson, Wendell Holmes. *Isaac Franklin: Slave Trader and Planter of the Old South. With Plantation Records.* University, Louisiana State University Press, 1938.

Stern, Curt. "The Biology of the Negro," *Scientific American,* October, 1954.

Still, William. *Still's Underground Railroad Records. With a Life of the Author Narrating the Hardships, Hairbreadth Escapes and Death Struggles of the Slaves in Their Efforts for Freedom. Together with Sketches of Some of the Eminent Friends of Freedom, and Most Liberal Aides and Advisors of the Road.* Philadelphia, William Still, Publisher, 1886.

Stoddard, Lothrop. *The Rising Tide of Color against White World-Supremacy.* With an Introduction by Madison Grant. New York, Charles Scribner's Sons, 1922.

Stout, Wesley Winans. "Little Eva Is Seventy-Five," *Saturday Evening Post,* October 8, 1927.

Stowe, Charles Edward. *Life of Harriet Beecher Stowe.* Compiled from her Letters and Journals by her Son. Boston, Houghton, Mifflin and Company, 1889.

────── and Lyman Beecher Stowe. *Harriet Beecher Stowe. The Story of Her Life by Her Son . . . and Her Grandson. . . .* Boston, Houghton Mifflin Company, 1911.

Stuart, James. *Three Years in North America*. New York, J. & J. Harper, 1833.

Sydnor, Charles Sackett. *A Gentleman of the Old Natchez Region: Benjamin L. C. Wailes*. Durham, Duke University Press, 1938.
Slavery in Mississippi. New York, D. Appleton-Century Company, 1933.

Talbot, William. "Uncle Tom's Cabin: First English Editions," *American Book Collector*, May-June, 1933.

Tandy, Jeannette Reid. "Pro-Slavery Propaganda in American Fiction of the Fifties," *South Atlantic Quarterly*, Vol. XXI, pp. 41-50, 170-78.

Taylor, Rosser Howard. *Slaveholding in North Carolina: An Economic View*. The James Sprunt Historical Publications . . . Department of History and Government, The University of North Carolina. Vol. 18, Nos. 1-2. Chapel Hill, University of North Carolina Press, 1926.

Thomson, William. *A Tradesman's Travels in the United States and Canada*. Edinburgh, Oliver Boyd, 1842.

Trent, William P. *William Gilmore Simms*. American Men of Letters. Boston, Houghton, Mifflin and Company, [1892].

Trollope, Anthony. *North America*. Edited with an Introduction, Notes and New Materials, by Donald Smalley and Bradford Allen Booth. New York, Alfred A. Knopf, 1951.

Trollope, Frances. *Domestic Manners of the Americans*. Edited, with a History of Mrs. Trollope's Adventures in America, by Donald Smalley. New York, Alfred A. Knopf, 1949.
The Life and Adventures of Jonathan Jefferson Whitlaw: or, Scenes on the Mississippi. London, Richard Bentley, 1836.

United Nations: Department of Public Information. Press Release UNESCO/220/Add.1. 18 July 1950. *Full Text of Unesco Report on Race*.

United Nations Educational, Scientific and Cultural Organization. *What Is Race? Evidence from Scientists*. Paris, Imprimerie Georges Lang, 1952.

van Buren, A. de Puy. *Jottings of a Year's Sojourn in the South*. Battle Creek, Mich., 1859.

van Evrie, J. H. *The Dred Scott Decision: . . . also an Appendix Containing an Essay on the Natural History of the Prognathous Race of Mankind Originally Written for the New York Day-Book by Dr. S. A. Cartwright at New Orleans*. New York, Van Evrie, Horton & Co., 1860.
Negroes and Negro Slavery: The First an Inferior Race, the Latter Its Normal Condition. 3d ed. New York, Van Evrie, Horton & Co., 1863.

Walker, Jonathan. *Trial and Imprisonment of . . . at Pensacola,*

Florida, for Aiding Slaves to Escape from Bondage. With an Appendix, Containing a Sketch of His Life. Boston, The Anti-Slavery Office, 1846.

Ward, Christopher. *The War of the Revolution.* New York, The Macmillan Company, 1952.

Warner, Charles Dudley. "The Story of Uncle Tom's Cabin," *Atlantic Monthly,* September, 1896.

Washington, Booker T. *The Story of the Negro: The Rise of the Race from Slavery.* New York, Doubleday, Page & Company, 1909.

Up From Slavery: An Autobiography. New York, Doubleday, Page & Company, 1907.

Watson, Henry. *Narrative of . . . a Fugitive Slave.* Boston, Bela Marsh, 1849.

Watts, Ralph W. *History of the Underground Railroad in Mechanicsburg.* Reprinted from the Ohio Archeological and Historical *Quarterly* for July, 1934. Columbus, F. J. Heer Printing Co., 1934.

Weeks, Stephen B. *Southern Quakers and Slavery: A Study in Institutional History.* Baltimore, The Johns Hopkins Press, 1896.

Weinstein, Alexander. "Heredity," *Encyclopedia of the Social Sciences.*

Weld, Charles Richard. *A Vacation Tour in the United States and Canada.* London, Longman, Brown, Green, and Longmans, 1855.

Weld, Theodore Dwight. *American Slavery as It Is: Testimony of a Thousand Witnesses.* New York, Published by the American Anti-Slavery Society, 1839.

Wendell, Barrett. *A Literary History of America.* 3d ed. New York, Charles Scribner's Sons, 1901.

Wertenbaker, Thomas Jefferson. *The Old South: The Founding of American Civilization.* New York, Charles Scribner's Sons, 1942.

Patrician and Plebian in Virginia: or the Origin and Development of the Social Classes of the Old Dominion. . . . The Michie Company, Charlottesville, Va., 1910.

Wesley, Charles H. "The Concept of Negro Inferiority in American Thought," *Journal of Negro History,* October, 1940.

White, Walter. *A Man Called White: The Autobiography of . . .* New York, The Viking Press, 1948.

A Rising Wind. New York, Doubleday, Doran and Company, 1945.

Rope & Faggot: A Biography of Judge Lynch. New York, Alfred A. Knopf, 1929.

Williams, Eric. *Capitalism and Slavery.* Chapel Hill, University of North Carolina Press, 1944.

Williams, George W. *History of the Negro Race in America from 1819 to 1880.* Negroes as Slaves, as Soldiers, and as Citizens; together with

Preliminary Consideration of the Unity of the Human Family, an Historical Sketch of Africa, and an Account of the Negro Governments of Sierra Leone and Liberia. New York, G. P. Putnam's Sons, 1883.

Wilson, Edmund. "Harriet Beecher Stowe." *New Yorker,* September 10, 1955.
"No! No! No! My Soul Ain't Yours, Mas'r!" *New Yorker,* November 27, 1948.

Wilson, Forrest. *Crusader in Crinoline: The Life of Harriet Beecher Stowe.* Philadelphia, J. B. Lippincott Company, 1941.

Wilson, Joseph T. *The Black Phalanx: A History of the Negro Soldiers of the United States in the Wars of 1775, 1812, 1861-'65.* Hartford, Conn., American Publishing Company, 1890.

Winterich, John T. *Books and the Man.* New York, Greenberg, 1929.

Wittenberg, Philip. "Miscegenation," *Encyclopedia of the Social Sciences.*

Wittke, Carl. *Tambo and Bones: A History of the American Minstrel Stage. Durham,* Duke University Press, 1930.

Witty, Paul A., and Martin D. Jenkins. "The Educational Achievement of a Group of Negro Children," *Journal of Educational Psychology,* November, 1934.

Woodson, Carter G. *The Mind of the Negro as Reflected in Letters Written during the Crisis 1800-1860.* Washington, D.C., The Association for the Study of Negro Life and History, Inc., 1926.
The Rural Negro. Washington, D.C., The Association for the Study of Negro Life and History, 1930.

Woodward, C. Vann. *The Strange Career of Jim Crow.* New York, Oxford University Press, 1955.

Woofter, T. F., jr. *Black Yeomanry: Life on St. Helena Island.* New York, Henry Holt and Company, 1930.

Wright, Richard. *Black Boy: A Record of Childhood and Youth.* New York, Harper & Brothers, 1937.
Black Power: A Record of Reactions in a Land of Pathos. New York, Harper & Brothers, 1954.
A Million Black Voices: A Folk History of the Negro in the United States. Text by . . . Photo-Direction by Edwin Rosskam. New York, The Viking Press, 1941.

Wulsin, Frederick R. "Hot Weather and High Achievement," *Florida Anthropologist,* December, 1953.

Wyman, Lillie B. Chace. "Harriet Tubman," *New England Magazine,* March, 1896.

Index